Cotton Coated

CONSPIRACY

BOOK ONE

JOHN McFERREN'S WORD

An investigative series on the death of
DR. MARTIN LUTHER KING JR.

John Roberts

Clear Lens Publishing, LLC

Cotton Coated Conspiracy
Book One: John McFerren's Word

For information contact:
info@clearlenspublishing.com
https://www.clearlenspublishing.com

ISBN: 978-1-7352296-2-1

First Edition: May 2021

10 9 8 7 6 5 4 3 2 1

In loving memory of

John McFerren

From the Cambridge University Dictionary

cotton: the threads that grow around the seeds of a tall plant grown especially in the U.S., China, and South Asia

coated: thickly covered

conspiracy: the activity of secretly planning with other people to do something bad or illegal

Contents

Introduction

Before lifelong Fayette County resident John McFerren passed away at the age of ninety-five, he regularly told one of our investigators, "Everything happens for a reason. There is a purpose behind everything that happens in this world, good and bad. All of it happens because God wills it to. He is in control of everything, and no matter how long it takes, or how much pain we go through, the Lord will always make sure the truth comes out in the end."

When I was considering how to begin this introduction, Mr. McFerren's now transcendent voice kept replaying in my mind, and the word "purpose" embedded itself within the fabric of my soul. The word itself and its definition first reminded me of the catchy lyric "every purpose under heaven" repeated by the Byrds in their famous 1965 song, "Turn! Turn! Turn!". After some light internet digging, I quickly discovered that the popular melody was first written by legendary folk singer, songwriter, and recording artist Pete Seeger in the late 1950s, a full six years before David Crosby and his pals turned the tune into a national hit.

But then I was floored to learn that Seeger's prior talents once touched on an issue much closer to home. In 1961, he also wrote, performed, and recorded "Fayette County," a folk song about the plight of a small African-American community of civil rights activists who lived right here in West Tennessee, one of whom was John McFerren himself. Still, it was Seeger's immutable lyric "and a time to every purpose under heaven" that kept haunting my thoughts. Interestingly, the phrase dates back even further than Seeger's writings. In the first and second verses of Ecclesiastes 3, the Bible declares:

> To every thing there is a season, and a time for every purpose under the heaven; a time to be born, and a time to die; a time to plant, and a time to pluck up that which is planted.

How incredibly apropos. If ever there were narratives that best describe the purpose of the following story, it's Seeger's previous songs and the two verses above. Indeed, this book is a true-life account of Fayette County, its cyclical seasons of cotton planting and harvesting, the multi-generational struggles the county's African-American residents have endured, and the joyous births and tragic deaths that have occurred in West Tennessee under God's eternal heaven. In John McFerren's own words, "There is a purpose behind everything that happens in this world, good and bad. All of it happens because God wills it to." As such, I emphatically believe that the time has come, according to the Almighty's divine purpose and will, to finally convey the true, untarnished story of John McFerren and his testimony regarding Fayette County's involvement in the assassination of Dr. Martin Luther King Jr. Under that primary purpose of conveying unadulterated truth, however, several other secondary purposes for the creation of this book must too be explained.

First, it is our intention to simultaneously educate and entertain. While all of the dry, Dr. King and James Earl Ray facts and figures contained in the following pages were thoroughly researched and corroborated by historical documentation, the proceeding text was written in a dramatic style that we believe lends itself to keeping you, the reader, engaged. And the vehicle for that drama was the creation of true-crime investigator "Randall Stephens" and whistleblower "Marcus Holmes" It is, therefore, of the utmost importance that, in the spirit of first expressing profound truth, we also include a full disclosure; The characters of "Randall Stephens" and "Marcus Holmes" are a conglomeration of several private researchers who toiled over a period of nine years to vet this story. There was no single "Randall Stephens" or "Marcus Holmes" nor are those names the genuine titles of anyone who worked on this project. While all of Mr. Stephens' and Mr. Holmes' actions, conversations, and conclusions actually took place as described in this book, those endeavors were performed by a multitude of separate individuals. To be clear, "Randall Stephens" and "Marcus Holmes" are fictitious, umbrella monikers assigned to a group of willfully anonymous men and women who executed the intense investigative narrative you're about to read.

With that single instance of dramatic license aside, the second underlying purpose of this book is to provide unrelenting clarity and accuracy. A great deal of methodical research and data mining went into ensuring that precise names, dates, and locations were used within the proceeding text. Unlike some other King and Ray narratives, no misspelled derivatives of individual names or pseudonyms (other than "Randall Stephens" and "Marcus Holmes") were used. In addition to our staunch desire to provide a painfully accurate record of historical events, it is also our hope that these exacting details equip other researchers with the essential breadcrumbs needed to conduct and/ or verify their own investigations. What's more, we also invite those same researchers and untold number of future critics to form their own conclusions by fact-checking our work. While we are confident that we have portrayed said events as truthfully as possible, we are not immune to making mistakes and welcome scrutiny and verifiable corrections. Quite simply, it is our hope that this book is viewed as a highly accurate investigative guide that inspires others to initiate their own research.

Third, it is our utmost desire to honor the legacy of John McFerren. Through the printed communication of his long-consistent assertions, we intend to publicly reveal the uncomfortable truths John prayed would someday come to light. By exposing these shocking realities, it is our intention to also refute, once and for all, the less than honest individuals who have tried to silence Mr. McFerren throughout the decades. Stated simply, it is the purpose of this book to posthumously honor John McFerren by providing him with a modicum of long-overdue justice.

It is our intention, through the accurate portrayal of John McFerren's well-recorded testimony, to shed light on James Earl Ray's willing involvement in the 1968 conspiracy. We intend to demonstrate that Ray, in his thirst for quick cash and ultimate freedom, found himself entangled with powerful government officials and organized crime figures who were deeply rooted in the racist South. But it is also our contention that, because of this unholy alliance, Ray was unfairly sentenced to life in prison for a crime that he was at least partially innocent of.

Finally, it is our goal to honor the memory of the late Dr. Martin Luther King Jr. Through this body of work and our intense evaluation of John McFerren's evidence, we prayerfully hope to enlighten the otherwise ill-informed public as to why the civil rights icon was assassinated and who orchestrated his murder, thereby providing Dr. King with a degree of justice as well. In conclusion, we simply believe that it is our predestined purpose to honor historical fact for future generations, and we believe that now is the time to do so.

JOHN ROBERTS

Prologue

ACCIDENTAL INVESTIGATOR

October 2015
Memphis, Tennessee

IT WAS UNSEASONABLY warm as Randall Stephens meandered down the gently sloping pavement of East Butler Avenue toward Mulberry Street. Encamped at the base of a wooden utility pole, on the sidewalk corner ahead of him, the permanent vigil of Ms. Jacqueline Smith cast a disapproving shadow over the touristy foot traffic. Final resident and self-appointed guardian of the former Lorraine Motel, Ms. Smith was evicted from the modest motor lodge in 1988, twenty years after Dr. Martin Luther King Jr. lost his life there.

The building's entrails, minus its unaltered west-facing façade, were being transformed into the National Civil Rights Museum/ NCRM at the time of her expulsion, and as such was necessary, the motel's last living piece of history had been summarily dumped on the sidewalk outside. Incredibly, she stayed there and demonstrated for the next twenty-seven years. After waving politely in the direction of the steadfast African-American protester he knew only as "Ms. Jackie," Stephens crossed Mulberry and entered the well-manicured grounds of the museum, a place once home to both the Lorraine Motel and its now-exiled final occupant.

After making his way from the western edge of the NCRM's brick-inlaid courtyard, Stephens stopped at the waist-high barrier built of additional bricks and painted steel, raised his head, and set his solemn gaze upon the infamous, still-preserved second-story balcony where Dr. King was struck down by an assassin's bullet on April 4, 1968. It was a decisive blow, handed down by a society still entrenched in the Jim Crow South; a bullet with a decisive message, born of hate, intolerance, and fear. The death slug, it seemed, had traveled through time, from slavery, past Reconstruction and Emmett Till, to the Freedom Rides, through Selma, Alabama, and Philadelphia, Mississippi, into white-only schools, through segregated restaurant doorways, past a sanitation strike in Memphis, and into the neck of the world icon. After pondering the final tragic moments of Dr. King's life, Stephens' thoughts drifted off to another, albeit far lesser, injustice in the recent past.

Marcus Holmes, an African-American construction contractor and friend of Stephens, had just recently been sent back to prison. Stephens and his family had moved to Somerville, the intimate, rural centerpiece of Fayette County, Tennessee, a number of years earlier, and had often called upon Holmes to do repair work on their home. It was during that frequent interaction that Stephens and Holmes soon stuck up a long-lasting friendship. Just an hour's drive east of Memphis and its parent jurisdiction of Shelby County, Holmes' hometown of Somerville had been his own family's stomping ground since before the Civil War.

To the outsider looking in, Fayette County's Rockwell-esque town capital was the ostensibly tranquil, rural little sister to the nearby urban, heaving and clawing, trouble-making Memphis. The quiet county that surrounded Somerville was, and still is today, marked by vast family farms, dense clusters of hardwood timber, and small-town monuments dedicated to the area's former war heroes. Bisected by Highway 64, the same path that saw hundreds of Native Americans driven from the Southeast by President Andrew Jackson, Fayette was full of cotton and history, less akin to cities like Memphis and Jackson, Tennessee, and more in line with Mississippi and its slave-holding delta.

Fayette County's wealthy elite did not look favorably upon the smallest legal infractions, nor did they tolerate even the slightest challenge to their archaically antebellum way of life, especially by those living within the local African-American community. As a result, Holmes, a black man and perceived troublemaker throughout his nearly fifty-year life, often found himself on the losing end of countless legal battles with Fayette County's despotic, notoriously corrupt law enforcement community.

Then, in the late summer of 2015, during a surprise vehicle inspection at the office of his parole officer, state law enforcement and prison officials found small traces of marijuana in Holmes' truck. Initially, Holmes' parole officer released him immediately after the finding with little more than a verbal reprimand. But less than twenty-four hours later, the officer was telephoning his recently freed parolee to warn him that Tennessee state officials within Fayette County were steadfastly opposed to the recent release and that an arrest warrant was imminent.

Before the warrant could be served, Holmes took heed of the tip. Fearing this was perhaps his last opportunity to blow the whistle on Fayette County's more devious transgressions, the soon-to-be fugitive scheduled a secret meeting at a nearby hotel with Randall Stephens. Over the next two days and late into the uninterrupted hours of the successive starlit nights, Holmes revealed the jaw-dropping evidence he had gathered throughout his lifelong predicament in Somerville, explaining to Stephens what he had personally uncovered regarding Fayette County's involvement in the assassination of Dr. Martin Luther King Jr.

Holding nothing back from the sometimes confused and often dubious Stephens, Marcus handed over countless official documents, played Stephens several audio recordings, and rattled off dozens of names, locations, and dates. Tapping upon the thin plastic keys of his laptop computer, Stephens worked feverishly to keep up with the fast-talking Holmes, sometimes taking notes, other times searching the internet to validate his impromptu witness's assertions.

At the end of their clandestine, multi-day huddle, the two men emerged, mentally exhausted. After providing much-needed prayers for the now-wanted Holmes, Stephens shook his friend's hand and gave his word that he would dig deeper into the seemingly implausible allegations just revealed to him. Unfortunately, it was the last time he would speak with Marcus in person for the next several months. Only two weeks later, the Tennessee State Parole Board voted to rescind Holmes' parole status, thereby sending him to prison for the second time in his nearly fifty-year life. Stephens could do little in late September of 2015 as his friend was sentenced to yet another lengthy prison term, this time for the trivial violation of possessing only small amounts of cannabis.

As he concluded the painful reminiscence, and his thoughts returned to the present, Stephens again focused his eyes on the second-story balcony in front of room 306 at the former Lorraine Motel where Dr. King/MLK had been shot and killed. Perhaps there was more to Stephens' future than just a simple promise to look into Holmes' claims. Perhaps he was being led to achieve something far greater. Had the late MLK been robbed of the justice he, too, so obviously deserved?

Stephens knew little about the thirty-nine-year life of the famed civil rights leader or the cowardly act that cut it tragically short. His only real knowledge of MLK's murder was that James Earl Ray, the accused shooter who proclaimed his innocence until dying in 1998, was the only person to be sentenced for the 1968 slaying. In addition, Stephens was even less familiar with the details surrounding the wide speculation that Ray was not the actual gunman but a mere patsy. The story of Dr. King's death at the hands of Ray was simply a topic that had never crossed Stephens' radar.

Yet, since his last meeting with Holmes, a glimmer of curiosity had been slowly stirring within Stephens' mind. If he followed the small breadcrumbs that had just been laid out before him, maybe he could somehow provide the much-needed justice Dr. King never received. And if Ray was nothing more than a scapegoat, as many believed, perhaps Stephens could posthumously vindicate him as well.

The glaring absurdity of the notion was immediately apparent, and Stephens quickly laughed at himself as he tried to push the delusions of grandeur from the forefront of his mind. Not only was he still reeling from a previous combat tour in Iraq, but Stephens was already engrossed in the management of his own struggling business. More to the point, he was acutely aware that he lacked the basic knowledge and research skills essential for taking on the monumental task. It was apparent that a number of other, more well-equipped investigators, lawyers, and authors had already trekked this path years before. What could he possibly add to the mountain of previously amassed information?

Despite his grave misgivings, Stephens' thoughts kept returning to the promise he recently made to Holmes. Even if he doubted his own abilities, Stephens could not escape his conscience nor the reality of his previous vow to the now incarcerated man. To backpedal at this point could signal the final death knell for the already demoralized prisoner. With a sigh of anticipatory angst, Stephens clenched the glossy gray railing in front of him. As if to shore up his resolve, he glanced up one final time at the second-story balcony in front of room 306, gathered his emotional strength, turned around, and headed for home to finish the arduous process of sorting through Holmes' disorganized collection of physical documents and digital files.

After several days of reviewing, copying, and organizing the shocking material he was recently entrusted with, Stephens saved the data to portable hard drives and then hid the devices at separate undisclosed locations. His next step was to dive headfirst into the vast sea of public information already available on the case. Initially, he limited his scope of study to brief online articles and documentary films in order to grasp the fundamentals of Dr. King and the shooting. It was only later that Stephens delved into the countless books written on the tragic subject. After reading dozens of publications, it became clear that all of the titles fell into one of two categories; those that claimed Ray was an ardent racist and the lone assassin, and those that painted him as an innocent patsy unwittingly manipulated by a high-level government conspiracy.

Stephens was torn. He didn't completely buy the theory that Ray was the shooter. Nor was he convinced that Ray acted alone as a raving bigot. But he also couldn't swallow the notion that Ray was a blameless victim who suddenly found himself accused of a crime he knew nothing about. Could the reality possibly lie somewhere in the middle, hidden beneath the array of misinformation scattered between the oversimplified official story and wild conspiracy theories?

Before long, it became obvious to Stephens that he would not be able to cut corners by merely relying on what other authors had researched and published in the past. There were just too many inconsistencies tucked between the stacks of battling narratives. In order to get to the truth, and perhaps vet what had been previously written, he would have to begin his digging inside the various archives spread across the internet and the city of Memphis. Stephens ultimately decided that it was essential to base his entire investigation on nothing less than hard documentation derived from original witnesses, law enforcement officials, government authorities, journalists, and the independent investigators who were in Memphis and at the Lorraine Motel at the time. He also made the decision to remain objective. Due to his lack of allegiance to Memphis, Shelby County, Somerville, Fayette County, and those involved in the case, it mattered little to Stephens who he exposed for wrongdoing, or whether Ray was guilty or not. He simply decided early on that the discovery of untarnished facts would be his only goal.

The learning curve was steep. But after several clumsy telephone calls, countless online searches, and numerous trips to the Bluff City's various archival institutions, the accidental investigator was soon unearthing Memphis Police Department/MPD reports, Federal Bureau of Investigation/FBI 302 reports, Shelby County court records, Department of Justice/DOJ interviews, House Select Committee on Assassination/HSCA transcripts, and all manner of news articles. By mid-October 2015, Stephens' digital collection had grown into a respectable database of government documents, newspaper clippings, Facebook photos, video archives, and previously recorded audio clips.

His next and certainly most difficult mountain to climb was the painstaking process of tracking down and interviewing the long list of witnesses who were still alive and willing to speak. And as Marcus Holmes had already learned through years of dedicated trial and error, it would take several long weeks before the first person on Stephens' list felt comfortable enough to begin revealing his well-guarded secrets regarding the murder of Dr. Martin Luther King Jr.

Part One

BACKGROUND RESEARCH

Chapter 1

A MAN NAMED McFERREN

MARCUS HOLMES REVERED the ninety-one-year-old John McFerren on an intensely profound level. In previous decades, Mr. McFerren had refused to speak to scores of unofficial investigators and self-absorbed writers whose only desire was to glean his dramatic testimony. But through the unpretentious gesture of long-term kindness and genuine friendship, a young Holmes was slowly granted the rare privilege of becoming McFerren's most-trusted student. Since the forging of the two men's bond in the early 1990s, Holmes had spent countless hours inside McFerren's gas and grocery business, hanging on every word the reclusive former civil rights leader uttered about his role as an unintended witness in the assassination of Dr. Martin Luther King Jr.

Before his departure to one of Tennessee's numerous state correctional facilities, Holmes was adamant in his assertion that McFerren held the key to unlocking the 1968 assassination mystery and that, if Stephens was to learn additional details about Fayette County's involvement, it was imperative to earn McFerren's seldom-granted trust. But unlike Holmes, Stephens knew that he would be starting from square one with McFerren. While he had accompanied Holmes on a handful of visits to Mr. McFerren's business and was already a slightly familiar face, Stephens certainly had not invested in the type of relationship with the enigmatic black man that Holmes had. His only possible inroad to a potential rapport with McFerren was the topic of their mutual friend. Perhaps, he could build a foundation of trust with the grocer by regularly discussing Holmes' most recent legal calamity and current prison stay.

Forging a Friendship

It wasn't long before he found himself standing in front of the double doors of the McFerren Grocery and Oil Company. Located at the three-way intersection on Highway 195 just south of downtown Somerville in Fayette County, the orange-brick building's faded red trim was in dire need of fresh paint, and the four analog gas pumps that lined its face, obviously decades old, looked longingly toward the oblivious highway traffic just beyond. To Stephens' right, a pair of local African-American men sat on overturned pickle buckets near the station's outside northeast corner, loudly chuckling while drinking forty-ounce beers hidden in brown paper sacks. He pulled on the right-side door's stainless-steel handle, but the main entrance was locked.

As he peered through the dusty window, Stephens could see the gas station's proprietor sitting atop a stool behind a turquoise-colored service counter. Before the strange, pasty-faced visitor had the opportunity to knock, a watchful John McFerren began his snail-like journey off the tall stool and around the counter to unlock the doors. The pace with which the elderly African-American man moved gave Stephens a discouraging glimpse into the long process ahead of him. Eventually, McFerren, hunched over, was standing before him on the other side of the glass, twisting and yanking on the door's lock.

His leathery, light-brown skin, which hung loosely over an antique frame, was immensely crevassed and dotted. His face, although clean-shaven, had been worn by the elements of time, weather, and most certainly deep-cutting pain. In addition to the pair of cloudy eyeglasses that sat atop his nose and in front of his piercing blue eyes, McFerren also wore a non-descript black baseball cap. Creeping out from beneath the edges of his dark head covering was a thick layer of salt-and-pepper hair. Rounding out his ensemble, McFerren also wore a long-sleeve, dark blue button-down shirt, black pants, a pair of equally ebony-colored suspenders, and two worn-out tennis shoes, each layered with strips of tattered duct tape. Stephens watched patiently, heard a metallic click, and then opened the unlocked door behind the now slowly retreating, still hunched-over McFerren.

Despite Tennessee's comfortable fall warmth, the station's indoor common area was stifling. As McFerren headed back behind the counter to his original perch, Stephens quickly looked around and spotted a familiar item. Resting on a shelf along the southern interior wall was the grease-smudged, tanned pith helmet he recently witnessed a much younger John McFerren wearing in the 1989 documentary film, *Inside Story: Who Killed Martin Luther King?* As the frail gas and grocery store owner once more took his seat, Stephens approached the service counter, stood across from McFerren, and began his well-rehearsed introduction.

"Hi, Mr. McFerren. I'm not sure if you remember me, but I'm a friend of Marcus Holmes."

Without making eye contact, the elderly black man replied with a straightforward and exceedingly drawn-out "Alright," devoid of any emotion or acknowledgment of who Holmes was. Due to either a lack of breath or an unwillingness to confirm information he believed to be private, it was clear the blue-eyed man was not going to make it easy on Stephens by elaborating.

The pale-skinned stranger continued undeterred, "Okay, well, he asked me to come by here and tell you that he's been sent back to prison."

In spite of McFerren's famously stoic nature in front of less-than-familiar faces, it was clear that he was both surprised and alarmed at the news. "Prison? Again? Wha—what he get hemmed up in this time?"

The sharp reaction was both a relief and a curse. While he was glad to hear an authentic, multi-word response from the notoriously guarded McFerren, Stephens also hated delivering news that caused such obvious distress.

As the out-of-place visitor went on to explain the recent circumstances surrounding Holmes' return to prison, McFerren exhibited only confusion, disbelief, and anger. After several minutes of repeating the same previously outlined details, Stephens concluded with an assurance that he would return in a few days to update McFerren about their mutual friend's plight. Despite his selfish desire to immediately begin questioning McFerren about the King case, Stephens recognized the distraught grocer's need to process the new development. In the eyes of the hesitant messenger, there was little more to say.

It was a minor victory, but a victory, nonetheless. Although it would take several more visits before McFerren let his guard down, Stephens had his foot in the door and was pleased with their initial meeting. He departed the southern outskirts of Somerville that day feeling cautiously optimistic that, as a future conduit between McFerren and Holmes, he could eventually earn the Fayette County man's confidence.

In the following days, Stephens quickly learned when it was okay to stop by the store to chat or when McFerren "had eyes watching him." He was also told who the local "snitchers" were and who was there simply to hang out at the building's northeast corner to get drunk. As Stephens would eventually discover, McFerren had long believed that specific area residents, all of whom were black, visited his gas station only to spy on him on behalf of Fayette County's racist white leadership. But Stephens would also come to learn that these suspicions weren't unfounded.

Week after monotonous week, Stephens made regular visits to McFerren's combination grocery and gas station to relay small bits of information about their friend's current and future prison status. As was typical, their conversations almost always centered on McFerren's continued worry about Holmes and what the rulers of Fayette County had done to destroy him yet again. The guarded civil rights leader even sometimes suspiciously questioned Stephens himself as if he was a possible contributor to Holmes' recent demise. As much as Stephens tried to assure the man that he had been sent there by their imprisoned friend, McFerren remained stubbornly leery of the newcomer.

Stephens soon realized that he would need to up his game if he was going to glean the vital information he was looking for. After a few weeks of simply lingering around the Fayette County business, discussing the same topic over and over again, he started bringing his young daughter around on evenings and weekends. Her presence seemed to lighten the mood, and McFerren clearly enjoyed her giggly company, often calling her "little lady." In front of McFerren, Stephens also made it a point of describing to his daughter the elderly man's past achievements as a World War II combat veteran, civil rights leader, and iconic hero of Fayette County. Admittedly, however, these appeals to McFerren's ego did little to coax him into additional discussions, and Stephens started to harbor feelings of guilt for his shameless attempts at manipulation, especially since he had begun to grow genuinely fond of the man.

Eventually, he changed tactics. During subsequent visits, Stephens began to tote a number of MLK books, each one outlining various versions of McFerren's role as a witness in the shooting conspiracy. Astonishingly, McFerren had little inkling he had been written about. As Stephens recited the different sections, it became clear that a number of titles were highly inaccurate in the mind of the aging eyewitness. Yet, despite his frustrated assertions regarding the mistakes in each narrative, McFerren was still unwilling to correct either the narrator or the authors themselves by offering up accurate details. Most often, his only response was, "That ain't right!", a simple denial of what had just been uttered.

It became clear to Stephens that he wasn't going to get anywhere as long as Holmes was absent from the meetings. If the two of them were free to work as a pair, then maybe McFerren would open up. But as long as Holmes was behind bars, Stephens was on his own. It was time to focus some of his efforts elsewhere. While continuing his regular trips to McFerren's Fayette County business, the accidental investigator returned to his recently obtained archival documents, focusing first on the area's dark history, John McFerren's background, and the same civil rights leader's often contentious relationship with the county's white establishment.

Fayette's Founding Fathers

Made up of thick tracts of hickory, walnut, poplar, cypress, and oak woodland initially belonging to Shelby County in the west and Hardeman County just to the east, Fayette County was founded on September 29, 1824. Just like the other six Fayette Counties established throughout the mushrooming United States before it, Tennessee's newest jurisdiction was named in honor of Marquis de LaFayette, a French general and statesman who had been an ally of the American colonists during the Revolutionary War. Before the ink had a chance to dry on the articles establishing Fayette County that September, local and state officials were also choosing a name for its future seat of government. By the next month, the state legislature had passed an act declaring that the county's new capital be named in honor of a U.S. military officer who had fallen in the 1814 Battle of Horseshoe Bend.

Also known as the Battle of Tohopeka, the brutal past offensive was led by Tennessee attorney and Major General Andrew Jackson in March of 1814 against a faction of the Creek Indian tribe known as the Red Sticks. Opposed to the white man's expansion into their centuries-old, southern-held territory, the Red Sticks fought bravely against Gen. Jackson's Tennessee militia in what is now the State of Alabama. After their overwhelming defeat on the 27th of that month, the Red Sticks' 800 native corpses, now scattered across the battlefield, were pillaged by Jackson's soldiers. The Tennessee militia fashioned bridle reins from thin strips of the Red Sticks' skin, conducted body counts by slicing off the tips of their noses, and shipped the natives' blood-soaked clothing back to the "ladies of Tennessee" as souvenirs. On October 16, 1824, a little more than ten years after the violent clash, Fayette County's new seat of power was officially named in honor of Lieutenant Robert Somerville, one of the officers killed in the horrific assault against the butchered Red Sticks.

Settled soon after by more than forty Scotch-Irish families intent on clearing the land and becoming wealthy slave and cotton plantation owners, the 704 square mile county ballooned rapidly from a population of just 265 white residents in 1826 to more than 5300 by 1830. Using pre-surveyed gridlines, dirt paths, rocky creeks, and the winding banks of the Loosahatchie and Wolf Rivers as boundaries, state and local officials sectioned off and granted vast blankets of rich uncultivated earth to white homesteaders who had either staked an original claim or paid other land speculators for rightful ownership.

One of Fayette County's original homesteaders was a Scotch-Irish Methodist minister named William Meek McFerrin. By 1836, the young Reverend McFerrin and his new wife had settled in Somerville. Under the direction of West Tennessee's Methodist leadership, William Meek quickly began his ministry within the local "Somerville African Mission." As a circuit rider assigned to this specific field of service, McFerrin spent the next several years traveling the dirt trails of the area, calling on neighboring farms and large plantations, and preaching to Fayette County's exploding population of spiritually downtrodden African-American slaves.

In contrast to his noble Christian work with members of the county's subjugated black community, Rev. McFerrin was a slaveholder himself. But after President Lincoln's Union troops defeated the Southern Confederacy in 1865, the family members of the pious Methodist minister were forced to free their African-American captives. These formerly enslaved men, women, and children had, by that point, adopted their white owner's moniker and went on to pass down the misspelled derivative of the "McFerren" family name to numerous generations in the future. Historical documents indicate that one of John McFerren's paternal forefathers, a former slave, was once the property of the Rev. William Meek McFerrin.

Today, oral history also suggests that a young Native-American girl settled in Fayette County after fleeing the Trail of Tears procession that snaked through Somerville in the winter of 1838. Local legend held that, upon her escape from John Bell's parade of native captives, the frightened girl hid in the dense brush along the dirt roadside of what is today Highway 64. Now wandering the area aimlessly and alone, the cold and hungry American aborigine was taken in by a nearby family of empathetic African-American slaves who lovingly raised her as their own. Many years after the woman's marriage to another Fayette County slave, the interracial couple's children and grandchildren, sometimes referred to by historians as "Black Indians," went on to become additional members of John McFerren's subjugated lineage.

Making of a Man

Eugene and Estella McFerren were an impoverished, albeit hardworking, African-American married couple who lived on their own farm near the rural outskirts of Somerville. But despite their economic hardships, the two happily gave birth to a baby boy named John on October 28, 1924. The McFerrens' new progeny eventually earned a reputation amongst his siblings and childhood peers for being an intelligent, industrious, and wholeheartedly honest young man. It was said that, from the first moments following his birth, John McFerren's piercing blue gaze never lost sight of his admired father, Eugene. The young boy spent his formative years watching the elder McFerren intently, studying every move the wise patriarch made. It was through this close relationship with his father that John quickly learned the vital importance of a relentless work ethic, financial independence, and accurate record keeping.

At some point in John's childhood, a local white physician named Dr. John W. Morris, with rusty kerosene lantern in hand, appeared unexpectedly on the McFerren family's wooden doorstep late one night. As an angry Dr. Morris demanded to be financially compensated for a costly horse saddle Eugene had previously purchased, Mr. McFerren hurriedly found and then brandished a handwritten bill of sale, supplying proof that he had already finished paying for the item in question. It was widely whispered by members of the area's black community at the time that Dr. Morris, a prominent Somerville citizen, wealthy business owner, and landholder, was the furtive leader of the Fayette County klavern, a nearby branch of the Tennessee Ku Klux Klan. According to the local rumor mill, it was also claimed that the good doctor had seized control of the county's top KKK position several years prior by way of a deadly gun duel with an opposing Klan member.

In spite of Dr. Morris's obvious embarrassment and damaged white pride that evening, a brave Eugene watched calmly as the

Fayette County physician handed back the piece of paper and then silently departed the McFerren homestead in peace. Mr. McFerren used the heart-stopping, potentially fatal encounter with the notoriously greedy and racist doctor to teach John a valuable lesson; never eat from the white man's trough, always keep a written record of your agreements with people, and always remain loyal to the truth.

After sustaining a severe injury while working as a part-time carpenter, Eugene McFerren became permanently disabled and ultimately unable to maintain the family's farm. At the age of thirteen, a selfless John McFerren dropped out of school to begin supporting his ailing father, mother, and the married couple's other young children. In addition to working in the nearby cotton fields, John also tinkered with rusty farm equipment and discarded engines, becoming a bit of an expert welder and mechanic.

He also earned extra money by selling wild quail. His daddy had raised him up to be a stealthy shot, and John regularly used the family's 22-caliber rifle to harvest the brown and white spotted fowl. After filling his satchel with their warm bodies, the young McFerren would make the day-long horseback ride into downtown Memphis and then sell his feathered bounty to the kitchen staff at the famous Peabody Hotel. Once delivered, the plump birds were hand-plucked, gutted, artfully roasted to a glistening golden brown, garnished with vibrant delectables, and then served under a steaming air of pomp and circumstance to the hotel's discerning guests.

The Burton Dodson Affair

There had been countless white-on-black slayings in Fayette County before. Typically, after the local lynching, the victim's grotesquely disfigured body would be tossed into the back of a horse-drawn wagon or pick-up truck bed, hauled to the southern fringes of neighboring Haywood County, and then unceremoniously dumped to rot away in the stench and muck of "Hatchie Bottom," the dark, snake-infested swamps located on the edges of the Hatchie River. The phrase "I'll take you up to Hatchie Bottom if you ain't careful!" was commonly used by Fayette County's white tormenters when threatening members of the rarely defiant black community. That's why, when a local sixty-year-old African-American man was being hunted down by an angry white mob on the still-darkened morning of Saturday, March 23, 1940, the elderly fugitive knew what his ultimate fate would be if caught.

Intent on capturing Burton Dodson, a black man accused of assaulting a white resident from the area, dozens of newly deputized white men led by Fayette County Sheriff W. H. Cocke surrounded the Dodson family's rural cabin, ordering Mr. Dodson to come outside. But when he refused to surrender and tried to flee the scene, several gunshots were fired, and in the moonlit melee, a forty-six-year-old Fayette County Sheriff's deputy named Olin B. Burrow was struck and killed by a stray bullet. Miraculously, Mr. Dodson fled the area on foot, escaped to the North, and lived in East St. Louis, Illinois, under an assumed name for the next eighteen years. What no one could have possibly predicted at the time was the impact the Burton Dodson affair would have on the future life of John McFerren and the area's race relations.

Local Leader

During World War II, John McFerren braved the blood-soaked trenches of France as a drafted service member in the United States Army. Throughout his combat tour in Western Europe, Mr. McFerren and his fellow segregated African-American soldiers were regularly ordered to hand-deliver heavy ammunition cans to their white counterparts, who were themselves fighting on the frontlines against Adolf Hitler's racist Nazi regime. But the often life-threatening and undeniably arduous work eventually took its toll on John's small frame. In the spring of 1945, he was shipped back to the United States, where he recovered from a war-related back injury. Following an honorable discharge from the military, John returned to his rural birthplace, and in 1950, married a Fayette County high school senior named Viola Harris. For the next eight years, the McFerrens kept their heads down, attended church, and worked diligently on the family's meager eight-acre farm to support themselves.

But in the late summer of 1958, a dark chapter in Fayette County's long and divisively racist history resurfaced, ultimately sparking something profound within the lives of John, his young wife, and those residing in the local black community. On September 3, 1958, a seventy-eight-year-old black man by the name of Charlie "Unk" Taylor was apprehended in East St. Louis by special agents of the Illinois FBI. After a routine fingerprint check, it was soon determined that Mr. Taylor was, in reality, Burton Dodson, the same fugitive now wanted in Fayette County for the murder of Deputy Olin B. Burrow eighteen years before.

As time would tell, this was to be one of the first in a long series of future collaborations between J. Edgar Hoover's powerful G-Men and Fayette County's corrupt law enforcement officials. From the moment of his extradition back to Tennessee on September 25, 1958, through his indictment on November 24, until the start of his Fayette County murder trial in early April 1959, Mr. Dodson remained behind bars while his attorney, a Memphis African-American man named James F. Estes, prepared for his defense.

Before his participation in the liberation of Europe in 1944, and just by coincidence, John McFerren had already met and befriended James Estes while the two soldiers were stationed together in the midwestern United States. As a teen growing up in the tightly-knit Tennessee county, John had also heard the amazing legend of Dodson's heroic 1940 escape from the sheriff's white lynch mob and pursuing bloodhounds. So when Attorney Estes, a former Army buddy of John's, arrived unexpectedly at the Fayette County Courthouse in downtown Somerville to represent Dodson, the inquisitive thirty-four-year-old McFerren could not be kept away from the hometown proceedings. Due to the Jim Crow laws of the day and the white-only seating, the standing-room area at the back of the dust-filled courtroom was packed with local African-American onlookers, among them, John McFerren and his neighboring friend and brother-in-law, Harpman Jameson.

Since being a registered voter within Fayette County was an official prerequisite for sitting on the twelve-man jury, and only a handful of African Americans in the county were registered to vote, Attorney Estes was forced to defend his client in the black-on-white murder trial in front of an all-white jury. Despite Estes's fiercely noble and equally brilliant rhetoric in the courtroom as the area's first black defense attorney, and the eyewitness accounts indicating that Deputy Burrow had not been shot by Dodson in 1940 but was instead the victim of friendly fire, the accused seventy-eight-year-old man was found guilty of second-degree murder on Thursday night, April 2, 1959, and then sentenced the following week to twenty years in prison. But the heartbreaking courtroom drama had a more enduring, conversely positive, effect on the area's black population.

Estes used Dodson's unjust, racially motivated conviction to highlight the need for African Americans to serve as future jury members, and therefore privately pushed McFerren to encourage other black Fayette County residents to become registered voters. By that summer, James Estes, John McFerren, and Harpman Jameson had unknowingly taken up their personal crosses as leaders in the South's new civil rights movement.

The Blacklist and Tent City

Following the South's overwhelming defeat at the end of the Civil War in 1865, millions of recently freed slaves were faced with a difficult decision; travel hundreds of miles with nothing in hand to the unfamiliar yet progressive North, only to start from scratch, or stay in the South and work on familiar farms, alongside familiar black neighbors, under the direction of familiar white families, who lived in familiar small towns. For many, the prospect of leaving the only source of food, shelter, and community they had ever known was too daunting a task to even consider. As a result, thousands of freed slaves remained in Fayette County and continued to work for their former slave owners, not as free labor, but this time as underpaid tenant farmers, sharecroppers, housekeepers, butlers, cooks, and nannies. By 1959, more than 16,900 African Americans lived in Fayette County. In comparison to its white residents, black families comprised almost seventy percent of the county's total populace. Consequently, when this long-disenfranchised majority began to organize that year under the leadership of John McFerren, the potential shift in racial power terrified the white minority.

As the founders of the county's new social justice organization, the Fayette County Civic & Welfare League/FCCWL, James Estes, the McFerrens, the Jamesons, and other black leaders from the area launched a voter registration drive on behalf of Fayette's African-American community. The results were immediate. They arrived by foot in worn-out shoe leather, packed inside dented cars, and loaded into the backs of rusted pick-up truck beds. They suffered under Tennessee's unrelenting heat and humidity, only to then endure bureaucratic stonewalling, verbal harassment, and physical assaults. In the months following the Dodson trial in April, hundreds of brave African-American men and women lined up, one by one and reticently proud, on the outdoor steps of the Fayette County Courthouse in downtown Somerville to register as official voters in the region's upcoming elections. But the new League's push to upend the white community's ruthlessly racist stranglehold on local politics quickly caught the fearful attention of government officials in Somerville, the Fayette County Sheriff's Department, and the area's wealthy white business and agricultural establishment.

Unified under the gleaming robe of the county's White Citizens Council, dozens of upper and middle-class landowners, merchants, politicians, judges, and law enforcement officials met in secret, strategized, and ultimately implemented a scheme to thwart the black voting efforts. First, West Tennessee Democratic Party leaders and Fayette County election officials audaciously, and in violation of constitutional law, barred hundreds of already registered African Americans from entering the polls during the local primary on August 1, 1959. In a letter distributed to precinct officials by representatives of the local Democratic Party, it was stated, "If any Negroes should ask to vote in your district, they are to be informed that this is a White Democratic Primary and not a general election." In turn, Attorney Estes, McFerren, and the FCCWL submitted an official complaint to the DOJ's Civil Rights Division, and on November 16, 1959, a federal lawsuit was filed against Fayette County's Democratic Executive Committee.

It was immediately clear to the local white leadership that a more devious method for eliminating the county's black voter base was needed. As a means of quietly circumventing the recent legal action taken by the federal government while also forcing the black registrants to move out of Fayette County en masse, the White Citizens Council next initiated an economic embargo. After a list of names of Fayette County's black voters was compiled, this new "blacklist" was copied and then quietly distributed to each of the area's commercial and industrial establishments. By the spring of 1960, dozens of white business owners, including physicians, insurance agents, grocers, bankers, auto mechanics, and gasoline distributors, had joined the embargo, secretly agreeing to deny much-needed products and services to the county's African-American voters. Then, when that wasn't enough to push them out of the area, the county's white cabal dealt yet another, even more, devastating blow.

As 1960 drew to a close and the bone-chilling months of winter set in, the blacklist was once again used for nefarious purposes, this time to evict numerous families from the only homes they had ever known. Many of Fayette County's black citizens were tenant farmers at the time. As such, these families, in exchange for working on white-owned farms, lived rent-free in barely inhabitable shanties located on the same white farm owner's property. As part of this repugnant tenant-farming and sharecropping system, it was also necessary for the black families to take out crop loans from their white landlords in order to pay for the initial supplies required for a profitable future harvest. But as the individual tenant farmers and sharecroppers became registered voters, and the blacklist was circulated amongst their white Fayette County landlords, early repayment of these crop loans was angrily demanded in full, and numerous men, women, and children were thrown out of their tenant-farming homes.

In response to the crisis, a black farmer and landowner named Shepard Towles permitted dozens of now homeless families to live in canvas tents on his open field south of Somerville. The encampment, ultimately led by respected civil rights leader and Towles' friend John McFerren, quickly earned the nickname "Tent City." John and other industrious black leaders from the area quickly provided the Tent City residents with kerosene lighting, heat from oil and wood-burning stoves, and solid flooring made of wooden pallets and layered sheets of cardboard. Many of the tenants were happily overwhelmed by the new tents. When compared to the drafty shacks they had suffered in for generations, the canvas accommodations were a vast improvement in keeping out the weather. Despite the harsh winters and drenching rains, a lack of proper bathroom, laundry, and cooking facilities, drive-by-shootings at the hands of local white teens and Klansmen, and the continued pressure of the economic embargo, scores of African American residents from Fayette County remained in Tent City for the next three years.

The McFerren Grocery and Oil Company

Robert McFerren, John's more educated sibling, had long been the owner and manager of the McFerren Grocery and Oil Company. The rural enterprise, located on the west side of Highway 195, looked out over the three-way merging of Highways 195, 76, and Lagrange Road about a mile and a half south of the Somerville town square. It was a small and simple structure, built from drab cinder blocks, topped with sheets of corrugated metal, and painted all in white. Serving as its primary signage, propped up just above the business's main entrance and crumbling wooden canopy, a five-tiered, pyramid-like facade had been constructed of shiplap and was hand-painted with the words "McFERREN GRO." In the gravel parking lot in front of the building, two bulbous gas pumps stood attentively like wet nurses from the antebellum past, waiting obediently for a thirsty visitor in need of nurturing and feeding. Due to the business's popular locale near Somerville's black community and the three-way intersection's frequent in-and-out-of-town traffic, Robert McFerren consistently earned a respectable annual income.

But just months after the Dodson trial in 1959, all hell broke loose. At first, the area's white leadership believed that it was Robert who was stirring up all the trouble. After all, they wondered, how could an illiterate, uneducated black farmer like John McFerren start a voter registration drive that large? It didn't seem possible. Consequently, it was the other McFerren, the more successful and academically trained

Robert, who was mistakenly blamed for instigating the county's racial upheaval. In the months that followed, Robert's entrepreneurial endeavor became one of the many targets of the white merchants' embargo. It began with only small items. First, the local Coca-Cola bottler refused to stock Robert's cold storage with soft drinks. Next, the nearby dairy stopped delivering milk, butter, cheese, and ice cream.

Eventually, a wealthy Fayette County farmer, banker, and Somerville Gulf Oil distributor dealt the most damaging blow. A nearby white man by the name of Reuben "Rube" Scott Rhea Sr. began halting large shipments of fuel to Robert's gas station. Adding insult to injury, Mr. Rhea, who legally owned the underground tanks and fuel pumps at Robert's business, later ordered that the equipment be physically removed from the property to ensure that Robert never sold gasoline again. In quickstep, large earth-moving equipment under the direction of Rhea arrived at the three-way gas station and dug up Robert's fuel tanks. With a rapidly dwindling supply of goods to offer to his neighboring black customers, Robert, now defeated and demoralized, eventually threw up his hands, closed the business, and moved away.

The fallout weighed heavily on John's shoulders. In truth, he had been the catalyst of Robert's undoing. And although he was desperate to make it up to his brother, there were additional factors that contributed to John's final decision. In the weeks following Robert's forfeiture of the business, John was encouraged by other black leaders from the area to reopen the establishment as a way of supplying the goods and services the white embargo had since denied to the black community. By 1960, John and Viola McFerren had gone into business for themselves and were renting Robert's old building from him for $50.00 a month. But because of the continued embargo, John was forced to make day-long trips into Memphis to buy the essential supplies he could then sell at his store.

It was a rough haul, and he often had to flag down delivery trucks along the side of the road or secretly approach them in back alleyways in order to purchase crucial items such as bread, milk, and beef. During his starlit trips back into Fayette County, he was often confronted by large motorcades of patrolling Klansmen. But the crafty driver was several steps ahead of the notorious lynch mobs. Predicting their future efforts to stop him at every corner, John routinely slipped in and out of town by navigating Macon Road and the other bumpy backroads of Fayette County. He also re-equipped his clunky, 1955 black Ford Fairlane with a high-powered Thunderbird engine, a pair of four-barreled carburetors, and a custom-designed suspension system that allowed him to make high-speed turns when being chased. Much like the local moonshiners of the day, and the Southern stock car racers they eventually spawned, John became an ace at modifying his getaway car and outrunning the enemy.

The next, much larger hurdle to overcome was the issue of the business's lack of fuel tanks, fuel pumps, and the unavailability of local fuel shipments. Undeterred by the seemingly insurmountable challenges before him, John spent most of the McFerren couple's savings on two new tanks and pumps to replace the ones that had been taken from Robert. Then, on cue, the White Citizens Council reared its ugly head yet again. When John finally got the two 6000-gallon tanks buried underground and then ordered the first fuel shipment to be delivered from Memphis, a local Fayette County Sheriff's deputy named Thomas Edward "Ted" Davis stopped the out-of-town fuel tanker as it entered the county. According to past reports, Davis pulled out his gun and threatened the truck driver with bodily harm, ultimately forcing the man to turn the tanker around. It was only after secret negotiations with the NAACP, the DOJ, and a distant fuel refinery several months later that John and Viola finally acquired the gasoline needed to fill their new tanks.

Encouraged by their business's hard-fought success from early 1960 through 1961, the married entrepreneurs ultimately set out to construct a larger, more modern building that would serve as a combination gas station, grocery, café, maintenance garage, and laundromat. Faced with FCCWL infighting, frivolous lawsuits meant to disrupt their personal financial standing, and the denial of local financing, the McFerrens finally secured a large business loan from Dr. James A. Dombrowski, a liberal social activist and Executive Director of the Southern Conference Educational Fund in New Orleans. In 1963, and much to the chagrin of the area's white coveters, John completed construction of the new McFerren Grocery and Oil Company next door to Robert's former building. Sometime later, the couple obtained another loan through the Small Business Administration which they used to pay back Dr. Dombrowski's organization. Still, the McFerrens and their new building were the continued targets of frequent drive-by shootings, harassing telephone calls, and various threats at the hands of the local KKK.

In spite of the constant pressures, the McFerren Grocery and Oil Company remained at the epicenter of the civil rights movement in Fayette County for the next decade. From the moment they took over Robert's old building, John and Viola's business became the local black community's primary meeting place. It was there that area residents traveled to contact the leadership of the FCCWL (later, the Original FCCWL) when in dire need of assistance. Quickly, the grocery and gas station also established itself as the main drop point for donated clothing and food distributions to those living in Tent City. It was also used as a staging area for the 1.6-mile civil rights marches the McFerrens regularly led from southern Somerville, north along Highway 76, and onto the steps of the Fayette County Courthouse. And finally, the destination was a safe haven where area activists frequently held secret strategy meetings and quietly exchanged sensitive local information.

Attention and Assistance

They journeyed day and night to reach their destinations. They drove without rest to the urban meccas of the more progressive North, determined to convey their message to those who might listen. They left their frightened wives and children behind for days at a time. They pounded the concrete sidewalks of Washington, D.C., Chicago, Newark, and New York City in search of sympathetic ears, media attention, and hopefully legal and financial assistance. Throughout their struggle to gain racial equality and individual freedom, Attorney James F. Estes, John McFerren, Harpman Jameson, and other West Tennessee African Americans traveled hundreds of miles to meet with some of the most influential government and social leaders of the era.

In January 1960, the brave black leaders made the lengthy trip to the nation's capital to attend the Volunteer Civil Rights Commission hearings hosted by a number of organizations including Dr. King's Southern Christian Leadership Conference/SCLC. In a deeply emotional question and answer session led by the Rev. James Lawson, John McFerren spoke candidly at the hearings about the plight of Fayette County's black community.

During his lengthy comments, John outlined the violence his mother had recently suffered at the hands of a local white dairy truck driver. It was his contention to the Rev. Lawson that Mrs. Estella McFerren, while standing in her own front yard, was run down by a delivery driver who worked for the nearby Cedar Hill Farms dairy. It was also McFerren's claim that the accident was most likely intentional. Worse yet, when the Tennessee Highway Patrol reached the scene of the incident at Mrs. McFerren's home just south of Somerville, no charges were filed against the dairy truck driver.

Not long after his return home from the January hearings in D.C., John encountered the same patrolman who investigated the prior calamity. After being pulled over by Tennessee Highway Patrolman Jerry

Simmons near the McFerrens' business, John was interrogated about his recent comments in Washington and then threatened by Patrolman Simmons. According to a February 17, 1960 article in the *Memphis World* (a now-defunct locally-owned African-American newspaper), Simmons told McFerren:

> The reason nothing was done is because that is the way I saw it. You talk too much. What you need is a good head-whipping, that would shut your mouth up. What you need is for me to catch you out one night and give you a good head-beating.

While local and state newspapers such as *The Commercial Appeal*, *Tri-State Defender*, *Memphis World*, *The Jackson Sun*, and *The Nashville Tennessean* published regular pieces on the Fayette County conflict in 1959, it wasn't until the summer of the following year that the national press picked up the story. In August of 1960, African-American journalist Ted Poston wrote a series of hard-hitting editorials for the *New York Post* focusing on the social kettle that was boiling over in Somerville. Not long afterward, numerous other publications raced to cover the salacious saga, including *TIME*, *Jet*, and *Ebony* magazines. In the case of *Ebony*, a full six-page spread was dedicated to the issue in its September 1960 edition. In the article entitled "Cold War in Fayette County," numerous black-and-white photographs, including one of Winfrey Bottom, Somerville's detestable black ghetto, accompanied a photostatic copy of the infamous blacklist. In the *Ebony* article, John McFerren himself was quoted as saying:

> I was born and raised in Fayette County. It was 18 years before I was taken into the army and before I even knowed I had a country. I came back here and made a home. I think it is as important for me to fight a war here as it is for me to go over there and fight. This war is just as important as World War II.

As a result of the national news coverage, a wave of both private and federal assistance poured into Fayette County. Over the course of the next several years, throngs of civic-minded college students from the North made the annual pilgrimage to volunteer at Tent City. High-profile civil rights organizations such as the NAACP and Dr. King's SCLC donated money and provided free legal assistance to the FCCWL. Well-known black civil rights leaders and attorneys from Memphis, such as the Rev. James Lawson, Dr. Benjamin Hooks, Russell Sugarmon, and A.W. Willis, risked their lives to bail out jailed activists in Somerville. The Invaders, a now-disbanded black militant group from Memphis, occasionally provided aid.

Jimmy Hoffa's International Brotherhood of Teamsters (Local 97 in Newark, New Jersey) gladly gave much-needed food and clothing. Even a Memphis-based sect of the Nation of Islam and communist groups linked to the Soviet Union approached the McFerrens to offer assistance. Luckily, the patriotic and freedom-loving John and Viola were wise enough to recognize, at least most of the time, the dark political strings that were attached to some of these more radical organizations, and therefore declined their help.

But most important to the McFerrens, Jamesons, FCCWL, and the members of Fayette's black community was the powerful support granted by the White House and the Department of Justice. During his first filmed press conference on January 25, 1961, a newly sworn-in President John Fitzgerald Kennedy was asked by African-American reporter Alice Dunnigan:

Does your administration plan to take any steps to solve the problem in Fayette...uh Fayette County, Tennessee, where tenant...tenant farmers have been evicted from their homes because they voted last November, and must now live in tents?

President Kennedy then responded:

> We are uh...the Congress, of course, enacted legislation which
> placed very clear responsibility on the executive branch, to protect
> the right of voting. I am extreme...I supported that legislation. I am
> extremely interested in making sure that every American is given
> the right to cast his vote without prejudice to his rights as a citizen.
> And therefore I can, uh state that this administration will, pursue
> uh, the problem of providing that protection, uh...with all vigor.

Even before America's version of Camelot seized control of
Washington's gilded reins, James F. Estes, the McFerrens, and the
FCCWL were in constant communication with the DOJ's Civil
Rights Division under the Eisenhower administration. But it was
only after President Kennedy's inauguration that the U.S. government
supercharged its efforts to extinguish the racial firestorm
that had engulfed Fayette County. At the new President's
direction, a large stockpile of federally-funded food was sent to Tent
City in the summer of 1961. The President's younger brother, Attorney
General Robert F. Kennedy, also directed U.S. Assistant Attorney
General John Michael Doar to double his efforts in resolving the issue
of the economic embargo and exiled tenant farmers. With the assistance
of fellow Civil Rights Division Attorney J. Harold "Nick" Flannery
Jr., Doar ultimately settled the federal lawsuits in a Cincinnati, Ohio
courtroom in 1962. The federal court's consent decree included a stern
warning to Fayette County's white merchants and landowners never to
harass the McFerrens and other black residents again.

Desegregation and the DOJ

As the old segregationist adage goes, they were "separate but equal."
Yes, it was true; public schools in the nineteenth and twentieth centuries

were separated by race, little white boys and girls over here, little black boys and girls over there. But in reality, the education offered to African Americans living in the alleged separate-but-equal Jim Crow South was repugnant, to say the least. Unlike their white counterparts, the school year for black children was not dedicated to providing them with an adequate education, but instead scheduled around the cotton planting and harvesting seasons. When they weren't toiling under the blistering sun, chopping cotton alongside their tenant-farming parents, hundreds of youngsters were stuffed into overcrowded ramshackle school houses barely fit for livestock. They lacked desks and school books, and what materials they were afforded were worn-out hand-me-downs donated by neighboring white schools.

In Viola Harris's hometown of Michigan City, Mississippi, a small community less than a mile from the Tennessee border, there wasn't even a school for African-American teenagers to attend. Hungry to learn, she walked five miles every day across the state line into Fayette County just to catch a bus in LaGrange, Tennessee. From there, she and her fellow passengers were driven several additional miles to the Fayette County Training School in Somerville. Even after her marriage to John McFerren in 1950, the determined young wife and eventual mother continued to look toward the horizon by attending Jackson State Community College and Memphis State University, a school known today as the University of Memphis. Clearly, the attainment of a proper education was extremely important to Mrs. Viola Harris McFerren.

Consequently, when she and John became parents, it was paramount to Viola that her own children be provided with suitable academic opportunities. In 1965, the McFerrens sought the help of the DOJ's Civil Rights Division once again. In yet another effort to end the area's despotic segregationist traditions, John, Viola, and numerous other African-American parents filed a federal desegregation lawsuit in June of that year against the Fayette County school board. Cited as "*McFerren v. County Board of Education of Fayette County, Tennessee*," the federal action was named in honor of one of the lawsuit's many plaintiffs, John and Viola's first son, John McFerren Jr.

Although school integration in Fayette County was eventually achieved, the challenges facing the newly integrated black students were almost unbearable. School bus rides were torture. Pennies were pelted at the heads of the black boys and girls, and they were repeatedly called the "N-word" by opposing white students. Fights broke out in school hallways, and local white administrators, teachers, and other staff members regarded the African-American children with utter contempt. Due to their previous school environment, most were behind academically and struggled to catch up to their white peers. But unlike the underprivileged white children who were also integrated into the new public education system, Fayette County's more affluent and middle-class white families found an avenue for avoiding the fiery issue altogether.

Immediately following the July 1965 submission and recognition of the new desegregation plan, an all-white private school called Fayette Academy was established in the heart of the county. Along with the sudden blossoming of other private schools in West Tennessee that year, Fayette Academy's enrollment quickly swelled. Funding the school's development was not a problem, and much-needed start-up cash flowed in through private tuition payments and the financial backing of numerous white landowners, businessmen, bankers, and government officials in Somerville. Unquestionably, Fayette Academy, while claiming it provided a private "Christian Education," was created solely to prevent impoverished African-American children from attending the costly institution, thereby allowing white parents and their own children to evade the impending federal school desegregation judgments.

In 1966, just a year after its inception, the new all-white school was provided with a large tract of land located on the south side of Highway 64 just west of downtown Somerville. Eager to assist Fayette Academy and its future growth, wealthy landowner, banker, and businessman, Reuben "Rube" Scott Rhea Sr. sold thirty-three acres of agricultural real estate to the private institution's school board. In the end, Fayette Academy became an exclusive haven for Fayette County's middle and upper-class white community. During a hearing held in Nashville on April 6, 1971, Federal District Court Judge Robert N. McRae staunchly asserted that Fayette Academy was a "beautiful building sitting on top of a hill as a monument against the black people."

But while the U.S. court system and other federal agencies, specifically the DOJ's Civil Rights Division, were professed allies of the African Americans who called Fayette County home in the 1960s, another subsidiary of the DOJ was, at the exact same time, diametrically opposed to the McFerrens and their unrelenting civil rights endeavors.

Chapter 2

HOOVER'S MEN

FROM THE MOMENT of its formation in 1924, the Federal Bureau of Investigation was focused on two social ills: crime and communism. In response to the latter, the FBI, under the authority of its founding director, J. Edgar Hoover, initiated the now highly controversial Counterintelligence Program or "COINTELPRO" in 1956. In a paranoid effort to combat political and social organizations he deemed as communist, radical, subversive, or "anti-American," Hoover authorized FBI field offices throughout the country to conduct covert and often illegal surveillance on United States citizens, specifically those leading the burgeoning and perhaps communist-linked black civil rights movement. Once an adequate degree of warranted intelligence was accumulated through these surveillance endeavors, the FBI would then deploy counterintelligence measures to disrupt the inner workings of said civil rights groups. Just a few years after COINTELPRO's inception, a number of African-American civil rights activists living in Fayette County were targeted by an unofficial derivative of this secret FBI program.

History of Opposition

Randall Stephens uncovered his first clue regarding John and Viola McFerren's acrimonious relationship with Hoover's men in a pair of newspaper clippings published in September and October of 1959. In the articles, two employees of the Memphis FBI field office, Special Agent Franklin Lewis Johnson and his supervisor, Special Agent in Charge Frank C. Holloman, were accused by the FCCWL's attorney, James F. Estes, of secretly using their positions as federal civil rights investigators under the DOJ to spy on the area's black activists. The articles went on to claim that private information provided by the activists to Special Agent Franklin L. Johnson had mysteriously made its way into the hands of the county's racist white leadership, specifically the local sheriff's department. In a separate document chronicling the same issue, Stephens learned that McFerren was himself questioned by Special Agent Johnson, and then immediately threatened once his statements to the FBI reached the Fayette County Sheriff's department. Due to Attorney Estes's complaints, authorities inside the Civil Rights Division at the DOJ ultimately removed both Special Agent Franklin Johnson and Special Agent in Charge Holloman from the Fayette County inquiry, replacing them with other investigators.

While it was not completely evident to Estes and the McFerrens at the time, their suspicion that the local FBI office was in collusion with the county sheriff had merit. According to several FBI memos discovered by Stephens, Fayette County Sheriff Clarence Edward "C.E." Pattat Jr. regularly coordinated with the Bureau in a combined effort to spy on the county's black citizens. In one example dated January 29, 1961, Sheriff Pattat called the Memphis FBI field office to advise them that several out-of-town whites had traveled to the immediate area to assist the families living in Tent City. In the three-page memo, the license plate numbers, names, campus activities, and political leanings of the five college students from Texas and Michigan were eventually investigated and thoroughly detailed by the Bureau based on the information Sheriff Pattat provided.

Stephens' next indication that the McFerrens and FBI were on opposing sides came by way of a Sunday, September 12, 2010 article published in *The Commercial Appeal*, Memphis's primary newspaper. Written by investigative journalist Marc Perrusquia, the shocking story revealed that famed civil rights photographer, MLK friend, and Memphis resident Ernest Columbus Withers had been paid by the FBI for more than a decade to spy on his friends and fellow activists. As an African American, former Memphis police officer, and subsequent confidential informant, Withers, who was designated as informant "ME 338-R," secretly provided the Memphis FBI field office with photos and intelligence on organizations led by his closest allies. Among the countless black leaders Withers spied on were the McFerrens in neighboring Fayette County.

Eventually, Stephens obtained and examined several declassified FBI documents outlining personal conversations between the prying Withers and an unwitting John McFerren. From 1961 on, Withers regularly spoke with the McFerrens and other Fayette County activists about public and private matters and then relayed those conversations to Special Agent William H. Lawrence at the FBI field office in Memphis. Outside the FBI's official COINTELPRO channels, Agent Lawrence was also running his own Memphis-based surveillance initiative, which he simply named the "interview program." Included with the mountain of local and national intelligence Withers routinely provided Lawrence through the FBI agent's COINTELPRO offshoot, the photog reported on John McFerren's tenuous connections to Nation of Islam leader Elijah Muhammad and alleged Communist Dr. James A. Dombrowski.

In a third and incredibly shocking case, Stephens also uncovered documented evidence verifying that one of the McFerren's own

Fayette County neighbors, a trusted friend and local black civil rights ally, was yet another confidential informant for the FBI. According to a July 17, 1978 declassified government memo, former Fayette County school teacher and NAACP President Allen Yancey Jr., designated in the federal document as informant "ME 339-R," began spying on his friends and fellow activists as early as 1965. Undoubtedly, the targets of Yancey's work would have included the leaders of the Fayette County movement, John and Viola McFerren. After providing the intelligence to his succession of handlers at the FBI field office in Memphis, Yancey was most certainly given cash payments as compensation for his clandestine efforts.

As time went on, the McFerrens, when battling the closely-knit band of white authorities who ruled over Fayette County and West Tennessee, continued to naively call upon Hoover's FBI and the federal employees who worked under Attorneys General Robert F. Kennedy, Nicholas Katzenbach, and Ramsey Clark. But it was John McFerren's well-recorded encounters with Hoover's men in April of 1968 that Stephens was most interested in.

Room 561

As a much younger man, he had schlepped fresh quail across the Fayette and Shelby County border for extra money. But while he had been a frequent visitor to the lower guts of the majestic Memphis establishment before, this was the forty-three-year-old McFerren's first time seeing the inside of one of its lavish guest rooms. In a secretly hatched plan to protect his anonymity and safety, John found himself sitting across from several white men inside room 561 at the famous Peabody Hotel during the predawn hours of Monday, April 8, 1968. According to an MPD Departmental Communication dated April 12, 1968, and a partially redacted FBI 302 report dated April 11 of the same year, the group included McFerren's friend and civil rights comrade; the Rev. Sidney Baxton Bryant, who was a white Methodist minister and head of the Tennessee Council on Human Relations; and ACLU Attorney David Earl Caywood from the Burch Porter & Johnson law firm.

Also present were Memphis FBI Special Agent Orville Vernon "O.V." Johnson and Memphis Police Chief Homicide Inspector Nevelyn E. "N.E." Zachary. Born in Lambert, Mississippi, in 1922, O.V. Johnson was eventually assigned to the Memphis FBI field office and was one of the primary special agents investigating Dr. King's recent murder. N.E. Zachary was also born in Mississippi, just a year after Johnson in 1923, employed with the MPD since 1948, and was a 1964 graduate of the FBI Academy. No doubt cut from the same cloth, the two law enforcement officials from Mississippi worked the hotel room that morning like well-seasoned partners.

Stephens learned early on in his research that someone from McFerren's past, although not an official participant in the interview process, may have attended the hotel meeting as well. It was McFerren's decades-long assertion that newly appointed Memphis Police and Fire Director Frank C. Holloman was also inside room 561 that morning. As fate would have it, this was the same Frank Holloman who was summarily dismissed from the DOJ's Fayette County civil rights investigation after Estes and McFerren complained in 1959.

Frank Catchings Holloman was an FBI G-Man, through and through. Like O.V. Johnson and N.E. Zachary, he originally hailed from Mississippi. Born on July 8, 1914, Holloman had been with the Bureau since the late 1930s and was J. Edgar Hoover's right-hand man at the FBI Director's office in Washington, D.C. from 1949 to 1959. Following his service at the nation's capital, Special Agent in Charge Holloman took over the Memphis FBI field office. Immediately upon Holloman's arrival in 1959, Special Agent William H. Lawrence began reporting to him that first year and continued to work alongside the former Special Agent in Charge from 1960 to 1964, even after Holloman was demoted by Hoover. It was during this multiyear collaboration between the two special agents in Memphis that Lawrence, with the assistance of his Bluff City confidential informant, Ernest C. Withers, regularly spied on John McFerren on behalf of the FBI.

If since-retired FBI Special Agent and eventual MPD Director Frank Holloman was, in fact, present during the hotel interview as McFerren claimed, then the former federal agent would have most likely remembered the Fayette County black man as one of the troublemaking activists he and Lawrence had dealt with numerous times before. To Stephens, this prior contention between the local FBI and the Fayette County civil rights leader was sufficient cause to believe that Holloman would have been secretly hostile toward McFerren and the information he eventually provided. Nevertheless, McFerren went on to furnish the law enforcement officials in the hotel room that morning with the following details.

April 8, 1968 Interview

As outlined in both N.E. Zachary's MPD Departmental Communication and Special Agent O.V. Johnson's FBI 302 report, McFerren stated that approximately a week before the assassination of Dr. Martin Luther King Jr., he overheard several men making incendiary remarks about Dr. King while gathered together at the Liberto, Liberto, and Latch/LL&L Produce Company. At the time, LL&L occupied a large concrete block and metal warehouse located inside the 814 Scott Street farmers market in Memphis. McFerren claimed that the owner of the LL&L Produce Company, a man McFerren believed to be of possible "Puerto Rican extraction" who had gapped teeth and weighed approximately 300 lbs., could be heard barking to four other men, "They ought to shoot the son-of-a-bitch." When the truculent produce owner then turned his attention to the nearby McFerren and asked,

"What do you think about King and his mess?", McFerren humbly replied, "I tend to my own business."

During the same April 8 interview, McFerren also furnished the MPD and FBI investigators with information on two additional conversations he had overheard at the LL&L warehouse, this time occurring the very day of Dr. King's horrific murder. McFerren claimed that on the morning of April 4, 1968, he again made his regular Thursday trip from his business just outside of Somerville to Memphis to purchase supplies for his Fayette County grocery store. At approximately 4:20 p.m., after shopping throughout the morning and afternoon, he began driving toward his last stop of the day, the same 814 Scott Street farmers market he had patronized the week before. After purchasing a sack of potatoes from one of the market's small outdoor vendors, McFerren parked his vehicle and walked into the LL&L warehouse at approximately 4:45 p.m.

As he entered the large concrete and steel building through its dock entrance, McFerren peered through the small open door just off to his right and witnessed the same heavyset produce owner sitting at a desk inside the warehouse's main office. The heavyset man was speaking on the telephone at the time and had not noticed McFerren walk up behind him. In that instant, McFerren heard the heavyset man scream into the telephone, "Kill the son-of-a-bitch on the balcony and get the job done. You will get your $5,000."

Without warning, the second owner of the produce business, a thin white man with a scar on his right cheek, walked around the corner and confronted McFerren. When asked what he was doing there, McFerren calmly replied that he wanted to buy some produce. After being told to help himself, the unassuming shopper proceeded to the back of the warehouse to pick out his items. Only a few minutes later, while perusing the colorful assortment of fruits and vegetables, McFerren heard the loud ring of the office telephone echo throughout the concrete and metal building. This time, the thin white man with the scar could be overheard picking up the receiver and answering the call.

As Stephens read on, he noted that in both the MPD and FBI 302 reports, it was indicated that McFerren didn't clarify what the thin, scarred man said to the caller at the time. Nevertheless, it was evident to McFerren that the second business owner made some kind of statement just before quickly handing off the telephone receiver to the heavyset man. It was then that McFerren overheard one side of yet a second heated telephone exchange. Once again screaming, the heavyset business owner told the caller, "Don't come out here. Go to New Orleans and get your money. You know my brother."

At the conclusion of the second, albeit brief, telephone conversation, McFerren approached the office to ask the scarred thin man about purchasing two bushels of apples. After being told that he would have to buy the apples elsewhere, McFerren quickly paid for his items, departed the building, and began the hour-long drive back to his Fayette County business. According to his calculations, McFerren was inside the Scott Street warehouse approximately ten minutes that day, heard both telephone conversations sometime between 4:45 and 5:15 p.m., and was back at his Somerville store by 6:15 p.m. when he learned of the 6:01 p.m. shooting of Dr. King in Memphis.

McFerren continued his account that April 8 morning by advising the investigators that on April 6, the Saturday following the shooting, McFerren's wife, Viola, noted that a hand-drawn composite and a written description of Dr. King's suspected assassin had been published in *The Commercial Appeal*. After reviewing the sketch artist's rendering of the unknown assailant and listening to Viola read the description, McFerren immediately believed that the man depicted was a former employee of the same 814 Scott Street business.

According to McFerren's Monday morning statement to the MPD and FBI, the suspect first began working for both business owners at the LL&L Produce Company sometime in the summer of 1967.

McFerren also went on to state that the former employee was a cross between an Indian, a Cuban, a Mexican, or a Puerto Rican, exhibited a "very yellow complexion," and that he had contracted on his neck what McFerren stated was "jungle rot." McFerren then claimed that the suspect he saw was 5'9" or more, weighed 140 lbs., had a slender build, and was approximately twenty-five years old. McFerren concluded his April 8 interview with the MPD and FBI by stating that, out of extreme caution, he had only revealed his beliefs to his wife and their family friend, Baxton Bryant.

April 18, 1968 Interview

After thoroughly examining the MPD and FBI's April 8, 1968 interviews, Stephens shifted his attention to the next official statement given by McFerren, this time recorded ten days later on Thursday, April 18. Unlike the single redacted copy of the FBI's Peabody Hotel inquiry, this time, Stephens had the benefit of examining two different versions of the same 302 report. Hidden amongst the hundreds of unorganized documents Marcus Holmes had hurriedly donated, an unredacted copy of McFerren's second statement was found by Stephens. No doubt given to Holmes by McFerren, the 302 report listed specific names, addresses, and other important details that would have normally been redacted by federal agents during the declassification process. However, some of the report was extremely faded and, therefore, illegible.

Thankfully, the second, partially-redacted version of the same 302 report that Stephens found online was clear and easier to read. While the online version failed to include the names and addresses listed in McFerren's copy, it did clear up the previously faded sections that Stephens was unable to decipher. When he placed the two versions side by side, Stephens was able to piece together an unredacted and unfaded April 18 interview that was complete and simple to read.

Unlike his first MLK interview, this time McFerren hadn't been required to travel under the cover of darkness into Memphis. Questioned only by FBI Special Agents Robert Fitzpatrick and Andrew Sloan, McFerren instead recounted his story from the privacy and relative safety of his Fayette County gas and grocery business. As he had on April 8, McFerren told the FBI investigators what he first witnessed on Thursday, March 28, while shopping at the Liberto, Liberto & Latch Produce Company.

But according to the typed 302 report authored by Fitzpatrick and Sloan, both the "heavyset man" and "the man with the scar" were now confusingly combined into the same individual. The scarred, heavyset man approached McFerren and inquired, "What do you think about your buddy?", at which time McFerren asked, "Who are you talking about?"

The heavyset man then replied, "Martin Luther King."

Doing his best to appear indifferent, McFerren answered simply with, "I tend to my own business."

Not satisfied with McFerren's passive response, and obviously intent on goading his black customer, the heavyset man pressed further: "Somebody ought to shoot the son-of-a-bitch!"

Again, appearing as submissively apathetic as possible, McFerren calmly repeated, "I tend to my own business."

McFerren then went on to describe his next experience at the warehouse the following week. McFerren told Fitzpatrick and Sloan that on the late afternoon of April 4, he eventually made his way to the LL&L Produce Company. As he entered the warehouse through "a garage type door," he witnessed a man sitting at a desk inside the office yelling into a telephone, "Kill the son-of-a-bitch on the balcony! I don't care how you get the job done, just get it done!" McFerren stated that, because the portly man was facing away from the large warehouse door, he didn't notice McFerren standing behind him during the telephone conversation. McFerren also explained that when he heard the man's exclamations, he didn't know what they meant at the time.

The heavyset man he overheard, the owner or manager of the LL&L Produce Company, had straight hair and gapped teeth, was about six feet tall, weighed approximately 250 to 300 lbs., and was wearing a red sports shirt at the time. Although McFerren stated that the heavyset business owner was white, he also asserted once again that he had "dark skin" and was of possible "Puerto Rican" or some other "foreign extraction."

McFerren then explained to Agents Fitzpatrick and Sloan that, as he was preparing to leave that day, he heard the office telephone ring, which was then answered by the scarred man. Stephens noted that the same 302 report now inconsistently referenced the scarred man as a second individual separate from the heavyset man. Nonetheless, Stephens continued to read McFerren's paraphrased account.

McFerren then told the FBI agents that, immediately after answering the telephone, the scarred man said something to the heavyset man just before handing him the phone receiver. At that moment, McFerren overheard the heavyset man scream into the telephone, "Go to New Orleans and get your $5,000, and don't bring your ass near my place, and don't call me anymore. You know my brother in New Orleans." Before he could complete his shopping at the warehouse, McFerren was told by the "nervous" managers that he would have to purchase his last items elsewhere. It was McFerren's assertion that he was inside the LL&L produce warehouse no more than thirty minutes on the day of April 4 and heard the second phone call sometime around 5:15 p.m.

McFerren then explained to the two FBI agents that, on the Saturday after the assassination, he observed a hand-drawn composite in the April 6 edition of *The Commercial Appeal* that depicted the unknown suspect. After listening to his wife read the description of the alleged shooter and then comparing that description to the published sketch, McFerren believed that the depicted suspect was the same person who had been employed at the LL&L warehouse sometime in the late fall or early winter of 1967.

According to McFerren, the former employee, although white, had a "light tan" or was a "Puerto Rican type individual" with long, straight, coarse black hair. The man also suffered from what McFerren again described as "jungle rot" on his neck, exhibited "dropped shoulders," and was of a slender build. McFerren estimated that the alleged shooter was between 5'10" and 5'11", weighed 160 lbs., was not a day over twenty-five years of age, and was a cross between an Indian, Cuban, and Mexican. McFerren also stated that he could possibly identify the alleged gunman despite the fact that he had not witnessed him working at the LL&L warehouse since the late fall or early winter.

But unlike the April 8 interview, McFerren included an incident that had occurred since his first MPD and FBI meeting at the Peabody. In fact, the unnerving event had taken place that very morning, the same day he was interviewed by Fitzpatrick and Sloan. Just a handful of hours before his second interview with Hoover's men, sometime between 8:30 and 9:00 a.m. on April 18, a beige, late model 1966 or 1967 Cadillac with a gold emblem affixed to its front license plate arrived at McFerren's home. According to John, a white man he recognized as a former resident of Somerville, named Robert Powers, exited the Cadillac and approached him as he stood in the McFerrens' front yard.

McFerren stated that Powers used to own and operate the Powers Store in Somerville. He also stated that about twelve years prior to 1968, Powers moved to New Orleans and opened an all-night truck stop at the junction of U.S. Routes 11 and 90. As described by McFerren, the Powers' truck stop property also included a collection of house trailers, although he did not elaborate on what their significance was.

Reaching out to shake hands, the visiting Powers stated that he was "glad to see him" just before asking McFerren about his plans for the day. Immediately suspicious of the sudden inquiry into his regular Thursday schedule, the now-uneasy McFerren lied to Powers, claiming that he was not headed into Memphis until sometime around 4:00 p.m. Powers continued his odd probe by asking McFerren if he was putting on weight, and if the former Powers Store Road still connected to "Old Macon Road" in Fayette County. Powers' mention of Macon Road was even more alarming, especially since John regularly used the route when making his low-key trips in and out of Fayette County.

Growing more uncomfortable with Powers' intrusive questions, McFerren stated that he "acted dumb" in front of the unwelcomed visitor. At the conclusion of his inquisition, Powers stated that he and his wife were leaving Somerville either that night or the night after, then re-entered his Cadillac and pulled away from the McFerrens' home just as inexplicably as he had arrived.

John went on to explain to the two agents that, while never outwardly threatened, he was very suspicious of Powers' questions and immediately assumed the encounter was connected to the telephone conversations he had overheard at the LL&L Produce Company two weeks earlier. McFerren's suspicions were further raised by Powers' overtly kind demeanor. According to the social norms of the era, it was unheard of for a white man to willingly reach out and shake the hand of a black man in Fayette County.

After Fitzpatrick and Sloan concluded recording all of McFerren's recollections, they presented him with photographs of six men, hopeful he could identify one of the photos as the alleged gunman. Five of the images shown to McFerren were of random individuals who had been arrested in various parts of the United States. They included Norman James Burkert, Folse Joseph Bertaut Jr., Joseph Frank Armone, Ronald Francis Scott, and Bert Vincent Patrem. The sixth and final photograph shown was of the suspected killer himself, Eric Starvo Galt.

McFerren was asked by the two agents if he could identify any of the photographed men as the same person he witnessed working at the warehouse between the late fall and early winter. According to the Fitzpatrick and Sloan 302 report, McFerren immediately eliminated the images of Scott, Patrem, and Galt. Looking closely at the three remaining photos, McFerren then intimated that Burkert looked like the man he saw temporarily working for the two produce owners but that he may have been "too short." While he claimed that Burkert exhibited similar features to the man he witnessed, McFerren ultimately refused to provide the agents with a signed statement due to his uncertainty.

The FBI's 302 report continued by stating that McFerren was then informed that Galt was the man the authorities were seeking for the murder of Dr. King. Fitzpatrick and Sloan's report claimed that McFerren, despite eliminating the Galt photo three times, then changed his mind and began to imply that Galt looked like the temporary employee he had witnessed at the warehouse in late 1967. The report further claimed that McFerren believed the photos of Burkert and Galt shared certain similarities, but in the end, the black interviewee couldn't be sure.

Within the final section of the FBI's 302 report, and subsequently highlighted in bright yellow marker by Marcus Holmes, a typed comment had been included regarding the unwelcomed presence of a *TIME* magazine reporter. It was documented by the FBI report's author that during the questioning of McFerren in Fayette County, the unnamed journalist caused a distraction by photographing the two agents at work. It was at that time that Fitzpatrick and Sloan escorted McFerren away from the prying lens of the journalist's camera. Finally, in the righthand margin of the same highlighted section, Stephens noted that Holmes had scrawled the words "Bill Sartor" in red ink, thus naming the previously unknown *TIME* reporter.

Capture, Confession, Case Closed

On Wednesday, April 17, 1968, the day before Fitzpatrick and Sloan questioned John McFerren, the two agents' superiors in Washington, D.C. supplied the national news media with an update concerning their investigation into Dr. King's murder. According to the press conference held by Attorney General Ramsey Clark and leading officials at the FBI, a federal arrest warrant had just been issued for one Eric Starvo Galt, a.k.a. Harvey Lowmeyer, a.k.a. John Willard, in connection with the shooting conspiracy and death of Dr. Martin Luther King Jr. From the moment his photo was released to the public that Wednesday, Galt became the target of a nationwide, if not worldwide, manhunt.

Then, just two days later, the FBI's forensics lab, through apparent fingerprint analysis, discovered that Galt's real name was, in fact, James Earl Ray. During their startling announcement to the press on Friday, April 19, the day after McFerren's second FBI interview, federal authorities advised that Ray was a convicted armed robber who had been serving a twenty-year sentence inside the Missouri State Penitentiary in Jefferson City, Missouri, when he escaped on April 23, 1967. According to the announcement, Ray had been on the lam for nearly a year before allegedly assassinating Dr. King.

Then, on June 8, 1968, a little more than two months after the shooting in Memphis, the wanted Ray was stopped, questioned, and ultimately captured by British authorities inside London's Heathrow Airport as he tried to board a flight to Brussels, Belgium. After a few weeks of unsuccessfully fighting extradition back to the United States through the United Kingdom's judicial system, Ray contacted, met with, and retained well-known Birmingham, Alabama attorneys Arthur Hanes Sr. and Jr., who arrived in London on June 20 to discuss the impending Tennessee state criminal case against him.

Eventually, the alleged killer of Dr. King was legally extradited and then flown back to Tennessee under the close supervision of Hoover's men. On the still-darkened morning of July 19, 1968, the international flight and its handcuffed passenger arrived at the naval air base in Millington, Tennessee. The FBI's proud agents then handed over their prisoner, placing James Earl Ray in the physical custody of the awaiting Shelby County Sheriff, William Noel "Bill" Morris Jr. Sheriff Morris then personally escorted his new detainee under heavy guard to a jail cell inside the Shelby County Criminal Court building in downtown Memphis.

As a way of supposedly protecting his now-infamous prisoner from being murdered in the same way suspected JFK assassin Lee Harvey Oswald had been in 1963, Sheriff Bill Morris mandated before Ray's arrival that construction of a specially designed, windowless jail cell take place, one equipped with twenty-four-hour lights, video cameras, and microphones. Under these mentally and physically exhausting conditions inside the unique cell, Ray suffered innumerable sleepless nights for several months while awaiting his trial for Dr. King's murder.

Following Ray's extradition back to Memphis in July, the Hanes father and son legal team continued to represent their new client until he abruptly fired them on November 10, 1968. Immediately after his dismissal of the Hanes boys, Ray replaced them with high-profile Texas criminal defense attorney Percy Eugene "The Texas Tiger" Foreman. After the court's mandated addition of Memphis public defenders Hugh Stanton Sr. and Jr. in December to the legal team of the often-inebriated Forman, and several months of rampant speculation by the media that Ray was part of a much wider conspiracy, the alleged triggerman half-heartedly confessed in a Memphis courtroom on March 10, 1969, to being Dr. King's killer.

As Shelby County State District Attorney Philip Michael Canale Jr. and his triumphant prosecution team looked on, Judge Walter Preston Battle Jr. sentenced Ray to serve ninety-nine years in a Tennessee state prison as a part of a prearranged plea deal between attorneys Forman and Canale. But just three days after his confession,

Ray recanted on March 13, claiming that he had been unfairly coerced by his lead defense attorney, Percy Forman, into falsely admitting to the murder of Dr. King.

Despite Ray's flip-flop claim of innocence, his future endeavors to obtain a new trial, and the multitude of open-ended leads, the DOJ under Attorney General Ramsey Clark, the vast army of special agents under FBI Director J. Edgar Hoover, Frank Holloman's Memphis Police Department, and the Tennessee State authorities all closed the case, proudly standing by their joint claim that they had gotten the right man. In the view of federal, state, and local officials, Ray, a fervent racist unaided by outside individuals, was the lone gunman in the assassination of Dr. Martin Luther King Jr. Government officials instantly dropped all periphery investigations into the alleged conspiracy, including John McFerren's enduring assertion that he spotted Galt/Ray working for the racist fat man at the Scott Street market in Memphis several months before the shooting. In the years that followed, Ray and his long succession of defense attorneys would continue to deny his guilt, that he had ever traveled to Memphis before April 3, 1968, or that he had met with or worked for the Scott Street fat man before the assassination.

Conclusions and Questions

Stephens, now well versed on all of McFerren's previously recorded MPD and FBI statements pertaining to the tragic murder of Dr. King, immediately drew some compelling conclusions. First, nothing about McFerren's claims as recorded in either the April 8 or April 18 interviews seemed outlandish. On the whole, McFerren's clear and extremely plausible accounts impressed Stephens. Also, while there were additional details included in the second interview that were not outlined in the first, the duplicate information from each report almost never conflicted with the other. While

McFerren's statement was indeed expanded upon in the second interview conducted on the 18th, it rarely changed or contradicted the initial Peabody reports taken on the 8th, therefore remaining generally consistent throughout the two narratives.

Additionally, Stephens found it promising that McFerren, completely unaware at the time of Ray's criminal background, advised the authorities on April 8, 1968, that the individual he witnessed working at the Scott Street warehouse first appeared in the summer of 1967, which was only a few months after Ray's April 23 escape from the Jefferson City state prison in neighboring Missouri. Also, McFerren claimed that the jungle-rotting man he witnessed stood somewhere between 5'9" and 5'11". When Stephens checked the official records, he learned that Ray was, in fact, 5'10". Finally, he noted with confidence that the warehouse where McFerren overheard the telephone conversations was only seven miles from the Lorraine Motel where Dr. King lost his life. However, there were some glaring questions that remained in Stephens' mind.

First, he was perplexed by McFerren's consistent habit of assigning inaccurate ethnicities to the people he was describing, specifically the Puerto Rican portrayal of the heavyset business owner and his alleged employee, James Earl Ray. By now, Stephens had become extremely familiar with the names of everyone listed in McFerren's interviews and knew the heavyset man to be Frank C. Liberto. While Liberto was an Italian American and may have exhibited a slightly darker complexion, Ray was typically photographed exhibiting a light-to-medium skin tone. Were the Puerto Rican descriptions of both men just McFerren's way of saying that they looked darker? And if so, why would Ray have exhibited a swarthy complexion at the time?

Second, as reported by those who either knew or interviewed him, at no time did Ray exhibit pockmarks or scarring on his neck. So, what could McFerren have possibly observed that led him to believe that the alleged assassin suffered from what he called "jungle rot"? And more to the point, what exactly was the definition of "jungle rot" according to McFerren? In addition, John stated that he believed the alleged assassin to be no more than twenty-five, when Ray was, in fact, thirty-nine years old in 1967.

Third, Stephens was slightly confused concerning the wide range of time periods McFerren claimed Ray worked for Liberto. In his first interview on April 8, McFerren stated that the alleged gunman first began working at the warehouse in the summer of 1967. But then, in the second interview on April 18, he claimed that Ray worked there in the late fall or early winter of the same year. Did McFerren's two time periods contradict each other, or was his latter observation an addition to his first?

Next, there was the question of the heavyset Liberto versus the thin, scarred man who, according to numerous documents, was Memphis businessman James Latch. If these two men were physically distinguishable business partners, why were they briefly combined into a single entity in Fitzpatrick and Sloan's April 302 report? Was the confusion due to a mere notetaking mistake or typo made by one of the agents? Or had, as Stephens began to wonder, McFerren's limited education, vocabulary, and rural vernacular contributed to the possible breakdown in communication?

Then there was the atmosphere of distrust and contention between McFerren and members of the local FBI to consider. According to Holmes, the Fayette grocer had long claimed that the FBI lied about his alleged confusion during the photo lineup. Despite the two agents' contrary 302 report, it was McFerren's adamant assertion that he immediately chose the picture of Galt/Ray on April 18 as the person who worked for Liberto. Further, Stephens noted that there was a four-day gap between the time Fitzpatrick and Sloan interviewed McFerren on April 18 and the time their 302 report was typed on April 22.

What were the individual backgrounds of agents Robert Fitzpatrick and Andrew Sloan? Did either of the men have less than savory records? Had MPD Director Holloman influenced, in any way, the views and actions of his former coworkers at the Memphis FBI field office either before or after their second interview with McFerren? Also, was the newly-hired MPD director actually inside the 561 Peabody hotel room on the morning of the 8th as McFerren claimed? After discovering McFerren's past conflict with Holloman in 1959, as well as William H. Lawrence's efforts to spy on Fayette County's black leadership throughout the 1960s, it was Stephens' initial suspicion that the Memphis FBI's investigative waters had been muddied by racial hatred at the time of the inquiry. Simply put, Stephens first theorized that the MPD and local Bureau merely dismissed McFerren's allegations due to their ongoing civil rights conflict with him, and therefore fumbled their 1968 investigation into Liberto's possible connection to Ray.

Finally, as a result of studying the three April 1968 reports, Stephens was now faced with the need to investigate additional witnesses. Not only would he have to continue researching the countless records pertaining to John McFerren, James Latch, Frank C. Liberto, and James Earl Ray, but he now needed to look into New Orleans resident Robert Powers, *TIME* journalist Bill Sartor, Frank Liberto's yet-unidentified brother, and the various criminals portrayed in the April 18 photo lineup. As would become routine throughout Stephens' investigation, a few simple answers had now led to even more questions.

Chapter 3

DENOUNCED D.O.J.

PROMPTED BY THE national outcry over the still painful, unclearly explained assassination of President John F. Kennedy in 1963, the equally horrific murders of Dr. Martin Luther King Jr. and Senator Robert F. Kennedy in 1968, Daniel Ellsberg's leak of the Pentagon Papers in 1971, and President Richard M. Nixon's collusion in the Watergate scandal between 1972 and 1974, a long series of official fact-finding bodies were formed by President Gerald R. Ford and members of Congress. Orchestrated to appease their angry American constituencies, the new legislative committees focused much of their attention on the covert intelligence community, specifically the Central Intelligence Agency/CIA, National Security Agency/NSA, and FBI. By 1975, the Rockefeller Commission, Pike Committee, and Church Committee were in full swing; all launched to investigate the federal government's alleged involvement in illicit activities, both foreign and domestic.

The Church Committee

On November 1, 1975, William C. Sullivan, former Assistant Director of the FBI's Domestic Intelligence Division, testified before the Church Committee that from 1963 until the assassination on April 4, 1968, Dr. King was the target of operation COINTELPRO under the authority of FBI Director J. Edgar Hoover. Sullivan admitted that the long-term operation had been designed to neutralize the effectiveness of countless civil rights icons through a series of covert actions such as illegal wiretaps, blackmail, and various forms of harassment. Sullivan went on to explain to the Select Committee, chaired by Democratic Senator Frank F. Church of Idaho, that when it came to Hoover's counterintelligence war against Dr. King, it was no holds barred.

When the Church Committee's final report was released in April of 1976, it included a startling revelation related to Director Hoover's vile and racist contempt for Dr. King. As part of its investigation into the FBI, the committee discovered that Hoover, in an effort to permanently remove the black "messiah" from his globally influential position of radical leadership, sent MLK an anonymous letter in late November of 1964 that was intended to blackmail the civil rights icon into committing suicide. Hoover's intentionally misspelled and clumsily edited letter, which he paired with an audiotape allegedly depicting several sexual encounters involving MLK and his mistresses, was mailed to the King family's Atlanta, Georgia home through the handy work of COINTELPRO lackey William C. Sullivan. Hoover and Sullivan's 1964 blackmail letter to Dr. King stated:

KING,

In view of your low grade, abnormal personal behavoir I will not dignify your name with either a Mr. or a Reverend or a Dr. And, your last name calls to mind only the type of King such as King Henry the VIII and his countless acts of adultery and immoral conduct lower than that of a beast.

King, look into your heart. You know you are a complete fraud am a great Liability to all of us Negroes. White people in this country have enough frauds of their own but I am sure they don't have one at this time that is any where near your equal. You are no clergyman and you know it. I repeat you are a colossal fraud and an evil, vicious one at that. You could not believe in God and act as you do. Clearly you don't believe in any personal moral principles.

King, like all frauds your end is approaching. You could have been our greatest leader. You, even at an early age have turned out to be not a leader but a dissolute, abnormal moral imbecile. We will now have to depend on our older leaders like Wilkins a man of character and thank God we have others like him. But you are done. Your "honorary" degrees, your Nobel Prize (what a grim farce) and other awards will not save you. King, I repeat you are done.

No person can overcome facts, not even a fraud like yourself. Lend your sexually psychotic ear to the enclosure. You will find yourself and in all your dirt, filth, evil end moronic talk exposed on the record for all time. I repeat - no person can argue successfully against facts. You are finished. You will find on the record for all time your filthy, dirty, evil companions, male and females giving expression with you to your hidious abnormalities. And some of them to pretend to be ministers of the Gospel. Satan could not do more. What incredible evilness. It is all there on the record, your sexual orgies. Listen to yourself you filthy, abnormal animal. You are on the record. You have been on the record - all your adulterous acts, your sexual orgies extending far into the past. This one is but a tiny sample. You will understand this. Yes, from your various evil playmates on the east coast to [gap in sentence] and others on the west coast and outside the country you are on the record. King you are done.

The American public, the church organizations that have been helping - Prostestant, Catholic and Jews will know you for what you are - an evil, abnormal beast. So will others who have backed you. You are done.

King, there is only one thing left for you to do. You know what it is. You have just 34 days in which to do (this exact number has been selected for a specific reason, it has definite practical significant. You are done. There is but one way out for you. You better take it before your filthy, abnormal fraudulent self is bared to the nation.

DOJ Task Force

Given the terrifyingly dichotomous role the FBI played as both the secret saboteur of Dr. King and the investigative body tasked with solving his murder, the since-deceased Hoover and his Bureau's conflicting agendas came under severe public scrutiny in the mid-1970s. Now widely denounced by members of Congress, the national news media, and the American public for its negligent inability to curtail Hoover and the FBI's abhorrent campaign against Dr. King, the Department of Justice under the new U.S. Attorney General, Edward Hirsch Levi, moved swiftly to clean out its own closet.

In May of 1976, just one month after the release of the Church Committee's shocking and highly critical report, Levi formed a departmental task force. The attorney general quickly directed this new group of federal lawyers to investigate the DOJ's own subsidiary law enforcement arm, the FBI. As members of the DOJ's recently formed task force, federal Attorneys Fred G. Folsom and James F. Walker, along with their team of investigators, quickly descended upon numerous FBI field offices throughout the country to interview the Bureau's current and past agents. One of the men the Folsom and Walker team spoke with was FBI Special Agent Joseph C. Hester, the lead MLK assassination investigator in West Tennessee under 1968 Special Agent in Charge Robert Jensen. Not surprisingly, the next official document Randall Stephens examined contained Agent Hester's 1976 statement regarding John McFerren.

Hester and the DOJ

According to the typed interview notes obtained by Stephens, members of the DOJ task force sat down with Hester in Memphis on June 23, 1976, to review his involvement in the 1968 MLK murder investigation. After asking him several questions about his past work, the DOJ attorneys shifted their examination to Hester's opinion of McFerren's previous FBI interviews. In their notes, the DOJ wrote that:

> Hester eventually determined the LL&L Produce Company story to be a bogus lead. All relevant persons were interviewed in Memphis and New Orleans. There was no indication of any past racial or Klan activity. Nothing of interest was discovered. This in combination with Mr. McFerren's low credibility in the eyes of the Bureau led to a termination of this lead. The story was related to the Bureau after the fact and Hester viewed McFerren as a publicity seeker in light of his past involvement in demonstration activity. Nothing was uncovered to reinforce McFerren's allegations.

Initially, Hester's statement to the DOJ would have simply confirmed Stephens' earlier suspicion that the FBI field office in Memphis botched the 1968 MLK investigation. In the beginning of his research, Stephens merely theorized that agents at the local

Bureau failed to properly examine the purported Liberto and Ray connection as a result of their civil rights prejudice and nine-year battle with McFerren. However, based on his recent examination of Hoover and Sullivan's bloodthirsty desire to see Dr. King commit suicide, Stephens' initial conclusions were now evolving.

McFerren and the DOJ

In addition to the Hester interview notes, Stephens also obtained and examined Folsom and Walker's interview of John McFerren himself. As noted in their typed account, Folsom and Walker traveled to Fayette County on July 9, 1976, entered the McFerren Grocery and Oil Company, and introduced themselves to its proprietor. As was now customary, McFerren escorted the two well-dressed men into the privacy and safety of the building's back room, offered them a seat at a makeshift conference table, checked their official credentials, and commenced with the retelling of his past observations.

Without hesitating, McFerren began the interview by blurting out his belief that "[Alabama Governor George C.] Wallace was in on it," and that "the same man that killed President Kennedy killed Dr. King." McFerren followed up the bold declarations by informing Folsom and Walker that he had recorded his evidence onto a series of audiotapes, one of which he had already mailed to the DOJ. McFerren then stated that when the tape was returned to him undelivered, he sent it again, this time using certified mail. It was his claim that after remailing the same audiotape, the DOJ finally took receipt of it.

Without responding to his new allegations, Folsom and Walker quickly steered both the interview and their subject's attention back to his original 1968 allegations. Happy to oblige the two DOJ investigators, McFerren again outlined his Liberto and Ray claims. McFerren stated that, for approximately eight years before the shooting, he had been a regular customer at the LL&L Produce

Company. Extremely familiar with the warehouse, he went on to describe its physical layout and drew a crude diagram for the two federal attorneys, which they attached to their typed interview notes.

As he had before, McFerren then explained the first telephone conversation he overheard on April 4, 1968, his momentary encounter with the scarred man, and his steps to and from the produce bins at the rear of the warehouse that same day. But this time, McFerren stated that, after the scarred man answered the second telephone call, he (McFerren) overheard him tell Liberto, "Ray wants to speak to you." After Folsom and Walker pointed out that he had not included Ray's name in the original 1968 interviews with the FBI, McFerren simply acknowledged the fact by stating that he had not mentioned any of the men's names under questioning, but gave authorities only physical descriptions.

Attempting to bolster his Ray and Liberto conspiracy theory, McFerren informed the two attorneys that Ray, while working at LL&L, once helped him load supplies into his (McFerren's) truck either before or after Christmas in 1967. Again, McFerren went on to describe Ray as a thin man with coarse black hair and fungus on his neck called "jungle rot." He also stated that, in 1968, he believed Ray to be a Mexican or an Indian rather than a white person. McFerren then again indicated that he left the LL&L warehouse on April 4, sometime around 5:15 p.m., and arrived back at his gas and grocery business close to 6 p.m. Finally, he concluded the assassination-day portion of his account by stating that, after discussing the situation with his wife, he eventually decided to report his observations to the authorities.

McFerren then moved on to the April 18, 1968 portion of his account. Although Folsom and Walker recorded the man's last name as "Powell" in their 1976 interview notes, it was clear to Stephens that there had been yet another miscommunication between interviewers and interviewee. McFerren was obviously detailing his encounter with the man he originally named as "Powers." As before, John described the man as a "small time gangster of New Orleans" who suspiciously approached the McFerrens' home two weeks after the shooting of Dr. King.

McFerren then outlined several new events with Folsom and Walker, ones that had transpired since his 1968 interviews with the MPD and FBI. First, he described a violent encounter with three black men who had traveled to his store in an attempt to shoot him. Next, he stated that approximately six months to a year after Dr. King's murder, he was again attacked, this time by five black men near the steps of the Fayette County Courthouse in downtown Somerville. McFerren then handed Folsom and Walker a typed letter dated January 10, 1970, which he believed supported his theory that the five men were paid to assault him. Stephens was thankful that McFerren's letter was also attached to Folsom and Walker's DOJ interview notes.

McFerren then went on to inform the two investigators that he was suspicious of a white West Tennessee attorney named Russell X. Thompson. According to McFerren, Thompson used to represent the Memphis chapter of the NAACP but was now the legal counsel for the Memphis Police Union. In addition, McFerren stated that his wife, Viola McFerren, had also retained Thompson in an effort to file for divorce. It was McFerren's belief that the Memphis police had been involved in the conspiracy to assassinate Dr. King and that Thompson was using his position as Viola's attorney to destroy McFerren's marriage on behalf of the involved officers.

Next, McFerren explained his previous friendship with *New York Post* journalist Ted Poston who passed away in 1974. He then provided Folsom and Walker with a copy of a March 15, 1969 news article written by the since-deceased reporter. Titled "King Murder: A Mystery Call," the article explained the telephone conversations McFerren overheard at the LL&L Produce Company as well as the immediate fallout. In addition, McFerren told the investigators that he had sent Poston an audiotape containing pertinent evidence and that Poston's widow could possibly give the DOJ access to it. As they had done with the previous items supplied by McFerren, the DOJ attorneys included a copy of Poston's article with their typed notes.

McFerren continued his interview with Folsom and Walker by stating that a lot of money had been collected in Somerville on behalf of James Earl Ray. When the two investigators inquired about the source of his information, McFerren stated that the African-American cooks who worked for the mayor and other white families in the area regularly provided him with detailed information. McFerren went on to state that he used a pocket-size audio recorder to tape his conversations with the black informants and then transferred all of the recordings to a master tape. As he tried to convey at the beginning of his interview, McFerren again told the investigators that he previously mailed several copies of the master tape to various locations throughout the country, including the copy he sent to the two attorneys' own DOJ.

Rounding out the interview with Folsom and Walker, McFerren communicated his belief that his store's telephone had been wiretapped or, in his words, "bugged." He also asserted that after hiring someone from an "electronics company" to conduct an inspection, his suspicion of telephonic surveillance was confirmed. It was due to this surveillance that McFerren avoided discussing specific or sensitive matters over the telephone.

Then, on November 16, 1976, almost five months after his interview with Folsom and Walker, McFerren himself contacted the DOJ investigators by telephone. When Walker returned his phone call later that day, McFerren explained that he had just spent eight days in the hospital due to a September 10 gun attack. He also relayed his ongoing concern about Russell Thompson's involvement in Viola's decision to file for divorce. After describing to Walker the circumstances surrounding the recent shootout and Viola's legal efforts, McFerren intimated that the police were somehow involved in the recent Fayette County shooting, but he refused to speak in specifics over the telephone. After inquiring if the DOJ was prepared to investigate, McFerren was told by Walker that the attack "appeared to be a purely local matter involving his local activities" and that he should "pursue the matter through the local sheriff's office."

Twisted Narrative

Another document Stephens unearthed pertaining to the 1976 DOJ inquiry was a curious memorandum sent from the FBI to the Assistant U.S. Attorney General at the Civil Rights Division on December 21 of that same year. In the memo, McFerren's original 1968 statements to the FBI were clumsily entangled with several new allegations provided by a mid-1970s anonymous source, a man Stephens later discovered was a criminal and part-time confidential informant named Morris Davis. According to the 1976 memo, Davis spoke of an underworld figure named Frank Laberto (phonetic), who ran "a truck stop in New Orleans named the Lake Pontchartrain Restaurant," who "owned an unnamed truck stop on Lake Pontchartrain," and who used to be the "head of the Greek Mafia in New Orleans."

Immediately following Davis's peculiar secondhand claims was a summary of McFerren's still consistent statement about Frank C. Liberto. The memo went on to state that Liberto was interviewed by the FBI on April 19, 1968, and "emphatically denied having any knowledge of the identity of the person responsible for the death of King on 4/4/68." The memo also stated that New Orleans members of Liberto's family were oblivious to anything involving the MLK shooting. The memo's summary regarding McFerren and Liberto then concluded with the FBI author's own statement: "New Orleans Office advised in December, 1975, that there is no Pontchartrain Restaurant in New Orleans."

Aside from not knowing the name of the FBI agent who authored the memorandum, Stephens was immediately troubled by some very glaring mistakes. First, McFerren's descriptions of Frank Liberto, the Memphis produce business owner, and Robert Powers, the New Orleans truck stop owner, had obviously been confusingly commingled into the same person by either Morris Davis or the memo's FBI author. McFerren was very clear about who Frank Liberto and Robert Powers were and the distinct role each man played in the past. Second, McFerren never claimed that Liberto, an Italian American living in Memphis, used to be the "head of the Greek Mafia in New Orleans." That was again false information that was later included by either Davis or the FBI. Next, Davis provided an erroneous name for Powers' truck stop, the "Lake Pontchartrain Restaurant," a name McFerren never claimed to know. But most troubling to Stephens was that the FBI agent who wrote the memo concluded the summary by attributing the inaccurate statement about the restaurant's name to McFerren's 1968 account, even though it was Davis who provided the false information, not McFerren.

Despite his best efforts, Stephens could find no additional documentation regarding McFerren's interactions with the 1976 DOJ inquiry. Not only did the DOJ's final January 11, 1977 report fail to mention Liberto, it also did not include any reference to McFerren or his statements to Folsom and Walker. Again, it was time for Stephens to sift through what was consistent in McFerren's statements and what needed further vetting.

Conclusions and Questions

As illustrated in the DOJ's June 23, 1976 interview notes, it was clear Memphis FBI Special Agent Joseph C. Hester thought little of McFerren and his 1968 claims. As he had done earlier, Stephens again mulled over the Memphis FBI field office's apparent mishandling of the grocer's account. But by this time, Stephens was considering a new possibility. At first, he believed only that, due to their obstinate disdain for Dr. King, the McFerren family, and the black civil rights movement as a whole, Hoover's men had simply prejudiced themselves when looking into various leads, therefore discrediting McFerren's allegations about Liberto and Ray. But now, Stephens was considering an alternate theory, one that took into account Hoover's ravenous desire to see Dr. King perish.

Perhaps the FBI, or at least rogue employees inside the Memphis FBI field office, were engaged in an intentional cover-up of the assassination conspiracy. Perhaps the local special agents and the MPD did not fumble their murder inquiry but instead worked together as the primary on-the-scene investigative team to convolute the evidence and hide McFerren's claims. Of course, this theoretical whitewash by the West Tennessee authorities would have undoubtedly required the participation of a number of individuals, including that of FBI Special Agents Joseph C. Hester, O.V. Johnson, Robert Fitzpatrick, Andrew Sloan, as well as MPD Chief Homicide Inspector N.E. Zachary, and MPD Director Frank Holloman.

Next, Stephens evaluated McFerren's own July 9, 1976 interview with the DOJ. It was now obvious that all of the information McFerren relayed to Folsom and Walker about Liberto's screaming telephone conversations aligned with what was earlier described to the MPD and FBI in April of 1968. And after examining the attached sketch of the 814 Scott Street LL&L warehouse and comparing it to current photos of the building's exterior and interior, it was clear McFerren was accurate when describing where he and Liberto were located at the time.

Furthermore, McFerren never vacillated when describing Ray's physical appearance. Although it would have been obvious to everyone by 1976 that the now-incarcerated Ray was not Hispanic nor that he exhibited permanent scarring on his neck, McFerren repeated the same ethnic and jungle rot descriptions, unafraid that his comments would conflict with what Ray was known to look like. Was this simply an example of a misinformed McFerren being stubborn in 1976, unwilling to admit to an earlier error? Or was there a kernel of truth about who and what he saw eight years before?

Finally, McFerren once more asserted that he witnessed the swarthy and jungle-rotting Ray working at the LL&L warehouse before and after Christmas. This was again consistent with his earlier statement that he saw the alleged gunman in the late fall and early winter of 1967. Then came the new revelations Stephens needed to sort out.

First, he returned to the issue of McFerren's audacious remarks concerning Governor Wallace and President Kennedy. Once his initial eye-rolling subsided, Stephens began to wonder if there was any truth to McFerren's opening statement. Obviously, there was little the small-town grocery store owner could have done between 1968 and 1976 to research the two monumental issues on his own. Had McFerren heard the theories from an independent investigator or journalist and simply repeated them to Folsom and Walker? Despite the surface-level outlandishness, the possible connections between King, Wallace, and Kennedy intrigued the presently doubtful Stephens, prompting him to dig deeper.

Stephens also realized he would have to tackle the question of whether or not James Latch spoke Ray's name before handing the telephone receiver off to Liberto. Did McFerren actually hear the name of the alleged assassin verbalized on April 4? When McFerren responded to the 1976 discrepancy by telling Folsom and Walker that he did not mention anyone's name to the FBI but gave the authorities only physical descriptions, he was telling the truth. After analyzing the previous April 1968 interviews again, it was clear that McFerren never uttered anyone's name, including Liberto and Latch's. Did McFerren perhaps know everyone only by their first names or nicknames, and, therefore, out of fear of supplying the authorities with inaccurate information, simply withhold the names when speaking to Hoover's men? A deeper probe into McFerren's surface-level inconsistencies and Ray's chronological use of aliases was essential.

There was also the issue of whether or not Ray loaded produce into McFerren's truck. While it would have been natural for an LL&L dockworker to have done so, Stephens was troubled by the fact that McFerren again failed to mention it in his initial 1968 interviews. Was it an exaggeration that had slowly developed over the last eight years to support his previous claims? And if he had stood that close to Ray, how could McFerren have mistaken him for a Cuban, Mexican, or Puerto Rican?

In addition, while it was clear that a typo or misquote had occurred, Stephens was now slightly unsure as to the real name of the April 18 visitor from New Orleans. Was the man's last name Powers or Powell? While he had already placed all of his chips on the Powers name, Stephens wasn't going to leave anything to chance.

There was also the confusing reference attributed to McFerren in the December 1976 FBI memorandum regarding the Lake Pontchartrain restaurant or truck stop to deal with. As Stephens would later discover, the business in question was indeed located near Lake Pontchartrain, but it was not called the Pontchartrain Restaurant; hence the reason the New Orleans FBI field office could not find a registered business with that name. Yet, because of the odd secondhand account by confidential informant Morris Davis and the FBI memo's twisted narrative, the DOJ most likely blamed McFerren for the inaccurate information while failing to investigate the real truck stop owner.

With the so-called facts being communicated by the FBI to the DOJ in the biased and disorganized manner in which he observed, Stephens began to quickly understand why McFerren's narrative had been so severely misunderstood and therefore dismissed through the years. But was this 1976 confusion due to pure negligence, or was it by design? Stephens still needed to pin down the specific name, location, and exact owner of the New Orleans restaurant. A separate and more thorough investigation into Morris Davis, the New Orleans FBI field office, and the enigmatic Robert Powers, or Powell, was paramount.

Finally, Stephens still needed to confront the slew of post-assassination topics in the 1976 DOJ memorandum, including the various physical assaults against McFerren, the possible connection between Ray and a yet unnamed mayor, the alleged involvement of Attorney Russell X. Thompson, the *New York Post* article written by Ted Poston, McFerren's belief that his phone had been bugged, and the audiotapes McFerren described to Folsom and Walker.

Stephens was already familiar with Marcus Holmes' long-standing proclamation that McFerren had secretly recorded several private conversations between himself and other key individuals, and that those recordings revealed vital evidence about Dr. King's death. But were these the same tapes McFerren gave to the DOJ and Poston? Despite the growing entanglement of loose ends dangling overhead, Stephens was determined to tie them together into a complete narrative.

Chapter 4

CONCERNED CONGRESS

ALMOST CONCURRENT WITH the U.S. Department of Justice's paternal attempts at cleansing the Federal Bureau of Investigation of illicit behavior, yet another official investigative body was gearing up in Washington, D.C. But unlike the previous federal inquiries into the FBI and CIA's internal dysfunctions, this time, the concerned members of Congress sought to investigate the specific assassinations of President John F. Kennedy and Dr. Martin Luther King Jr. On September 17, 1976, the United States House of Representatives voted 280 to 65 to establish the House Select Committee on Assassinations, also known as the HSCA.

Evolution of the HSCA

After months of partisan squabbling between House Democrats and Republicans and the passage of various congressional bills authorizing federal funds, the twelve-member committee's investigation got underway in late 1976. Under the direction of the HSCA's first chairman, Virginia Democrat Thomas N. Downing, and its first chief counsel and staff director, Attorney Richard A. Sprague, eleven additional U.S. representatives, along with numerous federal attorneys, congressional staff members, and law enforcement officials began what would be a two-year study of the deaths of President Kennedy and Dr. King. Then, following Downing's retirement in January 1977, he was replaced as the HSCA's chairman by Texas Democrat Henry B. González. But immediately after taking up the position on February 2, 1977, González tried to sack Sprague as the HSCA's chief counsel. After a month of bitter infighting between González, Sprague, and the other members of the HSCA, the second chairman resigned from the Committee on March 1, 1977, calling Sprague "an unconscionable scoundrel."

The third and final chairman of the Committee, Ohio Democrat and Congressional Black Caucus member Louis Stokes, eventually convinced Sprague to step down on March 30 of 1977. In addition to Chairman Stokes, three additional representatives from the Black Caucus were included on the final twelve-member Select Committee. Among these African-American representatives were Walter Fauntroy of Washington, D.C., a past friend of Dr. King; Yvonne Burke of California; and Harold Ford Sr., a Democrat from Memphis, Tennessee. Throughout the course of Randall Stephens' investigation, he eventually learned that, just prior to Ford's 1974 ascent to the Capitol Building in Washington, the U.S. Congressman also served four years as a representative in the Tennessee General Assembly, a fact that would later become vital in Stephens' search for the truth.

Along with Chairman Stokes and his eleven other committee members, the HSCA was ultimately led and advised by its second chief counsel and staff director, George or G. Robert Blakey, a federal attorney and law professor who first taught at the University of Notre Dame, then at Cornell University, and then again at Notre Dame a number of years later. Attorney Blakey was also a well-known fixture in Washington and had served in numerous government capacities as a legal expert on organized crime and racketeering. From 1960 to 1964, he worked at the Criminal Division of the DOJ under Attorney General Robert F. Kennedy. Then, under the watchful guidance of U.S. Senator John McClellan, Blakey went on to draft the 1970 *Racketeer Influenced and Corrupt Organizations Act*, popularly known as the RICO Act. The RICO Act Blakey authored was used in later decades by the DOJ, the FBI, and other law enforcement agencies to indict, prosecute, and convict the leaders of the Italian Mafia in the United States. But after the forced resignation of Chief Counsel Sprague in the final days of March 1977, it was Cornell Professor Blakey's popularity and legal expertise in evaluating mob-related conspiracies that earned him the HSCA's chief counsel position that following June.

Under the leadership of the HSCA and its succession of chairmen and chief counsels, a large team of federal attorneys and investigators was also sanctioned by Congress to canvas the country and question past witnesses. Among these team members were two additional African Americans, a man, and a woman, both named Johnson. Gene Randolph Johnson, yet another attorney from the DOJ, was hired early on in the HSCA's investigation by Richard Sprague. Then, in February of 1978, G. Robert Blakey, Sprague's successor, promoted Mr. Johnson to replace the departing Robert Lehner as the Select Committee's deputy chief counsel in charge of the King investigation subcommittee. In addition, a twenty-three-year veteran detective with the Washington, D.C. Metropolitan Police named Ernestine Gary Johnson was also assigned as one of the HSCA's King subcommittee investigators.

On March 12, 1977, the pair of Johnsons (not related) made their way to a backwater town in Tennessee to question a witness who had been involved in the periphery of the 1968 King murder inquiry. And just like the two DOJ investigators who preceded them less than a year before, Gene and Ernestine Johnson entered the witness's rural business, introduced themselves, and began their first interview of John McFerren.

McFerren's Affidavit

Were it not for the close friendship between McFerren and Marcus Holmes beginning in the 1990s, Randall Stephens would have been forced to read only the federal government's summarized interpretation of McFerren's 1977 and 1978 HSCA statements. In their infinite wisdom, and based on claims of national security, the HSCA deemed much of their investigation too sensitive for public eyes. Volumes of evidence and recorded witness testimony were therefore sealed until 2029, including McFerren's sworn statement. But because the Gene and Ernestine Johnson investigative team was required to provide McFerren with a signed copy of his affidavit in June of 1978, and because McFerren had graciously given that affidavit to Holmes, Stephens now had the rare privilege of reviewing, word for word, McFerren's actual sworn statement, one that would have otherwise been off-limits to the King research community.

What's more, unlike the faded photocopy of McFerren's unredacted April 18, 1968 FBI interview, the HSCA documents were not duplicates. The physical papers Stephens held in his hands were the original pages given to McFerren by the Johnson team. Knowing what the Tennessee civil rights leader meant to Fayette County and the nationwide circle of people who had investigated the MLK assassination, Stephens felt deeply honored to be holding McFerren's seldom-seen contribution to U.S. history. Starting with the simple, one-word title, he began reading the browned and timeworn pages aloud:

AFFIDAVIT

JOHN MCFERREN, being duly sworn, makes oath as follows:

That on April 4, 1968, I travelled from Somerville, Tennessee, where I live, to Memphis, Tennessee, for the purpose of picking up supplies for my grocery store located in Somerville.

That during the course of this trip I went to the LL & L Produce Company located at 814 Scott Street, Memphis, Tennessee at approximately 4:30 p.m. for the purpose of purchasing supplies.

That while at LL & L Produce Company I initially overheard a loudly uttered statement which I recall as consisting of the following words: "Kill the son-of-a-bitch on the balcony; I don't care how you get the job done; just get it done" - or words to that effect.

That this statement was made by an individual known to me as Frank Liberto, a large, heavy-set, white male also known to me as one of the operators of LL & L Produce Company, as that person spoke over the telephone in an office of the building which housed LL & L Produce Company.

That immediately after over hearing this statement I was approached by another large - but not so large as the first - white male with a scar on the right side of his neck, also known to me as one of the operators of LL & L Produce who asked me what I wanted and who then advised me to help myself.

That several minutes later as I was exiting the building after making a purchase in the rear I heard the telephone in the office ring. I observed the white male with the scar on his neck who had previously spoken to me hand the receiver to the heavy-set white male known to me as Frank Liberto whom I had overheard earlier. I, then, overheard the following words spoken into the telephone receiver by Frank Liberto: "Go to New Orleans and get your $5,000; you know my brother; don't come here." - or words to that effect.

That the approximate time of the latter phone call was 5:15 p.m.

That after overhearing this second conversation I left LL & L Produce Company and returned home to Somerville where I learned at approximately 6:15 p.m. that Dr. King had been shot.

That approximately four days later I described to Inspector N. E. Zachary of the Memphis Police Department the aforementioned incident.

That approximately ten days thereafter I was interviewed by agents of the Federal Bureau of Investigation with respect to this incident at which time I was shown several photographs one of which I immediately chose as closely resembling an individual whom I had seen working at LL & L Produce Company for a short period of time during the preceding fall or early winter. This individual was a lightly tanned or Puerto Rican type individual with black hair, slender build, and a height of approximately five feet, nine-to-ten inches, readily recognizable due to skin abrasions on his neck which I would most accurately describe as "jungle rot." The photograph which I chose was identified to me by the FBI agents as being that of someone other than James Earl Ray.

That this individual closely resembled a sketch of Dr. King's assassin which appeared in the Commercial Appeal on April 5, 1968.

That about a week prior to Dr. King's assassination while at LL & L Produce Company I was told by the large white male with a scar on his neck with reference to Dr. King: "Somebody ought to shoot the son-of-a-bitch."

That in and about 1968, I maintained an underground intelligence network composed of cooks, butlers, and bellboys from which I learned that former-Mayor Yancy of Somerville, Tennessee, a friend of former-Mayor Loeb of Memphis, collected money from local businessmen to pay for the assassination of Dr.

King; made two trips to London, England, to assist James Earl Ray; and harbored James Earl Ray for the two days immediately prior to Dr. King's assassination.

That I have been threatened, beaten, and shot since the aforementioned incident and believe these threats, beatings, and shootings to be related to my observations at said LL & L Produce Company on April 4, 1968, and my relation of these observations to law enforcement authorities.

That I have been interviewed by staff members of the House of Representatives, Select Committee on Assassinations on several occasions including March 12, 1977, May 13, 1977, and February 9, 1978 during which times I have communicated to them the extent of my knowledge concerning circumstances which I believe to be connected to the assassination of Dr. Martin Luther King, Jr.

Further affiant saith not.
John McFerren

Sworn and subscribed to before me on this 22nd day of June, 1978.

Ora Towles
Notary Public
My Commission Expires:
May 20, 1981

Stapled to the back of McFerren's four-page affidavit were two additional items. The first was another hand-drawn sketch of the Scott Street market. As he had done with McFerren's 1976 DOJ drawing, Stephens methodically examined the crude diagram and noted its accuracy to the known layout of Frank C. Liberto's former business. While the drawing was not directly referenced in the affidavit by the Johnson team, it was clear to Stephens that McFerren was once

again the artist. The second item was a single piece of five-by-eight
notebook paper pulled from a yellow legal pad. Scrawled in blue ink
on the face of the single page were the words:

April 3, 1978
3:26 PM

Received from John McFerren one tape speed 3¾ (reel to reel)

Those present:
Gene R. Johnson
John McFerren
Ernestine G. Johnson

It was immediately evident to Stephens that the handwritten note
was a makeshift receipt acknowledging that McFerren had given a
copy of his earlier referenced audio recordings to the Johnson team.
And on the surface, nothing about the crude handwritten receipt
should have raised red flags. But because of an earlier in-depth
discussion with Holmes, Stephens already knew that the combined
matters of McFerren's secret tapes, the HSCA's investigation, and the
yellow handwritten note were in desperate need of further inquiry.
The amateur sleuth jotted down yet another important reminder to
himself.

Hester's Return

In the course of Stephens' investigation into McFerren's
interactions with the HSCA, a familiar name reared its ugly head.
On November 21, 1977, FBI Special Agent Joseph C. Hester met
with HSCA investigators in Washington, D.C. and once more
conveyed his opinion regarding McFerren's poor credibility. This

time, however, his negative commentary was actually affirmed by the HSCA interviewers themselves. Within the detailed documentation, Stephens was shocked to discover that, immediately after Hester again disparaged McFerren's previous Liberto statements, the unnamed HSCA interviewer "agreed that they had not believed McFerren to be a very reliable witness."

Findings on John McFerren

While the HSCA noted that Frank C. Liberto, his family members, and his business partner James Latch all denied having involvement in the death of Dr. King when interviewed in 1968, the combination of Liberto's Memphis residence and known racial bias compelled the Select Committee to revisit McFerren's allegations. After conducting new interviews with the Libertos and checking their various backgrounds through the FBI and municipal police departments, the HSCA discovered an "indirect link between Liberto's brother, Salvatore, and an associate of New Orleans organized crime figure, Carlos Marcello." In stark contrast, the HSCA then immediately qualified their discovery by stating that "no evidence was found to substantiate the claim that Frank Liberto or Carlos Marcello were involved in the assassination."

The Committee also interviewed local police and FBI agents in West Tennessee who had past dealings with McFerren. Based on those interviews, it was determined that McFerren had a reputation for supplying information that could not be validated. But the HSCA also admitted that McFerren's reputation amongst local law enforcement officials might have been tainted by his past complaints of police brutality and his work as a black civil rights activist.

The HSCA went on to assert that both their 1978 investigators and the FBI agents in 1968 found inconsistencies in McFerren's allegations that could not be reconciled. To bolster their evaluation of

McFerren's purported low credibility, the committee members pointed to his unsubstantiated claim regarding Ray's employment at the Scott Street market in the fall or early winter of 1967 as well as John's account of Ray's physical appearance at the time. The committee argued that, because investigators found no evidence supporting Ray's 1967 presence in Memphis or the past skin affliction, the allegations made by McFerren must be erroneous.

In addition, the committee also raised the issue of McFerren's inaccurate identification of Galt/Ray during the FBI's 1968 photo lineup. It was noted that, although McFerren claimed he had positively identified Galt/Ray, the FBI 302 report stated that McFerren actually eliminated all of the photographs, including Galt/Ray's, as the person he witnessed working at LL&L. Ultimately, the HSCA's 1979 report stated, "on the basis of witness denials, lack of corroborating evidence and McFerren's questionable credibility, the Committee concluded that his allegation was without foundation and that there was no connection between his story and the assassination of Dr. King."

Conclusions and Questions

Despite the HSCA's findings, the first thing he was struck by was McFerren's unflinching consistency. Stephens was once more impressed by the continuity of his research subject's past statements. Barring the alleged admission that he chose the wrong photo during the second 1968 interview, McFerren's 1978 sworn affidavit to the Johnson team was a near duplicate of his past claims to the Memphis police, FBI, and DOJ, right down to the precise times, dates, and physical descriptions of those he claimed to have witnessed.

The next item Stephens took note of was the new interview of FBI Special Agent Joseph C. Hester by members of the HSCA's investigative team in Washington, D.C. Although he predicted Hester's continued attack on McFerren's credibility, Stephens was appalled when the unnamed interviewer recklessly voiced their endorsement of Hester's opinion. To the dumbfounded Stephens, it was apparent that, what was supposed to be a one-sided and altogether objective examination of a witness by a theoretically professional HSCA investigator, had been, in reality, an unethical swapping of personal views between two federal cohorts. With still another government official relying on a biased FBI agent like Hester to summarize McFerren's veracity, it was obvious to Stephens that the HSCA's investigation was tainted.

Stephens was also intrigued by the similarities and general overlap of the Kennedy and King subcommittee investigations. As outlined in their final report, the HSCA found that both Lee Harvey Oswald and James Earl Ray were guilty of being the lone assassins in each murder, that both men were most likely involved in conspiracies, but that neither the Kennedy nor King subcommittee could ascertain the exact number or identities of the two assassins' purported co-conspirators. In addition, neither subcommittee could find conspiratorial involvement by nefarious elements of local, state, or federal government, nor could they pinpoint the involvement of organized crime. But what fascinated Stephens most was that both subcommittees investigated many of the same key figures, most notably New Orleans crime boss Carlos Marcello. Was this a possible validation of McFerren's 1976 claim to the DOJ that "the same man that killed President Kennedy killed Dr. King?" To Stephens, the rural grocer's once eye-rolling comment didn't seem as outlandish anymore.

In spite of his growing confidence in McFerren, Stephens still wrestled with a growing list of pressing questions. First, his interest had been piqued upon discovering that U.S. Representative Harold Ford Sr., one of the twelve members of the Select Committee, was a former Tennessee state assemblyman from Memphis. Who was the young Ford, what was his background in West Tennessee and Nashville politics, and what were his known associations? Stephens made a note to find out.

Next, he decided to investigate and eventually contact the HSCA's last chief counsel. G. Robert Blakey had earned a well-regarded reputation by first working as an attorney at the DOJ and was a sought-after expert on legal issues pertaining to organized crime. Curiously, the HSCA was still unable to confirm either the Mafia or Marcello's suspected connection to both the Kennedy and King conspiracies, even with Blakey's astute insight and leadership. Stephens began to grow suspicious of Blakey's perhaps divided loyalties to the DOJ, FBI, and HSCA. He also wanted to know what Blakey went on to achieve after the 1976-through-1978 inquiry and if the law professor was still reachable.

Another knot Stephens sought to unravel was the inaccuracy of McFerren's interview dates as published in the HSCA archives. According to both the typed and handwritten pages included in McFerren's unpublished affidavit, he first met with the Johnson team on March 12 and then again on May 13, 1977; February 9 and April 3, 1978; and finally on June 22, 1978. But when Stephens compared all of the dates listed on the stapled pages to the dates listed in the public archives, he found that they did not coincide. The version the HSCA published instead indicated that McFerren was interviewed on May 10, 1977, but omitted both the May 13, 1977 interview date and April 3, 1978 audiotape receipt date. Why were the dates changed or left out? Had the Johnson team swapped out their original May 13 interview notes for ones dated May 10? And why was the handwritten receipt date of April 3 or the subject of the secret tapes not referenced in the public archives?

That issue, of course, led Stephens to his next mystery; why hadn't the crudely fashioned receipt been formally typed and included in the original pages of the notarized affidavit? To Stephens' untrained eye, the Johnson, McFerren, and Johnson signatures located at the bottom of the yellow legal paper were all written in a different hand, decreasing the likelihood that the receipt was somehow forged after the HSCA investigators concluded their interviews with McFerren. Also, Stephens recalled an earlier discussion with Holmes about the same handwritten note, the Johnson investigative team, and McFerren's claims about the secret recordings.

Holmes asserted that McFerren never knowingly gave the tapes to the HSCA. In fact, it was Holmes' belief that, because of McFerren's inability to read in 1978, he was unaware of what the Johnson team had written on the yellow page and was therefore oblivious to what he was signing. While Holmes had already provided a plausible answer as to how the HSCA obtained the highly coveted audiotapes without McFerren's knowledge, it was now clear to Stephens just how vital it was to reinvestigate the matter.

An additional obstacle that needed to be breached was McFerren's alleged confession to the Johnson team that he failed to identify Ray during the April 18, 1968 photo lineup conducted by FBI Special Agents Robert Fitzpatrick and Andrew Sloan. It now seemed extremely unlikely to Stephens that the steadfast McFerren would have admitted to such a thing, even if he had been earlier told of his alleged mistake. As before, Stephens was reminded of McFerren's illiteracy. Was it possible the HSCA investigators simply typed a false admission within the affidavit, knowing full well McFerren would not have known what he was reading or signing on June 22, 1978?

Stephens noted that a brief misidentification made by the Fitzpatrick and Sloan team in '68 had been repeated verbatim by the Johnson team. As referenced in chapter two of this book, Fitzpatrick and Sloan had mistakenly, although momentarily, combined the scarred James Latch and heavyset Frank Liberto into a single person, one who stated on March 28, 1968, "Somebody ought to shoot the son-of-a-bitch." Astonishingly, the Johnson team made the exact same mistake. According to McFerren's final HSCA affidavit, he allegedly stated to the Johnsons:

That about a week prior to Dr. King's assassination while at LL
& L Produce Company I was told by the large white male with a
scar on his neck with reference to Dr. King: 'Somebody ought to
shoot the son-of-a-bitch.'

McFerren had been very clear during his initial interview at the
Peabody as to the physical differences between Latch and Liberto and
the distinct statements each business owner had made in the past.
Additionally, Stephens was highly doubtful that McFerren had even
vocalized the original inaccuracy to Fitzpatrick and Sloan in 1968,
let alone a second time to the Johnsons in 1978. It was now extremely
obvious that Gene and Ernestine Johnson did not legally obtain
several portions of their so-called 1977-through-1978 interviews from
McFerren, but instead copied the FBI's April 22, 1968 302 report,
thereby inserting inaccurate sections of the said report into the final
pre-typed, partially forged affidavit McFerren unwittingly signed on
June 22, 1978. Based on this fast and loose handling of McFerren's
statements by the Johnsons, Stephens also concluded that this could
account for the discrepancy between the May 10 and 13th 1977
interview dates. If the Johnsons were simply adding bits and pieces
of past FBI interviews to McFerren's 1978 affidavit, then the specific
dates of said HSCA interviews could have also been easily confused
and therefore falsified.

By this time, Stephens was also aware of McFerren's opinion of
the Johnson team. According to information relayed by Holmes, Mr.
McFerren had felt deceived and mistreated by the pair, specifically
Gene Johnson, during their last interview together. In fact, it was
McFerren's assertion that the Johnsons had led him to believe that he
would be given the opportunity to testify in front of the House Select
Committee during their public hearings in Washington. It wasn't
until June 22 or immediately thereafter that a notably abrasive Gene
Johnson told McFerren that he would not be needed in D.C. Given

the government attorney's past employment at the DOJ and highly questionable handling of McFerren, it was clear to Stephens that a thorough investigation into the Johnson team was essential.

Another item that begged to be examined was McFerren's 1978 disclosure regarding the previously unnamed mayor. As outlined in his affidavit, McFerren believed that the former mayor of Somerville, Isaac Perkins Yancey, also known as I.P. Yancey, was involved in the conspiracy to assassinate Dr. King, having assisted Ray at various times both before and after the shooting. Stephens pondered the possible connections between I.P. Yancey and the other rumored Bluff City conspirators, specifically Liberto. Also, Stephens wondered if it was possible to corroborate Ray's association with Yancey or the Somerville mayor's trips to London.

Finally, there was the all-encompassing issue of the HSCA's alleged inability to connect Frank C. Liberto and Carlos Marcello to the shooting of Dr. King. Were it not for McFerren's now verified claim that Liberto had a brother living in New Orleans, the HSCA's investigative team would not have pursued the Liberto and Marcello angle in the first place. Clearly, it would have been virtually impossible to have known about Salvatore Liberto's secondary association to Marcello unless McFerren had accurately overheard Frank on April 4, 1968.

Yet, despite their discovery of an "indirect link between Liberto's brother, Salvatore, and an associate of New Orleans organized crime figure Carlos Marcello," the Select Committee and Chief Counsel Blakey remained unified in their declaration that they could not identify any of Ray's possible co-conspirators, including members of organized crime. Now astonished by the glaring contradiction, Stephens was determined to nail down the exact details of who Salvatore Liberto was and how he was indirectly linked to Marcello.

By and large, it was the third time that federal authorities had either dismissed or purposely discredited McFerren in just over a decade. In their final estimation, the HSCA asserted that he was unreliable and that no evidence could be found to support his allegations. But to Stephens, the federal investigators' purported failure to locate the required evidence did not automatically devalue McFerren's trustworthiness. How hard had the investigators looked? How much weight did the previous findings of the FBI and DOJ carry in the HSCA's decision? And why were former employees of the already denounced DOJ permitted to work within the top levels of the HSCA in the first place? Stephens continued to ponder these issues while pressing on.

Chapter 5

PEPPER SHAKER

BY THIS POINT in his investigation, Randall Stephens had slowly familiarized himself with a number of key players in the King and Ray saga. One of these stand-outs was Bill Pepper, a colorful, publicity-seeking New Yorker who went on to become James Earl Ray's last lead attorney. In addition to the incalculable hours Stephens dedicated to investigating Pepper's background, Marcus Holmes had also researched, emailed, and met with the pale-faced attorney prior to Stephens' involvement. But what was most crucial to Stephens' current inquiry was Pepper's decades-long, curiously close relationship with Holmes' Fayette County friend, John McFerren.

William Francis "Bill" Pepper

Born August 16, 1937, William Francis "Bill" Pepper was raised and college-educated in the northeastern United States and went on to become a loud proponent of several progressive and human rights causes, one of which was the end to the U.S.'s involvement in the war in Southeast Asia. In the spring of 1966, the twenty-eight-year-old Pepper flew to the battle-torn country of South Vietnam as a member of the American news media to photograph and document his observations.

Immediately following his six-week tour and return home, Pepper authored an anti-war article entitled "The Children of Vietnam" for the January 1967 issue of *Ramparts* magazine. The seven-thousand-word piece, a critique focusing on the atrocities suffered by Vietnamese women and children, was endorsed by the well-known author, liberal child welfare advocate, and pediatrician, Dr. Benjamin M. Spock. Through his relationships with *Ramparts'* pugnacious editor, Warren Hinckle, and Dr. Spock, who wrote the article's preface, Pepper eventually met with additional figures within the progressive national civil rights and anti-war movement, one of whom was Dr. Martin Luther King Jr.

By that summer, Pepper and Dr. King had become acquaintances, unified in their shared, outspoken disdain for the U.S.'s involvement in Vietnam. Pepper and Dr. King sat shoulder to shoulder at the Palmer House Hotel in Chicago, Illinois, on the evening of August 31, 1967. It was there that Dr. King gave the keynote speech on behalf of the National Convention of New Politics, or NCNP, a radically liberal and anti-war organization that was believed by conservative government officials to be a front for communist politics.

Also in attendance at the NCNP gathering were Dr. Spock, Pepper and King's mutual friend and colleague; popular black comedian and civil rights activist Dick Gregory; and the Rev. Ralph Abernathy, who was King's best friend and second-in-command at the Southern Christian Leadership Conference. Despite the NCNP's political failures and the shocking murder of Dr. King on April 4 the following year, Pepper continued to maintain relationships with members of the SCLC and other figures who were close to the now-deceased civil rights leader.

Over the next nine years, Pepper went on to become embroiled in several controversies. After being accused of falsifying his academic record to avoid being drafted into the U.S. military, and grossly mismanaging several private and public child education ventures, he was forced to answer to allegations of child sexual abuse. In addition to authoring a child psychology book in 1973 entitled *The Self-Managed Child*, Pepper also became a licensed attorney in the State of New York in January 1977.

Then, sometime in the early months of that year, the recently licensed Pepper became inexplicably involved in a long, albeit private, investigation into James Earl Ray's possible innocence in the slaying of Dr. King. During his hushed 1977 inquiry, Pepper supposedly took it upon himself to question Attorney Richard A. Sprague about Congress's MLK investigation "shortly after" the former HSCA chief counsel stepped down on March 30. Subsequently, in "late 1977," and at the request of King's former SCLC associate and friend, the Rev. Ralph Abernathy, Pepper also initiated the process of scheduling a "face-to-face meeting" between Abernathy and Ray. Stephens was immediately curious as to the kind of connection, either direct or indirect, that Pepper had to Ray in late 1977 that would have prompted Abernathy to ask the New York attorney if he could arrange a "face-to-face meeting" between the two men. Interestingly, Pepper's private inquiry beginning in early 1977 continued well into the next year until he personally traveled to central Tennessee to interview the imprisoned Ray on October 17, 1978.

The very next month, Pepper finally stepped out of the King and Ray shadows and into the HSCA spotlight. Because of the obvious conflict of interest, James Earl Ray's most recent legal counsel, New York Attorney Mark Lane, was unable to represent both James and his brother Jerry Ray at the House Select Committee on Assassination's forthcoming public hearings. Consequently, Pepper was asked by Lane and several others close to the case to represent the embattled sibling. With outspoken civil rights activist and co-counsel Florynce Kennedy at his side, Pepper went on to defend Jerry Ray as he was publicly questioned by members of the HSCA on November 30, 1978.

Throughout the late 1970s and into the early 1980s, Pepper again found himself within the eye of several public storms. When he wasn't burrowing into the King and Ray case, the New York attorney devoted his energies to uncovering other high-level government conspiracies, holding incendiary press conferences, and fending off undying claims of sexual abuse involving male children. By early 1981, Pepper and his former HSCA co-counsel Florynce Kennedy had also co-authored and published the book *Sex Discrimination in Employment*. Then, in June of that same year, Pepper abruptly uprooted himself and his immediate family and moved to England.

But his new residence across the pond did not dissuade Pepper from continuing his legal practice or investigating the U.S. government's orchestration of several clandestine schemes, including the federal intelligence community's alleged use of James Earl Ray as an unwitting patsy. Between 1981 and 1987, the eternally inquisitive Pepper, now a British barrister, continued to make frequent trips back to the continental United States to research his suspicions and speak to the news media. Then in 1988, he agreed to take on his most important role yet, the legal defense of Dr. King's alleged murderer, James Earl Ray.

Shaking Things Up

Just as Ray's previous high-profile attorney Mark Lane and comedian Dick Gregory had attempted to achieve through public appearances, news interviews, and the April 1977 release of their co-authored King assassination conspiracy book, *Code Name Zorro*, Pepper also wasted little time in attracting national attention on behalf of himself, his new client, and the King assassination case. As a result of his repeated efforts within Tennessee's judicial system

and numerous public relations endeavors, Pepper eventually made a
name for himself as the conspiracy community's lead authority on
everything Ray and King.

One of Pepper's first forays into the media spotlight as Ray's newest
counsel was his collaboration with U.K. independent film producer and
director John Edginton and British Broadcasting Corporation/BBC
journalist John Sergeant. With Pepper's eager assistance as a starring
figure in their documentary film, Edginton and Sergeant's *Inside
Story: Who Killed Martin Luther King?* began production in January
of 1989, was released to the British public in September, and aired on
U.S. cable television in March of 1990.

Randall Stephens had viewed the film in 2013 prior to beginning
his research, but only as a semi-curious bystander who had been tipped
off by Marcus Holmes. Now, with DVD remote control in hand,
Stephens revisited and scrutinized every frame of the British-made
documentary, specifically its portrayal of the three-hour non-interview
Pepper allegedly conducted with John McFerren. A little more than
forty minutes into the somewhat grainy film, Stephens began his
analysis of what was said about the Fayette County business owner.
He watched as Pepper, from behind the wheel of his rented maroon
Chrysler, spoke to the onboard documentary team while driving east
from Memphis on Highway 64 through the rural town of Oakland,
Tennessee.

The two-lane country highway Pepper was filmed traveling
on was the same road that had been used between the early and
mid-nineteenth century to transport African-American men, women,
and children from the downtown slave markets in Memphis to the
cotton plantations of Fayette County. It was the same road John Bell
used when escorting more than 650 Native Americans west through
Somerville during the Trail of Tears in late 1838. It was the same road
where two-hundred Fayette County white men lynched and hanged an
African-American man named Thomas Brooks from a trestle of the

Nashville Chattanooga and St. Louis Railway bridge in April of 1915. It was the same road John McFerren sometimes used when making his way west to Frank Liberto's produce warehouse in Memphis during the 1960s. And in the 1989 film, it was the same road Pepper and his British passengers used when traveling east toward McFerren's Fayette County store.

Stephens was immediately struck by how Pepper, even from the outset of his hour-plus drive from Memphis to Somerville, characterized McFerren to the back-seat interviewer and passenger-side cameraman:

> I've found a very fearful man with John. I found him very fearful then, and I find him now increasingly fearful. The first night I saw him he insisted on retiring to a room in the back of the garage general store, and sitting with the lights out. I saw him again and he always reminded me that he wasn't really unduly paranoid, but that, in fact, he had been shot at, and people had attempted to kill him, and he had been beaten up. He, at one point, was hospitalized. There is a basis for his profound uneasiness.

When asked by the off-camera interviewer if he thought McFerren would speak to them once they arrived, Pepper replied simply with, "I don't know whether he'll talk to us this afternoon. He vacillates." While the attorney's remarkable ability to predict McFerren's fearful reluctance to speak on camera seemed suspect to Stephens, what he observed next on his television screen set off alarm bells.

The scene immediately following the film crew's arrival depicted Pepper entering McFerren's business alone. In addition, it was shot by the small film crew from a great distance away. Clearly, McFerren's gas station property had not been approached by either the faceless British interviewer or his crew members, who instead filmed the scene from the far east side of the three-way intersection using a high-zoom lens. Even though the camera was able to capture, through the gas station's large plate-glass windows, a much younger McFerren speaking to Pepper inside the building, Stephens was troubled by the absence of audible dialogue. No recording of the two men's conversation was included. Curiously, the only audio Stephens heard was a portion of the film's musical score; a corny blues riff made by an electric guitar. Did Pepper fail to bring a microphone with him to the meeting? Or did he purposely not include proof of what he discussed with McFerren?

After the two men's behind-the-scenes, purported three-hour conversation, Pepper then reappeared outside the gas station in front of the camera lens alone, explaining to the off-camera interviewer why McFerren was unwilling to be filmed. Now standing in the south end of the parking lot, off to the side of the gas and grocery store, and conveniently out of view of the building's large front-facing windows or McFerren's watchful blue eyes, Pepper stated in a contrived British accent, "Well, we have a very frightened man. He's just very, very afraid to come on-camera and to say anything about this matter." When prompted by the interviewer, Pepper then went on to paraphrase the account McFerren gave in 1968:

On April 4th, 1968, at 5:15 in the afternoon, John McFerren went to Liberto and Latch Produce Company to do his shopping. It was his last stop of the day before coming back to Somerville. Shortly after he entered the place, he heard a man he originally called the fat man, Frank Liberto, on the telephone. Heard Liberto say words to the effect, "Shoot the son-of-a-bitch when he comes on the balcony. Don't come round here. Don't call me here. Go to New Orleans and pick up your money from my brother." The conversation ended at that point. McFerren didn't think too much about that conversation until 6:30 p.m. when he heard that Martin Luther King had been assassinated shortly after 6:00. Then it all made sense to him. He gave a statement to the FBI, the Memphis Police Department investigators, and eventually to the House Select Committee on Assassinations. They all disregarded his comments and ignored him. I've known John for ten years. I believe John had a crucial bit of information that was never looked at properly, never followed up, and disregarded. And the only reason it would have been disregarded was because it was inconvenient to the scenario that became, in effect, the official story.

Stephens was suddenly forced to conclude his analysis of the McFerren segment as the filmmakers abruptly cut to an entirely new scene; an aerial shot of CIA Headquarters in Langley, Virginia. Where was the rest of McFerren's portion of the film? Conspicuously absent from Pepper's final summary was any hint of what was discussed with McFerren during their alleged three-hour chat. Furthermore, no mention was made whatsoever by the on-camera orator regarding McFerren's other important allegations, specifically his past account of Liberto's 1967 relationship with Ray.

In addition to the 1989 documentary, Stephens also studied Sergeant and Edginton's March 1, 1990 *Chicago Reader* newspaper article entitled "The Conspiracy to Kill Martin Luther King." As they had done in their film featuring Pepper and his McFerren synopsis, the two British authors also portrayed John as being "afraid" and "reluctant to repeat his story." And as with their film, Sergeant and Edginton's article was also devoid of any reference to McFerren's belief that Liberto was connected to Ray.

Throughout the 1990s, Pepper continued to embark on a number of projects meant to shed light on Ray's alleged innocence as an unwitting patsy. By late January of 1993, he had started production on yet another cable television show. This time, Thames Television in London, United States-based Home Box Office/HBO, and British television producer Jack Saltman were behind the endeavor.

Titled *Guilt or Innocence: The Trial of James Earl Ray*, the three-hour video was billed as a mock trial of King's alleged killer and staged by a host of players including Pepper, Ray, federal prosecutor William Hickman Ewing Jr., Judge Marvin Frankel, and several past 1968 witnesses and law enforcement officials. Timed perfectly to coincide with the 25th anniversary of King's murder, HBO aired the heavily edited show on April 4, 1993. Interestingly, Stephens quickly discovered upon watching the rapidly decaying VHS tape that John McFerren had not appeared in the three-hour television court drama.

To Pepper's publicity-craving delight, other high-profile stories pertaining to Dr. King's murder also began to emerge in the media the same year the HBO trial aired. One of these stories pertained to a 1968 witness and former Memphis tavern owner. On December 16, 1993, Loyd Jowers, the elderly former proprietor and manager of the now-defunct Jim's Bar and Grill on S. Main Street, appeared with journalist Sam Donaldson on ABC's *Primetime Live* television news program to publicly confess to his alleged collusion with Frank Liberto in the murder of Dr. King. Not surprisingly, Shelby County State District Attorney John Pierotti made headlines the day after the airing of the *Primetime Live* episode by cynically announcing that he would open a limited investigation into Jowers' claims.

Orders to Fool

By September of 1995, Pepper's first-authored work on the topic of Dr. King's murder and Ray's alleged innocence, *Orders to Kill*, was waiting patiently on bookstore shelves to be gobbled up by the conspiracy-hungry masses. Distributed by former New York publishing house Carroll and Graf, the five hundred-plus page book perpetuated several former assassination conspiracy theories while simultaneously revealing a myriad of previously unheard ones.

Among its overwhelming cast of old and new characters, the book detailed Pepper's assessment of John McFerren's 1968 assertions as recounted throughout their fifteen-year friendship. Like before, Stephens also began his own assessment of Pepper's recorded claims.

According to *Orders to Kill*, it was well-known civil rights leader Rev. James Lawson who provided the introduction between Pepper and McFerren. And while it was true that Rev. Lawson was a longtime friend and Memphis civil rights colleague of both the late Dr. King and McFerren family, Stephens would later question the book's claim that the black civil rights leader advised Pepper to contact John in the late 1970s.

Pepper further claimed in his book that he, along with Mark Lane's former legal associates April Ferguson and Barbara Rabbito, met McFerren for the first time at his Fayette County business on the afternoon of February 8, 1979. As he had in the 1989 documentary, Pepper claimed in *Orders to Kill* that McFerren eventually retold his entire Frank Liberto telephone account. But also like the documentary, Pepper again failed to include the second half of McFerren's allegations, which consisted of seeing Ray working for Liberto at the 814 Scott Street produce warehouse in 1967. Also absent from the book was any mention of McFerren's highly coveted audiotapes, the same audiotapes that allegedly linked Ray to the former mayor of Somerville, I.P. Yancey.

Pepper also took the liberty of explaining to his would-be readers the extent of McFerren's debilitating trepidation as the lawyer and U.K. film crew arrived to interview John in 1989. In the sixteenth chapter, Pepper wrote:

> At John McFerren's general store/gas station one afternoon, Edginton's production unit waited for three hours while I tried unsuccessfully to persuade McFerren to talk. His fear was still strong enough to prevent him from coming forward again.

In an effort to underscore his friend's unrelenting sense of terror, Pepper went on to describe McFerren's purported flight from Memphis back to Fayette County during the filming of the 1993 HBO mock trial. In chapter twenty-four, Pepper wrote that, after making the hour-plus drive to the Memphis courthouse to testify, McFerren abruptly "fled in fear and couldn't be persuaded to return to give evidence." The *Orders to Kill* author further elaborated on his friend's propensity for running away by writing in chapter twenty-seven that during a return trip to Memphis in January of 1994, Pepper was promised by McFerren that, "this time he would not 'chicken out' and that he was ready to sing like a bird."

Just as he was perplexed by Pepper's repeated depiction of a fearful McFerren, Stephens was skeptical of another of the attorney's characterizations, this time regarding McFerren's memory. In chapter twenty-eight, Pepper wrote, "Over the years McFerren had become unable to remember the details of the incident." Regardless of the incident in question, Holmes had always asserted that McFerren, even as late as 2015, possessed an uncanny memory and the quickness of recall to match. So why would Pepper portray one of the key witnesses in his own conspiracy theory as being forgetful? Something seemed terribly amiss.

Finally, Stephens took note of the numerous MLK witnesses Pepper claimed to have heard about or met through McFerren. Among the names listed in the 1995 book were Ezell Smith, who worked in Memphis; Fayette County resident Tommy Wright; and Jackson, Tennessee Attorney H. Ragan. Also mentioned were "Old Pal," whose real name was Robert Tyus; O.D. Hester, who was nicknamed "Slim,"; Freddie Granberry; Columbus Jones; and someone known simply as "Tango." While he had seen several of the same names highlighted in Holmes' array of documents, there were several monikers Stephens didn't recognize. The list of people he would need to research was growing daily.

Conclusions and Questions

The first issue Stephens felt compelled to grapple with was Pepper's checkered past. While it was clear the liberal attorney could have been the target of federally-backed smear campaigns, a likely result of his criticism of the U.S. government and its military-industrial complex, the multiple fingers that had been pointed at Pepper's propensity for illicit and deceptive behavior over the years was still a factor Stephens needed to strongly consider. Next, he was troubled by the hazy explanation Pepper provided in his 1995 book regarding why he initiated his personal 1977 involvement in the HSCA's King inquiry. Surely, Stephens thought, there had to be more behind Pepper's impromptu curiosity and personally costly inquest.

It also seemed suspicious that Pepper had cultivated such a trusting and enduring relationship with McFerren over the past several decades. Point of fact; McFerren had accused Ray, Pepper's own client, of conspiring with organized crime figures in Memphis and New Orleans to assassinate Dr. King. What then, Stephens wondered, was Pepper's motive for becoming so cordial with someone who should have been a witness for the prosecution had Liberto and Ray ever been positively linked by law enforcement?

Furthermore, it was inconceivable to Stephens that Pepper left his 1989 foreign film crew, one that would have been on a tight and financially draining schedule, sitting outside McFerren's store for three hours, and then return with nothing related to his lengthy conversation with John. In addition, not only did it appear to Stephens as if the pith helmet-wearing grocer was being filmed without his knowledge, but McFerren himself eventually confirmed to Holmes that he had not been aware of the camera across the road at the time and that he was never asked by Pepper to speak to the outdoor film crew.

Conveniently, Pepper was then afforded the privilege, due to McFerren's previously predicted fear, of speaking in front of Edginton and Sergeant's camera alone on behalf of John. As previously described, the film crew and Pepper set up their camera on the southern outdoor side of the business where they could not be seen by its indoor owner. In addition, during his summation of McFerren's Liberto story, Pepper combined the two separate telephone conversations into one, never communicating the brief period of time that elapsed between them.

Was this done simply for the purpose of filming and time constraints, or was there a reason Pepper didn't want the audience to know that McFerren had, in fact, overheard two separate conversations? Stephens was again reminded of McFerren's 1976 claim that James Latch spoke Ray's name in between the two calls. And as noted earlier, at no time did Pepper discuss with the film crew Ray's possible connection to Liberto as alleged by McFerren. By now, it was becoming difficult for Stephens to dismiss the theory that Pepper had deceived the public and manipulated McFerren throughout the years in order to place Ray in a less guilty light.

Then there were the claims in Pepper's 1995 book that needed to be dealt with. From the beginning, it was clear that a conflict existed between the details Pepper had alleged and what McFerren asserted was the truth. In the opening narrative regarding McFerren, it was Pepper's claim that he, along with April Ferguson and Barbara Rabbito, first met McFerren in February 1979. Yet, while it may have been Ferguson and Rabbito's first meeting with the Fayette County grocer, both Holmes and Stephens knew it was not Pepper's.

Based on Holmes' previous research, Stephens believed that Pepper became acquainted with McFerren sometime in 1977. Pepper admitted in the eighth chapter of *Orders to Kill* that he himself, for reasons still unknown, questioned Attorney Richard A. Sprague, the HSCA's first chief counsel, about the federal inquiry into Dr. King's death "shortly after" Sprague's forced departure from the Select

Committee on March 30, 1977. In the same chapter, Pepper also stated that in "late 1977," and at the behest of King's former SCLC associate and friend, the Rev. Ralph Abernathy, the New York lawyer began the process of setting up a "face-to-face meeting" between Abernathy and Ray. Stephens had earlier wondered what kind of access Pepper had to Ray in late 1977 that would have led Abernathy to believe that the same New York attorney could facilitate a "face-to-face meeting" between the two men.

Eventually, this request by Abernathy required Pepper to travel from New York to Tennessee on October 17, 1978, to interview Mark Lane's still-imprisoned client, James Earl Ray. It seemed highly improbable to Stephens that Pepper would have forgone a visit to the Lorraine Motel crime scene between April of 1977 and October of 1978 before questioning Ray, meaning Pepper would have been in extremely close proximity to McFerren at the time of the suspected trip to Memphis. Pepper's mysterious post-March 30, 1977 interview of Sprague, his late 1977 personal coordination with Mark Lane and James Earl Ray at the behest of Abernathy, and his subsequent October 17, 1978 trip to Tennessee, along with other evidence detailed later in this book, eventually convinced Stephens that Pepper had, in fact, met with McFerren much earlier than 1979. However, the reason for the *Orders to Kill* author's large gap in memory and inaccurately recorded chronology was yet to reveal itself.

Adding to his growing sense of skepticism, Stephens noted yet another troubling claim in Pepper's book. If McFerren had already permitted Pepper to record his allegations with two strangers present in 1979, Ferguson and Rabbito, why was he then too afraid to speak with Pepper in front of the unfamiliar two-to-three-person film crew later in 1989? It made little sense to Stephens that McFerren was perfectly willing to be interviewed by Pepper's legal team, but then spent three hours arguing with the very same man ten years later as to why the small Sergeant and Edginton crew couldn't do the same.

Pepper's portrayal of McFerren's fearful lack of participation in the HBO mock trial was the next item Stephens mentally tackled. As he had done so many times before, Holmes stepped into the information vacuum, providing Stephens with McFerren's side of the story. According to a previous discussion between John and Marcus, McFerren stated that after his brief testimony on the witness stand in 1993, the court adjourned for a break and that he was then dismissed by Pepper, who led him to believe that he was no longer needed in the courtroom. Holmes once again asserted that McFerren, while cautious and oftentimes guarded, was by no means afraid. He further argued that the Fayette County grocer, since being denied his right to speak at the HSCA hearings in 1978, had eagerly awaited for fifteen years to sit on the witness stand and explain his side of things, and by no means would have passed up the opportunity to do so in 1993.

Again, it also made little sense to Stephens that McFerren would have made the one-hour drive all the way from Somerville to downtown Memphis only to then turn and run in fear. Did any missing footage of McFerren's testimony exist? Did McFerren say something in court that Pepper didn't want cable television audiences to see and hear and was, therefore, edited out of the final program? Were there any court transcripts available that detailed McFerren's partial testimony? Would any of the show's past participants talk about who was on the witness stand and who wasn't? Stephens was determined to solve the mystery.

Holmes was also angered by yet another one of the author's deceptions. In his book, Pepper wrote that Ezell Smith, a longtime friend of McFerren's, had died in the mid-1990s before he could be tracked down and questioned by Pepper's Memphis private investigators. However, Holmes discovered through his own research that Ezell's whereabouts were not only known to Pepper between the late-70s and mid-90s, but that the lawyer's West Tennessee private eyes actually interviewed Ezell during the period that Pepper claimed they were supposedly looking for him. Holmes believed that Pepper lied within the pages of *Orders to Kill* about the private eyes' inability to locate the man because Ezell had been unwittingly involved in the preparation of a Browning 30.06 rifle for Frank C. Liberto just before the 1968 shooting. This fact, of course, would have been potentially damning to Pepper's book narrative and long-term defense case since Ray's alleged murder weapon, a Remington 30.06 rifle, was found near the crime scene stuffed inside a Browning cardboard box. In short, Ezell's account about the Browning might have helped link Ray to Liberto and was, therefore, omitted from the book by Pepper.

It was also becoming increasingly difficult for Stephens to believe that, over the course of fifteen to seventeen years, McFerren never once outlined his Ray allegations to Pepper. And even if he hadn't, the nosey attorney would have been well aware of the claims based on his study of McFerren's previous interviews with news reporters and the authorities. Additionally, Holmes had also personally trekked this same avenue of questioning with McFerren and was thoroughly convinced that his friend had spoken to Pepper on numerous occasions about seeing Ray working at Liberto's business. But again, the *Orders to Kill* author made no mention of this crucial detail within the pages of his so-called authoritative, truth-seeking book.

Finally, Pepper was also involved in covering up yet another element of McFerren's evidence. Based on Holmes' lengthy analysis of his friend's secret audio recordings, there was now zero doubt that Pepper knew about the tapes and did everything in his power to ensure that the general public never heard them. Moreover, both Holmes and McFerren were adamant that Pepper had been provided a copy of the tapes as early as 1977. If the recordings did indeed contain secret information implicating both Ray and Somerville Mayor I.P. Yancey in the alleged conspiracy, then it was crystal clear to Stephens why Pepper failed to reference the tapes in his book.

In the end, an entirely new picture of deceit and cover-up had appeared before Stephens' eyes. Except, this time, the lies hadn't been heaped upon the naive public by local, state, and federal authorities. This time, the mound of deception had been piled high by the very person tasked with uncovering the truth for those who disbelieved the government's official story. Aside from his well-deserved infamy for mixing the absurd with known facts, it was now clear that Pepper intentionally cherry-picked parts of McFerren's story to suit his biased agenda. And after discarding what was inconvenient to the narrative needed to defend Ray, he intentionally discredited McFerren just as the official opposition had by claiming that the Fayette County grocer was too afraid to speak. Worse yet, McFerren was now publicly chained to Pepper's outlandish, spotlight-seeking antics, therefore adding even more distortion to McFerren's already vilified claims and reputation. Just like the centuries of other white men who had traveled the backwater lanes of Highway 64 to exploit the African-American population of Fayette County, so too had Bill Pepper done to John McFerren.

Chapter 6

RENO'S REDUX

ON MARCH 27, 1997, the youngest son of the late Dr. Martin Luther King Jr. met with his father's alleged killer inside a conference room at the Tennessee State Prison system's Lois DeBerry Special Needs Facility in Nashville. Cleverly choreographed by Bill Pepper, the well-publicized media event consisted of a lengthy face-to-face question-and-answer session between Dexter Scott King and a gravely ill James Earl Ray. As expected, Pepper's client was again paraded out in front of news reporters just before declaring his innocence. Immediately after the meeting, a sympathetic Dexter made national headlines by stating that he believed Ray's claims and supported his right to a new trial.

But exactly one year later, Shelby County State District Attorney Bill Gibbons and Assistant D.A. John Campbell announced that the investigation initiated by their predecessor, Shelby County D.A. John Pierotti, was over. Between 1993 and 1998, the team of Tennessee state prosecutors and investigators looked into the alleged 1968 collusion between Loyd Jowers and Frank Liberto as well as the previous evidence against Ray. In his March 27, 1998 statement to the press, state D.A. Bill Gibbons said, "There is simply no credible evidence to support a new trial for Mr. Ray." The district attorney went on to state that "the evidence against him is overwhelming" and that their investigation into the case did not "cover allegations that are so far-fetched as to be beyond the bounds of credibility." Gibbons punctuated his thoughts on Ray's and Pepper's lengthy endeavors by stating, "We will leave those theories to the tabloids."

As a result of Gibbons' official announcement, the successful efforts made by other Tennessee state officials to deny Ray a new trial, and the urgency caused by his failing health, the King family directed new pleas for assistance at the White House. On April 2, 1998, Mrs. Coretta Scott King, Dr. King's widow, stood in front of her murdered husband's tomb in Atlanta, Georgia, and made a public appeal to President Bill Clinton. In her statement before the national press, Mrs. King called for a meeting with the President to discuss Pepper's so-called new evidence and the possibility of forming an investigative commission to examine the matter. Desperate to obtain answers and closure before Ray's quickly-approaching death, she buttressed her plea by stating, "My family and I are still appealing for justice."

Within a matter of days, the President formally asked U.S. Attorney General Janet Reno to meet with Mrs. King and her adult children. On April 8, 1998, thirty years to the day John McFerren first spoke to the FBI, the head of the Department of Justice once more intervened in the assassination case by meeting with the King family. But on the 23rd of that same month, the ailing James Earl Ray died of liver failure along with any hope he might one day reveal his untold secrets. Then in a startling turn of events, Reno formally announced on August 26 that the DOJ would indeed conduct a limited investigation into the past and present claims that Dr. King had been killed as a result of a high-level government conspiracy and not by Ray.

Another DOJ Investigation

In the past, Bill Pepper had attempted, albeit unsuccessfully, to persuade Reno to form a federal grand jury to look into his accumulation of new evidence. But with the additional public pressure being mounted on the Oval Office by Pepper's powerful friends in the King family, the attorney general reluctantly agreed to a limited investigation that would cover most of the old evidence as well as the new allegations purported by Pepper, Jowers, and others. In an effort to appear fair and impartial, Reno first recused the already-criticized FBI from participating in the investigation, and instead formed an inquiry team made up of federal employees from the DOJ and other federal agencies.

Leading the surprisingly small seven-person team was Barry Kowalski, an attorney at the DOJ's Civil Rights Division. Also joining the team from Kowalski's division were attorneys Lisa J. Stark and Seth Rosenthal. From the DOJ's Criminal Division, Attorney Jerry Massie was also asked to assist. Recruited from the United States Marshals Service was Inspector Yvonne Bonner, along with Special Agent Brad Farnsworth from the Bureau of Alcohol, Tobacco, and Firearms/ATF. Finally, Robert Nolan Carwell, who was an inspector at the United States Postal Service, rounded out the team.

As Randall Stephens began his examination of the public report detailing the DOJ's 1998-through-2000 investigation, several glaring omissions immediately roused his suspicion. While the individual names of the seven-person team and their respective agencies had been made available for open review, at no time did Reno disclose her team's investigative notes, witness affidavits, or typed memorandums. More alarming still was the report's complete lack of even the most basic information, including which of the seven investigators canvassed Shelby and Fayette Counties, which witnesses each of the seven investigators individually interviewed, and the specific dates those interviews were conducted. Just like G. Robert Blakey's HSCA investigation between

1977 and 1978, Reno and her team conducted their government business under a shroud of secrecy.

Particularly disconcerting to Stephens was the obvious absence of detail regarding the team's alleged interview of John McFerren. None of the names of his interviewers or the exact dates he was interviewed could be tracked down, and except for the DOJ's statement in the affirmative, no proof existed that federal authorities had even questioned McFerren in March of 1999. The only item available for Stephens to analyze was Reno and Kowalski's final June 9, 2000 report, which was nothing more than the DOJ team's own interpretive summary and conclusions.

Findings on John McFerren

Incredibly, nearly all of the so-called new findings on McFerren and his allegations were, at best, a mere rehash of previous government conclusions. After summarizing his initial two 1968 statements regarding the connection between Liberto and Ray, the June 2000 DOJ report simply endorsed the Memphis Police Department and FBI's past criticisms of McFerren by reiterating the Bureau's inability to locate corroborating evidence at the time. The only bits of previously unheard information Stephens noted were the unconvincing accusations that McFerren supposedly did not hear Liberto utter the words "on the balcony," and that the Italian-American business owner was not present at the Memphis Scott Street warehouse on April 4 at the time McFerren said he was there.

As described in the report, David E. Caywood, the previous Burch Porter & Johnson law firm attorney who represented McFerren inside the Peabody Hotel room, apparently told Reno's DOJ investigators that he didn't remember hearing McFerren say the phrase "on the balcony" prior to the MPD and FBI's interview that Monday morning. The 2000 DOJ report also went on to assert that when questioned by MPD homicide detectives after April 8, 1968, Liberto claimed that he left work early on April 4 due to a previous finger injury, and that he was not inside the warehouse at the time McFerren accused him of screaming into the telephone. Liberto was able to present the 1968 MPD detectives with a doctor's note indicating that he had his finger lanced on April 3, the day before the shooting. And when both James Latch and Liberto's wife, Gladys, were asked about Frank's whereabouts on the April 4 day of Dr. King's death, both of them backed up the produce owner's alibi by asserting that he was resting quietly at his Memphis home that evening.

Next, the DOJ outlined and backed their own 1976 investigation. Just as Stephens predicted, Reno's team focused their harsh spotlight on McFerren's past statements, specifically his comment that the person who killed President Kennedy also killed Dr. King. They further tried to highlight his alleged paranoia and unreliability by repeating his 1976 belief that his phone had been tapped and that people "were out to get him." The report also reinforced the DOJ's previous insinuation that McFerren presumably exaggerated his 1976 statement when he said that James Latch spoke Ray's name just before handing the telephone receiver off to Liberto.

Reno and Kowalski's team also criticized McFerren's past claim to DOJ investigators that, despite the contrary assertion in the Fitzpatrick and Sloan 302 report, he had positively identified Ray in the 1968 FBI photo lineup. Additionally, his 1976 reassertion that he witnessed Ray working for Liberto around Christmas in 1967 was lambasted. The report also took aim at McFerren's 1978 House Select Committee on Assassinations affidavit by belittling his belief that Ray was assisted by Somerville Mayor I.P. Yancey. Then, after their lengthy re-evaluation of everything McFerren stated between 1968 and 1978, Reno's team finally began their own analysis of what he claimed during their alleged interview of him in March of 1999.

One of the first items that immediately jumped off the page at Stephens was the investigative team's own admission that McFerren was unwilling to reveal certain information to them "until he could testify for Dr. Pepper in court." Astonishingly, the same report went on to contradict that statement by detailing McFerren's alleged disclosure of the complete Somerville and Memphis conspiracy. In one instance, the report stated, "Finally, he repeated his erroneous assertion that Ray had stayed at the mayor's home in Somerville (McFerren's hometown) before the assassination." Then in an effort to demonstrate his propensity for communicating conflicting narratives, the report criticized McFerren's eventual failure to mention Ray while on the witness stand during the *King v. Jowers* civil trial held in November 1999 (discussed in the next chapter).

The investigators, apparently unable to extract any new information from the tight-lipped McFerren in March of '99, dedicated the rest of their June 2000 public report to attacking his soundness of mind and reputation. The DOJ filled the remaining word space by claiming that, during their team's 1999 interview of him, McFerren exhibited "quirky behavior" by locking his door and asking them to speak quietly as he placed a paper bag over his allegedly "bugged" telephone. They also cynically noted that the grocer declared he had access to an "intelligence network," believed the KKK and Mafia were still "after him," and "that he was in great danger because of his knowledge of the connection between the King and Kennedy assassinations."

In the end, it was the finding of Reno's team that McFerren was extremely unreliable. They concluded their harsh denouncement of him by stating that he exhibited "peculiar behavior," that the investigators could not ascertain any evidence to defend his "bizarre, uncorroborated claims," and that his accounts "contradict known facts."

Conclusions and Questions

Stephens was immediately dismayed by Reno and her team's so-called impartial investigation. It was apparent to him that the DOJ had not improved its track record nor accomplished anything groundbreaking that would warrant a reversal in confidence. In Stephens' eyes, the 1998-to-2000 inquiry was just another in a long series of governmental whitewashes, abhorrently conducted by the very same federal agency that skirted its duties under Attorney General Ramsey Clark more than three decades before. As previously alluded to, Stephens was also frustrated by the immense vacuum of supporting material. At no time was he able to locate the DOJ's notes, memorandums, or notarized witness affidavits as were available for previous investigations. It was still unclear exactly who on the seven-person team interviewed McFerren and when. All previous federal investigators had been required to give McFerren a dated copy of his statement. So why hadn't he been given a dated copy of this one?

Just as troubling were the new investigators' extreme reliance on old information. If Reno and her team set out to conduct an entirely fresh, independent, and unbiased inquiry, separate from the efforts of the original federal inquests, then their actions and final report failed to reflect it. Upon a lengthy word count and subject analysis, Stephens was shocked to discover that, mixed in with the report's visually deceiving section on McFerren, Reno's team used 615 words to review his original 1968-to-1978 statements while dedicating only 335 words to his alleged 1999 interview. In short, the DOJ devoted nearly two-thirds of their McFerren report to regurgitating and re-criticizing his prior accounts.

What's more, these rehashed criticisms still did not rise to the level of adequately refuting McFerren's reliability. To Stephens, the denouncements from the past only indicated that the government bodies who looked into McFerren's former claims either failed or chose not to find the needed evidence to prove him correct or incorrect at the time. As before, Stephens could not help but wonder why Reno and Kowalski's team focused so much of their time and energy on reworking McFerren's old interviews. Were members of their 1999 team unable to extract anything revelatory from the famously guarded Fayette Countian?

Stephens' mind shifted to the DOJ's own documented admission that McFerren was not as cooperative with their investigators as he had been in the past. If, after many years of manipulation, Bill Pepper had managed to convince McFerren to stay quiet about certain topics, then Stephens had zero doubt that the stubbornly-loyal grocery store owner from Fayette County would have honored the New York defense lawyer's request. Was it possible that, because of his naive commitment to Pepper to remain silent until the *King v. Jowers* trial in November, McFerren simply stonewalled Reno's team earlier in March? Was the DOJ left with little choice but to reuse John's '68-to-'78 statements in place of what they failed to retrieve in '99?

Aside from their support of former federal criticisms and their June 2000 rebuke of his unwillingness to speak, the DOJ went to incredible lengths to openly and ruthlessly assassinate McFerren's character based on what little material he supposedly provided them. Virtually none of the 1999 portion of John's alleged statements covered anything new or of substance regarding his knowledge of the conspiracy. Instead, the final one-third of the report's word space was filled with the DOJ team's personal opinions of McFerren. Using inflammatory language such as "quirky behavior," "peculiar behavior," and "bizarre, uncorroborated claims," the team ravaged John's name and integrity, thereby portraying him as a crazy person to anyone who studied the report.

During one of several jailhouse phone calls, now regularly occurring between the accidental investigator and Marcus Holmes, Stephens mentioned the incendiary remarks in Reno's report. Often playing devil's advocate, he asked Holmes if it was possible that McFerren, because of his age at the time, the repeated traumatic attacks he had endured over the years, or maybe his rural vernacular, ever exhibited unwarranted paranoia or perhaps senility. Without hesitation, Holmes declared his undying confidence in his friend's past and present mental faculties. At no time, he stressed, had he witnessed or known of an instance when McFerren lost his mind, said something grossly inaccurate, or was disproportionately fearful.

In addition, Holmes was unyielding in his forceful assertion to Stephens that McFerren never mentioned being interviewed in 1999 by the federal government, nor had he supplied any documentation to indicate it. The only inquiries McFerren had described at length or shown proof of were the ones that occurred in '68, '76, '78, and with Pepper in later years. Holmes firmly believed that the March 1999 interview never actually took place. But the still-imprisoned sleuth wasn't finished yet. He went on to direct Stephens' attention to several documents located in his previously compiled files. Buried within the stacks of government reports, newspaper clippings, and various photocopied books he recently passed along to Stephens, Holmes had included paperwork that illustrated the exact anecdotes the DOJ might've borrowed to fabricate their 1999 interview with McFerren.

In one example, Holmes discovered that true-crime Kennedy and King author Gerald Posner, in his 1998 book *Killing the Dream*, interviewed attorney David E. Caywood about his allegation regarding McFerren's supposedly erroneous "on the balcony" statement. In this case, Holmes learned that the DOJ investigative team was already aware of Posner's book and Caywood's allegation prior to their '98-through-2000 inquiry. Holmes eventually tracked down Caywood himself at his Memphis law office in 2013 and questioned the still-practicing attorney about the very same comment.

In another example, Robert Hamburger's 1973 *Our Portion of Hell*, a book detailing the civil rights struggle in Fayette County, recounted McFerren's own claim that he once placed "two paper sacks...over the receiver" of his store's indoor payphone to prevent government eavesdropping. Holmes thought it likely that Reno or members of her team obtained a copy of Hamburger's obscure, now out-of-print book either before or after their failed attempt to interview McFerren. Again, over the telephone, Holmes told his partner where to find a photocopy of Hamburger's book and his interview notes on Caywood.

By now, Stephens' head was spinning. Had McFerren really been questioned again or had his old statements simply been plagiarized and inserted into the June 2000 report? Would a high-level government agency like the DOJ really create a counterfeit interview in order to paint someone as unreliable? Immediately, Stephens recalled his previous discovery of plagiarism by Gene and Ernestine Johnson within the pages of McFerren's 1978 affidavit to the HSCA.

The last issue in Reno's report that Stephens needed to address was Liberto's injured finger. Unfortunately, Stephens had not yet tracked down the MPD homicide department's documented interview of Liberto, the typed interview Reno's team most likely had access to. Stephens first considered the possible identity of the "detective" who went unnamed in Reno's report. Who was the MPD employee who questioned Liberto? Was Frank Holloman's chief homicide inspector, N.E. Zachary, the law enforcement official who spoke to the Scott Street business owner? Stephens contemplated Zachary's April 8 interview of McFerren at the Peabody and then began to wonder how much information the inspector may have relayed to Liberto when questioning him in the days afterward. And if it wasn't N.E. Zachary who spoke to Liberto, it most certainly would have been one of Zachary's underling homicide inspectors.

Next, Liberto apparently provided proof from his doctor that his infected finger had been lanced on Wednesday, April 3, 1968. But even if that was true, Stephens thought, why would a simple cut on his finger, one that had been medically treated the day before, prevent Liberto from running his highly lucrative business on Thursday? Although Liberto's wife, Gladys, and his business partner, James Latch, backed up the alibi when interviewed by the MPD, the entire story seemed thoroughly flimsy to Stephens, and he was immediately suspicious of the corroboration by Frank's wife and business partner. Furthermore, the '68 and '99 authorities' quick willingness to swallow the story without a second thought also seemed suspect. Now extremely interested in Reno's personal and professional relationships, and those of her small team of tightly-knit investigators, Stephens began to wonder if any of them maintained close connections to individuals from Tennessee or Shelby and Fayette Counties, individuals who had both the influence and vested interest in discrediting McFerren.

Chapter 7

WITNESS STAND

ON THE EVENING of December 16, 1993, American conspiracy enthusiasts sat spellbound in front of their television sets as former Memphis bar and grill owner Loyd Jowers; his local attorney, Lewis Kuykendall Garrison; and an African-American associate of Jowers named Willie Akins, spoke to journalist Sam Donaldson on the ABC news program, *Primetime Live*. During his interview, the sixty-seven-year-old Jowers made the brow-raising confession that he had been paid in 1968 by Memphis produce dealer Frank Liberto to find someone to shoot Dr. Martin Luther King Jr. Jowers also intimated during the interview that he had, in fact, hired an assassin on behalf of Liberto to carry out the murder, although Jowers did not publicly name the purported shooter at the time. But most intriguing was his assertion to Donaldson that James Earl Ray was not the gunman in the April 4, 1968 assassination.

Faced with mounting failure in Tennessee's criminal court system along with Ray's deteriorating health, Attorney Bill Pepper labored frantically, even before the 1993 televised confession, to draw the assumption of guilt away from Ray and toward Jowers and his alleged involvement. Now, with little hope that Janet Reno's Department of Justice would find new evidence that incriminated Jowers or exonerated the since-deceased Ray, a desperate Pepper made one final attempt in the fall of 1998 to exploit the questionable 1993 confession. Working in close collaboration with Jowers and his attorney, Pepper ultimately sold Dr. King's widow and her adult children on the idea of filing a wrongful death civil suit against the self-professed conspirator, cleverly billing it as the King family's last chance to hold an official trial that might expose the truth.

King v. Jowers

Running concurrent with Attorney General Reno's investigation into the assassination of Dr. King, jury selection in the wrongful death civil trial of *King v. Jowers* got underway on November 15, 1999, in a downtown Memphis courtroom. Representing the plaintiffs, which included Mrs. Coretta Scott King, Martin Luther King III, Bernice King, Dexter King, and Yolanda King, was none other than James Earl Ray's former attorney, Bill Pepper. For the defense, Lewis K. Garrison represented Loyd Jowers and "other unknown co-conspirators."

Apart from his highly unethical role as the King family's new attorney, Pepper also convened several closed-door meetings that included one of his plaintiffs, the opposing defense attorney, and the defendant himself. Astonishingly, Pepper, Dexter King, Garrison, and Jowers met at least twice as a group even before the trial began to discuss the case, ultimately forming what can only be assumed was a well-rehearsed conspiratorial narrative.

With District Thirteen, Division Four Circuit Court Judge James Swearengen presiding, and the newly selected twelve-member jury listening intently in the wings, Pepper's highly choreographed courtroom spectacle lasted a total of fourteen days. Following the testimony of nearly seventy witnesses, closing arguments and deliberations began on December 8, 1999. After only two and a half hours, the jury returned to the courtroom at 3:02 p.m., unanimously finding that Jowers did "participate in a conspiracy to do harm to Martin Luther King." In the end, the King family was awarded their symbolically requested $100 in damages.

Then in April of 2009, nearly a decade after the verdict, one of the 1999 court reporters hired to transcribe the proceedings published *The 13th Juror*, a 750-page paperback book marketed as the full and unedited transcript of the *King v. Jowers* civil trial. It wasn't long after Randall Stephens began his own investigation in 2015 that he purchased a copy of the thick, powder-blue book, and began analyzing McFerren's transcribed testimony for himself.

Pepper's Direct Examination

On November 16, 1999, the opening day of official testimony in the *King v. Jowers* trial, Mrs. Coretta Scott King became the first person to testify under oath regarding her late husband's horrific murder. Following Mrs. King on the witness stand were Coby Smith and Charles Cabbage, two former leaders of the Invaders, the same black militant group from Memphis that once participated in the civil rights movement in Shelby and Fayette Counties. Then, sometime after 2:00 p.m., John McFerren became the fourth person to testify. Since his original statements to the Memphis Police Department and Federal Bureau of Investigation in 1968, his interview with the DOJ in 1976, his revoked invitation to speak before the House Select Committee on Assassinations in 1978, his alleged flight from Pepper's HBO mock trial in 1993, and his theoretical interview with Reno's DOJ investigators eight months before, this was to be McFerren's first and last opportunity to testify on the witness stand.

After being politely encouraged by Judge Swearengen to "sit back and relax," the seventy-five-year-old, well-dressed McFerren began answering Pepper's direct examination questions by first stating his name and address. Pepper then led McFerren down a testimonial path that, to Randall Stephens' surprise, started almost a full decade before the 1968 assassination occurred. Having nothing to do with Dr. King's murder, one of Pepper's first questions to the witness was, "John, did there come a time in 1959 or 1960 that you became involved in civil rights activity, voter registration activity, in Fayette County and the area of Somerville?"

From that point forward, and as evident in the published transcript, McFerren went on to describe in painfully rambling detail his past leadership of Fayette County's first two social justice organizations. For what seemed to be an inordinate amount of time spent in court, Pepper persisted to question McFerren at length about his life in the late 1950s and his struggle to operate his Fayette County gas and grocery business throughout the next decade. Then, after devoting nearly half of his direct examination time to McFerren's pre-1968 life and work, Pepper finally moved on to topics relevant to the King case. By asking McFerren where he used to purchase his grocery store's inventory, Pepper eventually opened a line of questioning that led to the issue of why McFerren was inside the 814 Scott Street produce warehouse on April 4, 1968.

However, as soon as McFerren began to describe his weekly visits to Frank Liberto's Memphis business, Pepper interjected by asking, "So you bought produce from a warehouse run by...a man framed Frank Liberto. In 1996?" The now extremely confused Stephens halted his reading of the transcript. Did Pepper mean "named" instead of "framed"? Was the oddly placed word simply a typo made by the court reporters? And what was the 1996 date about? According to Pepper's own 1995 book, *Orders to Kill*, the tomato salesman known as Frank C. Liberto supposedly died in 1978. If that was true, why on earth,

Stephens wondered, had Pepper knowingly vocalized a contradictory date while questioning his own witness?

Making matters worse, McFerren, unfazed by Pepper's strange question, then confirmed the contradictory date by replying, "That's correct. I did before then. See, I knew him way before then. Around about 1960, 1960 or 1961, I got to know him real well." Now exceedingly agitated, Stephens scribbled a quick note in the margins of the thick book, used a neon marker to highlight the troubling text, and continued his study of McFerren's alleged 1999 testimony.

McFerren's specific recollection of what he observed on April 4, 1968, was the next item in the transcript. As he had done countless times before, the aging Fayette Countian again explained the details surrounding what he overheard during Liberto's two telephone calls. But while McFerren's telephone eavesdropping testimony was consistent with his past accounts, no mention whatsoever was made during the trial by either Pepper or his witness regarding James Earl Ray's possible association with Liberto before Dr. King's death.

Following his description of what transpired at 5:15 p.m. on the day of the assassination, McFerren then went on to outline his 1968 interviews with local and federal investigators. Now accustomed to hunting down the often overlooked irregularities hidden within "authoritative" texts, Stephens quickly located another problem in the 2009 book. He knew by now that FBI agents Robert Fitzpatrick and Andrew Sloan had visited McFerren on April 18, 1968, a date which fell on a Thursday. Yet, based on the 1999 transcript, McFerren stated that the interview between himself, Fitzpatrick, and Sloan occurred on a Monday.

Next, McFerren described the subsequent reprisals he endured after the shooting, the first of which was his unnerving morning encounter with New Orleans truck stop owner Robert Powers. Stephens quickly noticed two more troubling anomalies. Just like in the DOJ's 1976 interview notes, Robert Powers' last name was potentially misspelled as "Powell" in the 1999 transcript. In addition, McFerren once again stated the incorrect day on which the event occurred. While the Powers encounter happened on the same Thursday as McFerren's interview with Fitzpatrick and Sloan, April 18, 1968, this time, John stated it transpired on a Tuesday.

Unfortunately, the second reprisal McFerren described to Pepper was no less challenging for Stephens to make sense of. According to the published text, McFerren claimed that because of his April 1968 statements to authorities, his mother had been intentionally run over by the driver of a Dean's dairy truck as she stood by the roadside, presumably somewhere in Fayette County. But by this point in his research, Stephens was already extremely familiar with the dairy truck incident involving Mrs. Estella McFerren, John's mother.

Based on hard documentation, the delivery man in question was not employed by Dean's but by Cedar Hill Farms, a former dairy business that once straddled the Fayette and Shelby County line near Collierville, Tennessee. Furthermore, the accident, which transpired in front of Estella's Fayette County home, could not have possibly been a post-MLK-whistleblowing act of vengeance since it took place in January of 1960, more than eight years before Dr. King was assassinated. Stephens now wondered if McFerren, perhaps confused by Pepper's earlier line of irrelevant questioning, was simply trying to communicate all of the reprisals he had endured since beginning his civil rights work, and not just the ones he had faced after Dr. King's death.

While on the witness stand, McFerren also discussed the apparent beating he received in 1969 at the hands of several black men, most of whom were the Anderson brothers of Fayette County. Once again, the 1999 transcript conveyed some muddled semblance of a story Stephens was already versed on. But as was now routine, two of the key masterminds behind the Anderson assault were misnamed in the published text. The name of the first mastermind McFerren mentioned, printed as "Marion Yancy," should have been transcribed by the court reporter as "Mayor Yancey," the former white mayor of Somerville who McFerren believed financially assisted Ray both before and after the murder of Dr. King. As for "Rue Grady," the next misprinted name in the transcript, that was undoubtedly meant to be "Rube Rhea," the since-deceased white businessman, banker, and landowner from Somerville, who was a friend of Yancey and indignant enemy of the McFerren family.

Pepper then followed up McFerren's 1969 beating testimony by asking, "John, were you put in the hospital as a result of that?" At the detriment of his already teetering credibility in the eyes of the jury and future readers of the transcript, McFerren quickly answered the question by launching into yet another eccentric elucidation, this time focusing on a rural home remedy he used after the beating. To Stephens' chagrin, the transcript outlined McFerren's open court explanation of how he healed his potentially fractured bones by applying an old slave-invented balm made of boiled mullet, petroleum jelly, and iodized salt.

Pepper's monotonously long, direct examination of McFerren finally concluded with the topic of the 1978 congressional assassination hearings held in Washington, D.C. In a shamelessly duplicitous attempt at highlighting how the government stifled McFerren's statements throughout the years, the equally guilty attorney inquired, "Were you ever asked to go to Washington and testify before the House Select Committee on Assassinations and tell what you have told us here today?" McFerren again replied by describing the situation that occurred between himself and Select Committee investigator, Gene Johnson. McFerren testified that Johnson had been cordial during their first several interviews, but ultimately became "hostile" when the two men spoke for the last time. McFerren then finalized his direct examination testimony by explaining to the court how Johnson had prevented him from speaking at the 1978 hearings.

Garrison's Cross-Examination

After a fifteen-minute recess, McFerren settled into the witness stand once more, this time to be questioned by Loyd Jowers' defense attorney, Lewis K. Garrison. Garrison's cross-examination of McFerren was brief but telling in the eyes of Stephens. In an exchange that could not have lasted more than five to six minutes in total, Garrison began his line of inquiry by stating, "Mr. McFerren, you and I have talked before about all of the things that you know." The attorney then asked McFerren if he knew Liberto for "quite a long time…over a period of years."

In a puzzling response that further exacerbated Stephens' prior confusion, McFerren again confirmed, "I know him from 1960 up until 1996, I was in his business once or twice a week." Garrison then asked, "Okay. After the assassination of Dr. King, did you ever see him anymore after that?" McFerren again replied, "I never did see him personally after that."

The meticulous reader stopped again, his mind working intensely through the newest conundrum. Not only was Stephens confounded as to why McFerren confirmed the 1996 year to Garrison, but he also wondered what Garrison's motive was for asking McFerren if he saw Liberto after April 4, 1968. Did Jowers' defense attorney already know the 1996 date conflicted with Liberto's 1978 death as asserted in Pepper's book? Was Garrison hinting at the apparent inaccuracy while cross-examining Pepper's witness? And if so, why didn't he challenge McFerren's faulty testimony and memory? Then it dawned on the researcher. Quickly recalling his own suspicions of pretrial tomfoolery between Pepper, Dexter King, Garrison, and Jowers, Stephens came to believe that McFerren had been unwittingly spoon-fed the contradictory date even before entering the courtroom and that Frank Liberto's true death date had been deliberately obscured during the trial by both attorneys.

Garrison proceeded with his inquiry by asking McFerren if he had ever overheard Liberto mention Jowers' name, to which McFerren answered in the negative. Then, in yet another line of questioning that caused Stephens' brow to furrow, Garrison asked, "Do you know Mr. Liberto visited Somerville—are you aware that he visited Somerville on occasion?" In still another erratic, long-winded, backwater oration, McFerren answered:

He would—I wouldn't say every Saturday morning, but he would visit John Wilder's office, which is on the east side of the courthouse. Now, let me explain this to you so you'll understand. When the assassination committee of Dr. King was going on in Washington, getting ready to go on, he went to visiting John Wilder's office regular. Now, the way I got ahold of it, I had some of our underground watching. Two to three weeks before James Earl Ray broke pen out of Brushy Mountain, I called Washington and told the Select Committee that they was going to kill James Earl Ray or something was going to happen to him. I talked to Mr. Gene Johnson, which I've got his phone numbers, I've got Mr. Flanders' phone numbers in my pocket now, I've got Mr. Dole's phone numbers in my pocket now. I was in correspondence with all of them. The Justice Department, what I said before, the Justice Department covered it up. When I said they covered up the barnyard, I mean they covered it up. Now, if you look at the records, the assistant to the United States Attorney General at that time was—it was under the Nixon administration. He had a heavy voice. I talked to him one time. I says, I know Dr. King's killings, who is in it, they trying to set me up to get me killed. Mitchell, that was his name. If you ever talked to him on the phone, he has got a gross voice like a bullfrog.

Stephens halted his reading for the umpteenth time, once more bombarded by misspelled names and chronological inaccuracies. Not only had the names of well-known DOJ civil rights attorneys J. Harold "Nick" Flannery Jr. and John Michael Doar been incorrectly printed by the court reporter as "Flanders" and "Dole," but Stephens was well aware that John Mitchell ended his tenure as attorney general in 1972, several years before the House Select Committee's investigation got underway. While Stephens believed that McFerren had indeed spoken with Mitchell over the telephone, it was obvious the two men's discussion took place while Mitchell was still employed at the DOJ, not after.

But what truly caught Stephens' attention was Garrison's question about Frank Liberto's trips to Somerville, Tennessee. As a part of McFerren's response to Garrison, he twice mentioned the name of a prominent Somerville attorney and high-ranking Tennessee state official. Not by accident, the Fayette Countian whom McFerren named was an individual who had already popped up on Stephens' radar. Fixing his bitter gaze on the name printed in the transcript, Stephens quickly recalled the notorious reputation of John McFerren's long-time nemesis, John Shelton Wilder. McFerren and Marcus Holmes had long asserted that John Wilder was, among other things, the friend of Somerville Mayor I.P. Yancey and Rube Rhea, as well as the personal attorney of Frank C. Liberto.

After his suspicious failure to press McFerren about the relationship between Liberto and Wilder, Garrison wrapped up his cross-examination by inquiring if the witness had ever been shot at since initiating his civil rights efforts. Confirming the past attempts on his life, McFerren explained the circumstances surrounding an individual named "Benefield" who, despite being hired to do so, ultimately decided against killing McFerren. But during his answer, the Fayette Countian mentioned a well-known historical figure that the court reporter once again failed to accurately identify. "Gerald Estes," the incorrectly printed name in question, was no doubt intended to be "James F. Estes," the former African-American civil rights leader, FCCWL attorney, and friend of McFerren, who Stephens had long heard about.

Pepper's Redirect Examination

In an incredibly abrupt and altogether redundant redirect examination, Pepper again took the floor, this time asking McFerren simply, "Is it true that almost thirty-one years ago you told the same story that you have told to this jury and this Court this afternoon?" After a quick, "That's correct," from McFerren, Pepper followed up with, "And have you ever had an opportunity to tell this story before in a court of law?" Following his equally brief reply of "This is the first time," McFerren was then thanked by the King family's attorney and allowed to step down by Judge Swearengen.

Conclusions and Questions

His final impression of *The 13th Juror* was stark. Never mind the author's inept introductory claim that James Earl Ray passed away in 1996 instead of 1998. Stephens now joined a number of other authors and critics in their belief that Jowers and Garrison, fully aware that Jowers would not face any actual criminal or financial penalties as a result of the civil trial, perpetuated a false conspiratorial narrative in order to profit from an eventual book or movie deal. And waiting happily in the wings was Bill Pepper, the other crafty lawyer who used Jowers' greed and erroneous Liberto story to serve a biased agenda. More than willing to collude with the opposing defendant and defense attorney, Pepper helped shift the assumption of guilt away from his deceased client, James Earl Ray, and onto the still-living Loyd Jowers, the self-confessed, so-called accomplice of Frank C. Liberto.

Stephens was now highly critical of the published transcript. Indeed, the 1999 narrative had left a painfully indelible mark on McFerren's already vilified credibility. From the outset, Pepper spent an inordinate amount of time in court questioning McFerren about his civil rights past. Based on Stephens' calculations, that initial, entirely irrelevant line of questioning took up approximately eleven minutes of Pepper's total twenty-three-minute direct examination. In other words, Ray's former attorney dedicated nearly half of his time to questioning McFerren about topics that had nothing whatsoever to do with the conspiracy to kill Dr. King. Accordingly, Stephens eventually formed the opinion that Pepper intentionally asked McFerren these immaterial questions for two reasons.

First, this line of inquiry naturally ran down the clock as McFerren sat on the witness stand, thus depriving him of the opportunity to disclose the more pertinent information Pepper obviously wanted left unheard. Second, Pepper was fully aware by this point that the aging, illiterate, often overly eager McFerren had a habit of using long-winded, chronologically rambling answers laced with rural vernacular. While Pepper still depended heavily on McFerren's brief testimony about Frank Liberto's telephone calls, it ultimately benefited the lawyer if McFerren's memory and ability to articulate could be called into question at a later date. Clearly, McFerren was deliberately provided with the questions and time needed to undermine his own credibility, therefore ensuring his lack of participation in any potential anti-Ray, anti-Pepper inquiries held in the future.

Then there was the discrepancy between Liberto's 1978 and 1996 death dates that needed to be dealt with. Once again, Stephens had previously taken at face value Pepper's *Orders to Kill* claim that Frank C. Liberto died in 1978. In the twentieth chapter of his 1995 book, Pepper stated:

The first Frank Liberto (Frank Camille Liberto), the primary target of the investigation, was the produce dealer overheard by John McFerren who died in 1978.

Yet, more than once during the trial, it was alleged that the Scott Street produce dealer lived until 1996. Was this simply a transcribing error that had been made by the court reporter more than once that day? Or was the erroneous 1996 date actually verbalized by both Pepper and McFerren? Based on Pepper's previous propensity for self-serving deception, it was now becoming clear that it benefited him to cloud the issue of Liberto's true death date. In his 1995 book, Pepper also admitted that during the late 1960s, Memphis was home to several businessmen named Frank Liberto. In the same chapter and paragraph just cited, Pepper also wrote that:

> The investigation of the Liberto connections to the killing was complicated by the fact that in 1968 there were no fewer than three Frank Libertos in Memphis alone, each with extended family connections in New Orleans. The first Frank Liberto (Frank Camille Liberto), the primary target of the investigation, was the produce dealer overheard by John McFerren who died in 1978. The second Frank Liberto had also been dead for over ten years. In 1968 he owned Frank's liquor store and the Green Beetle Tavern on South Main Street, just up the block from Jim's Grill. The third and probably wealthiest Frank Liberto was over 80 in 1992. Barksdale told me that despite his age he was still active in his automobile business.

If Pepper wished to hamper any future investigations into the conspiracy involving his since-deceased client and Liberto, what better way to accomplish such a feat than to confuse the public regarding which Frank Liberto was involved. McFerren was very clear that, after the shooting in 1968, he immediately stopped purchasing produce at the Scott Street market. So, if McFerren no longer met with the tomato salesman he knew as Frank Liberto, it would have been very easy for him to assume that the same Liberto was still alive in 1996, especially given the number of Frank Libertos living in the area at the time.

Knowing full well how to exploit his witness's gullibility, illiteracy, physical isolation, and age, Pepper took advantage of the multiple Frank Liberto angle by intentionally feeding McFerren the wrong date both before and during the Jowers civil trial. By blindly following Pepper's lead, McFerren's testimony then went on to become a matter of public record, ultimately obscuring Ray's conspiratorial connection to the now hard-to-pin-down Frank Liberto. But Pepper was not the only guilty player in this courtroom charade. Lewis Garrison was a willing accomplice as well.

As a Mid-South native and legal professional representing Memphis clientele for multiple decades, Garrison would have been keenly aware of exactly who the infamous Frank C. Liberto was, as well as the differences between him and the other Memphis businessmen who shared his name. In addition, the resourceful, well-seasoned attorney had complete access to the official Shelby County records and newspaper clippings that determined the correct date the real Liberto died. Yet Garrison never challenged McFerren's claim about Liberto's 1996 death, a tactic that, as Jowers' courtroom defender, Garrison should have immediately employed as a way of discrediting Pepper's witness. As he previously speculated, Stephens was more positive than ever that McFerren unknowingly adopted the incorrect date as a result of Pepper and Garrison's collusive manipulation.

Next, Stephens scrutinized the absence of Ray's alleged association with Liberto in McFerren's 1999 testimony. Just as predicted, Pepper successfully prevented McFerren from mentioning Ray's name in connection with Frank Liberto. But like the purposely shrouded issue of Liberto's death date, Pepper's so-called legal opponent was again complicit in the guise. Unquestionably, Garrison was well aware that McFerren had previously implicated Ray in the conspiracy. Yet, as a defense attorney allegedly tasked with drawing the assumption of guilt away from Jowers, Garrison neglected to press McFerren on his knowledge of Ray's work with the Scott Street produce owner.

And just as Pepper and Garrison almost certainly planned, McFerren went on to be publicly chastised for his documented omission and theoretical unreliability. Approximately six months after the December 1999 verdict, the transcript of the *King v. Jowers* trial was cited by Attorney General Janet Reno. In the same June 2000 government report described in the previous chapter, Reno's DOJ team stated:

> During King v. Jowers, McFerren again related Liberto's alleged telephone conversation. He did not, however, repeat his contention that Liberto's partner named Ray as the caller. In fact, McFerren did not mention Ray in his testimony at all. Since McFerren focused on Ray for years, including during our interview of him in March 1999, this recent omission further undermines his credibility. Indeed, it seems McFerren may have tailored his testimony to fit the theory advanced by Dr. Pepper at trial—that Ray was not involved in the assassination.

What Reno's DOJ report failed to mention was that, during the trial, not once did Pepper or Garrison ask McFerren about Ray's possible involvement. Stephens was now absolutely certain that, in an effort to protect their well-crafted portrayal of Ray as the innocent victim, both of the *King v. Jowers* civil trial attorneys barred McFerren from speaking about Ray's role in Liberto's plot.

Next on the list of yet-to-be-decrypted irregularities was McFerren's mention of incorrect days. By this time in his evaluation, Stephens had to concede that McFerren probably made some mistakes during his 1999 testimony. One of these errors was his claim that FBI Special Agents Fitzpatrick and Sloan interviewed him on a Monday. Another, of course, was McFerren's claim that the unwelcomed visit by Powers occurred on a Tuesday. Based on official documentation, Stephens knew that both events transpired on April 18, 1968, which fell on a Thursday.

But Stephens was also fully aware that McFerren had been entangled in a countless number of historically significant events. Without a doubt, it would have been difficult for a normal person to keep track of the precise details surrounding every incident, let alone a seventy-five-year-old man like McFerren. Furthermore, Stephens viewed McFerren's mistakes as minor in comparison to his overall testimony.

The issue of misprinted words and names within McFerren's portion of the transcript was the next enigma Stephens tackled. According to his analysis of the published text, Stephens tracked down at least eight items that were incorrectly recorded, although there could have been more. While the word "framed" as spoken by Pepper was undoubtedly intended to be "named," the final seven misprinted words were proper names that were crucial to McFerren's testimony. Given the gravity of who some of those people were within the context of the assassination of Dr. King, Stephens was extremely frustrated by the team of court reporters' lack of accurate transcribing. Additionally, one of the members of the court reporting team waited until 2009 to author and publish *The 13th Juror.*

From the moment the verdict was read by Judge Swearengen in 1999 until the transcript's publication in 2009, the same court reporter neglected to correct the seven misprinted names. The customary errata sheet (the legal document used to correct court transcript errors) was either never generated by the various lawyers and court reporters following the trial or was simply not used by *The 13th Juror* author when compiling the book. Given Pepper's thorough knowledge of who McFerren was specifically referring to during the trial, as well as the close working relationship Pepper and Garrison continued to maintain with the same court reporter/book author in the decades that followed, McFerren's potentially muddled pronunciation of the names in 1999 could not be used as an excuse for the 2009 misprints.

Stephens was now highly suspicious of the three legal professionals and their failure to rectify McFerren's misprinted testimony within the ten-year period they were afforded. Worse still, less than diligent MLK researchers and authors would later use the 2009 publication as a baseline for their own investigative narratives. As of the publication of this book, author Phillip F. Nelson and former MLK investigator Gary Revel have both clumsily cited McFerren's misquoted court testimony in their individual written works, thus propagating the chronologically inaccurate events and misprinted names as fact.

Finally, Stephens made an attempt to wade through the still-murky waters of Lt. Gov. John Wilder's relationship with Frank Liberto. Even before reading McFerren's cloudy testimony concerning the Saturday meetings between the tomato salesman and the Somerville attorney, Stephens knew about the two men's purported connection due to Holmes' own chats with McFerren. In contrast, however, the Liberto-Wilder narrative that Stephens was told differed slightly from the one that was described in court. According to Holmes, McFerren had received word from a Mid-South local man named T.R. Wright, also known as Tommy Wright, that Liberto met regularly with Wilder in Somerville to discuss private matters, not only during the HSCA's investigation in the late 1970s, but even before the 1968 assassination of Dr. King took place.

What's more, while Garrison was the only attorney in the courtroom to broach the Liberto-Wilder subject, Stephens was well aware that Pepper also knew about the connection, having already hinted at it in his 1995 book. In the twenty-seventh chapter of *Orders to Kill*, Pepper wrote that McFerren:

...said that he recalled hearing from a local man, Tommy Wright, that on Saturday mornings Liberto would meet with a high-level Tennessee state official at his law office in Fayette County. Tommy said that they would meet regularly on Saturday mornings.

Naturally, Holmes and Stephens had long been suspicious of Pepper's cagey handling of the Wilder issue. One, why did Pepper fail to actually name the "high-level Tennessee state official" in his 1995 book? And two, why was Garrison, the opposing defense attorney, the only person in the courtroom on November 16, 1999, to indirectly ask McFerren about Liberto's connection to Wilder? It only took Stephens a second or two to mull over these questions before the singular answer came into focus.

If Wilder, who was still alive and politically powerful in 1999, was both Liberto's attorney and Mayor I.P. Yancey's friend, and Ray had been in contact with both Liberto and Yancey, then Wilder may well have been at the hub of the conspiratorial wheel. And if Pepper had made a strong case against Wilder as one of the potential ringleaders in the Liberto conspiracy to kill Dr. King, the consequences for Ray's long-crafted legacy as an unwitting patsy could've been disastrous. In short, Wilder most certainly would have exposed Ray's real involvement in the conspiracy if Pepper had tried to implicate the Somerville lawyer. A more penetrating investigation into both the lieutenant governor's past and Pepper's reluctance to publicly point a finger at him was now a foregone conclusion.

After considering the totality of the 2009 published transcript, Randall Stephens was now one hundred percent convinced that the so-called uncertainty and misinformation surrounding John McFerren's 1999 testimony was part of a calculated plan to denigrate him. Even before reading McFerren's testimony, Stephens believed that, as James Earl Ray's attorney, Bill Pepper had sidled up to McFerren for the sole purpose of manipulating the grocer and his statements. But now, the evidence was clear.

In addition to his overall orchestration of the *King v. Jowers* show trial, Pepper was guilty of deliberately silencing, confusing, misquoting, and ultimately discrediting the same man who had long considered the New York attorney a trusted friend and ally. And because he knew the isolated and aging Fayette Countian struggled with illiteracy, Pepper placed his faith in McFerren's inability to eventually discover what was transcribed during the trial. The only question Stephens was left asking was, how many more of the seventy-plus witnesses did Pepper also manipulate in 1999?

Chapter 8

SECRET TAPES

RANDALL STEPHENS FIRST heard small mentions about John McFerren's secret tapes from Marcus Holmes in June of 2012. After his own extensive analysis of the forty-two-year-old audio reels in question, as well as interviews with numerous witnesses, including McFerren himself, Holmes became convinced that the tapes contained vital information regarding the plot to kill Dr. King. Additionally, Holmes was also of the opinion that the United States government had colluded with a number of other individuals to keep the existence of the tapes hidden from the American public.

Over the next several weeks, Stephens worked tirelessly to decode the multifaceted issue of the audio recordings' content and history. And like Holmes before him, it eventually became clear to Stephens why McFerren made the tapes, what the tapes revealed, and who had worked to keep them a secret.

Somerville Strife of '69

Immediately following his interviews with the Memphis Police Department and FBI in April of 1968, the threats against John McFerren's life, family, and business grew in frequency and ferocity. As the verbal and physical attacks mounted, so did McFerren's defenses. Then on March 15 of the following year, journalist Ted Poston splashed John McFerren's name across the front page of the *New York Post*, publicly identifying him as the once anonymous witness who overheard Frank Liberto's "Mystery Call." Aggravating the nationally-named black whistleblower's already growing hypervigilance, racial tensions were also reaching a fever pitch in rural Fayette County.

Following more than a century of festering strife between the county's wealthy white minority and subjugated black proletariat, the proverbial fire was lit on the afternoon of August 12, 1969, when three African-American women, all members of the Hobson family, were viciously assaulted while standing in their own Fayette County front yard. Their white attackers were local grocery store owners Julian and Gerald Pulliam, a father-and-son duo who had earned a nefarious reputation in the area for being violent racists. A teenage Gerald Pulliam had been driving recklessly in downtown Somerville that day. After almost colliding with Vester Hobson, Gerald was confronted by the young woman who made an extremely brief criticism to the boy. Only minutes later, both of the Pulliams showed up at the Hobson family's home, confronted Vester, her sister, and the two girls' mother, and then furiously beat all three of the ladies.

The Pulliams' attack on the Hobson women set off a five-month series of high-profile demonstrations and physical skirmishes between the local African-American community and Fayette's all-white law enforcement agencies. Under the leadership of the McFerren family and their close friend and political ally, the Rev. Baxton Bryant, numerous rallies were held on the steps of the Fayette County

Courthouse that year. One of these large demonstrations took place on September 27, 1969. Led by both Bryant and a visiting Dick Gregory, the same well-known African-American comedian and civil rights advocate who would later co-write the 1977 book *Code Name Zorro* with Mark Lane, the demonstrations were covered by a number of news outlets. In spite of Bryant and Gregory's best efforts at achieving social justice for the black community in Fayette County that summer and fall, the ongoing tensions and violent clashes would continue well into the winter.

On December 15 of that year, a forty-five-year-old John McFerren and newspaper journalist McCann L. Reid were walking north together along Highway 76 toward the Fayette County Courthouse. Moments later, both men were verbally threatened, chased down, and physically separated from each other by five local black youths. Thankfully, McFerren spotted a Tennessee Highway Patrolman slowly circling the courthouse square. But after John asked for assistance, the indifferent patrolman told him he was too busy to intervene. Despite the presence of the state law enforcement officer, McFerren was then chased again from the courthouse to the front yard of a nearby home, savagely beaten, and held at gunpoint by the young men.

Mrs. Fair and her family were the longtime owners of the Fair Theater, a stage and movie cinema located on the northeast corner of the Somerville town square. With gun drawn and her housecoat only half-buttoned, a loudly barking Mrs. Fair sprinted from her house to break up the scuffle that had just erupted on her front lawn. A few moments later, a white Somerville police officer named Alton Feathers arrived on the scene. After giving a quick wink to one of the five assailants, Officer Feathers half-heartedly broke up the unprovoked attack and arrested the five youths as well as McFerren, charging all six men with disorderly conduct. At the conclusion of the subsequent court hearings, local white grocery store owner and judge, J.L. Howse, acquitted the bruised McFerren while imposing only a $5 fine on each of the guilty assailants. Immediately following the brutal attack and fizzled legal fallout, rumors began to swirl within the local African-American community as to why the attack on McFerren occurred and who was behind it. Eventually, word reached McFerren that the five black delinquents had been paid by members of the county's wealthy white establishment to injure or perhaps even kill him.

McFerren Investigates

From the outset of John and Viola's participation in the local civil rights movement in 1959, the two recognized the vital importance of obtaining accurate, often undisclosed information from their white oppressors. In an effort to strengthen their cause, an unofficial underground network of African-American informants composed of local cooks, maids, farmhands, and other laborers soon emerged. Before long, numerous men and women from around the county were making regular trips to McFerren's gas and grocery business to convey confidential information they had overheard while working for their white employers. It was through this now ten-year-old network that McFerren first caught wind of the December 15, 1969 conspiracy to cause him harm. Only days after the attack, locally accumulated intelligence started pouring in regarding the beating and who had orchestrated it.

With new details emerging daily, coupled with his outrage over the trivial penalties handed down by Judge Howse, the seasoned McFerren did what came naturally: he took matters into his own hands by launching a personal investigation. Hoping to provide attorneys at the Department of Justice and various journalists with verifiable statements about the beating conspiracy, McFerren quickly devised a simple yet effective method for discreetly recording any future conversations that might arise between himself and his regular rotation of informants. Using a heavy-duty utility garment outfitted with large cargo pockets, a portable cassette tape recorder, and a handheld microphone, the resourceful grocer fused together a wearable mechanism that would easily and discreetly record his future discussions.

Equipped with his new eavesdropping attire, McFerren wasted little time in putting his plan into action. Within a matter of days, he was again meeting with his eagerly loose-lipped moles. As they had done before, McFerren's revolving door of local spies provided him with specific names, dates, and other details related to the December 15 beating. But this time, he was prepared. With the subtle click of a button, McFerren was now capturing every word spoken by his unsuspecting informants. To his surprise, however, the small-town civil rights leader recorded far more than he originally anticipated.

Emboldened by the unexpected new evidence he believed he had acquired, McFerren worked quickly to implement the next step in his plan. With the assistance of a nearby tech-savvy friend and fellow civil rights activist named Hayward C. Brown, McFerren copied, combined, and transferred his multiple cassette tape recordings to large 3¾ audio reels. Numerous duplicates of those audio reels were then mailed through the local postal service to members of the national news media and attorneys at the DOJ's Civil Rights Division. Leaving nothing to chance, McFerren also backed up the recordings by dictating an official statement through his wife, Viola. As McFerren spoke on January 10, 1970, his academically trained spouse took dictation by typing a two-page document that would someday find its way into the hands of DOJ attorneys Fred G. Folsom and James F. Walker in 1976, Marcus Holmes in 2012, and Randall Stephens in 2015.

Audio Analysis

From their inception in 1970, John McFerren's secretly compiled audio recordings had been ignored, deemed as irrelevant, or kept quiet by nearly everyone he submitted them to. But then, in June 2012, Marcus Holmes, after tracking down and buying a vintage SONY TC-102 reel-to-reel audio device, played the somewhat distorted recordings under the watchful eye of McFerren. Realizing the profound historical significance of what he had just listened to, Holmes eventually convinced McFerren to travel with him to a Memphis recording studio to have the slowly decaying reels remastered and safely converted to MP3 digital audio files. Then in 2015, just before his second impending departure to prison at the hands of Fayette County's angry law enforcement machine, Holmes gave copies of the digitally remastered MP3s to Randall Stephens to analyze for himself.

Sitting quietly alone in front of his office computer in the late hours of a December 2015 evening, Stephens took a sip of his overly-doctored coffee, opened a blank *Word* document, placed a pair of headphones over his ears, clicked on the virtual play button of his *Windows Media Player*, and began typing a series of notes based on McFerren's forty-six-year-old confidential conversations. Admittedly, the recordings contained multiple, albeit brief, sections that were distorted and therefore inaudible. Stephens also noted that in between the secretly recorded conversations, McFerren sometimes spoke directly into the microphone. Beyond the earshot of his informants, the Fayette County grocer occasionally provided verbal footnotes and other supporting details to assist his future listeners.

Finally, while Stephens was certain the recordings were made between the December 15, 1969 beating and early 1970, there was no way of narrowing down the precise dates the individual conversations occurred. By the end of the two-and-a-half-hour audio and note-taking session, Stephens had typed a four-and-a-half-page outline that included subject titles, names of Fayette County participants, event dates, locations, and corresponding audio timestamps.

Participants, Payments, and the Pontiac

Based on Stephens' careful analysis, approximately two hours, or eighty percent, of the recordings were devoted to the 1969 beating McFerren endured. According to the various informants' audiotaped accounts as well as McFerren's 1970 typed statement, Anderson brothers Otha Lee, Alex, Alfonzo, Robert Lee, and their friend W.C. McNeil were all hired by members of Somerville's local white establishment to either severely injure or kill McFerren.

McFerren's informants also provided the names of the white donors and donation collectors who fronted the contract money that was eventually paid to the five black youths. The list included McFerren's former arresting officer Alton Feathers; Feathers' fellow Somerville Police Department comrade Tom Day; Somerville Police Chief Paul Burrow (the son of the late Olin B. Burrow who was allegedly killed by Burton Dodson); Fayette County Special Deputy Billy Doyle; General Sessions Judge Paul R. Summers Sr.; Ku Klux Klan member Kyle Wilbourne; local residents Frank Boswell, Sam Parsons, Dean Gammel, Harmon Havercamp, Reuben "Rube" Scott Rhea Sr., and of course, Somerville Mayor Isaac Perkins Yancey. Among the numerous Fayette County officials, businessmen, and wealthy landowners named in the beating conspiracy, it was clear to McFerren that Rhea and Yancey were the primary ringleaders of the '69 attack.

Not only was Rube Rhea Sr. one of the wealthiest cotton planters in the county, but he was also part founder and director of the First State Bank of Fayette County, a highly lucrative financial institution in Somerville. He was also the owner of the Rhea Oil Company, a Gulf Oil distributorship in Somerville. This, of course, was the same Rube Rhea oil distributorship that successfully shutdown Robert McFerren's gas station business in 1959. Yancey, on the other hand, was one of the primary targets of Stephens' MLK research. In addition to being Somerville's leading city official, Yancey was the owner of a local Chevrolet car dealership and maintenance garage, and a longtime board member of the Somerville Bank and Trust Company, another extremely profitable financial firm located on Somerville's downtown square.

In the end, it was indicated by McFerren's informants that, together, the highly affluent Rhea and Yancey compensated the Andersons and McNeil for the beating by giving them $300 in cash and a used white and green 1961 Pontiac from Yancey's Chevrolet car lot.

Host and Handler

The remaining thirty minutes of the secret recordings were dedicated to a topic he did not expect to capture on tape. To McFerren's surprise, his local informants also divulged several details regarding Mayor Yancey's 1968 association with an out-of-town traveler named James Earl Ray. As the Ray portion of the 1970 tapes began to play inside his headphones, Stephens could make out a somewhat indistinct conversation between McFerren and an informant concerning a third person, a Fayette County pastor from Oakland, Tennessee. Based on McFerren and the informant's crudely recorded discussion, the Oakland pastor was told by a mysteriously unnamed "white man" two days prior to the April 4, 1968 assassination that "King was going to get killed this time."

Then, about fourteen minutes into the recorded section pertaining to the MLK assassination, Stephens overheard Ray's full name referenced in connection with Yancey's. According to the informants, Ray's parked Mustang had been spotted at Yancey's Chevrolet maintenance garage by more than one person exactly two days before Dr. King was killed. Stephens began to wonder if Yancey had, in fact, hosted Ray on the evening of April 2. As the tape continued to play, Stephens listened to a second informant state that Yancey had twice flown to London in 1968. As the twenty-eight-year-old African-American son of Yancey's private cook, the informant asserted that his mother had, while working in the home of the mayor, learned that her employer had unexpectedly boarded a roundtrip flight to London shortly before April 1968 and then again approximately three or four weeks after Dr. King was murdered.

Having discovered through his cursory look into Ray's documented travels, Stephens already knew that the alleged shooter flew out of Toronto, Canada on May 6, 1968, and then arrived in London on May 7, a little more than four weeks after the shooting. The cook's son also stated that his now-petrified mother had been approached by special agents of the FBI. As the informant outlined on the audiotape, the unidentified agents asked his mother several questions about Yancey's past travels, recent guests, professional associations, and personal habits.

Nearing the end the informant's statement, Stephens overheard the faint voice of a young child in the background of the audio recording. As he listened closely, it soon became apparent that the voice belonged to the informant's young son. McFerren could then be heard interrupting his crucial interview with the father in order to bestow some momentary kindness on the little boy. After the grocer asked the child what his name was, the shy, delicately innocent voice replied simply with, "Gerald."

While it was of little consequence to Stephens at the time, he would later discover the deeply heartbreaking future the young Gerald would eventually face at the hands of Fayette County's crushing law enforcement machine.

McFerren's Final Plea

At the conclusion of the audio, McFerren could be heard once again making a private, chronologically rambling aside in his rural dialect. After first introducing himself, he confirmed that his previously heard informants were unaware that their statements had been recorded at the time. The assertive and desperate-sounding narrator then rushed headlong into a lengthy diatribe outlining his ten-year battle with Fayette County's financially and politically influential white cabal.

As asserted by McFerren in the recording, some of the same individuals who orchestrated the December 1969 attack were also defendants in the Tent City landowners case beginning in 1960. McFerren then went on to record his account of the county's white conspirators' 1960 efforts to shut down his entrepreneurial endeavors. In addition, he recorded his version of the 1963 events in which he was falsely accused of fathering a young girl with a married black woman who was not his wife. Facing a publicly and financially damning paternity suit, it was McFerren's adamant claim that he had not engaged in intercourse with Emma Jean Frazier and could present the court with a local man who had been romantically involved with her at the time. Despite McFerren's best efforts, a scientifically-limited blood test (blood tests determining exact DNA were not available in 1963) conducted by Somerville physician and fervent racist, Dr. John W. Morris, helped seal the accused adulterer's fate. Fayette County Juvenile Court Judge T.V. Luck found McFerren to be the father of Angela K. Frazier and, therefore, financially responsible for her. Shortly after the verdict, Emma Jean fled to Milwaukee, Wisconsin, with Angela and another daughter, never to be seen by McFerren again. To buttress his accusations, McFerren went on to state in the recording that West Tennessee had been controlled by a "syndicate" since 1960.

The narrator's next recorded statement centered on the reprisals he had faced since overhearing the plot at Liberto's warehouse to murder Dr. King. Claiming that "more pressure has been applied to me," McFerren continued to detail the specific events that occurred on the afternoon of December 15, 1969. Based on the 1970 recording, it was McFerren's recollection that during the assault, one of the black assailants aimed a "double-barreled Derringer" at him while the others kicked him in the head and beat his stomach and back. After the description of the violent encounter with the Anderson brothers and McNeil, Stephens listened as McFerren matter-of-factly declared, "...for some reason, I've come out, so far, lucky I would consider..."

But it was the next audio recorded claim that stood out. As he had been previously led to believe by his numerous informants, McFerren stated that the Fayette County orchestrators of the 1969 beating were in coordination with the Memphis conspirators who handled the 1968 contract-killing of Dr. King. But was there any truth to this slightly implausible implication? Stephens' mind shifted to McFerren and Holmes' recent assertion that Somerville Mayor I.P. Yancey was indirectly linked to Memphis businessman Frank Liberto through their alleged lackey, James Earl Ray, and mutual friend, John Shelton Wilder.

McFerren's recorded voice continued to emphasize the purported connection by stating, "...every time uh, they even move any around with...with James Earl Ray, I can tell immediately, two or three days afterwards, a repercussion of pressure on me." It was already obvious to Stephens what McFerren was referring to. Since his allegedly coerced confession in March of 1969, Ray continued to attract news media attention throughout the local area, especially when he was transferred to one of Tennessee's numerous state prison facilities. It was McFerren's complaint that those newspaper articles, in turn, reminded the Somerville and Memphis conspirators of his own 1968 whistleblowing efforts, thus prompting a fresh set of reprisals against him.

The next topic McFerren outlined for his future listeners was the involvement of a Memphis attorney named Russell Thompson. After McFerren's audiotaped description of the man, Stephens confirmed that Thompson was once a prominent lawyer in Memphis who had been involved in the King case. Not long after McFerren's statements to the MPD and FBI regarding Ray and Liberto, Thompson questioned John and Viola at their Fayette County business. Then, sometime after his initial meeting with the married couple, Thompson returned to cryptically warn John to "keep it quiet...to yourself." After explaining on the recording Thompson's belief that the merchants of Somerville were again plotting to kill the black grocer and his wife, McFerren stated that he no longer ventured out into public with Viola and the children for fear of the future attack. Stephens' memory was triggered again. Surely, this had to be the same Russell X. Thompson who McFerren later accused in 1976 of assisting Viola with her divorce proceedings.

In addition to the affluent Thompson, McFerren also described the indirect connection a local African-American man had to the MLK conspiracy. As asserted in the recording, McFerren had been advised that his Fayette County neighbor and fellow struggling business owner, "John Thomas," was being harassed by the same West Tennessee power structure that placed the contract out on Dr. King's life. According to the audio, John Thomas's brother had been recently arrested for illegal alcohol transportation and distribution. As it turned out, Thomas, whose real name was John Hardy Thompson, told McFerren that he believed the "underworld gang" his brother had been smuggling for was identical to the group that conspired to kill King. Stephens' interest was again aroused. Could the organized crime figures who ran Memphis's illicit alcohol industry in the late 1960s be the same individuals who paid to have Dr. King murdered?

McFerren began to wrap up his lengthy 1970 lecture by stressing the severity of the situation he and his family were facing. In his final recorded plea for outside assistance, McFerren stated that "...if you study this recording close, we have no police protection, no judge protection, the mayor...there's no protection from him. They're all in a cahoots together!" McFerren continued by declaring, "...sooner or later, I'm going to get a knife through my stomach or get my head blown off, 'cause it's too clear that there's no question about it, that there's a conspiracy that's formed to kill me and kill my wife!"

As he had done so many times throughout his impassioned speech, McFerren again implored the future tape recipients at the DOJ to "take immediate action." Just after declaring that he was also sending the audio reels to his various newspaper contacts around the country, the Fayette County grocer and civil rights leader concluded his impassioned appeal by reminding the audience of the unique information they had just listened to. The forty-five-year-old McFerren finished with, "I never will, I imagine, be able to get such information on a tape, like I got this time. I thank you."

Conclusions and Questions

Stephens was both inspired and haunted. While he was uplifted by the narrator's bravery and proactive efforts to back up his accusations with witness corroboration, it also chilled Stephens' bones to hear the voice of a much younger McFerren plead for the assistance that would never come. Indeed, the DOJ ignored McFerren's tapes, never answering his calls for help. Although the outspoken activist survived another life-threatening attack in 1976, his saga still ended sadly. As the years drifted by, McFerren grew more estranged from his family and was eventually divorced by his once supportive wife, Viola. As the isolated, eccentric shut-in of Fayette County, McFerren eventually spent the rest of his meager existence living inside the gas station that he would continue to quietly operate into the next millennium.

Despite the inaudible sections of the recording and McFerren's folksy, chronologically wandering dialogue, nothing about the audio bothered Stephens. Not a single second of the narrative seemed staged or outlandish to him. In fact, the inaudible distortions and other imperfections only added to the tapes' mystique and sense of unscripted authenticity. As for McFerren's informants, it was obvious none of them knew they were being taped at the time. Also, while McFerren prompted his informants by asking them specific questions, he was never the person heard filling in the gaps with details. McFerren's inquiries were short, and he allowed his interviewees to speak at length.

After carefully considering the matter of the 1969 beating and examining both the audio recording and accompanying January 10, 1970 document typed by Viola, Stephens came to believe that Mayor Yancey never intended to compensate the Andersons or McNeil for the preplanned assault. According to the details in the aforementioned document, W.C. McNeil was provided a gun by the white conspirators before the attack. Further, one of McFerren's informants overheard Otha Lee Anderson complaining a number of days after the beating that neither he nor the others had received the cash and Pontiac they were promised. It was only after Otha Lee threatened to expose the conspiracy that the five-person gang was paid by the reluctant instigators. This simple but revealing timeline spoke volumes to Stephens about Yancey and Rhea's original intentions.

As with other well-documented, prearranged black-on-black assaults involving civil rights leaders, McFerren's attackers were no doubt assured by their white financiers that they would be protected by the local authorities and then paid after the attack. However, as in most cases, the white orchestrators already knew that their unwitting flunkies would be sent to jail or prison, especially if the intended victim was murdered in the assault. This, in turn, would extricate the wealthy white contractor from having to pay the now-imprisoned black killer or killers.

Stephens was now close to convinced that Yancey and Rhea expected McFerren to be murdered in December of 1969, hoping their five hired hoodlums would then be sent to prison and therefore unable to collect the bounty. But when McFerren survived and the five youths were released, Yancey and Rhea had no choice but to keep their end of the deal or be exposed by Otha Lee. This scenario compelled Stephens to consider Yancey's level of motivation in seeing McFerren murdered. Was the 1969 beating merely a coincidental outcropping of the racial strife in the area at the time, or was that racial strife used as a convenient cover by Yancey and company to get rid of the Liberto conspiracy tattletale? After years of putting up with John's local civil rights activities, why did Yancey finally decide in the winter of '69 to have the local black agitator killed?

Stephens was again reminded of the *New York Post* article that had been published just nine months before McFerren's attack. As described earlier, Ted Poston publicly named McFerren in the March 1969 article as the once anonymous 1968 "Mystery Call" whistleblower. While Liberto's name was not actually mentioned in Poston's story, Stephens now wondered if Yancey was afraid that he would be the next MLK conspirator to be indirectly exposed in the national press by McFerren.

Moreover, there was the issue of Dick Gregory's September 1969 work with the Rev. Baxton Bryant and McFerrens in Somerville to consider. Given Gregory's close connection to the late Dr. King, Bryant, and Fayette County's civil rights leadership at the time, coupled with the same comedian's brash outspokenness, popularity, and national audience, it's quite possible Yancey's MLK paranoia was being further agitated that year by Gregory's high-profile involvement.

Shockingly, McFerren's investigation into the 1969 beating inadvertently opened the door to something far more sinister in the good mayor's closet. Based on the corroborating nature and number of independent, candid conversations linking Yancey to Ray, Stephens had zero doubt that McFerren's informants at least believed the information they were providing was true. Just like his belief in local informant T.R. "Tommy" Wright's efforts to relay accurate details about the meetings between John Wilder and Frank Liberto,

Stephens was also confident in the overall level of honesty and reliability McFerren had cultivated with the other members of his Fayette County underground.

More than one person on the audio claimed to have witnessed Ray's Ford Mustang parked at Yancey's garage. Also, it made sense that Yancey would, believing the Mustang blended in with his other vehicles, take advantage of his dealership's packed sales lot in order to obscure the eventual getaway car's presence. And if Yancey did indeed finance and steer the Andersons and McNeil into a criminal assassination conspiracy in '69, the probability that he would have done the same as a host and handler of Ray in '68 was extremely high.

As confident as he was in the seeming credibility of McFerren's Yancey and Ray narrative, Stephens was still faced with a number of unanswered questions. First, what was the slightly inaudible name of the Oakland pastor as recorded on the tapes, and who was the unnamed white man who confessed to him? Was the unidentified Caucasian, in fact, James Earl Ray, or was it another Fayette County conspirator whose conscience got the best of him? Second, Stephens needed to track down Ray's documented whereabouts for the evening of April 2, 1968. Could the since-deceased convict's location be narrowed down for that period? Third, Stephens was already aware that the alleged shooter had fled to London on May 6, 1968. But was there a way of verifying if Yancey was in London or Europe at the same time, just as the informant's mother claimed? And did agents from the FBI actually interview Yancey's cook after the mayor's alleged flights?

Also, was it possible for lightning to strike more than once in the same place? In other words, was it likely that McFerren would have been in the right place at the right time to learn of the multiple connections between the various MLK conspirators? Despite his natural propensity for skepticism, Stephens had to acknowledge the weight of the circumstantial evidence. McFerren had long been able to somewhat multiply his singular set of eyes and ears through the use of his well-established network of informants. It was important for Stephens to remember that the humble Fayette Countian, while physically present to witness the first conspiratorial connection between Liberto and Ray, was only able to learn of the second Yancey-and-Ray-conspiracy link due to his underground spies. Next, more than a handful of local black informants, primarily T.R. Wright, knew of the third connection between John Wilder and Liberto as well as the obvious fourth Somerville connection between Wilder and Yancey. Then there was a possible fifth conspiratorial link, one Stephens had only briefly considered until now.

Thinking back on his collection of previously examined documents, Stephens recalled that in the 1978 affidavit to the House Select Committee on Assassinations, McFerren stated, "former-Mayor Yancy of Somerville, Tennessee, a friend of former-Mayor Loeb of Memphis, collected money from local businessmen to pay for the assassination of Dr. King." Mayor Henry Loeb had long been suspected by those in the MLK research community as having also played a role in the West Tennessee conspiracy to kill Dr. King. But were Loeb and Yancey indeed friends? This fifth connection was not far-fetched. Since both men were elected leaders of neighboring municipalities, it would have been completely natural and most certainly probable for the two city mayors to cross paths at different times. After only some light digging, Stephens eventually located a *Jackson Sun* newspaper article dated September 16, 1960, confirming both Loeb and Yancey's simultaneous attendance at the Mayor's Day Dinner hosted by the West Tennessee District Fair. Finally, if Yancey did, in fact, help orchestrate the failed murder of McFerren, what was the likelihood he would have also assisted Loeb in the murder of Dr. King? Undoubtedly, the chances were better than good.

Aside from his need to look deeper into the Oakland pastor issue, the multiple allegations regarding Yancey and Ray, the role of Memphis attorney Russell X. Thompson, and the possibility that

Memphis's illegal liquor industry helped finance the assassination, Stephens felt enlightened by the amount of questions and ambiguities McFerren's recordings now clarified. The next items to clear up fell under the heading of, "Who knew about the tapes, and when did they know about them?"

Chapter 9

TIMELINE OF THE TRAVELING TAPES

WHEN IT CAME to the Martin Luther King Jr. assassination conspiracy, Marcus Holmes' greatest achievement by far was his work involving John McFerren's secret audiotapes. Not only had the insatiably inquisitive man provided Randall Stephens with digitally remastered versions of the recordings, but Holmes also spoke with some of the key individuals who were involved in the initial creation and distribution of the antique audio reels. After an intense degree of study, Stephens pieced together McFerren and Holmes' well-documented evidence to form a coherent, multi-decade timeline that explained exactly who ignored or suppressed the information contained within McFerren's traveling tapes.

Hayward C. Brown - 1970

After wrapping up the recorded interviews with his underground informants, McFerren entrusted his numerous cassette tapes to

Hayward C. Brown, a faithful local friend and technically skilled entrepreneur originally from Michigan. Together, McFerren and Brown copied the cassette recordings and transferred them to several 3¾ audio reels. Pleased with the stack of duplicate reels he now had in his possession, McFerren left the original cassettes with Brown for safekeeping. However, the newly transplanted Yankee from Michigan was also feeling the unbearable heat of the South's racial fire at the time.

Powerless against the white establishment's efforts to block the construction of his all-black Fayette County factory and co-op, Brown mailed numerous letters to the DOJ and members of Congress, one of whom was a U.S. representative from Illinois named Donald Rumsfeld. But when his multiple requests for assistance were left unanswered by the Nixon-era government, Brown ultimately abandoned his dream of financially empowering his Fayette County brethren through the development of the co-op, packed up his family belongings along with McFerren's cassettes, and moved far from Fayette County and the state of Tennessee.

Hoping McFerren's original cassette tapes were still in existence, Holmes spent a number of weeks in 2012 trying to locate Hayward Brown or his next of kin. But after an exhaustive and ultimately unsuccessful search, Holmes called it quits.

DOJ - 1970

Before Brown's flight from the area, he and McFerren mailed several copies of the new audio reels to various organizations throughout the country in January of 1970, the first of which was the Civil Rights Division at the DOJ in Washington, D.C. Because he had been assured at the close of the federal Tent City and landowners case in 1962 that Fayette County's white defendants would face harsh penalties if they violated his civil rights in the future, McFerren believed he could depend on the DOJ to protect him again in 1970. Confident in the federal safeguards he was once promised, McFerren wasted little time in requesting that the DOJ investigate the December 15, 1969 attack. After mailing his packaged audio reels to his long-standing contact at the Civil Rights Division, Attorney J. Harold "Nick" Flannery, McFerren waited patiently for a response in mid-January of 1970.

Just two weeks later, however, the unopened package was returned. Unbeknownst to McFerren at the time, Flannery, as a result of his displeasure with President Nixon's lack of civil rights support, had already resigned his position at the DOJ in October of 1969 and was therefore unable to take receipt of the personally addressed parcel. Determined to get the attention of federal investigators, the steadfast McFerren sent the package again, this time using certified mail. Although federal attorneys eventually received McFerren's tapes, his pleas for help fell on deaf ears. While it's unclear exactly when their discussion took place, McFerren stated in the Jowers trial that he even spoke about the issue over the telephone with Attorney General John Mitchell. But as history now indicates, the fight for civil rights was the furthest thing from the minds of those working in the Nixon administration, especially Mitchell's.

Ted Poston - 1970

While it is unknown how many other audio reels were distributed and to whom, journalist Ted Poston of the *New York Post* was one of the few who received a copy in the mail from McFerren. After Poston's honest hard-hitting coverage of both the African-American struggle in Fayette County during the early 1960s and the issue of Frank Liberto's 1968 telephone calls, McFerren viewed the New York newspaper writer as a trusted friend and confessor. Believing Poston would see the newsworthiness in his recordings, McFerren mailed a copy of the reels to him in New York and waited. Sadly, the journalist thought little of the tapes and therefore declined to publish a story about the 1969 beating or Mayor Yancey's alleged role in the King assassination. From that disheartening point forward, McFerren kept his singular set of duplicate audio reels under lock and key at an undisclosed Fayette County location.

Holmes' efforts to make contact with Poston's family in June of 2012 were just as futile as his previous attempts at reaching Hayward Brown's. Unable to question the deceased reporter's wife or children, Holmes ultimately concluded that sometime after Poston began listening to the tapes for himself in 1970, the New York journalist dismissed their relevance due to the two hours focused on issues other than the Martin Luther King conspiracy. Holmes believed that Poston most likely grew tired of the lengthy 1969 beating portion of the recordings and then gave up, never listening to the last half hour of the informant dialogue detailing Mayor Yancey's 1968 handling of Ray.

Robert Hamburger - 1971

When Poston declined to write a story based on the 1969 beating and 1970 recordings, an undaunted McFerren approached a young civil rights activist and future author from New York named Robert Hamburger. In the spring of 1965, the idealistic Hamburger made his first journey to Fayette County to volunteer in the local civil rights movement, and by 1971 had become a welcomed presence and close friend of the McFerren family. In preparation for his future book based on the local struggle, Hamburger began interviewing and tape recording the closely-knit circle of African-American activists living in the area at the time. As one of the primary subjects of the forthcoming book, John McFerren's personal accounts were recorded by Hamburger on a number of occasions between 1971 and 1972.

Perhaps reminded of his own use of a cassette tape recorder in the recent past, McFerren eventually pulled Hamburger aside and told him about his own audio recordings. But although an extensive composition covering the 1969 beating was ultimately printed in Hamburger's *Our Portion of Hell*, the book was published in 1973 without any mention of McFerren's actual audiotapes.

Remarkably, the search for Robert Hamburger was a quick success. With the help of an internet savvy associate, Holmes eventually tracked down a New York address and phone number for the *Our Portion of Hell* author. Before reaching out to Hamburger, however, Holmes carefully studied the pages of the 1973 book and came across some very interesting details. Despite Hamburger's failure to write about McFerren's own private recordings, it seemed suspicious to Holmes that the author did, in fact, write about several people who were aware of the tapes' physical existence and content. In addition to briefly referencing Ted Poston's early 1960s coverage of Fayette County, Hamburger conducted a lengthy interview with Hayward Brown. In his recorded account, Brown explained his personal opposition to the white establishment's hold on the local economy, his efforts to contact the DOJ and members of Congress, and the 1969 beating McFerren endured. In his recorded account, Brown told Hamburger:

> The mayor of Somerville, the police force of Somerville in collaboration with the sheriff, and the grocers put up money to these black folks to beat or kill McFerren when he came to town. And the Police Department called them when he come to town.

After reading Hamburger's interview of Brown, as well as his similar interviews with John and Viola concerning Mayor Yancey, Holmes began to question the New York author's motives and failure to write about McFerren's audio reels. Then, Holmes found another curious account between McFerren and Hamburger, one not related to Yancey and the 1969 attack. This time, the Fayette County grocer's complaint centered on his store's new payphone:

> However, our phone stays outa fix a whole lot. And I have a strong reason to believe the phone is tapped because I took two paper sacks and put one inside of the other one and put it over the receiver and hang it up. And all of a sudden, outa the deep blue sky, the phone'd ring and I'd go there to answer the phone and the operator'd ask if the phone was outa fix. By havin the paper sacks twisted over the receiver they couldn't hear no sounds outa the store and that's why they would call up and ask if the phone's outa fix.

Immediately recalling his previous research, Holmes was certain that the bugged telephone and paper-sack anecdote in Hamburger's 1973 book had been plagiarized by Attorney General Janet Reno's DOJ team and deceptively used as a part of their alleged March 1999 interview of McFerren. As described in their June 2000 report, the DOJ investigators stated that:

> McFerren's account also appears unreliable because of his quirky behavior and beliefs. When members of our investigative team spoke to McFerren, he locked his door and asked that we speak quietly because his phone was "bugged." He then placed a paper bag over the telephone receiver to prevent the conversation from being overheard.

When contact was finally made with Hamburger, the New York author indeed confirmed to Holmes that he had once considered listening to and writing about McFerren's audiotapes. It was Hamburger's claim that upon hearing the incredible account from McFerren in 1971, and how he could obtain a copy of the audio reels, the burgeoning author returned to New York and quickly contacted his neighboring writer, Ted Poston. But by the end of Hamburger's conversation with the pessimistic Poston, his enthusiasm had been deflated. Hamburger told Holmes that Poston convinced him of the tapes' seemingly tenuous value. It was the author's claim that without listening to the recordings himself, he blindly heeded the advice of the elder *New York Post* journalist and dismissed McFerren's previous 1971 story.

Yet, when Holmes pressed Hamburger further about the tapes, as well as the topics of John Wilder, the McFerren family, and the possible use of the paper-sack story by the DOJ, the New York author became extremely nervous and evasive. By the end of their telephone conversation, Holmes was wondering what Hamburger was hiding.

DOJ - 1976

On July 9, 1976, the federal government finally came knocking in search of information on the past conspiracy to kill Dr. King. But to McFerren's surprised disappointment, DOJ attorneys Fred G. Folsom and James F. Walker weren't interested in his 1969 beating account, his ongoing belief that his store's phone was "bugged," nor his allegations about the connection between Yancey and Ray. Unaware of the tapes' possible existence inside their own Washington archives, the two DOJ investigators seemed caught off guard when McFerren tried to explain the issue. Even after detailing the relevance of the tapes to the attorneys and naming the New York journalist's widow whom they could obtain a copy from (Poston died in 1974), McFerren was still dismissed out of hand.

Then, on September 10 that same year, the Fayette County grocer once more became the victim of an attempted murder plot. As he began to close up his rural business for the evening, several individuals pulled up in front of McFerren's gas station, parked their vehicle, stepped outside, and fired a gun through the building's large plate glass windows. One of the bullets struck McFerren in the stomach. Having been tipped off beforehand, however, the now-victimized McFerren expected the attack and was prepared. Unfazed by the round now lodged in his abdomen, John fired back with his own sidearm, wounding the unknown assailant who immediately fled the scene with the others.

After an eight-day stay at St. Joseph's Hospital in downtown Memphis and a lengthy recovery elsewhere, McFerren finally called Walker at his Washington office on November 16 to advise him of the recent development. Assuming Folsom and Walker were his new contacts at the DOJ, McFerren anticipated swift action from the recently inquisitive MLK investigators. But as was routine by that point, McFerren was again brushed aside by federal authorities. The aloof Walker encouraged John to take his complaint to the racist members of the Fayette County Sheriff's Office.

Decades later, when Stephens looked into the 1976 shooting, it became immediately apparent to him that the very same week McFerren was wounded, the national news media was covering a story about the 94th U.S. Congress and their continuing debate over H.R. bill 1540. Then, just one week after McFerren was struck by an unknown gunman's bullet, H.R. 1540 finally passed the House of Representatives on September 17, authorizing its members to form the House Select Committee on Assassinations, the same HSCA that would question McFerren about Frank Liberto for the next two years. While Folsom and Walker's notes included details about McFerren's seemingly unrelated September 10 attack, the DOJ's final January 11, 1977 report failed to include a single word about McFerren, Liberto, Yancey, or the still-secret audiotapes.

Bill Pepper - 1977

Depending on the person telling the tale, Bill Pepper first traveled to Fayette County, Tennessee, to investigate McFerren's Frank Liberto allegations in either 1977 or 1979. As McFerren repeatedly asserted to Holmes, the New York attorney's first trip to the humble country gas and grocery business occurred sometime in 1977. However, according to the account in *Orders to Kill*, Pepper did not question McFerren about Liberto until after February 8, 1979, when the attorney first showed up in Fayette County with two of Mark Lane's previous legal associates, April Ferguson and Barbara Rabbito.

According to McFerren's version of events, he and Pepper became slowly acquainted with each other from 1977 through early 1979 before the two men finally agreed that the official February 8 interview could be conducted. Disappointed before by other investigative journalists and attorneys, the tight-lipped McFerren spent a substantial period of time vetting the pale-faced Northeastern stranger. As McFerren tells it, it was during this 1977 courtship phase that he eventually told Pepper about Liberto, Ray, John Wilder, and Yancey, as well as the previously recorded audio reels. Recognizing the potential significance of the recordings and McFerren's refusal to release his last and only copies, Pepper made arrangements for the former Liberto whistleblower to meet with a Memphis musician, recording engineer, and part-time private investigator named Kenneth Herman.

With the 676 North Graham Street address scrawled on a piece of paper and his recordings in tow, McFerren drove from his Fayette County business to Herman's multi-use Memphis home and recording studio in 1977. After the flamboyantly red-haired Herman duplicated the 1970 audio reels, he boxed up the newest version of the recordings on behalf of Pepper as McFerren took back possession of the originals. It was McFerren's recollection that just before departing the Graham Street residence and music studio, he was told by Herman, "You've got the goods on them now, John."

Then in 2012, after divulging the existence of his secret tapes for the first time in several decades, McFerren called Pepper in front of a now-shocked Marcus Holmes. Eager to provide his friend with a confirmation of his recent claim, McFerren dialed a New York cell phone number and immediately reached his longtime contact. Abruptly, the then eighty-seven-year-old McFerren blurted into his outdated cellular flip phone, "Pepper, where are the copies of my tapes!?" As McFerren held his cell phone up to Holmes' ear, the raspy-voiced Pepper could be overheard assuring his aging Fayette County witness that he would visit Memphis again soon and that they would discuss the issue of the tapes in person. Not long afterward, Holmes himself contacted Pepper to ask about the status of the duplicate recordings. To his amazement, Holmes was told simply and coolly by the attorney, "Don't let anyone hear John's tapes." Apparently, Pepper believed he could mollify Holmes the same way he had McFerren in the past. He was wrong.

Within days of his failed questioning of Pepper, Holmes tracked down Kenneth Herman's most recent address and telephone number in Florida. During a long-distance phone conference between McFerren, Holmes, and Herman, it was disclosed by the Florida resident that upon making the copies in 1977, he eventually mailed a final version of the tapes to the DOJ at Pepper's direction. McFerren was dumbfounded. It was now obvious to both he and Holmes that Pepper not only squelched the existence and contents of the tapes, but that the New York attorney was also coordinating in some fashion with members of the DOJ and HSCA in 1977. Yet, it was still unclear why Pepper lied about being in Fayette County before 1979.

During his own in-depth investigation, Stephens discovered a number of arguably weak clues that pointed to Pepper's possible presence in the area during '77 and '78, just as McFerren had claimed. First, Pepper himself vaguely admitted in *Orders to Kill* to starting his MLK assassination research as early as April 1977, and then visiting the imprisoned James Earl Ray in late 1978. At the time, Ray was incarcerated at Brushy Mountain State Penitentiary near Petros, Tennessee. Was it conceivable the nosey attorney would have traveled from New York all the way to Tennessee to interview the accused assassin in October of '78 without first making the trek to Memphis in '77 or early '78 to walk the crime scene, question past witnesses, and investigate other pertinent details in the Bluff City? It seemed unlikely to Stephens. Second, Pepper may have unknowingly authored another revealing clue regarding his first meeting with McFerren. In the fourteenth chapter of his book, Pepper wrote:

When we reached McFerren's store around 6:15 p.m., I was immediately struck by the impression of a place under siege. The huge plate glass window in front of his store was cracked from top to bottom and taped together, the result, McFerren said, of a drive-by shooting, one of many he had experienced since 1968. Not long ago, he told us, he shot and wounded a man contracted by the Mafia to kill him.

Based on official documentation, the shooting Pepper was referring to in his book occurred on September 10, 1976, just as James F. Walker had outlined in his typed interview notes. As indicated in both the DOJ and Pepper's accounts, McFerren returned fire through the window in the direction of the assailant in front of the store. In addition, Pepper wrote that the window was "cracked from top to bottom and taped together." Stephens was doubtful that McFerren would have allowed the building's cracked plate glass windows to remain unreplaced from September of 1976 to February of 1979.

Additionally, Pepper used the phrase "not long ago" to describe the span of time between the gas station shooting and his first visit to McFerren's business. Could a two-and-a-half-year time frame be truly considered "not long ago"? Stephens didn't think so and was now certain that Pepper's narrative unknowingly illustrated the same shooting McFerren communicated to DOJ Attorney James F. Walker on November 16, 1976. This, of course, further supported the claim that Pepper was in West Tennessee in 1977 "not long" after the September 1976 shooting. This scenario also supported Holmes' 2012 belief that Pepper supplied the DOJ and HSCA with McFerren's secret tapes.

HSCA – 1978

According to the HSCA's published report and McFerren's own copy of his unpublished HSCA affidavit, federal investigators Gene R. Johnson and Ernestine G. Johnson interviewed the Fayette grocer about Liberto, Yancey, and Ray on several occasions between March of 1977 and June of 1978. However, the list of interview dates outlined within the two versions did not match. Attached to the sworn witness's private copy, a yellow piece of handwritten legal paper, dated April 3, 1978, had been included, although not mentioned anywhere in either the typed affidavit or the published report.

As Randall Stephens noted earlier in his investigation, the handwritten sheet of yellow paper had served as a makeshift receipt indicating that the Johnson team had signed for and taken custody of McFerren's 3¾ audio reels. But according to McFerren's somewhat panicked admission to Holmes in 2012, he had been unaware at the time of what he was signing due to his illiteracy and most certainly did not recall giving his only recordings to either one of the Johnsons. So, the previous questions remained: How did the two investigators obtain another copy of McFerren's well-guarded tapes? Why was the crudely fashioned receipt written in blue pen on a separate sheet of paper instead of typed as a part of the official affidavit? And why didn't the HSCA reference the audio reel receipt in their public report?

By April 1978, the Johnson team would have been just as oblivious to the potential existence of the audiotapes inside the DOJ

archives as Folsom and Walker were two years earlier. Also, Ted
Poston had since passed away in 1974, most likely bequeathing his
dismissed copy of the audio reels to an unaware next-of-kin. The
only other possible source of the recordings was Bill Pepper and his
Memphis-based MLK investigator, Kenneth Herman. As Herman
himself told Holmes in 2012, he was instructed by Pepper to mail
a copy of their duplicate recordings to the DOJ. And as historical
fact now dictates, the HSCA, while officially functioning under
the untrained eyes of twelve elected politicians, was technically
controlled by several past employees of the DOJ, including HSCA
Chief Counsel G. Robert Blakey and his second in command, Deputy
Chief Counsel Gene R. Johnson.

Stephens eventually concluded that the Johnsons were most
likely given the 1977 duplicates in secret by either their contacts
inside the DOJ, who received them from Kenneth Herman at
Pepper's direction, or perhaps directly from Herman himself. Unable
to admit that they had received McFerren's tapes from the opposing
camp, the HSCA and Gene Johnson no doubt duped the unwitting
McFerren into signing over, and therefore acknowledging, the
federal government's receipt of the ill-gotten recordings. In the end,
a conspicuously hostile Gene Johnson told McFerren sometime after
June 22, 1978, that he would not be needed at the public hearings in
Washington, and no mention was ever made publicly by either the
HSCA or the opposing defense attorneys concerning the ever-silent
audio reels.

Now thoroughly suspicious of the former federal investigators,
Randall Stephens looked deeper into the backgrounds of Gene
Johnson and his HSCA partner, Ernestine Johnson. Eventually,
Stephens called the now-retired Gene Johnson at his Maryland home
just outside of Washington, D.C. Upon being asked about McFerren
and the Johnsons' unorthodox method of taking receipt of the tapes
in 1978, the former DOJ attorney immediately barked at Stephens

in a curiously defensive tone, stating that he didn't remember signing for any tapes, but that his former Fayette County witness was "a liar and a fool!" Stephens found it bizarre that while Johnson was unable to recall the tapes or his own signature on the sheet of yellow legal paper, the ever-hostile attorney could still vividly remember McFerren. Not long after the heated, albeit brief, telephone conversation, Stephens conducted a focused investigation into Mr. Johnson that covered his background both before and after his DOJ and HSCA work. The evidence Stephens ultimately obtained was nothing less than jaw-dropping, evidence that not even Johnson's former HSCA superior, G. Robert Blakey, could defend when later questioned about it. As for the all-important question of why Pepper leaked the tapes to the DOJ and the HSCA, that answer would come a short time later.

Bill Pepper - 1989

As the late 1970s drew to a close and a majority of the 1980s also drifted into recent memory, Pepper found himself personally responsible for the ongoing legal defense of James Earl Ray in 1988. By the next year, Pepper, along with U.K. television and film producers John Sergeant and John Edginton, had completed production of the made-for-cable documentary film, *Inside Story: Who Killed Martin Luther King?* As described earlier, McFerren never spoke for himself in the cleverly filmed and edited documentary. Instead, Pepper conveniently summarized his witness's 1968 account for Edginton's camera. Along with Pepper's erroneously dramatic portrayal of McFerren as a man who was still "very, very afraid," the attorney and burgeoning celebrity also failed to mention that McFerren heard two separate telephone calls, the name that was allegedly spoken by James Latch in between those two calls, the details regarding Ray's possible connection to Liberto, Yancey, and Wilder, or the audiotapes he (Pepper) had been in possession of since 1977.

Bill Pepper - 1993

Amid the recent election of a skirt-chasing baby boomer to the White House and a national economy that mirrored the robust opulence of the Reagan era, Ray's attorney embarked on his second major cable television production. In the late months of 1992, Pepper once again partnered with a U.K. television producer, this time a man named Jack Saltman. During their January 1993 filming of the HBO mock trial entitled *Guilt or Innocence: The Trial of James Earl Ray*, McFerren apparently made the lengthy drive from his Fayette County business all the way to a Memphis courthouse in order to appear in front of Saltman's lens. Yet, contrary to McFerren's recollection of events, Pepper later asserted that the Fayette County grocer's fear got the best of him again and that McFerren immediately turned around and fled the courtroom shortly after arriving. Fortunately for the spotlight-seeking attorney, his witness was not in the well-staged courtroom that day to discuss Liberto, Wilder, Yancey, Ray, or the 1969-to-1970 recordings.

Bill Pepper - 1995

Pepper's highly anticipated *Orders to Kill* hit bookstands across the country in 1995. But along with the publication's numerous deceptions and grossly unresearched inaccuracies, the extent of McFerren's account was once again limited to overhearing Liberto scream into a telephone receiver. As he had in the past, Pepper mysteriously failed to reference all of McFerren's allegations and evidence, which included seeing Ray work for Liberto in 1967, Yancey's alleged role as both a host and handler of Ray in 1968, the secret audio recordings that were created in 1969 and 1970, and the role of "high-level Tennessee state official" John Wilder as a central figure in the overall conspiracy to assassinate Dr. King.

Bill Pepper - 1997

Produced as an update to his December 16, 1993 Loyd Jowers piece, host Sam Donaldson revisited the topic of the conspiracy to kill Dr. King in an April 2, 1997 episode of ABC's *Primetime Live* television news program. Approximately seven minutes into the Jowers and Dr. King sequel, John McFerren appeared on screen with the nationally renowned reporter. Speaking directly to Donaldson in front of the same 814 Scott Street produce warehouse he stopped patronizing in 1968, McFerren firmly and fearlessly summarized his account of Liberto's telephone calls.

However, upon the conclusion of McFerren's short appearance on the small screen, no mention was made of Ray's connection to Liberto and Yancey or Wilder's link to the same group, nor was the topic of the 1970 audio recordings broached. Unbeknownst to the national television audience that evening, Pepper had accompanied Donaldson and McFerren to Liberto's former business and was standing just off-camera during the prerecorded interview. In an effort to confirm Pepper's role as the master of ceremonies during the taping of the *Primetime Live* segment, Marcus Holmes obtained a 1997 black-and-white photograph of McFerren, Donaldson, and Pepper posing together in front of Liberto's notorious warehouse.

Interestingly, Donaldson's network colleague, journalist Forrest Sawyer, also produced a segment for ABC the following June that highlighted Pepper's King and Ray claims. This time appearing on the news program *Turning Point*, Pepper was surprised, challenged, and ultimately embarrassed on national television when Sawyer introduced him to retired Army officer Billy Ray Eidson. Pepper, as it turned out, had made the ludicrous claim in *Orders to Kill* that Eidson, as part of a military-backed operation to kill MLK, was directly involved in the assassination conspiracy and most likely committed suicide as a part of the cover-up. The episode featuring a still-breathing and now incredibly angry Eidson confronting Pepper aired on June 19, 1997, and had an immediate impact on the author's already paper-thin credibility. Stephens' 2015 suspicion that Pepper twisted and obscured other parts of the King and Ray case, separate from the lawyer's manipulation of McFerren, had already been confirmed by ABC and Forrest Sawyer in '97.

Bill Pepper - 1999

It goes without saying that Pepper used his well-honed influence over McFerren to steer the impressionable grocer's 1999 court testimony toward a predetermined, and most certainly vague conclusion. Despite McFerren's best efforts to communicate his knowledge of Fayette County's role in the conspiracy to murder Dr. King, Pepper and his so-called opposing counsel worked diligently to guide the seventy-five-year-old witness down a dead-end road during the *King v. Jowers* trial. When McFerren tried to explain the involvement of the Anderson brothers and W.C. McNeil in the 1969 beating, Pepper allowed only a brief and muddled mention. Before McFerren uttered the names of Liberto and Mayor Yancey in the courtroom on November 16, Pepper no doubt suppressed any inclination by his witness to verbally connect the two men to James Earl Ray. And when the name of Tennessee's powerful lieutenant governor was referenced by McFerren in connection to Liberto, Pepper cowardly avoided the topic by saddling Attorney Lewis K. Garrison with the unpleasant task of broaching the John Wilder question. Finally, of course, McFerren was never asked about the secret tapes that both he and Pepper still had in their possession in 1999.

DOJ - 2000

Attorney General Janet Reno and her MLK investigating attorney Barry Kowalski completed and published their final DOJ report on June

9, 2000. Within the voluminous document, Reno and Kowalski's investigative team severely criticized John McFerren's credibility and thirty-two-year-old claims. Unlike Pepper, however, it should be noted that the DOJ was at least forthcoming about the entirety of McFerren's Liberto and Ray accusations. Still, their harsh rebuke of the humble Fayette Countian rang as personally vindictive in some strange way while simultaneously lacking any evidential substance. And although they did indeed reference, albeit negatively, McFerren's belief that Mayor I.P. Yancey assisted James Earl Ray in 1968, it was unclear exactly how the DOJ attorneys discovered the information contained on McFerren's 1969-through-1970 tapes or what evidence they used to support their critical conclusion. Stephens considered the possibilities.

Beginning in 1970, McFerren mailed several copies of his secretly recorded tapes to various locales around the country, the first of which was the Civil Rights Division at the DOJ. Did Reno and her team manage to unearth the original package as it lay buried inside some cobweb-infested Washington catacomb? It didn't seem logical. Next, DOJ attorneys made notes in 1976 about the Somerville mayor's possible involvement. However, Folsom and Walker's typed summation never actually named Yancey, was extremely ambiguous, and without context. That also didn't seem like a possibility to Stephens. Perhaps the 1998-to-2000 team used the HSCA materials. Within McFerren's 1978 signed affidavit, he did indeed state:

That in and about 1968, I maintained an underground intelligence network composed of cooks, butlers, and bellboys from which I learned that former-Mayor Yancy of Somerville, Tennessee, a friend of former-Mayor Loeb of Memphis, collected money from local businessmen to pay for the assassination of Dr. King; made two trips to London, England, to assist James Earl Ray; and harbored James Earl Ray for the two days immediately prior to Dr. King's assassination.

Founded on his belief that the 1977 DOJ and/or HSCA obtained copies of McFerren's tapes through Pepper, coupled with the statement concerning Yancey's handling of Ray in McFerren's 1978 affidavit, Stephens ultimately concluded that Reno's team had accessed and therefore referenced McFerren's still sealed HSCA evidence. However, McFerren was adamant in his assertion to Holmes that he did not speak to federal investigators in March of 1999. Surely, Stephens thought, Reno's team had not relied exclusively on the tapes and the 1978 Yancey accusation to determine whether or not McFerren's beliefs were inaccurate. It would have been essential for the DOJ to also conduct a background investigation in order to properly vet and therefore criticize McFerren's audio reels and 1978 claim. Stephens was at a loss. Did Reno's team somehow acquire their supporting, anti-Yancey-and-Ray-collusion information from another source, one McFerren and Holmes were not aware of? Was there another person in March of 1999 who had knowledge of and access to McFerren's personal recordings?

Not satisfied with the quagmire of corruption, conspiracy, and cover-up they had unearthed at the hands of the DOJ and HSCA in the late '70s, Holmes and Stephens also probed deeply into the backgrounds of Attorney General Janet Reno and her 1998-through-2000 MLK investigation staff. The two men soon realized that between 1999 and 2001, Reno was in extremely close contact with a former Fayette County native who not only knew McFerren personally, but who was a friend of both Robert Hamburger and John Wilder. This individual was also well-versed on the paper-bag-over-the-telephone anecdote in Hamburger's book, the revelations regarding Mayor Yancey and James Earl Ray, and the existence, general location, and content of McFerren's well-guarded tapes.

Marcus Holmes - 2012

His inflamed curiosity had reached a boiling point. Incensed by the past collusion amongst Bill Pepper, the DOJ, the HSCA, and those living within Shelby and Fayette Counties to silence McFerren, Holmes took to the bumpy backroads, wooded alcoves, and rich rural fields of his hometown in June of 2012 in search of corroborating information about Mayor Yancey's former cook, her informant son, and their past allegations regarding James Earl Ray. It wasn't long before Holmes found himself standing in front of a genteel local African-American man named Karl Mosby. Still living just northwest of downtown Somerville on a gravel strip of earth aptly called Karl Way, Mosby seemed apprehensive at first of the black stranger knocking on his front door. But after learning of Holmes' friendship with McFerren, the Fayette County native eventually relaxed and told his Yancey story, plus much more.

Karl Mosby confirmed that he was, in fact, the informant son of Mayor Yancey's former cook, a since-deceased woman named Mrs. Edna Coe. The now seventy-year-old Mosby also confirmed that his mother had become privy to Yancey's two flights to London in 1968 and that she was later questioned by two well-dressed white men whom she believed to be agents of the FBI. Just as McFerren earlier explained to Holmes, Mosby also stated that Mrs. Coe was subsequently fired by Yancey not long after being questioned by the federal agents and that McFerren helped finance her rapid departure out of town. Mosby then confessed that both he and his mother believed that Yancey had bankrolled James Earl Ray's escape to London in May of 1968.

Abruptly changing subjects on Holmes, Mosby then slumped into a heartbreaking lament regarding the recent 2011 passing of his beloved son, Gerald. Holmes thought for a second and then was stunned. The elderly man was describing the very same little boy who McFerren had acknowledged during the secretly recorded conversation with Karl in early 1970. In the altogether separate issue, Holmes went on to inadvertently learn from Karl about the mysterious death of Gerald Mosby at the hands of Fayette County jailers and local Sheriff James Robert "Bobby" Riles.

At the apex of Holmes' research in the late summer of 2012, the local rumor mill was in full swing. Word eventually leaked out that McFerren and Holmes had teamed up to research Fayette County's connection to the Martin Luther King Jr. assassination. It was also being vaguely whispered among members of the local African-American community that the pair was engaged in some kind of clandestine work involving old audiotapes. During a trivial visit to McFerren's store to purchase a cold drink and a snack, a local black youth named Kendrick Chearis spotted Holmes' old-fashioned SONY reel-to-reel audio player sitting on the store's front counter.

Assuming the unique looking device held innate monetary value, and intent on stealing it from the business owner, Chearis returned on September 27 and broke into McFerren's store through a small window at the back of the building around 4:00 p.m. With McFerren still using the building as his primary residence, the napping grocer awoke to the sound of breaking glass, confronted the intruder, and chased the startled Chearis away. Upon calling the sheriff's department and making an identification later that evening, Kendrick Chearis was arrested and sent to Sheriff Riles' infamous detention center. It was not long after the break-in and attempted robbery that McFerren and Holmes agreed to have the singular version of the brittle audiotapes remastered, converted to digital audio files, copied to multiple electronic devices, and safely hidden at various locations.

Conclusions and Questions

McFerren's tapes had traveled a long and bumpy road since 1970. It was clear to Stephens by now that Fayette County neighbor Hayward

Brown played an unselfishly supportive role in the production of the audio reels, and that New York journalist Ted Poston's 1970 dismissal of said recordings most likely stemmed from a misunderstanding of what he was listening to. But it was also clear that *Our Portion of Hell* author Robert Hamburger, having first heard about the tapes in 1971, acted in an evasive manner under questioning by Holmes. Once again, what was the New York author hiding? Was there someone involved in the matter he was trying to protect? While it was unclear during the early stages of Holmes and Stephens' investigation, the bombshell truth lay just on the horizon.

Then there was the multi-decade involvement and cover-up by Bill Pepper to consider. Not only was it highly likely that Pepper shrouded his presence in West Tennessee in 1977, but all signs pointed to his collaboration with opposing federal investigators during the same period. But if McFerren was correct regarding the time frame Pepper first appeared in Fayette County, and the New York attorney and eventual English Barrister did, in fact, lie in his 1995 book, what was the reason for the deception? Stephens spent a significant amount of time performing various mental gymnastics in an effort to solve the mystery and eventually reached some rather profound conclusions.

By 1966, New York Attorney Mark Lane had garnered a well-deserved, nationally renowned reputation for being an intelligent legislator, a prolific civil rights lawyer, JFK assassination expert, ambitious author, and outspoken critic of the federal government's military-industrial complex and imperialistic agenda. And although he did not become Ray's defense attorney until late October of 1977, Lane had already been investigating the MLK case for a number of years. Furthermore, Lane met with a handful of future HSCA members in August of 1976 before the committee was actually formed, and then interviewed Ray in prison in December of that year. Then, in April of 1977, Lane and his co-author, Dick Gregory, published their Ray and King assassination conspiracy findings in the book

Code Name Zorro. Based on the number of remarkable parallels and corroborating details he uncovered, Stephens was now of the firm opinion that Pepper's unclearly explained, early 1977 initiation into the HSCA's King and Ray investigation was the result of his quiet work under neighboring New York friend, fellow civil rights attorney, and seasoned James Earl Ray advocate, Mark Lane.

It was now Stephens' unwavering belief that sometime in the opening months of 1977, the senior and more experienced Lane brought the newly licensed Pepper on board to serve as a kind of unofficial junior legal partner and private investigator. Now coordinating as a calculated pair in an effort to prove Ray's innocence, the two attorneys worked tirelessly to infiltrate the federal government's '76-through-'78 King investigation. This infiltration included the questioning of former HSCA Chief Counsel Richard Sprague by Pepper "shortly after" Sprague's departure on March 30, 1977. Eventually, this jockeying for a seat at the HSCA table also resulted in Lane becoming James Earl Ray's future HSCA attorney. At the urging of the senior New York lawyer, Ray fired Tennessee attorney Jack Kershaw and hired Lane as his lead defense counsel on October 25, 1977. With Kershaw out of the way, and Lane's new preeminence solidified in the HSCA spotlight as Ray's latest attorney, it was only then that the Rev. Ralph Abernathy, well aware of the two New York lawyers' partnership, contacted Pepper in "late 1977" to request a "face-to-face meeting" with Lane's new client.

Yet, at the core of Stephens' theory were the roles Lane, Pepper, Kenneth Herman, and the HSCA's Johnson team most likely played in the secret sharing of McFerren's audio reels between 1977 and early 1978. Stephens was now of the opinion that Dick Gregory, having been earlier tipped off by Baxton Bryant and McFerren while leading the 1969 demonstrations in Somerville, explained to his longtime friend and *Code Name Zorro* co-author, Mark Lane, what McFerren allegedly overheard at Liberto's warehouse in 1968. At the recommendation of Gregory, Lane then furtively directed Pepper to travel to West Tennessee in early 1977 to privately investigate a number of issues, one of which was McFerren's eavesdropping account.

Upon entering McFerren's gas and grocery business for the first time, Pepper noted the broken and taped plate glass windows that had been recently damaged in the September 10, 1976 shootout between McFerren and the Mafia-paid assailant no doubt sent by Liberto. Unwilling to spill his guts at their first meeting, McFerren's now-famous reticence forced Pepper to make several additional trips to Fayette County over the course of the same year. It was at one of these future 1977 conferences with Pepper that McFerren finally divulged the existence of the secret audio reels and his personal knowledge of the conspiracy involving Liberto, Ray, Mayor Yancey, and Lt. Gov. Wilder.

Instantly seduced by the idea that McFerren possessed never-before-heard audio recordings pertinent to the case, Pepper notified his New York legal partner immediately. After discussing the issue at length, Lane instructed Pepper to obtain copies of McFerren's recordings. It was then that the junior legal partner arranged for Memphis audio man and part-time private investigator Kenneth Herman to meet with McFerren to duplicate the reels. By late 1977, at least one copy of McFerren's tapes had been mailed by Herman to Pepper's New York address. Upon listening to the contents of the duplicate tapes together, Lane and Pepper eventually discovered that McFerren's candid recordings indicated not only a conspiracy (one that had long been denied by the federal government), but a conspiracy that involved a West Tennessee government official, Mayor I. P. Yancey. The two attorneys then decided at some point between late 1977 and April 3, 1978, to quietly use the audio recordings as a politically damning bargaining chip to gain leverage for themselves and their client.

The New York legal duo immediately realized that, if both Frank C. Liberto and Mayor Yancey could be positively and publicly tied to the long-denied conspiracy, then it would have taken little time for nosey members of the national news media to also begin knocking on the doors of other leading West Tennessee figures. This could have included Memphis Mayor Henry Loeb; Loeb's Police and Fire Director, Frank Holloman; Holloman's previous coworkers inside the Memphis FBI field office; and perhaps even Tennessee Lieutenant Governor John Wilder himself.

It is important to remember that during the HSCA hearings, numerous past agents of the FBI, organized crime figure Frank C. Liberto, and local officials Mayor Yancey, Mayor Loeb, Holloman, and Lt. Gov. Wilder were all still alive. Recognizing the explosive implications of McFerren's tapes, Lane and Pepper most likely believed at the time that they could frighten Chief Counsel G. Robert Blakey and the twelve congressional members of the HSCA into making some kind of deal that would benefit Ray and the entrenched members of Lane's anti-government camp. To be clear, Lane and Pepper tried to use the tapes to blackmail members of the HSCA and the United States Government, thereby cornering them into a position where they were forced to ask Tennessee State authorities to release Ray from prison.

As part of their plan, Pepper once more contacted Herman in Memphis, this time instructing him to mail another copy of McFerren's recordings directly to members of the DOJ. After the DOJ and HSCA's surreptitious receipt and examination of the audio reels sent by Lane and Pepper, the Johnson team was quickly instructed by a nervous Chief Counsel Blakey to return to Fayette County on April 3, 1978, to provide the illiterate McFerren with an unofficial receipt. This fraudulent receipt would obviously explain away to any of McFerren's present and future, potentially nosey, friends and family how the HSCA obtained copies of his recordings.

A little more than two months later, and fearful of what McFerren might reveal if given the opportunity to speak at the public hearings in Washington, Deputy Chief Counsel Gene Johnson, under the direction of Blakey, barred the humble grocer on June 22, 1978, or shortly thereafter, from testifying before the HSCA at the nation's capital.

Given Gene Johnson's unkind treatment of McFerren, Ray's ongoing incarceration at the conclusion of the HSCA, and the current vacuum of public information related to McFerren's still-secret audiotapes, it was obvious to Stephens that Lane and Pepper's attempts at quietly leveraging the recordings against federal and Tennessee state officials backfired, resulting in a multi-decade stalemate that still exists to this day. Since the tapes implicated Ray in the conspiracy as well, then neither Mark Lane nor the stubbornly combative G. Robert Blakey could use them in the court of public opinion as a way of forcing the opposing side into submission; hence the decades-long impasse and cover-up of McFerren's recordings by both sides of the MLK conspiracy debate.

Playing devil's advocate once again, Stephens then switched sides and deflected his own theory. There was little doubt that opposing critics would attack his HSCA-tape hypothesis by suggesting that Stephens was overinflating the importance of McFerren's recordings. But like any good strategist, Stephens quickly returned to his original position and volleyed back during the one-man mental tête-à-tête. If McFerren's secret tape recordings were unimportant and therefore lacked any content that was relevant, why didn't the HSCA or DOJ simply divulge their existence, publicly criticize them, and discredit McFerren? Yet, if the information revealed in his original interviews and audiotapes was central to uncovering the conspiracy's link to West Tennessee's white society, then numerous officials within local, county, state, and even federal government would have needed to work together to keep McFerren and his tape recordings quiet.

On the flip side, it was just as imperative that Lane and Pepper hide McFerren's knowledge about Ray's relationship with figures in West Tennessee, especially if Liberto's alleged April 4, 1968 telephone conversations were already a matter of public record. If Ray could indeed be tied to organized crime figure Frank C. Liberto or Somerville Mayor I.P. Yancey, who was a notorious racist, then it most certainly would have made the imprisoned scapegoat look more guilty, not less.

In addition, because he was in a hidden alliance with Lane as a member of Ray's legal defense team during the HSCA's existence, Pepper had no choice but to keep the conspiratorial connection between I.P. Yancey, John S. Wilder, Frank C. Liberto, and Lane's client a secret. It was, therefore, imperative that Pepper steer clear of the Somerville mayor and Memphis tomato salesman while the two West Tennessee men were still alive in '77 and '78. Having been already entrusted with McFerren's private account of the West Tennessee conspiracy and copies of the highly coveted audio reels, Pepper also went on to hide his knowledge of Ray's true involvement while representing the alleged shooter's brother, Jerry Ray, at the request of Mark Lane during the HSCA hearings on November 30, 1978. But this cover-up by the pasty-faced New York charlatan would continue in future decades, specifically during his role as Ray's newest attorney in 1988, his involvement in the 1989 Sergeant and Edginton documentary, his role as a thespian lawyer in Jack Saltman's 1993 HBO mock trial, and the publication of *Orders to Kill* in 1995.

Now backed into a corner, unable to provide his eventual 1995 readers with a logical explanation as to why he failed to at least approach Liberto before the tomato salesman's alleged death in 1978, Pepper was forced to conceal his early partnership with Lane and investigative presence in West Tennessee during 1977, the year Pepper truly spoke with McFerren about Ray, Liberto,

Yancey, and Wilder. To compensate for the overlap in time, the crafty attorney and author gave himself plenty of margin by falsely claiming in his 1995 book that he did not meet John McFerren until February 1979, an entire year after Liberto allegedly and conveniently died. And while it was most likely the first time Mark Lane's former associates, April Ferguson and Barbara Rabbito, had entered McFerren's business, the 1979 interview was not the first time Pepper had traveled to Fayette County; hence the discrepancy between McFerren's '77 recollection and Pepper's written claim about his first visit to McFerren's store in '79.

Of course, the cover-up of McFerren's recorded evidence and Ray's true connection to members of West Tennessee's racist white society continued in the years following the publication of *Orders to Kill*, specifically during Pepper's participation in the *Primetime Live* episode in 1997, and his role as the King family's attorney in the 1999 civil trial, the same trial at which Pepper concealed Liberto's death date and minimized the utterance of Wilder's name. But Pepper was not the only guilty party in the multi-decade cover-up of McFerren's evidence.

From their supposedly uninterested receipt of McFerren's package in 1970, through their unsubstantiated dismissal of his Yancey and Ray allegations in 2000, to the writing of this very book, the U.S. Department of Justice has never publicly acknowledged the existence or exact content of McFerren's audio recordings. As incomprehensible as it may have once seemed to Stephens, he could not run from the very real possibility that what he, Holmes, and McFerren had uncovered was nothing less than a two-way MLK assassination cover-up involving those who sought to keep Ray imprisoned and those working to set him free.

This possible theory led Stephens to ask even more hypothetical questions: Did Bill Pepper and John Wilder also work together in some fashion? Did the two attorneys forge a backroom deal that would be mutually beneficial to them and their individual clients? Did Pepper promise to steer the already public Liberto narrative toward a comfortably confusing and inconclusive finale if Wilder promised to hide his personal knowledge of Ray's willing participation in the conspiracy? It was time to take a hard look at Fayette County's esteemed state senator, powerful lieutenant governor, wealthy land and business owner, and Somerville attorney, John Shelton Wilder.

Chapter 10

FAYETTE'S FAVORITE SON

RANDALL STEPHENS FIRST heard the name John Shelton Wilder spoken from the mouth of a Fayette County Commissioner and former Shelby County Sheriff's Assistant Chief named Terry Leggett. Waxing nostalgic during a local public meeting, Leggett fondly recounted his past dealings with Wilder, noting the former Tennessee state senator and lieutenant governor's extraordinary ability to pick up his Somerville telephone and quickly get things done. Famous for his own penchant for the stench and squalor of the county's typically dirty politics, Commissioner Leggett grinned as he boastfully detailed the unrestrained power Wilder was once known to have wielded. But Leggett was by no means the only Fayette Countian and local politician who liked to place the late Wilder up on a pedestal.

It was not uncommon to overhear local white residents, especially those who sauntered in and out of Somerville's upper crust circles, proudly proclaim their desire for the good ole days when Wilder was somehow able to keep the long arm of the federal government out of "their county." Oblivious to what they were referring to at the time, Stephens later discovered that the local residents' comments were aimed at the issue of the county's poorly managed public schools. Under the thirty-six-year rule of the lieutenant governor, Fayette County was somehow allowed to maintain and operate an inadequately funded, racially segregated public school system. Inexplicably, John and Viola McFerren's 1965 federal desegregation lawsuit on behalf of John Jr. went unresolved for nearly five decades and continued to be a point of divisive legal contention within the halls of Fayette County government during Wilder's long political reign.

Without explanation, civil rights attorneys at the DOJ quietly recoiled from their former position of authority, and specific school integration criteria mandated earlier by the federal courts in 1975 was never fully implemented by Fayette County commissioners and school board members, even as late as 2010. It wasn't until sometime after the eighty-eight-year-old senator's death on January 1 of that year that the U.S. Department of Justice's Civil Rights Division finally put its foot down, demanding that the county commission and school board correct the vast racial disparities that divided Somerville's two early-learning institutions, Jefferson Elementary and Somerville Elementary.

According to one previous federal report, the racial demographics of Jefferson Elementary's student body consisted of 14 white and 168 black children as of 2007, while at the same time, Somerville Elementary was comprised of 203 white and 52 black children. Amazingly, both of these racially identifiable schools were located within the vicinity of Somerville, separated by a distance of only 3.5 miles. As one local African-American woman stated upon hearing of Wilder's 2010 passing, "Well, I guess they'll finally be able to fix the schools now!"

Still unacquainted with the local customs and Southern proclivities of the county's white establishment, and their longing for a bygone era when the senator's mysteriously uninhibited power could freeze time inside the county's Jim Crow bubble, Stephens one day made the mistake of correcting an elderly Somerville woman who referred to Wilder as "The Governor." After naïvely reminding her that the former Speaker of the State Senate was, in fact, the lieutenant governor, and not the actual leading government official of Tennessee, Stephens was chastised by the insulted woman who sternly snapped back in a Southern drawl, "Well, around here, we call him 'The Governor'!"

It wasn't until 2012 that Randall Stephens began to hear of another side of the recently deceased statesman, an even darker side. After becoming more familiar with Marcus Holmes and his stories about John McFerren, Stephens came to learn of a seldom talked about John Wilder, one who embodied unimaginable treachery and evil. By 2015, Stephens was investigating McFerren and Holmes' long-held assertion that Wilder conspired with both Somerville Mayor I.P. Yancey and Memphis organized crime figure Frank C. Liberto to assassinate Dr. Martin Luther King Jr.

But Stephens had little to run on. Unlike his access to McFerren's documented government statements and forty-five-year-old tape recordings, there was absolutely no hard evidence in Stephens' possession, for obvious reasons, that pointed to Wilder's involvement in Dr. King's murder. The only circumstantial information available was the private statements of Holmes and McFerren, along with what was already floating about in the public domain. So that was where Stephens would have to start.

The first item the investigator scrounged up was a 2007 biography written by two Southern college professors named Rodney E. Stanley and P. Edward French. Entitled *Tennessee's John S. Wilder: The Longest Tenured State Legislator in Tennessee History*, the book's biased account of Wilder's local history was quickly evident to Stephens. While the publication provided a great deal of fundamental background information, the two authors collaborated closely with Wilder during their research, and the lieutenant governor himself sanctioned the writing and publishing of the piece. It was soon apparent that very little of the book would reveal the numerous controversies Stephens had previously heard rumored about. In one brief, albeit extremely slanted, example on page thirty-six, Stanley and French wrote:

> In another show of political power, the Lieutenant Governor helped poor "tent city" farmers in his own county. From 1959 to 1963, over 700 residents who tried to vote were forced off their land in Fayette County, and Viola and John McFerren organized a tent city to help feed and shelter those displaced by white farmers. Wilder supported the registration drive for these residents, and his company refused to cancel crop loans made to African-American families.

Stephens was extremely familiar by this point with the voter registration and Tent City dispute between the area's wealthy white landowners and exiled black tenant farmers beginning in 1959. While the authors had painted the Fayette County senator, cotton planter, and gin owner as the kindhearted benefactor to numerous African-American families during the upheaval, McFerren had already thoroughly enlightened Holmes on precisely what the paternalistic Wilder's motives were at the time. Despite the slow start, Stephens was eventually able to piece together, through the accumulation of newspaper clippings and other archival materials, a relatively focused portrait of who the powerful cotton baron was and what his personal motivations were.

Cotton Coated

John Shelton Wilder was born on June 3, 1921, to John Chamblee and Martha Anne Wilder, two longtime residents of Mason,

Tennessee, a town located inside Tipton County on the northwestern border of neighboring Fayette County. Born a small, gangly-looking fellow, what the young Wilder lacked in size and physical strength, he more than made up for in personal ambition. From the very beginning, it was said that what John Wilder sought most in this world was unlimited power. After high school, the wavy, auburn-haired Wilder married Marcelle Ann Morton on December 31, 1941. Less than two years later, on June 1, 1943, the pair gave birth to their first son, John Shelton Wilder Jr. Then, upon his enlistment in the United States Army, the new father served as a stateside cook, somehow avoiding a life-threatening foreign deployment during World War II. Following the conclusion of the war and his military service in Green Cove Springs, Florida, the restless veteran returned to his wife and son who had settled on a piece of the Wilder family's property in Longtown, a small municipality located just inside Fayette County south of Mason.

After the March 19, 1947 birth of his second son, David Morton Wilder, John enrolled that year at the University of Tennessee to pursue an agricultural degree. As the heir to his father's vast nineteenth-century cotton plantation, twentieth-century cotton ginning business, and highly profitable Longtown Supply Company, the young John Wilder spent the next several years managing his family's rural empire. But he was still unsatisfied. Determined to forge his own path, Wilder attended part-time classes at Memphis State University, now The University of Memphis, and graduated with a law degree in 1957. He also went on to parlay his family's immense wealth into several banking and businesses establishments throughout the county and elsewhere. Among these future enterprises was Wilder's private law firm located just a stone's throw east from the Fayette County Courthouse on Somerville's bustling town square.

In addition to Wilder's ongoing role as an agricultural and soil conservation official, the up-and-coming Fayette County Democrat was elected to the Tennessee General Assembly in 1958 and began his first two-year term in Nashville as a state senator in early 1959. Not long after taking office, however, the newly elected Wilder found himself embroiled in the hometown turmoil known as Tent City. Historically championed as one of the few wealthy white planters who refused to call in the crop loans held by Fayette County's black farmers, it was even rumored by some that Wilder went so far as to secretly provide the actual canvas tents that were used by the displaced Tent City residents. As the whitewashed story goes, Wilder, due to his unflinching moral integrity and generosity, lost his next bid for the same senate seat in the August 1962 Democratic primary. Because of his inability to attract the local white voters who were still angry over his previous stance, Wilder remained on the outer fringes of state politics for the next three and a half years.

Miraculously, Wilder regained his state senate seat in the 1966 election. Then, in January 1971, the state senator was elected by his General Assembly peers to the Senate Speaker and lieutenant governor's position, a leadership role he would continue to maintain well into the next millennium. Applauded as a shrewd bipartisan negotiator who regularly made deals with members of both parties, Wilder was fondly nicknamed by those in Nashville's hobnobbing circles, "The Wilder-Beast," meaning the lieutenant governor was a political hybrid, half Democrat, half Republican.

Among the many accolades the citizens of West Tennessee eventually bestowed upon the second-highest official in the state, Somerville's state-run juvenile detention facility was renamed the John S. Wilder Youth Development Center in 1975; Wilder's name was affixed in 1991 to the outer face of the National Civil Rights Museum (the former Lorraine Motel where Dr. King was slain); the Brister Library building on the campus of the University of Memphis was renamed the John S. Wilder Tower in 2003; and a bronze bust of the statesman was placed on permanent display in the rotunda of the Fayette County Courthouse on January 10, 2004.

All of the surface-level material Stephens could find on John Wilder was just that, surface-level. Where were the details regarding his mysterious ability to keep the DOJ out of Fayette County's public schools? Where was the real story about his involvement in Tent City? Where was the inside scoop regarding his contentious relationship with John McFerren? And how was Stephens going to connect the good senator to the King assassination? The semi-hopeful detective knew there was far more lying beneath the fluffy-white portrayal of Fayette County's stately cotton planter, attorney, and politician. But how was he going to find it? If Stephens was going to get to the root of who Wilder was, he was going to have to look underneath West Tennessee's thick blanket of white cotton-coated deception and dig in the blackened dirt, the ancient antebellum dirt still soaked with the warm blood, sweat, and tears of Fayette County's past African-American slaves and tenant farmers.

Digging in the Dirt

In the beginning of his investigation, the only items Randall Stephens could find that resembled anything close to being critical of John Wilder were the published anecdotes regarding the senator's quirky way of referring to himself in the third person, his obscure public comments on the numinous aspects of the cosmos, and his sometimes laughably reckless landing of "Jaybird," the 1971 twin-engine Piper airplane that Wilder owned and personally piloted on his commutes between the State Capitol in Nashville and his private Longtown airfield. But then Stephens located his first solid piece of hard-hitting journalism about the lieutenant governor.

On December 6, 2001, *The Tennessean* printed an article on page twenty entitled, "Wilder gained land at expense of blacks, Winbush charges." The article outlined accusations that Wilder's father and grandfather illicitly obtained large tracts of farmland previously owned by freed slaves. During his formal speech before the Tennessee General Assembly, Fisk University Professor Dr. Raymond Winbush stated:

> Lt. Gov. John Wilder's entire wealth, and that is not an exaggeration, was derived by systematically taking land from African Americans by his grandfather beginning in the latter part of the 19th century. We are going to document that and publish the results.

The fallout after Dr. Winbush's public comments was fierce and swift. Irate members of Nashville's powerful white political constituency cried foul. Wilder's portly Chief of Staff Pat Miller quickly came to the defense of his boss, stating in the same December 6 article that Winbush's comments were "outrageous and possibly slanderous allegations against Lt. Gov. Wilder and his family."

Intrigued by the story and its possible implications, Stephens tracked down Dr. Winbush and asked him about his past research, his 2001 public speech, and the immediate backlash thereafter. During his extremely pleasant and candid conversation with the professor, Stephens learned that Dr. Winbush received several death threats immediately following the publication of his Wilder comments. Tired of the constant harassment and lack of organized African-American political action in Tennessee, the professor resigned his position at Fisk and moved to a different area of the country.

When Stephens asked about his research, Winbush again asserted the validity of his 2001 findings. It was Winbush's claim that while he still possessed the archival documents that corroborated his conclusions, he never pursued the matter further, nor did he publish his findings due to the verbal harassment he received. Willing to pass the investigative torch, so to speak, Winbush then put Stephens in touch with a member of the Brewer family, a Memphis relative involved in one of the near century's old Wilder land disputes.

Hoping the Wilders' theft of the Brewers' land could be finally made public, the anonymous family member agreed to meet with Stephens. Over a steaming cup of overpriced coffee at an upscale Memphis bistro, the family member spoke candidly about the past and present plight of West Tennessee's African-American community. Then, the Brewer relative graciously provided Stephens with copies of old land deeds once belonging to Alex Brewer and his wife Priscilla, partially confirming Dr. Winbush's research and 2001 public comments.

Beginning in the latter part of the nineteenth century, the evil practice became commonplace throughout the South, especially in Fayette County, Tennessee. When freed slaves began purchasing small tracts of land after the Civil War in which to do their own farming, jealous former Confederates viewed the acquisition of their previous real estate by local African Americans as yet another post-war slap in the face, not to mention an obvious affront to their future financial status in the community as proud white Southerners. Keenly aware of the illiteracy that permeated the local black community, as well as the need for the impoverished black farmers to take out crop loans in order to pay for farming supplies, the wealthy white financiers devised a devious plan.

When black planters requested cash loans from neighboring white land and business owners to help pay for much-needed seed and other agricultural necessities, the white financial backers secretly included terms in the written loan agreements that were purposely beyond what the black farmers could achieve when it came time to pay off the loan. These terms most often included using the African-American farmers' privately owned land as collateral. As a result, when the illiterate black planters unwittingly signed the loan agreements, and then failed to meet the near impossible and previously misunderstood terms at harvest time, their land was forfeited to the neighboring white backers who provided the initial cash or agricultural supplies.

Given the positions of other wealthy white men within the local court system at the time, the now landless, illiterate, and penniless African-American farmers were without any legal recourse.

Today, the Brewers' 1928-through-1932 land deeds prove that Lt. Gov. Wilder's uncle, a Fayette County native named James Wiggins Shelton, along with Wilder's father, John Chamblee Wilder, used their Longtown Supply Company partnership and contractual sleight-of-hand to cunningly pilfer thirty-three and a half acres from the Brewer family for a delinquent loan amount of only $387.50, the 2019 equivalent of $5,627.33. When examined closely, the Brewer deeds were no doubt proof of a John Chamblee that was a far cry from the father who Lt. Gov. Wilder liked to portray to the public. On page nine of Stanley and French's 2007 John Wilder biography, they sourced a 1995 *Nashville Scene* article entitled "The Other Governor." According to Stanley and French, the article stated:

> During the Great Depression, an African-American man named Mac Jarman approached John Chamblee Wilder one day pleading for groceries so he could feed his seven children, with the promise that he would pay Mr. Wilder back in a couple of weeks. Several weeks passed and once again Mr. Jarman came barefooted walking up the dirt road. He solicited Mr. Wilder again with the same story, asking if he could please get some more groceries for his family? The elder Wilder's response was the same as before-telling Mr. Jarman to go ahead and get his family some more groceries. The young Wilder turned to his dad and asked "why did you allow him to get more groceries when he has yet to pay you for the first batch?" His father replied, "he has seven kids and a wife to feed" and that it was simply the right thing to do.

When Stephens asked for a final comment regarding John Chamblee's son, the Brewer relative took another sip of coffee, paused, and then bluntly said of the former lieutenant governor, "My family said he was a dishonest and evil man." While the Brewer's small piece of property made up only a fraction of the thousands of acres the Wilder family eventually laid claim to, it was most certainly an indicator of the type of illicit dealings and theft that habitually took place between the wealthy, educated Wilders and the struggling, uneducated African-American families who once called Fayette County home.

As if on an archeological dig, the singular skeleton Stephens had just found quickly led to many others buried in the same vicinity. Now interested in Wilder's complete genealogy, Stephens went on to discover that Thomas Broom(e), the lieutenant governor's great-great-grandfather on his mother and uncle James Wiggins Shelton's side, was a wealthy Fayette County slave owner. But that was just the beginning.

Apparently, John Wilder's own views on race did not fall far from the proverbial family tree. In a March 4, 1959 article in the *Kingsport News*, the newly elected senator stated, "Integration cannot be effected in heavily Negro West Tennessee counties without wrecking the school system." Amazingly, this direct quote was again at diametric odds with the heartwarming story Lt. Gov. Wilder recounted to the authors of his 2007 biography. On pages eight and nine of their book, Stanley and French wrote:

As a boy, the Lieutenant Governor noticed two separate doors in a local theatre. one labeled for whites only and the other for the "colored". This perplexed the young boy because while living on the farm, John Wilder had been sheltered and was unaware of the racial animosities existing at this time in the south, The Lieutenant Governor wondered why two separate entrances to the movie theatre existed for these two groups. John Wilder knew that most of the farm hands were of African-American decent

[sic], and his father treated them like any other individual. At this moment, John Chamblee Wilder found it necessary to explain to his son about the racial inequalities that existed between blacks and whites at the time (1930's); but he urged his son to understand that color was only skin deep and that one could tell the worth of an individual by where his heart lies. The Lieutenant Governor recalls that his father emphasized to him and his brother that all people should be treated the same, no matter what color or ethnic background they may possess. Speaker Wilder contends that this early lesson from his father influenced his political decisions to oppose the ideologies of the "Dixie-Crats," when the Civil Rights movement began in the United States.

Disgusted by the blatantly whitewashed fabrications in Stanley and French's authored work, Stephens continued to dig feverishly. The next items he uncovered were official Department of Justice documents clearly indicating that Somerville Bank and Trust, James H. "Preacher" Shelton (the bank's president and Wilder's first cousin), Dr. John W. Morris, Judge Paul R. Summers Sr., Rube Rhea, Mayor I. P. Yancey, and John S. Wilder were all named among the original white defendants in the 1960 to 1962 Tent City landowners case.

As previously detailed, Wilder had long been portrayed in local folklore as the lone white savior of the county's African-American residents during the Tent City era, a popular but false depiction that Stephens knew angered John McFerren. During the countless conversations between Marcus Holmes and McFerren, the grocer explained that Wilder was smarter than the average racist. McFerren knew better than anyone that from 1960 onward, Wilder's seemingly philanthropic gestures had nothing to do with being respectful of the local black community.

The former civil rights activist understood on a deeply personal level that what Wilder liked more than anything was power, and that the senator's methodology for controlling the African-American population was based on a simple concept he learned from his father, John Chamblee. To paraphrase McFerren's no-eating-from-the-white-man's-trough analogy, Wilder believed that "if you ingratiate yourself by giving black people something small, you make them indebted to you, and then you can control them later on." With this strategy in mind, coupled with the overwhelming number of African Americans in the county who were becoming registered voters, Wilder cunningly changed with the times. In short, the good Senator didn't care about Fayette's African-American community; he simply wanted to control them for his own political benefit.

Subsequent to Wilder's ostensibly noble efforts at helping the local Tent City residents, the FBI, in conjunction with the Civil Rights Division at the DOJ, ultimately saw fit to remove his name from the list of white defendants in the federal landowners case. But the senator's "kindness" toward the black community still left many whites in the county scratching their heads. Unable to understand Wilder's wily strategic agenda, they angrily refused to give him their votes in the 1962 election. Making matters worse, Wilder also failed to garner the large cluster of black votes he believed his prior philanthropy would earn him. Because the fiercely independent and distrusting John McFerren continued to publicly voice his opposition to the Somerville politician's hidden manipulations, it soon became painfully obvious to Wilder that, if he was going to infiltrate the local civil rights movement in Fayette County and win its black votes in the future, he had to somehow dethrone their outspoken and uncontrollable leader.

The first phase in Wilder's well-crafted plan to get McFerren out of the way came less than a year after the Somerville attorney's 1962 senatorial defeat. According to the Fayette County Juvenile Court records given to Holmes by McFerren, Mrs. Emma Jean Frazier and her Somerville attorney, John Shelton Wilder, brought a paternity suit against John McFerren on June 17, 1963. As detailed earlier, this was the same paternity suit McFerren defiantly objected to in his 1970 secret audio recordings. Once again, Mrs. Frazier and Wilder, armed with the results of the questionable blood test, went on to win their paternity suit against McFerren. It should also be repeated that the physician who assisted Wilder in obtaining the blood sample from McFerren was Dr. John W. Morris, the same Dr. Morris who, along with Wilder, was named as a defendant in the federal landowners case just three years before. In the end, McFerren was ordered by Fayette County Juvenile Court Judge T.V. Luck to pay numerous court costs and paternity fees, including $150 to Wilder for his legal representation of Mrs. Frazier.

Not satisfied with the damage the successful suit had on McFerren's reputation and financial stability, Wilder slowly implemented the next phase in his plan. Based on his interviews with Holmes, it was McFerren's furious claim that Wilder began sidling up to Viola, John McFerren's wife, by way of the couple's gas station business telephone. Growing up a privileged young boy in the Wilder home, John Shelton no doubt learned several powerful lessons from his father John Chamblee. One of the lessons most certainly stressed by the elder Wilder was the potential control an educated white man could wield over an illiterate black man. Emulating his uncle and father's cunning ability to swindle land from African-American farmers who were academically ill-equipped to understand the contractual documents they were signing, Wilder knew he could weaken the illiterate McFerren's ability to function by driving a wedge between him and his academically astute wife, Viola.

The issue of Wilder's incessant phone calls became so heated that McFerren, at one point, asked his contacts at the DOJ to "bug" his store's telephone in an attempt to record the powerful attorney's discussions with Viola. Yet, in spite of Mr. McFerren's best efforts to thwart Wilder's ongoing manipulations, the highly influential attorney's coaxing eventually worked. Already weakened by the impact of the physical and emotional separation the McFerren couple experienced in the years following Dr. King's murder in 1968, Viola eventually succumbed to Wilder's suggestive power and filed for divorce by the mid-1970s.

McFerren also confided in Holmes that, within the midst of his extensive legal battle with his estranged wife, Viola was assisted by Wilder in her attempts at obtaining total ownership of the couple's shared gas and grocery business. It was McFerren's belief that this was, in fact, the last phase in Wilder's plan to utterly destroy his financial independence and personal strength. While McFerren was able to retain sole possession of his Fayette County enterprise, Wilder continued to coddle Viola and her children under the warmth and comfort of his paternalistic wing, and in 1980, the McFerrens' divorce was finalized.

Many years before McFerren's divorce, however, the Democratic candidate from Fayette County finally regained his senate seat in the Tennessee General Assembly. But Wilder's 1966 campaign and ultimate victory was marred by suspicion and controversy. In one of the rare occasions the authors divulged a provocative event in the lieutenant governor's political past, Professors Stanley and French wrote in their 2007 Wilder biography:

The controversy over this primary election emerged when 136 stolen ballots were found on the McNairy River in McNairy County. To the Lieutenant Governor's recollection, C.E. Pattal, Jr., Sheriff of Fayette County at this time, and Paul Summers, General Sessions Judge, were informed that the McNairy county voting precinct had failed to report the voting results for the 1966 Democratic Primary therefore causing a delay in the official calculation of the vote. The precinct directly informed both the Sheriff and the General Sessions Judge that someone had "taken" the ballot boxes before an official count could be made. After a brief visit to the voting site by Pattal, and Summers, a search took place and the ballet [sic] box was miraculously found in some bushes on the McNairy River, adding 136 votes to John Wilder's lead in his primary win over opponent William S. Cobb.

Immediately after reading the mysterious circumstances surrounding the recovery of the 1966 ballot boxes, a number of items popped into Stephens' mind. Besides the story's striking resemblance to the 1948 Texas controversy in which Democratic candidate Lyndon Baines Johnson miraculously won his U.S. Senate seat after the discovery of 200 additional ballots in the now-infamous "Box 13," Stephens also noted some familiar names in the narrative.

In addition to Judge Paul Summers Sr., the same Judge Summers who was named as a defendant in the federal landowners' case and by McFerren in his secret tapes, Stephens recognized a misspelled reference to the Fayette County sheriff. While Stanley and French wrote that it was "Pattal" who helped track down the McNairy County ballot boxes, Stephens knew the sheriff's name to be Pattat, the very same Sheriff C.E. Pattat Jr. who assisted the FBI in their clandestine spying operation on Tent City. Having a fairly thorough knowledge of the close working relationship and camaraderie that Wilder shared with Summers and Pattat at the time, the story helped confirm in some small way Stephens' growing understanding of Wilder's brazen willingness to conspire with others in the illicit pursuit of power. However, the 2007 narrative concerning Wilder's affinity for dirty politics would not be the only confirmation Stephens came across.

According to an elderly woman who spoke to Stephens during his investigation, Wilder was able to maintain his seat in the Tennessee General Assembly for the next several decades due to a rather unusual method of pandering to his African-American voting base. In an unrelated project Stephens became involved in, he met an elderly woman who enjoyed volunteering for social causes she deemed as important. After getting to know the kind woman, she agreed to babysit Stephens' daughter. In passing, he mentioned his Wilder research to the woman. As it turned out, Stephens' new friend was a former campaign worker for Lt. Gov. John Shelton Wilder, and she wanted to share a story.

It was the woman's assertion that as part of her campaign duties several years before, she was instructed by her superiors to deliver thick envelopes to the homes of various African-American ministers within Wilder's multi-county West Tennessee district. However, it disturbed her that she was specifically told to make the deliveries at extremely late hours in the evening, long after most people had gone to bed. Despite her apprehension at the time, she looked past the odd instructions and did what she was asked. But she explained to Stephens that later on, after giving the matter some serious consideration, she believed she was unknowingly delivering large sums of cash to the black ministers in an effort to bribe them. It was her belief that these ministers, having great influence over their all-black congregations, would then firmly encourage said churchgoers to vote for Wilder.

Stephens was dismayed but not surprised. He found the gentle woman to be both truthful and completely convincing. Flashing an immediate, somewhat nervous smile, the woman concluded her story by sweetly demanding that Stephens never mention her name in connection with the allegation, to which he agreed. But it was difficult for him not to consider some of the well-known African-American pastors in Fayette County as being possible recipients of Wilder's rather large tithes, specifically a notoriously corrupt Somerville minister and Wilder ally named Connie Wright. It had long been claimed by those who were close to the county's backwater underworld that, despite the politically-protected Wright's superficial Christian piety, he was, in fact, a small-time gangster who greedily and quietly dealt in illegal local rackets.

As his investigation dragged on, Stephens continued to hunt down various, admittedly small, bits of information that corroborated Wilder's fondness for using political strong-arm tactics and illegal backroom deals to achieve his goals. But by 2004, the aging Wilder's mind along with his well-crafted reputation was beginning to slip. According to a May 4 article in *The Tennessean* newspaper, several attendees at a public meeting were angered over an unguarded comment made by the guest-speaking lieutenant governor in which he stated, "Affirmative action has helped blacks and women find jobs at the expense of some whites." Although the comment was viewed by most as both racist and sexist, it was Viola McFerren who quickly came to Wilder's defense. In the same newspaper article detailing Wilder's bigoted remarks, John McFerren's ex-wife was interviewed and said in reference to the state senator, "I know a lot of African Americans who have found him to be helpful."

Then in 2005, allegations over Wilder's financial interest in an industrial "mega-site" real estate and construction project within the borders of Fayette County brought even more unwanted attention to the elderly senator. Finally, in 2007, the Tennessee General Assembly deemed it necessary, and therefore voted, to remove Wilder from the lieutenant governor's position. By the end of 2008, Faytte County's favorite son had left public office completely and on January 1, 2010, John Shelton Wilder took his final breath, never to bother John McFerren again. As of the writing of this book, the bronze bust of the former senator and lieutenant governor still sits on permanent display in the rotunda of the Fayette County Courthouse just yards from the office where Wilder used to practice law.

Conclusions and Questions

To Randall Stephens, the evidence was clear: Lt. Gov. John Shelton Wilder was, without question, a deceitful, unethical, racist politician who stopped at nothing to accumulate and maintain massive concentrations of power. Judging by Wilder's numerous fabrications and collaboration with other government authorities in illicit activities, Stephens could only conclude that the lieutenant governor did whatever he deemed as personally necessary to achieve his self-serving goals. Along with his likely 1966 participation in the stolen ballot box controversy, the Fayette County lawyer intimidated his outspoken political opponents, made illegal closed-door deals, and bribed his voters. With the support of his well-organized white power base in Somerville and Nashville, in addition to his bought-and-paid-for black constituency in West Tennessee, "The Governor" remained in office far longer than any other duly elected governor of the Volunteer State, therefore consolidating more political strength than any other state official who served during Wilder's own thirty-six-year reign.

Despite the local culture's popular portrayal of Wilder as the lone advocate of racial equality, the elder statesman was, in fact, a quiet proponent of racial segregation. What's more, not only did he view African Americans as mere commodities to be harnessed and exploited for his benefit, but he exhibited a cruel willingness and ability to destroy black leaders who would not submit to his authority, particularly John McFerren. And in an effort to appeal to his unwitting black voters while also ensuring his enduring legacy as the kindhearted descendant of uniquely forward-thinking white men, Wilder also helped rewrite his own family's history within the pages of numerous news articles and his 2007 biography. It wasn't until his mental faculties began to falter that the elderly state senator's previously restrained beliefs began to creep from his bitterly dried lips.

To label Wilder a narcissist or megalomaniac was far from hyperbole. Undoubtedly, Fayette County's favorite son fit the profile of someone who would have both desired and participated in the removal of an uncontrollably vocal African-American civil rights leader like Dr. Martin Luther King Jr. But this simple psychological sketch was far from proof that Wilder had anything to do with the 1968 assassination of Dr. King. Stephens' mind continued to stir. Who was Wilder socially and politically aligned with throughout his life? Could he be tied to any major suspects who were already named in other investigations? And how was the powerful senator able to keep the DOJ out of Fayette County's public school system until 2010? Stephens needed to dig even deeper.

Chapter 11

ALL DIRT HOLES LEAD TO WILDER

RANDALL STEPHENS HAD sculpted a relatively clear profile of Lt. Gov. John Shelton Wilder, but it was just the beginning. While he firmly believed that the former senator from Fayette County was more than capable of orchestrating a conspiracy to murder Dr. Martin Luther King Jr., what Stephens observed up to that point was by no means evidence, not even circumstantial. Perhaps he could discover more by confirming Wilder's past associations with several well-known names that had been brought up by John McFerren and other MLK researchers and authors. Based on the repeated tips McFerren provided, Marcus Holmes' own past research, and the public information readily available, Stephens started the next phase of his Wilder investigation with the number one suspected conspirator on everyone's list.

Frank C. Liberto

As he had reiterated to Holmes on countless occasions, it was McFerren's staunch belief that Somerville Attorney John Wilder was both the legal counsel and confidant of Memphis organized crime figure Frank C. Liberto. But what was the evidence? While New York attorney and author Bill Pepper meekly hinted at McFerren's claims about the Wilder and Liberto connection in the pages of *Orders to Kill*, McFerren also thoroughly detailed his assertions to Holmes between 2012 and 2015. In an effort to corroborate his elderly friend's claims, Holmes conducted his own inquiry.

Interestingly, McFerren's research partner could not find a single newspaper clipping nor a Memphis headstone that referenced the 1978 Frank Liberto death date Pepper firmly asserted in his authored work. And while Holmes did uncover a 1996 Memphis obituary for one Frank Liberto, just as Pepper had led McFerren to believe during the *King v. Jowers* trial, it was not for Frank C., but instead for Frank H., the Memphis car dealer who made a name for himself as the most successful Ford salesman in the country. Undaunted, Holmes proceeded with his efforts to confirm Wilder's multi-decade connection to Frank C. Liberto.

McFerren had long claimed that T.R. "Tommy" Wright, a former member of the local African-American underground, informed him that Liberto would regularly drive from Memphis to Somerville on Saturdays to meet with Wilder at the attorney's law office on the east side of the town square. In addition, it was claimed that Hughie Ragan, McFerren's former divorce lawyer based in Jackson, Tennessee, could confirm that Wilder had a personal fondness for rubbing elbows with Memphis Italian Americans who were less than savory in nature. In McFerren's words, "Ragan knew Wilder had ties to the Mafias." But by 2012, Mr. Ragan had been deceased for eight years, and T.R. Wright was nowhere to be found. Fortunately for

Holmes, McFerren was able to put him in touch with another person who was still breathing and could confirm the Wilder and Liberto connection.

Robert Lee Bell

In the midst of their intense 2012 MLK collaboration, McFerren introduced Holmes to a sixty-five-year-old African-American man from Memphis named Robert Lee Bell. Having lost one of his legs to diabetes, Bell maneuvered his wheelchair into McFerren's business one day to repay its proprietor some money he had borrowed. Just by chance, Holmes was also in the room at the time to observe the two men's quick financial transaction. As soon as Bell wheeled himself out of the building to be driven back to Memphis by his sister, McFerren blurted out to Holmes, "Now that's someone you should talk to." Following his mentor's advice, Holmes eventually met with the obliging one-legged man and spent several subsequent days interviewing him.

Bell was a teenager when he, his mother, and his young sisters were all kicked out of their tenant farming home in Grand Junction, Tennessee, during the Tent City era. Presiding as the unofficial mayor over the African-American encampment, John McFerren welcomed Robert and his family into the protective embrace of the local exiled community, providing them with much-needed food, warmth, and shelter. But only a few years later, a now-adult Robert Bell, disgruntled by the oppressiveness of the area's rural racism and economic hardships, moved out of Fayette County in search of a quick dollar. It didn't take him long to find what he was looking for in Memphis's nearby black market underworld, and one of the leaders of that underworld was none other than Frank C. Liberto.

Among the numerous audio recorded interviews he willingly conducted with Holmes, Bell claimed that in the summer of 1967,

Liberto instructed him and a fellow African-American lackey named Willie Green to drive to an abandoned cotton gin in Only, Tennessee, to pick up a white hitchhiker. Bell said that when they arrived in Only, "he thought the white man was so hungry, he might eat the covers right off the car seats." Following their boss's instructions, Bell and Green transported the man back to the Memphis Scott Street market and delivered him to Liberto.

Bell also explained that sometime in early 1968, Liberto ordered him to pick up a red Ford Mustang parked at a local car dealership. It was Bell's claim that he was then instructed to have the red Mustang painted white, which he did so with the assistance of a young local boy nicknamed "Mutt." As Bell's story goes, both he and Mutt hand painted the entire vehicle using nothing but spray cans, crude paint brushes, and simple latex paint. It wasn't until after the murder of Dr. King on April 4 that Bell realized the man he had chauffeured from Only to Liberto's Scott Street warehouse in Memphis was James Earl Ray, and that the recently-painted Mustang was most likely a decoy getaway car used in the initial seconds following the murder.

Bell then stated that in 1984, he was involved in a federal interstate theft case in which the FBI caught him illegally transporting several pallets of Frosted Flakes cereal boxes across state lines. According to Bell, the cereal in question had been stolen from Memphis's local Kellogg's manufacturing plant at the direction of Liberto. It was also Bell's contention that immediately after his arrest, he was visited by a Fayette County attorney who asked him what his "plans" were for the upcoming trial. Bell said he instinctively understood what the attorney was cryptically implying and then reassured him that he would keep his mouth shut and take the wrap for the stolen goods without implicating his Scott Street boss. Bell concluded his account to Holmes by stating that the attorney who visited him in jail that day was John Shelton Wilder.

Holmes was elated. Not only had he met and recorded an independent witness who could corroborate Liberto's relationship with Wilder, but Bell also confirmed Liberto's employment of Ray. Then there was the ever-present question of when Liberto died. If Frank C. indeed sent his Somerville lawyer to speak with Bell in 1984, then that meant that the infamous Scott Street produce dealer was most certainly alive several years after the 1978 death Pepper claimed in his book. Even more interesting, Bell went on to state that Bill Pepper himself, in search of information on Liberto, came to visit him sometime after 1986 while he recuperated in the hospital from his leg amputation.

Holmes considered the matter further. Why was there no mention of Robert Bell or his incredible story in Pepper's book? Then the answer hit him like a bolt of lightning. Once again, the sly New York attorney and author had to hide the truth from the general public regarding Liberto, Wilder, and their potential connection to Ray.

Fayette County Judge Paul R. Summers Sr.

Besides Rube Rhea, another Gulf Oil distributor and lofty member of Fayette's white establishment was Somerville attorney and county judge Paul R. Summers Sr. Like John Wilder, I.P. Yancey, and Rube Rhea, Summers had been named as a defendant in the 1960 Tent City landowners case. He also played a mysteriously key role in finding the stolen ballot boxes that helped Wilder regain his senate seat in 1966. In addition, McFerren had implicated the judge as one of the financiers of the 1969 Anderson and McNeil beating. But most importantly, Judge Summers was an extremely close friend of John Wilder. Both men practiced law in the tightly-knit country town of Somerville, each were wealthy land and business owners in Fayette County, and both were heavily involved in assisting the other in achieving their individual political ambitions. One might say the two men were like brothers. In a two-hour video-taped interview conducted on July 9, 1999, by his adult son, Judge Paul G. Summers Jr., the elder Judge R. Summers Sr. himself stated that John Wilder was "one of the closest friends I got."

That's why it didn't surprise Stephens when Holmes told him that John McFerren believed Summers had some periphery involvement in the King case. In search of clues pointing to Summers' involvement, Stephens forced himself into the shadowy trenches of Pepper's book once again to see if the crafty author had alluded to anything that might corroborate McFerren's claim. In the twenty-second chapter of *Orders to Kill*, Pepper did indeed write:

> Rosenson also stated that prior to an HSCA interview in Richmond, he was visited by a big man who told him he should admit to having known James when asked. It would solve many problems. Rosenson said he refused. The man was introduced to him as a high-level Tennessee state official.

Based on various reports, James Earl Ray stated that, sometime before the April 4 murder, he found a business card stuffed inside a cigarette pack near the passenger side floorboard of his 1966 Ford Mustang. Ray examined the business card and claimed that it had Randy Rosenson's name written on the back of it. It was theorized several years later by Ray and his series of lawyers that Rosenson could have had prior knowledge of the conspiracy and assisted in setting Ray up as the patsy. Rosenson was, therefore, located and subsequently entangled in the HSCA's investigation between 1976 and 1978.

Interestingly, Pepper also wrote in his 1995 book that the "high-level Tennessee state official" who tried to pressure Rosenson during the HSCA investigation was the same "high-level Tennessee state official" who regularly met with Frank Liberto in Fayette County. In chapter twenty-seven, Pepper again wrote:

He [McFerren] said that he recalled hearing from a local man, Tommy Wright, that on Saturday mornings Liberto would meet with a high-level Tennessee state official at his law office in Fayette County. Tommy said that they would meet regularly on Saturday mornings. Alarm bells went off. I recalled that Randy Rosenson had insisted that in 1978, around the time of his interviews by HSCA staff, he had been visited by the same high-level Tennessee state official, who tried to get him to say that he had been acquainted with James Earl Ray.

In other words, Pepper, without actually naming him, claimed that it was John Wilder who tried to get Rosenson to admit to knowing Ray. However, despite this seemingly clear-cut connection, Rosenson did refer to the high-level official as being a "big man." What did "big man" mean? Was it in reference to the elevated position the unnamed official held in Tennessee state government or was Rosenson making a claim about the official's physical appearance? Stephens grappled with the issue.

Wilder was, by no stretch of the imagination, a physically "big man," but his best friend in Somerville, Paul R. Summers, was indeed. By all accounts, Judge Summers was an extremely tall individual who commanded a physically dominating presence of authority whenever he stepped into the courtroom. Also, by the end of October 1976, the same time the HSCA was kicking off, Summers had been named as executive secretary of the Tennessee Supreme Court, making him a high-level Tennessee state official from Fayette County. Since naming Summers in his 1995 book would have been tantamount to naming Wilder, could it be that the fearful Pepper fused Wilder and Summers' roles together, merging the individual friends into the same anonymous "high-level Tennessee state official" from Fayette County as a means of simplifying the book's narrative or throwing its future readers off?

Finally, Stephens considered the implications: If Wilder did, in fact, send Summers on an errand to pressure Rosenson into confessing to knowing Ray, then what was his motive for doing so? But just as quickly as the question popped into Stephens' mind, so did the answer. Because Wilder was the legal counsel of Frank Liberto and personal friend of I.P. Yancey during the HSCA's nosey investigation, and the Somerville attorney needed to secretly put distance between Ray and the other conspirators at the time, it is likely Wilder sent Summers to force an admission out of Rosenson as a way of covering up Yancey and Liberto's roles as the true handlers of Ray.

Somerville Mayor I.P. Yancey

He had already committed a significant amount of personal energy looking into the mayor's background, but in his gut, Stephens knew there was much more to Isaac Perkins Yancey than appeared on the fluffy-white surface. As outlined previously, the area's longest-reigning mayor was a Chevrolet dealership owner and board director at the Somerville Bank and Trust Company. Not only was the town's leading public official named as a defendant in the federal Tent City landowners case along with John Wilder, Rube Rhea, and Paul Summers, but Yancey was quoted in the previously-mentioned 1960 *Ebony* magazine article as saying:

> We sell to both niggers and white folks [and] there are more niggers in this county than whites and we just have to do business with them or we aren't in business. What we're afraid of is some unscrupulous politician getting the majority group together and upsetting the welfare of our county—electing a nigger law-enforcement officer for example...

In addition to Yancey's well-known concerns regarding Fayette County's local economy, public safety, and racial pecking order, he was implicated in McFerren's 1970 secret audio recordings as the primary financial backer and ringleader in the 1969 assault carried out by the Anderson brothers and W.C. McNeil. But most crucial to Stephens' investigation was Yancey's potential ties to John Wilder and James Earl Ray.

It should be repeated that Yancey, according to McFerren's recorded informants, allegedly hosted Ray at his Somerville dealership on April 2, 1968. Several individuals claimed that Ray's Springtime Yellow (cream-colored) 1966 Ford Mustang was spotted at Yancey's Chevrolet garage on the evening in question. It was also stated by McFerren's friend and informant Karl Mosby that Mosby's mother, Mrs. Edna Coe, became aware that Yancey visited London without any apparent reason in both March and May of 1968. Then, after trying to explain Yancey's role to the DOJ and HSCA, McFerren was either ignored or silenced. And of course, Stephens' had to also factor in the added intrigue behind Bill Pepper's obvious unwillingness to make both the existence and content of McFerren's Yancey and Ray recordings a matter of public record.

As Stephens' research continued, he eventually confirmed the mayor's professional and personal relationship with Somerville attorney and Tennessee State Senator John Wilder. As verified by historical documentation, Yancey worked alongside Wilder's first cousin, Somerville Bank and Trust Company President James H. "Preacher" Shelton, as a ranking member of the bank's board of directors, and Wilder himself sat on the very same board with Yancey. Also, upon interviewing Yancey's adult son and daughter, Stephens learned that the senator and mayor were, in fact, good friends. Stephens now had to consider the tremendous pressure Wilder must've been under as the friend and legal advisor to both

Liberto and Yancey, each of whom aided and abetted Dr. King's alleged assassin, James Earl Ray. But Wilder and Yancey's friendship was not the only important connection. Stephens also verified that both the Somerville mayor and Fayette County senator socialized from time to time with Memphis's own top city official.

Memphis Mayor Henry Loeb

Almost from the moment Dr. King's life was selfishly taken from him by an assassin's bullet, rumors swirled that Memphis Mayor Henry Loeb participated in the alleged conspiracy. Today, those rumors are more widespread than ever. It has been charged by many, specifically those inside the pro-conspiracy research community, that Mayor Loeb purposely prolonged the heated negotiations between the city and its striking African-American sanitation workers as a way of keeping Dr. King in Memphis to be murdered. But aside from the conspiracy theories, it is a documented fact that the Memphis mayor held the same social and racial beliefs as the majority of whites who called West Tennessee home at the time.

Just as Wilder had successfully achieved with Fayette County's African-American community by the mid-1960s, Loeb also believed he could convince the nearly all-black sanitation employees in Memphis to return to work through a form of paternalistic cajolery. But his use of the benevolent father figure role did not work. Unlike Wilder's successful sidling maneuvers in neighboring Fayette County, Loeb's plantation-era-like efforts were staunchly resisted, and the defiant city workers stood their ground. The proud sanitation employees, under the leadership of group organizer Thomas Oliver "T.O." Jones, refused to return to work until their new union was recognized and their demands were met by Loeb. The African-American workers continued to wear their "I AM A MAN" placards as they picketed up and down the streets of downtown Memphis. And as the heaps of unattended garbage rose throughout the increasingly putrid city, so did the area's social and racial tensions.

In one iconic black-and-white photograph taken during the upheaval, the wooden stock of a long-barrel firearm can be seen peeking out from underneath Loeb's city hall desk as he shakes hands with unassuming African-American leaders from the local community. And during what would be his final public speech at a packed sanctuary in Memphis, the visiting Dr. King denounced the city's stubbornly racist, anti-union mayor. On the stormy night of April 3, 1968, at the Church of God in Christ headquarters inside Mason Temple, the iconic civil rights leader took a personal jab at Memphis's leading official by stating, "Mayor Loeb is in dire need of a doctor."

But by the time the shooting of Dr. King occurred at the Lorraine Motel the following evening, Mayor Loeb had already been in close communication with a number of other leading law enforcement and government officials who were also eventually suspected of orchestrating the conspiracy and subsequent cover-up. Among these officials were Loeb's handpicked Memphis Police and Fire Director Frank C. Holloman, the same Frank Holloman who most likely suppressed the Liberto and Ray account John McFerren gave at the Peabody Hotel on April 8, 1968. Shelby County Sheriff William N. Morris Jr., who supervised James Earl Ray's controversial jail accommodations between July of 1968 and March of 1969, was in constant contact with Loeb and Holloman and also suspected of being loosely complicit in the post-assassination cover-up. Finally, Loeb and Holloman were both in direct communication at the same time with Tennessee Governor Buford Ellington, another potential conspirator.

Stephens once again considered John McFerren's 1978 affidavit to the HSCA in which he stated that Somerville Mayor I.P. Yancey was "a friend of former-Mayor Loeb of Memphis." As outlined earlier, the meticulous researcher quickly located a September 16, 1960

Jackson Sun newspaper article that confirmed Loeb and Yancey's simultaneous attendance at the West Tennessee Mayor's Day Dinner. But more importantly, Stephens eventually came across an obscure, yet telling, personal communication between Loeb and Fayette County's favorite son. In a January 19, 1971 letter mailed to the Nashville office of the Honorable John S. Wilder, the Memphis mayor wrote:

Dear John:

I thought the enclosure was a real accolade to you, and that you might want an extra copy thereof. Don't forget my previous, and when you are in Memphis, and have a chance, please give me a call. Congratulations on what was written about you. Sincere best wishes.

Yours truly, Henry Loeb

It was obvious to Stephens upon reading the authentic archived letter that Loeb had found some kind of article or public statement recognizing Wilder's new appointment to the lieutenant governor's position by the Tennessee General Assembly, and therefore wanted to send him a copy. But more than that, the letter was a revealing piece of history that pointed to Loeb's personal kinship with Wilder. Clearly, the two men had forged some kind of mutual admiration and first name bond prior to Wilder's January 1971 ascension to the second-highest position in Tennessee state government.

But at the same time Senator Wilder was being congratulated by Mayor Loeb for his new seat inside the Tennessee General Assembly, another southern Democrat and well-connected politician in Nashville was handing over command of the state's top government office.

Tennessee Governor Buford Ellington

Born June 27, 1907, in Holmes County, Mississippi, Earl Buford Ellington began his political career in the mid-1940s as a resident of Marshall County, Tennessee, and by 1948 was himself a General Assembly member in the State House of Representatives. Four years later, in 1952, he managed the gubernatorial campaign of Frank Clement, who went on to become Tennessee's governor for the next six years.

Nearing the end of his combined two-year and four-year terms, Clement prepared to leave office, but not before throwing his public support behind his loyal friend and former campaign manager, Buford Ellington. On January 19, 1959, Ellington began his own first four-year term as the governor of the Volunteer State. By January of 1971, Governor Ellington had served two, four-year terms, having been simultaneously succeeded and preceded by his friend Frank Clement in between the state's mandatory four-year break from January 1963 to January 1967.

Stephens had heard rumblings before from other authors about Ellington's possible involvement in the 1968 MLK conspiracy and cover-up, but he was highly skeptical. Could something as heinous as conspiring to murder a man in cold blood reach the heights of the governor's mansion in Nashville? Determined to inspect every dirty rabbit hole he came across, Stephens burrowed in. It wasn't long before the Fayette County fact-finder located a newspaper clipping linking Ellington to John Shelton Wilder as early as the 1950s. According to the article printed in *The Tennessean* on December 2, 1953, the Tennessee State Commissioner of Agriculture, Buford Ellington, met with the Supervisor of Fayette County's Soil Conservation District, John Wilder. However, his 1953 meeting with Fayette's favorite son wasn't the only important political relationship Ellington forged throughout the 1950s.

As illustrated by a black-and-white photograph of the three men touring Tennessee's Union Carbide-managed Oak Ridge National Laboratory in 1958, Ellington eventually met with and befriended Tennessee Democrat and U.S. Senator Albert Gore Sr. as well as Texas Democrat and U.S. Senator Lyndon Baines Johnson. Over the next several years, Ellington and Johnson formed a deeply personal and politically powerful bond. So much so that during Ellington's gubernatorial hiatus from 1963 to 1967, then-President Johnson appointed him in 1965 as the Director of the Office of Emergency Planning in Washington, D.C.

Then, after faithfully serving President L.B.J. until 1966, Ellington stepped back into the Tennessee governor's mansion on January 16, 1967, to begin his second four-year term. But after his close coordination with Mayor Henry Loeb and Director Frank Holloman during the 1968 civil unrest in nearby Memphis, Governor Ellington was facing a major problem by March of the following year. According to John Avery Emison's book, *The Martin Luther King Congressional Cover-Up: The Railroading of James Earl Ray*, Tennessee State Commissioner of Corrections Harry S. Avery (a relative of Emison's) took it upon himself to investigate the now-imprisoned James Earl Ray and his role in the possible conspiracy to murder Dr. King.

But when word reached Ellington of Avery's unsanctioned 1969 pet project, the governor warned his corrections commissioner to cease and desist. Defiant of the governor's mandate, Avery continued digging into Ray's possible past involvement, and after a two-month scandal that involved intentional leaks to the local news media by the governor and an official inquiry headed up by the Tennessee Bureau of Investigation/TBI, Ellington fired Avery on May 29, 1969. It was Avery's later assertion that, during his unpopular investigation, the incarcerated Ray received several questionable letters through the prison mail that were deemed as "significant." Among the list of letters and corresponding postmarks described in Emison's book, one, in particular, jumped out at Stephens, one from New Orleans, Louisiana. This was not the first time Stephens had seen Ellington's name written in connection with The Big Easy.

In Governor Winfield Dunn's autobiography, entitled *From a Standing Start* (another book about Tennessee state politics), Stephens remembered reading about Dunn's recollection of a flight he took from Nashville to New Orleans. It was Dunn's assertion that just before he took office in mid-January, he was encouraged by outgoing Governor Buford Ellington to fly to New Orleans to watch the January 1, 1971 Sugar Bowl pig-skin game between the Air Force Falcons and University of Tennessee Volunteers.

After offering Dunn and his wife the use of the state's private gubernatorial airplane, Ellington also suggested that Dunn use the trip to get to know the leaders of both the state House and Senate, which at the time were House Speaker-elect James O. McKinney and Senate Speaker-elect John Wilder. In Dunn's autobiography, he included a curious description that stuck with Stephens. The former governor stated in his book that, after he and his wife invited McKinney, Wilder, and both of the men's spouses to join them on the trip:

> Both parties accepted and joined us for the flight down and back. Our time together consisted of that spent on the airplane and little more, since every party went its separate way while in New Orleans.

If the New Orleans flight and college football game was meant to be a political and social mixer, Stephens wondered why every party went its separate way once the airplane landed. Was that a choice made by only Dunn, McKinney, or Wilder, or did everyone agree to part ways until the return flight home? And what were Wilder and his wife Marcelle doing when not in the presence of the other two couples? Did Ellington use the official, government-funded trip as a way of quietly sending Wilder on a personal post-assassination errand? Whatever the case, the city of New Orleans had, once more, reared its colorfully intriguing head.

In addition to Frank Liberto's mention of the same city during his telephone conversations on April 4, 1968, and the indirect link discovered by the HSCA between Frank's brother and Carlos Marcello in New Orleans, McFerren also claimed that the elusive Robert Powers owned a truck stop there. Next, Stephens eventually discovered that Ray visited New Orleans at least twice just before the murder of Dr. King, while John Emison's book claimed that the imprisoned scapegoat received a "significant" letter from there in early 1969. Finally, a newly-elected Governor Dunn was encouraged by a departing Governor Ellington to arrange for John Wilder to travel to New Orleans on January 1, 1971. Little did Stephens know at the time, New Orleans, second only to West Tennessee, would go on to become one of the major focal points of his entire MLK investigation.

On April 3, 1972, just one day shy of the four-year anniversary of Dr. King's senseless murder in Memphis, the recently retired Governor Ellington passed away. During the stately processions that followed, Tennessee Lt. Gov. John Wilder attended the ceremonial departure of Ellington's casket, and former President Lyndon Johnson himself made an unannounced appearance at his old friend's funeral at the Lone Oak Cemetery in Lewisburg, Tennessee. However, there was one final historical item Stephens wanted to look into when it came to the relationship between President Johnson and Governor Ellington.

While still occupying the Oval Office in early 1965, President Johnson found it difficult to contact segregationist Governor George C. Wallace at the start of the civil rights marches led by Dr. King's SCLC staff in Selma, Alabama. Unable to track down a worthy intermediary between the White House and the Alabama governor's mansion in Montgomery, Johnson turned to his close friend and Wallace's former neighboring governor, Buford Ellington. On March 8, 1965, a day after the violent "Bloody Sunday" civil rights clash on the Edmund Pettus Bridge in Selma, Johnson called Ellington to ask if he would contact Wallace and negotiate calm over the racially heated chaos that had overtaken the Alabama city.

Stephens was again transported back to one of John McFerren's documented claims. At the time of his 1976 interview with the DOJ, McFerren made the simple statement that "Wallace was in on it" in reference to the Alabama governor's possible role in the conspiracy to murder his hated adversary, Dr. Martin Luther King Jr. Stephens quickly unearthed a *Tennessean* newspaper article dated July 14, 1956, confirming the simultaneous appearance of both Democratic party regulars, George Wallace and Buford Ellington, at an intimately small political gathering held in Atlanta, Georgia. But beyond the obvious notion that Governors Ellington and Wallace were longtime political allies prior to the 1968 shooting, could the somewhat eye-rolling remark made by the humble country grocer have any merit to it? Stephens began his journey down yet another squalid rabbit hole.

Alabama Governor George C. Wallace

On January 14, 1963, the newly elected Democratic governor of Alabama, George C. Wallace, stood on the steps of the State Capitol building in Montgomery and proudly proclaimed during his inaugural speech, "segregation now, segregation tomorrow, and segregation forever!" Then, on June 11 of that same year, Governor Wallace stood defiantly in the doorway of the Foster Auditorium on the University of Alabama campus. As a symbolic gesture in defense of his prior segregationist vow, Wallace temporarily blocked the entry of Vivian Malone and James Hood, two African-American students who wished to register for classes at the all-white university. Throughout the next several years, Governor Wallace continued to place himself at the epicenter of a number of racial firestorms, one of which included his public refusal to protect Dr. King and the enormous crowd of civil rights activists who eventually marched from Selma to the state capitol building in Montgomery between March 21 and 25th of 1965.

But specific to the MLK murder investigation, Stephens learned that James Earl Ray, while hiding out in California, was an unofficial volunteer for Wallace's U.S. presidential campaign in late 1967. Stephens found it strange that Ray, a convicted thief who had just escaped from a Missouri state prison, chose to draw attention to himself by publicly advocating for the election of a political candidate to the White House. Nevertheless, numerous authors and historians have since theorized Ray was convinced that, after his planned shooting of King, he would be pardoned by a future President Wallace, and therefore tossed caution to the wind by vocally promoting the Southern racist's political bid.

Was this simple tidbit of historical trivia what McFerren was referring to in 1976? Was the Fayette grocer's belief that "Wallace was in on it" based merely on Ray's well-known desire to see Alabama's leading government official elected to the Oval Office? Surely, Stephens thought, there had to be more to McFerren's bold, somewhat embarrassing assertion. Unbeknownst to Stephens at that moment, it was his own lack of faith in McFerren's knowledge that would ultimately become a source of embarrassment.

After a tremendous amount of research, a deluge of previously unseen circumstantial evidence finally flooded in, placing Wallace in extremely close contact with one of Stephens' primary suspects in the conspiracy to murder Dr. King. Stephens' first, admittedly inane clue was an innocent 1972 photograph published in *The Jackson Sun* newspaper. The black-and-white photo illustrated a visiting Governor Wallace speaking before the Tennessee House of Representatives with Lt. Gov. John Wilder standing in the background. The next item Stephens found was a photo of a wheelchair-bound Governor Wallace shaking hands with a smiling John Wilder in 1975. But there was more, much more. While looking into the potential Wallace and Wilder connection, Stephens was ultimately shocked to discover that Wilder's second son, David Morton Wilder, had become business partners with George Wallace's son-in-law, James Thomas Parsons, beginning sometime in 1977 or most likely before.

Barely dodging a previous 1977 FBI probe into possible acts of bribery and misuse of his father's government influence, David Wilder went on to ink a multimillion-dollar deal that same year with Parsons that also fell under heavy public scrutiny. As a March 23, 1983, *United Press International* news article would later reveal, the young Wilder and Parsons were accused of misusing the political power of Parson's father-in-law, Governor George C. Wallace, to obtain state permits in 1977 that allowed for the construction and operation of their Emelle, Alabama-based hazardous disposal facility, Resource Industries of Alabama, Inc. As a twenty-four percent shareholder in the controversial toxic waste site, David went on to gross millions in royalties. Today, the youngest son of John Wilder has parlayed his toxic dump fortune into several other business ventures throughout the Mid-South, and his former Resource Industries of Alabama, Inc. is listed as a previous donor to the University of Memphis, the same college that now brandishes the name of David's father on the campus's tallest building.

Besides David's privileged ability to utilize his father's past political connections to accumulate large sums of wealth, the extremely close relationship between the Wilders and the Wallaces gave Stephens a moment of serious pause. Not only was Tennessee Governor Buford Ellington on a first name basis with Alabama Governor George Wallace, but Tennessee Lt. Gov. John Wilder himself most certainly established prior ties to Wallace long before the financially cozy partnership between David Wilder and James Parsons blossomed.

When Stephens revisited the documented timeline, it occurred to him that Ellington and Wilder had become acquainted in December of 1953, nearly three years before Ellington and Wallace met in July of 1956. Did Ellington go on to introduce Wilder to Wallace sometime between 1956 and the late 1960s before Dr. King's death?

Then, as just mentioned, there was the strange affinity James Earl Ray had for Governor Wallace's presidential campaign between 1967 and 1968 to take into account. Also, it was a matter of public record that, prior to the death of Dr. King in April of 1968, Ray resided in Birmingham, Alabama, and purchased both his 1966 Ford Mustang and the alleged murder weapon from there. Additionally, Ray's first set of post-assassination defense attorneys, Arthur Hanes Sr. and Jr., were natives of Birmingham, well-known segregationists, and upper-crust government officials who were friends and political allies of Gov. Wallace. And fueling his growing speculation, Stephens also learned that, among the "significant" 1969 letters Harry Avery claimed Ray received while in prison, one of them was mailed from the same city the alleged killer previously lived in, Birmingham, Alabama. Had John McFerren been right all along? Was Wallace really in on the conspiracy to assassinate Dr. King?

Stephens began to hypothesize that Wilder and Wallace's conspiratorial subordinates inadvertently influenced Ray on a political level while maneuvering him from place to place, therefore turning him into a Wallace-for-President devotee. These clues would not be the last of the astounding Ray, Wallace, and Alabama connections Stephens unearthed.

Attorney Lewis K. Garrison

Immediately after his study of Attorney Lewis K. Garrison's highly questionable cross-examination of John McFerren in 1999, Stephens delved deeper into the background of the longtime Memphis attorney.

Among the portrayals of Garrison's slithery role in the *King v. Jowers* trial, Gerald Posner's *Killing the Dream* and the Stuart Wexler-Larry Hancock book *The Awful Grace of God* each contained narratives that Stephens viewed as being thoroughly accurate. While he disagreed with a great many of the details, arguments, and ultimate conclusions printed in the two books, Stephens believed that both texts provided an honest representation of Garrison's appalling effort to financially benefit by falsely painting his client, Loyd Jowers, as the guilty party in Dr. King's murder. Simply put, Stephens was of the firm opinion that Garrison knowingly promoted his client's manufactured confession in order to partner with Jowers in a future book or motion picture deal.

But what were Garrison's ties to the Mid-South? After only a light scratching of the mucky West Tennessee surface, Stephens discovered that Garrison, a practicing attorney in Memphis for fifty-nine years, had occupied his 100 N. Main Street law office since at least 1982. This confirmed Stephens' earlier belief that Garrison most certainly would have known who all of the Frank Liberto businessmen were in the downtown area, especially if Frank H. passed away in 1996 and Frank C. was still alive in 1984 just as Robert Bell had told Marcus Holmes. This, of course, led Stephens to his next question: Where did Garrison live? Lo and behold, Loyd Jowers' former attorney last resided in Oakland, Tennessee, a mere fifteen-minute drive west of Somerville. Before that, the Pepper collaborator lived in Eads, Tennessee, a town that straddles the border of Shelby and Fayette County. And, as recently as 2017, Garrison occupied an office located at 4550 Highway 64 in Eads, just a few minutes west of Oakland inside Fayette County.

Stephens wondered, with all of the attorney's residential and office addresses in Memphis, Oakland, and Eads, how did Garrison not have a working familiarity of who Frank C. Liberto and John Wilder were? It seemed incredibly unlikely to the MLK researcher that Wilder and Garrison, both attorneys living in the sparsely populated rural area of

Fayette County, would not have known each other. Further, what was the probability that Wilder used that relationship with Garrison to negotiate a deal that kept the real Liberto and Ray conspiracy outside the sphere of solvability? Without question, it was all conjecture, but it was conjecture based on solidly researched facts. Stephens continued to weave the thin threads together.

Attorney Bill Pepper

The same question kept rolling over and over again in Stephens' mind: What was Pepper's motive for skirting the John Wilder issue? With all of the in-person interviews he conducted with McFerren throughout the years, was it conceivable Pepper never once made the 1.6-mile drive north from McFerren's store to John Wilder's Somerville law office? And not only did the New York attorney and author fail to name Wilder as the "high-level Tennessee state official" in his 1995 book, but Pepper never asked McFerren a single question about the lieutenant governor during the 1999 civil trial. What's more, if Lewis Garrison did, in fact, know John Wilder, at least on a neighborly or professional basis, why didn't Pepper use the Fayette County connection to perhaps meet and interview Liberto's alleged lawyer? While he eventually formed some very solid conclusions, Stephens wasn't the first person to ask these questions. Holmes also broached the Wilder subject with Pepper during a face-to-face meeting in September of 2012, a meeting outlined in the next chapter.

Conclusions and Questions

The weighty significance of John McFerren's seldom-heard audiotapes and the need for the long perpetrated cover-up of said recordings by the U.S. government was now even more evident to Stephens. His lengthy burrowing, he felt, had enabled him to connect the multiple dead ends of the John Wilder rabbit holes together, thereby allowing Stephens to reach a rather explosive, albeit uncomplicated conclusion.

It was no secret by 1976 that McFerren had accused Frank C. Liberto of being James Earl Ray's pre-assassination coconspirator. The HSCA was already well aware of this fact when they began their investigation late that year. And by 1977, it would have also been an open secret in Washington, D.C. that Tennessee Lt. Gov. John Wilder was Liberto's legal counsel during the HSCA's inquiry. So when Mark Lane instructed Bill Pepper and Kenneth Herman to mail McFerren's tapes to the DOJ and/or HSCA, Chief Counsel Blakey became instantly petrified. If I.P. Yancey could also be tied to Ray, as McFerren's multiple informants claimed on the recordings, how long would it have taken to also connect the Somerville Mayor to Somerville state senator and lawyer John Wilder, the same lawyer who was representing Liberto?

Furthermore, if Lt. Gov. Wilder was openly implicated by the DOJ and HSCA, then the ruthless Somerville conspirator would have undoubtedly named in short order other high-ranking players. Simply put, the DOJ and HSCA could not possibly allow that publicly disastrous chain of events to occur, nor any official or unofficial investigations to reach that high. The devastating collapse of various beneficial, well-oiled political machines throughout the country, in conjunction with the resulting racial outrage and bloodbath on the already tense urban streets of the United States, would have been catastrophic; hence the past HSCA and current DOJ's multi-decade commitment to keep McFerren's tapes a secret.

This conceivable, extremely basic theory answered yet another question. If MPD Director Frank Holloman and/or rogue members of the FBI field office in Memphis, under the ostensible supervision of the DOJ, were indeed involved in the 1968 conspiracy and/or cover-up, then Wilder would have had dirt on the FBI and DOJ, just as they had dirt on him. It was now extremely clear to Stephens that Wilder leveraged this mutually damning relationship against the DOJ's Civil Rights Division in the decades that followed, thereby keeping the federal attorneys out of Fayette County's racially segregated public school system.

Stephens also concluded that Bill Pepper forged some type of closed-door deal with the Somerville attorney that benefited both men and their individual clients. As explained earlier, Wilder presumably agreed to keep Ray's true role in the plot to kill Dr. King a secret if Pepper vowed never to expose Wilder and Liberto's real connection to the conspiracy. In the years following his initial 2015 investigation, Stephens would go on to discover that among the three separate books Bill Pepper eventually authored on the King case, it was the last publication that specifically named John Wilder as Liberto's attorney, and of course, "bravely" did so only after the lieutenant governor's 2010 death.

Admittedly, he was beginning to see ghosts around every corner. Stephens had to concede that what he was theorizing was, by no means, definitive proof that John Wilder was involved in the murder of Dr. King. Obviously, the lieutenant governor from Fayette County was thoroughly well known by a number of people in various social and political circles. Several of the man's relationships would have been a natural outcropping of his high-profile position and did not necessarily implicate him in a conspiracy. Also, Stephens had to acknowledge the possibility that Wilder's indirect connections in Washington, D.C. through Governor Ellington were at the root of his later power in keeping the DOJ out of Fayette County's public schools.

But as exhaustive as his research had been up to that moment, Stephens would continue to unearth flabbergasting links between Wilder and other players in the Dr. Martin Luther King case. One name, in particular, continued to dart in and out of Stephens' investigation until the very end, a name associated not only with Wilder, but with Robert Hamburger, Attorney General Janet Reno, and John McFerren himself.

Chapter 12

SUSPECTED SHOOTER

DESPITE JOHN McFERREN'S unyielding belief that James Earl Ray was involved with Frank C. Liberto, Mayor I.P. Yancey, and John Wilder in the conspiracy that took Dr. Martin Luther King Jr.'s life on April 4, 1968, he was also just as adamant that Ray was not the actual assassin who fired the fatal shot. After decades of listening to members of his rapidly dwindling African-American underground, McFerren felt he had a pretty firm grasp on the fundamentals of the case and who did what. Informants Karl Mosby, Tommy Wright, Ezell Smith, and Robert Bell had all been instrumental in helping the humble grocer construct a basic framework of the conspiracy's West Tennessee inner workings. But while he had learned enough to know that Ray was a willing participant and simultaneous unwilling patsy, there was one component of the murder that seemed to always elude McFerren: Who was the real triggerman?

For a number of years, it was McFerren's suspicion that the actual shooter had been a young African-American man originally from Fayette County who used to work for Liberto alongside Robert Bell. However, that suspicion changed in 2012 when another former member of McFerren's fading civil rights underground came shuffling into his gas and grocery business.

White Pages, Black Print, Red Dot

As recounted by Marcus Holmes, McFerren had always heard that a specific, out-of-the-way rural road in Fayette County was key to the conspiracy, and that a man who lived on that road played a major role in the death of Dr. King. Then in the late summer of 2012, McFerren and Holmes' investigation kicked up enough local dust to grab the attention of one of McFerren's former black informants, also a resident of the same secluded rural road. After catching wind of the two men's MLK inquiry, the old man came forward with new information. Identified in this chapter only as "J.P.," the elderly man had been instrumental in assisting the exiled tenant farmers during the Tent City era, was a regular visitor to McFerren's store, and in the habit of keeping the business's proprietor abreast of local gossip.

On a sweltering day in August 2012, J.P. entered McFerren's store, hobbled precariously over to the business's turquoise-colored service counter, leaned across, and whispered something into his old friend's ear. After a moment or two, J.P. then asked to see McFerren's combination yellow-and-white pages phonebook. Picking up a red felt tip pen that was lying on the counter, J.P. began flipping through the residential section of the out-of-date 2005 BellSouth phonebook, stopped at a white page, and used the red pen to place a simple dot next to a specific man's name, address, and telephone number. After making the red dot, J.P. then pointed to the man's name printed in black ink, looked up, stared into McFerren's azure-saturated eyes with intense sincerity, and stated softly, "This is the shooter y'all been lookin' for."

Within a matter of days, McFerren informed his younger counterpart of the newest development and arranged for J.P. to return to the store when Holmes would also be there. Unaware of the stranger's future attendance, however, J.P. arrived and was immediately frightened by the sight of an unfamiliar Holmes looking through the same phonebook inside the store, turned around, and shuffled back outside just as quickly as he had entered, never speaking to Holmes or with McFerren again about the matter. With his already insatiable curiosity piqued once more, Holmes questioned McFerren further about the skittish black man, at which time the elderly grocer showed his young protégé the recently marked-up phonebook. Pointing his boney finger at the suspected shooter's printed name, the identical rural road he had always heard rumored about, and the blood-red dot made by his ever-loyal informant, McFerren recounted J.P.'s previous assertion to a now overly-excited Holmes.

Marcus's Moscow Meeting

As a part of several emails he sent to attorney and author Bill Pepper not long after watching the panicked J.P. scurry out of McFerren's store, Marcus Holmes eventually asked the New York resident about the person indicated in McFerren's phonebook. In his correspondence, Holmes asked Pepper if he was aware of the man's potential participation as the real assassin in Dr. King's murder. Almost instantly, Pepper replied to Holmes' email, hurriedly reassuring the nosey West Tennessee sleuth that the suspected man, while admittedly near the Lorraine Motel at the exact moment King was shot, had not been engaged in any part of the conspiracy. Holmes found it extremely revealing how quickly Pepper replied to his email, thus appearing frantic to quash any suggestion of the man's possible involvement. Both intrigued and irritated by yet another blatantly veiled attempt by the cagey New Yorker to lead him astray,

McFerren's 2012 fact-finding partner again took it upon himself to personally investigate.

To his amazement, Holmes quickly discovered that living in the same rural neighborhood as both J.P. and the alleged assassin was a longtime Holmes family friend. It wasn't long before he was sitting in the driver's seat of his dented work truck, steering the vehicle toward the familiar Fayette County address. On a whim, Marcus swung by his family friend's home on the relatively cool morning of Saturday, September 8, 2012, to ask about the supposed MLK shooter who lived just down the road. Immediately, the family friend knew who Marcus was asking about, and, in a reply that only fueled Holmes' already flaming curiosity, stated sternly, "Look here, you need to stay away from there! Besides, there's a woman living over there who looks after him, and she ain't gonna let you talk to him anyhow!"

The warning had the opposite effect on Holmes. Within seconds of leaving his friend's residence, Marcus pulled up to the nearby open front gate of the alleged assassin's modest country home. As he entered the bucolic property and drove down its gravel driveway, Holmes spotted a man wearing mirrored sunglasses, sitting in a wheelchair atop the wooden front porch of the residence, watching stoically over the front yard and road just beyond. Quickly realizing that the disabled man was the individual he had come to meet, Holmes' heart began to pump wildly. After a few pointless deep breaths to emotionally and physically stabilize himself, the would-be interviewer stepped from the relative safety of his truck, walked up the handicap-accessible ramp, and approached the subject of his inquiry. But just as the initial few words of greeting began to leave the geriatric man's lips, an older woman with bleach blonde hair darted out the front door, nervously grabbed the rear handlebars of the man's wheelchair, and whisked him back inside the house as she mumbled something to the effect of, "It's almost lunchtime, and he can't talk right now."

Bewildered by the oddly abrupt departure of the man and his apparent caregiver, Holmes tried knocking on the same door the pair had just retreated behind, waited for several minutes, and then dejectedly walked back to his mother's awaiting car. Realizing he had just been intentionally blocked from speaking to the man by the panicked-looking companion, Holmes pulled out of the driveway, turned right onto the same road he had just traveled, and headed south toward the scarcely surviving Fayette County town of Moscow, Tennessee.

Only seconds after turning left onto McKinstry Road, an already jittery Holmes observed an all-black unmarked police car approaching from the front. But just as the two vehicles passed each other, and his eyes sought out the reflection in the rearview mirror, Holmes could see the unmarked squad car make an immediate U-turn behind him. Flanked on either side of the isolated two-lane rural road by nothing but open fields and distant kudzu-covered tree lines, Holmes felt eerily alone, and his light one-handed fingering of the steering wheel became an instant ten-and-two-white-knuckled grip. His back stiffened and his pulse began to race. Despite the ice-cold air conditioning blowing across his brow, rivulets of sweat began to emerge from the top and sides of his hairline. After years of legal jousting with corrupt Fayette County and Tennessee state law enforcement officials, and a major buildup of MLK and Fayette County conspiratorial research, Holmes was teetering on the edge of paranoia and emotional unpredictability.

His immediate thought was that the nervous woman whom he just parted ways with probably overreacted and called the local authorities. Determined to eliminate any legal cause to be stopped by the charcoal-colored vehicle now tailing him, Holmes looked down at his gauges to ensure that he was traveling at the appropriate rate of speed. Still breathing heavily, the uneasy driver entered the city limits of Moscow and slowed to the required thirty-miles-an-hour. But at the moment he rounded the curve of McKinstry Road and Watermill

Street near the railroad tracks in downtown Moscow, Holmes again looked in his mirror and watched as the driver of the squad car turned on his emergency lights. Giving no thought whatsoever to his next actions, Holmes finally let paranoia and panic take over as he stomped on the accelerator, jumped the bumpy railroad crossing, and darted south toward Highway 57.

With the squad car now giving chase, Holmes turned right and began traveling west toward the Fayette and Shelby County line. For the next one-mile stretch of the two-lane portion of Highway 57, the brazen officer darted in and out of the oncoming lane, pulled up alongside Holmes, and looked over in an apparent attempt to obtain a physical description of his fleeing subject. Engines growled, the police car's siren screamed, and rivers of deceased grass clippings lying along the roadside suddenly sprang to life. Feeling increasingly threatened by the pursuing officer's unreasonably aggressive maneuvers, Holmes changed his intended route and made an immediate left onto Slayden Road in an effort to cross the nearby Tennessee and Mississippi state line.

Now heading south with the officer still giving chase, the panicked driver of the dusty truck continued for another four miles. But upon crossing over into Mississippi, Holmes looked in his mirror to see the now out-of-state officer still trailing behind him. Undeterred by the non-jurisdictional endeavor, the darkened police vehicle continued to follow Holmes with its siren and patrol lights activated until the two vehicles finally came to a halt at a gas station located on the corner of U.S. 72 and Slayden Road.

To Holmes' astonishment, the officer simply turned off his siren and flashing lights, kept his distance, stared at his suspect through the dusty windshield for a few moments, turned the squad car around, and then headed north on Slayden Road back toward the Tennessee state line. With no additional law enforcement called to the scene, and the former police vehicle now mysteriously out of sight, Holmes finally caught his breath. Now thinking somewhat clearly, he and McFerren discussed the heated incident over their cellphones while Holmes made his way back to the outskirts of Somerville by way of a less conspicuous route. Although Marcus's heart-stopping entanglement with the Moscow policeman was over, his troubles with the town of Moscow and the Fayette County authorities were just beginning.

On Wednesday, September 12, 2012, while dodging the new arrest warrant issued by the Moscow Police Department and Fayette County Sheriff Bobby Riles, a wanted Marcus Holmes drove to Birmingham, Alabama and checked into a hotel to lay low for a while while planning his next move. Then, on the morning of Thursday the 13th, Holmes' sister called to deliver some troubling news. After asking him where he had disappeared to, Marcus's sister informed him that, at the request of Fayette County's notoriously vindictive sheriff, the Cordova, Tennessee home of their seventy-eight-year-old father had been raided by Shelby County Sheriff's deputies around 2:00 a.m. that very morning.

Marcus's sister went on to explain that, in the course of the local manhunt initiated by Sheriff Riles, neighboring Shelby County Sheriff Bill Oldham's men had illegally stormed Mr. Holmes' home without a search warrant. Now infuriated by the unlawful and obviously upsetting invasion his elderly father had just suffered at the hands of the West Tennessee authorities, and determined to make the most of the short time he had left before his looming arrest, Marcus departed Birmingham and made the fifteen-hour drive north to the Big Apple to question James Earl Ray's last attorney, Bill Pepper.

Over the course of the two men's cordial Friday Manhattan lunch meeting, and Pepper's customary bottle of wine, Holmes pressed the red-nosed lawyer on a number of issues, including McFerren's secret tapes, John Wilder's possible involvement in the conspiracy, and the role of the alleged assassin who had been named by J.P. Unwilling to deviate from his well-rehearsed script, the only answers the stoic attorney cryptically provided through his raspy, artificial British accent were that "John Wilder loved money" and that the Fayette County suspect in question "only ran around the block at the time of the shooting." Leaving New York no more enlightened than when he arrived, it was apparent to Holmes that Pepper knew much more about the death of Dr. King than he would ever divulge.

Visitors

Subsequent to his eventual arrest on charges related to the Moscow police chase, Marcus was convicted in Fayette County's kangaroo court, sentenced to five years of probation, and then released from Bobby Riles' county jail in December of 2012. Only a few months later, in the spring of 2013, an undeterred Marcus Holmes launched the website FayetteFiles.com. More enraged than ever by the local establishment's unchecked ability to unlawfully rob him of his livelihood, reputation, and personal freedoms, the steadfast combatant began exposing the county's past and present offenses by posting official documents to the website as well as candid videos, brief segments of McFerren's secret audiotapes, and references to the alleged assassin named by J.P.

By that summer, the level of internet traffic FayetteFiles.com was attracting had reached record highs. But beyond the local Shelby and Fayette County views the site was drawing, Holmes and his webmaster began to track several surprising visits from someone using a federally controlled web server out of Washington, D.C. To be specific, in 2013, someone with access to the U.S. Department of Justice's online computer system began making regular visits to Holmes' whistleblowing website. But this wasn't the only brow-raising consequence of his online exposé.

Sometime in the late fall of that same year, as McFerren went about his routine of selling forty-ounce beers to the local gaggle of black "snitchers" and thirsty drunks, an out-of-place visitor walked in and introduced himself to the leery proprietor. The official-looking man was white yet slightly swarthy, tall, completely bald, and wearing a law enforcement uniform. According to McFerren, the visitor also started asking questions about the MLK shooting just before claiming that one of his own relatives was somehow connected to the April 4, 1968 event. After realizing he wasn't going to get anywhere with the tight-lipped grocer, the man left his business card and then departed the building. When McFerren relayed the story of his encounter to Holmes, he provided the man's business card as proof. Upon seeing the item, it became instantly apparent to Holmes that the man who tried interrogating McFerren was the son of Dr. King's suspected Fayette County shooter. The startled Holmes believed that the public content posted to his Fayette Files website pertaining to the alleged shooter's role most likely sparked something within the son, prompting him to make the unannounced visit and failed inquiry.

The circumstances surrounding the man's somewhat intimidating visit reminded McFerren of another similarly odd encounter. As he described to Holmes, McFerren stated that one of the sons of John Wilder had also made an eerily pointless visit to his store a number of years before. It was McFerren's claim that one day while he and Bill Pepper were standing inside the grocery's common area discussing the MLK case, Wilder's grown son walked through the front door with two Hispanic men, stared at McFerren for several minutes, and then walked back outside without any explanation. It was McFerren's belief at the time that the young Wilder somehow caught wind of Pepper's local visit and traveled to the nearby gas station to intimidate the two men into staying quiet. But with everything Holmes suspected about Pepper's relationship with the former lieutenant governor, he now began to wonder if the New York attorney hadn't tipped off the Wilders himself. Based on what he knew about both of Wilder's sons,

Holmes also speculated that it was most likely David who delivered the veiled threat to McFerren. But now Holmes pondered, did David Wilder and the alleged assassin's son perhaps know each other as well?

Facebook Fact-Finding

Holmes wasted little time looking into the backgrounds of the alleged MLK shooter's local friends and family, specifically that of his suspiciously inquisitive progeny. Through his friendship with another Fayette County resident, one who was connected to the burly-looking son through Facebook, Holmes was given permission to use his friend's personal social media account to browse the son's numerous family photos, genealogical information, work history, and details pertaining to his personal beliefs and friendships. By the time his secret hotel meeting with Randall Stephens got underway in September of 2015, Holmes had created a nickname for the suspected shooter based on a hunting photo and accompanying anecdote the son once posted to Facebook about his highly adored father. For the remainder of his investigation, Holmes would refer to the purported Fayette County assassin of Dr. King simply as "Very Very Dangerous."

Just prior to his second and hopefully last Tennessee prison stay, Holmes sat down with Stephens at the undisclosed hotel to go over a number of documents, audio recordings, videos, and other pertinent MLK evidence. It was at one of these late-night investigative sessions that Holmes gave Stephens the tattered 2005 publication of McFerren's much-talked-about BellSouth telephone book. Just as he had heard described, Stephens flipped to the page in question and observed a sloppily made red blob next to the alleged shooter's name. Stephens had laid eyes on Very Very Dangerous once before. During a weekend drive in late 2012 following his September arrest and release on bond, Holmes took Stephens to the scene of his earlier car chase with the Moscow police, thereby passing the alleged assassin's Fayette County home. To the two men's surprise, the same mirrored-eyed, wheelchair-bound man was resting quietly outside in the exact location Holmes had previously spotted him. But to now see the actual red dot the elusive J.P. created years before caused a tingling sensation to form on the back of Stephens' neck.

And then there was the issue of the suspicious photo Holmes and Stephens uncovered on the internet that same night. Again using his friend's Facebook account, Holmes scrutinized the various online profile pages of the Very Very Dangerous family, pointing out to Stephens a number of highly intriguing pictures. Within the frame of one recently photocopied, decades-old image, three people stood side by side, posing for an unknown photographer. At the left, an attractive raven-haired woman appeared to have shut her eyes at the last second, perhaps blinded by the flash of the camera. As Holmes claimed, this brunette was, in fact, the wife of Dr. King's true assassin. In the center, a portly man with thinning gray hair, identified only as "Tony Angelo," grinned proudly. And at the right of the group, also with dark hair, a short, somewhat stout Mediterranean-looking woman known simply as "Anna Mae" provided the camera lens with a mere half-smile, concealing the whites of her teeth. While it was unclear to the two sleuths at the time, Stephens went on to discover a number of weeks later that the Anna Mae and Tony Angelo seen posing with the alleged assassin's wife were actually natives of the same U.S. coastal city that kept popping up in other parts of the investigation, the city of New Orleans.

Conclusions and Questions

Once again, it was time for Randall Stephens to take stock of the intriguing list of items Marcus Holmes had thrown in his lap. After mulling over the issue of the phonebook and J.P.'s claim about the suspected shooter, Stephens investigated where J.P.'s Fayette County address was in relation to the home of Very Very Dangerous. According to official property records, J.P. and the man in question lived directly across the road from one another. Stephens began to theorize that the elderly J.P. was a trusted and welcomed visitor to his neighbor's home and that perhaps the two convalescent men struck up a conversation one day about the King murder. Was it possible Very Very Dangerous confided in his African-American friend? Did the slowly fading assassin have something he wanted to confess before taking his dying breath? Stephens also took into account J.P.'s anxiety as reported by Holmes. It would appear that his refusal to speak about the matter in front of a stranger indicated at least a genuine fear in McFerren's elderly informant.

Then there was Bill Pepper's ambiguous acknowledgment of the alleged assassin's physical location at the precise moment Dr. King was shot. In typical Pepper shaker fashion, Ray's former New York attorney confirmed his prior knowledge of the man's close proximity to Dr. King at the time of the murder, but sprinkled in a hasty denial of the same man's conspiratorial involvement. Stephens found it highly suspect that, of all the so-called gunmen Pepper had pointed his finger at through the years, none of them could be positively placed at the scene of the crime. Yet, here was a man who, according to official historical records, was less than one hundred yards from the Lorraine Motel at 6:01 p.m. on April 4, 1968, and Pepper never considered him a suspect?

The next issue Stephens dealt with was the strange warning from Holmes' friend to stay away from the purported shooter's home. What did the friend know about Very Very Dangerous that prompted the stern remark? Also baffling to Stephens was the altogether hasty refusal by the nervous blonde-haired caregiver to allow Very Very Dangerous to talk to Holmes. Who was she? And why was she so hell-bent against letting the wheelchair-bound man speak for himself? Did she know something about his alleged role and was perhaps worried he might let something slip out just as he had with J.P.? Furthermore, why was the Moscow police officer patrolling that far north, well outside his jurisdiction? Stephens was fairly certain that the panicked caregiver called 911, and that with the probable scarcity of Fayette County deputies in the area at the time, the officer in question heard the call by dispatch, knew no other officers could answer the request, and began driving to the non-jurisdictional scene just as Holmes vacated the property.

Stephens also began to question the role of the alleged shooter's son. As stated by McFerren, the man was wearing a law enforcement uniform when he entered the gas and grocery in late 2013. What was the purpose of his inquiry while on duty? Was he simply another history buff who was interested in meeting McFerren, or was he there to send a subtle message just as David Wilder had done several years before? Also, what were the exact details behind his mother's relationship with the Anna Mae and Tony Angelo from New Orleans? Who took the dated photo of the three friends standing together, and where was the photo taken?

Finally, Stephens pondered the possible connections between Very Very Dangerous and the other suspected members of the Shelby and Fayette County conspiracy. Could Frank C. Liberto be positively linked to the man in question? Were there any associations between John Wilder and the alleged shooter or the shooter's family? Did Wilder's high-level DOJ relationships help protect this man during the federal investigations that followed? And if so, did part of Pepper's suspected deal with Wilder include keeping the shooter's name a secret as well? While all of these considerations continued to tumble around in Stephens' already jam-packed brain, he again asked himself the broader, more relevant question: Could lightning really strike in the same place several times in a row?

John McFerren was either extremely lucky or the polar opposite. But whatever side of the coin was facing up after the toss, it was once more obvious to Stephens that McFerren always seemed to be in the right place at the right time. To any skeptic looking at the multitude of conspiratorial components the unpretentious Fayette County grocer was somehow able to accumulate, it might first appear that much of it was contrived.

First, McFerren swore that he witnessed James Earl Ray working for Frank C. Liberto in the months leading up to January 1968. Second, he overheard Liberto screaming at a paid assassin over the telephone, demanding that the contract killer shoot Dr. King on the balcony before retrieving the contract money from the Liberto brother in New Orleans. Third, McFerren received word that Mayor I. P. Yancey had harbored Ray just before the shooting. Then there were the multiple threads between John Wilder, Yancey, Liberto, Henry Loeb, Frank Holloman, Paul Summers, Buford Ellington, and George Wallace to contemplate. And finally, McFerren was presented with the name of the actual shooter who allegedly took Dr. King's life. Stephens grappled with the incredible odds and surface-level absurdity of the situation. Of all the experts who had looked into the 1968 murder and all the complicated high-level theories that permeated the alleged conspiracy, was it possible the humble grocery and gas station owner truly cracked the MLK assassination case?

According to one highly skeptical Memphis news journalist Stephens spoke with, the notion that McFerren, a rurally-isolated man with little education, could actually solve one of the biggest crimes of the twentieth century was so absurd, it was beyond even mentioning. In the journalist's tongue-in-cheek comment, he summed up his personal opinion by stating, "Hmm, McFerren seems to be Johnny-on-the-spot." Stephens had to admit; it was all an incredibly fantastic coincidence.

But then he reanalyzed the situation from the opposite perspective. How had the FBI or other intelligence organizations accomplished their missions in the past? If FBI Director J. Edgar

Hoover had been only one person, he would have failed at virtually every inquiry the Bureau made. But because he was able to duplicate himself hundreds of times over, using countless special agents and paid confidential informants throughout the country, Hoover's personal ability to glean vital information grew exponentially. Was McFerren's small West Tennessee underground any different?

African Americans, especially those living in the heat of the racially oppressive South, were raised by their parents and family members to never trust the local white authorities. In the case of Fayette County, this group of historically close-mouthed individuals relied on each other to investigate and deal with local matters on their own. And as the scorecard indicated, McFerren was only physically present to witness the Ray and Liberto events. The slew of other circumstances had been relayed to him by his own version of Hoover's special agents. Furthermore, because he was the primary leader of the local civil rights movement and one of only a handful of independent black entrepreneurs in the county, McFerren's gas and grocery business became the unofficial intelligence agency's physical headquarters, therefore enabling him to assemble and contextualize numerous pieces of separate information and evidence.

While the one-man jury inside Stephens' mind continued to deliberate, the mounting circumstantial evidence certainly prompted him to proceed with his research. By now, it was time for him to continue where he started. Just a few days later, Stephens again made the trip east to McFerren's business to attempt an in-depth interview with the typically tight-lipped proprietor. But this time, he had a plan in place to help ensure McFerren would talk.

Part Two

PERSONAL INTERVIEWS

Chapter 13

—— QR ——

STRAIGHT FROM
THE SOURCE

As RANDALL STEPHENS pulled up to the front of John
McFerren's Fayette County store on a cold day in January 2016, he
looked nervously down at his bulky iPhone's clock to make certain
he was on time. If all things went according to plan, Marcus Holmes
would be calling from a prison telephone inside the Turney Center
Industrial Complex only a handful of minutes after Stephens walked
through McFerren's gas station doors. Stephens and Holmes had spent
several days coordinating with each other telephonically, and multiple
items needed to occur in a precise sequence for their strategy to work.

First, Stephens had to show up at McFerren's business several
minutes before Holmes had promised to call. Second, Holmes would
need to somehow reserve a spot at one of the prison's busy payphones
at the predetermined time. Third, Stephens needed to be inside the
building and already speaking to an awake and alert McFerren before
the call came through. And finally, Holmes would need to be able to
clearly and swiftly convince McFerren of Stephens' trustworthiness

before the prison's automated telephone timer cut their conversation off.

With five minutes to spare, Stephens quickly exited his vehicle, walked up to the dusty metal and glass doors, and knocked several times. Cupping his hands over his eyes and the building's window to block out the sun's glare, he watched as McFerren slowly shuffled from the building's back sleeping room. As Stephens was now accustomed to, McFerren approached the opposite side of the doors, unlocked the deadbolt, turned around, and immediately hobbled back to a row of awaiting steel-and-vinyl cushioned chairs positioned in the middle of the store's main lobby. Without hearing a verbal invitation or seeing a welcoming gesture, Stephens automatically knew that it was his turn to simply enter the store, follow the slowly-departing McFerren, and take up a seat in one of the black vinyl chairs next to the now-winded proprietor.

As the second hand on his iPhone's digital clock slowly ticked down, and McFerren engaged in his typical small talk, Stephens continued to fumble with the cell phone to make sure there was a good signal and that its volume was turned up to the highest setting. Finally, after what seemed to be an eternity, he heard a familiar electronic jingle. Without looking at the caller I.D., Stephens answered the phone and immediately recognized the automated voice instructing him to press a specific number to accept the inmate's prepaid call. Within seconds, Holmes was on the line, and just as previously planned, Stephens placed his cell phone on speaker mode and handed it to McFerren. As Stephens listened in, Holmes tried to repeatedly assure McFerren that the white man sitting next to him was, without question, reliable, smart, and one hundred percent on their side.

Following a lengthy back-and-forth between a notably concerned McFerren and a constantly reaffirming Holmes, the prison's telephone system ended the call, and the two men's discussion was cut off mid-sentence. Then there was nothing but silence. McFerren handed the now quiet cell phone back to his guest. Stephens was hesitant to say anything for fear of putting undue pressure on McFerren. He wanted to be respectful by giving the elderly man time to think, and he didn't want to assume Holmes had accomplished his mission. Then, after several long uncomfortable moments, McFerren finally spoke up.

"Okay." McFerren inhaled, exhaled, took another long pause, and then slowly started again. "Come back in two days...so I can get all my information together, so I can show you exactly what you need to know. 'Cause when I tell somebody something, I don't tell no lies. When I say something, you can take it to the bank. And I'm gonna tell it to you straight."

As the color rushed back into Stephens' pale face, he let out a sigh of relief, and then smiled from ear to ear. "Thank you, Mr. McFerren! I won't let you down; I promise!" Stephens was immediately embarrassed by his own impulsive, overly excited reaction. For fear that his current overeagerness would scare McFerren into another bout of silence, causing him to change his mind before their first interview even started, Stephens tried to feign calmness, thanked his host once more, and assured him of his return in two days.

The would-be interviewer spent the rest of that day and the next preparing for his future Q&A. He again studied his collection of old documents and listened to Holmes' previously recorded interviews. Then, with a long list of questions now organized and typed, Stephens returned on a Monday to begin his much-anticipated, one-on-one interview with the typically enigmatic John McFerren. Despite his fear that the Fayette County business owner might suddenly have a change of heart, Stephens entered the building and was surprised to see McFerren perched behind the store counter, sitting over an awaiting cardboard box of old photographs and stacks of yellowing paper. From that extremely long day forward, McFerren and Stephens were inseparable. When the unlikely pair weren't inside the store going over important details surrounding the Dr. Martin Luther

King Jr. assassination, Stephens volunteered to help with all manner of tasks, both inside and outside McFerren's business.

When the Fayette County entrepreneur asked for assistance in getting his gas station's antique, soot-covered kitchen grill fixed, Stephens jumped at the opportunity by calling and personally meeting with an appliance repairman. When McFerren wanted to travel to Memphis to shop for a modern refrigerator, his new protégé was more than eager to act as chauffeur. And when the former civil rights leader needed a quick ride to the Food Rite grocery store in downtown Somerville to pick up a helping of his favorite fried fish, Stephens was happy to oblige. Worried that his stubbornly independent passenger might stumble or fall, the overly protective Stephens often insisted that the unsteady McFerren hold his arm when exiting the vehicle and walking in public.

After a number of weeks, Stephens began to view McFerren as the grandfather he never knew, and McFerren gave Stephens the nickname, "Big Fella." Suffice it to say; the middle-aged white man felt an intense sense of pride just being in McFerren's presence. But most importantly, Stephens was able to finally clarify a number of lingering questions about the MLK case. By the end of his multiple interviews with McFerren, Stephens had pieced together a relatively accurate summary of the unintended witness's forty-seven-year-old accusations.

Chapter 14

RAY AND THE FAT MAN

THE IDENTITY OF Frank C. Liberto was the first topic on his list. Based on all of the confusion surrounding who the real Frank was, when he supposedly died, and who McFerren actually overheard on April 4, 1968, Randall Stephens felt it vitally important to present McFerren with photographs of the produce owner in question. Upon seeing the glossy, black-and-white images, the Fayette grocer immediately confirmed that the man in the two portraits was "Fat Frank." McFerren then verified that James Latch had a scar near his ear and neck, was skinnier, and not the man depicted in the two photos. McFerren also confirmed that Liberto's parents and siblings lived in New Orleans, that the Italian-American produce owner only hired black men from Shelby and Fayette Counties to work at the warehouse, and that the 814 Scott Street address was a bustling hive of underworld activity. As McFerren put it, "From the first time I set foot inside the market around 1960 or '61, dope, booze, guns, and stolen property flowed outta that place like honey."

It was also John's assertion that countless members of the Memphis Police and Shelby County Sheriff's Departments hung around the warehouse on a daily basis and that virtually all of them were there to collect kickbacks or inquire about illicit side work. McFerren also claimed that on certain Thursdays when he would arrive to do his shopping, he would be warned by one of the warehouse's numerous African-American employees to avoid walking near the office since the "head man of the city's Mafia" was inside discussing matters with Frank.

When Stephens asked who Memphis's head Mafia man was, McFerren said he didn't know his name, but that he was a short fat little man with "no neck." McFerren claimed he would see him sitting in a chair inside Frank's office from time to time "hunched over in a little round ball." Stephens also inquired about who the familiar black workers were, and without hesitating, McFerren confirmed that it was Ezell Smith, Willie Green, and Robert Bell who usually passed along the warnings. When the issue of Bell and Green came up, Stephens used it as an opening to delve into their alleged connection to James Earl Ray.

McFerren stated that while he knew Bell and Green had picked up Ray in Only, Tennessee, and then delivered him to Liberto's warehouse in the late summer of 1967, he only became aware of it after the shooting. He stated that because of his friendship with Bell and the nature of Bell's work with Frank, McFerren never told government investigators about Bell's connection to Ray for fear of getting his friend in trouble with Frank and the mob. The aging civil rights leader also confirmed that Bell continued to work for Liberto up until 1984, just before being sent to federal prison for transporting the stolen pallets of Kellogg's Frosted Flakes cereal across state lines.

John also claimed that Ray continued to show up at Fat Frank's business from time to time throughout the fall and winter of 1967 and into early 1968. McFerren claimed that Ray stood out at the warehouse, seemingly out of place since Liberto only hired blacks. He also said that in late 1967, Ray showed up looking darker than before. Again, McFerren asserted that Ray looked like a "Puerto Rican" at the time and that his neck had developed some kind of bad skin irritation, which he called "jungle rot." When Stephens asked if he thought Ray was indeed Hispanic, McFerren was quick to correct him. "No, I just mean he looked like he was dark, like he was yellow, like he got a tan." And with regard to the "jungle rot," he clarified his earlier statement by telling Stephens, "It was all dried and flaky, like it was an old snakeskin he was shedding off."

The inquisitor pressed further. Curious about McFerren's 1968 belief that Ray looked twenty-five, when the alleged shooter was, in fact, thirty-nine by late 1967, Stephens asked for a comment. McFerren acknowledged that he had been incorrect about Ray's age, but that even after the alleged gunman's capture, McFerren always believed Ray looked younger than he really was. Again, McFerren reasserted his sincerity that it was James Earl Ray he saw working at the warehouse, and that the alleged Liberto employee once loaded produce into his truck and even sat next to him for a brief moment near the building's dock entrance to have a lighthearted chat.

Stephens wanted to verify a couple of chronological items just to solidify the foundation of McFerren's long-established association with Liberto. "John," Stephens began, "can you tell me again what year it was that you first started shopping at Liberto's warehouse and how often you went there?"

Almost as if he was anticipating the question, McFerren quickly replied, "I started goin' there around 1960 or 1961 when the blacklist was first goin' on around here. When the white merchants in Somerville stop sellin' to us 'cause of the voter registration drive and durin' Tent City, then I had to start drivin' all the way to Memphis regular to get my supplies. I made trips out there once or twice a week, mostly on Thursdays for about eight years. See, all of the folks around here got paid every Friday. So, I wanted to have a fresh stock before Friday mornin' just before the black folks would come in here to do their grocery shoppin'."

The next question Stephens asked was in reference to the Thursday, March 28, 1968 remarks McFerren overheard while shopping at Liberto's. Stephens continued, "What about the Thursday evening, the week before Dr. King was shot? Can you describe what happened at Liberto's warehouse that previous Thursday?"

Again, McFerren did not hesitate. "See, just like always, I was there around five o'clock to buy my vegetables and fruits. Now, Dr. King had been marchin' that day near the river, and a whole lotta trouble broke out in Memphis when he was here. Lots of young Negroes in the city wenta' breakin' up the windows and such."

McFerren took an audible breath and then continued. "So when I got there, at the warehouse, Fat Frank and all of his buddies was cursin' and hollern' about the mess, and was blamin' Dr. King for it. I was fixin' to finish up and was up at the office to pay and get my receipt, and Fat Frank started messin' with me, tryin' to get me to bite like a fish hungry for a worm, like Frank was fishin' for a fight. He started askin' me what I thought about my buddy, Dr. King, and all of his mess. But I had already knowed how to handle the white folks 'cause I was from Fayette County. So, I just played dumb and told him that I tended to my own business. Even though he kept tryin to get me to bite, I just stayed at peace and kept sayin' that I tended to my own business. And then he left me alone."

After listening to McFerren recount his experience at the warehouse on the March 28 day of Dr. King's now infamously failed protest in Memphis, Stephens asked the all-important question about the two telephone conversations the Fayette Countian overheard at Liberto's on the following Thursday. As he had countless times before, the former civil rights leader again repeated word for word the one-sided discussions he claimed Liberto had with someone over the phone approximately an hour before the shooting of Dr. King on April 4. McFerren stated once more that Liberto screamed into his office telephone, "Shoot the son-of-a-bitch on the balcony and get the job done," and then during a second call, yelled once more into the receiver, "Don't bring your ass around here again. Go down to New Orleans and get your $5,000 from my brother."

Determined to clarify the 1976 interview with the DOJ, Stephens asked if Latch actually spoke Ray's name before handing the telephone receiver off to Liberto during the second call. McFerren was unequivocal, "Yes. Fat Frank and the scarred man always called him Ray. I just never told the FBI and Memphis police any of them names in 1968." Stephens went on to ask McFerren why he never mentioned anyone's names to the MPD and FBI. McFerren asserted, "Some people I only knowed their first names, like Fat Frank, and I didn't want to say no names if I was wrong. Look, when I tell you something, I only tell you facts that I know and I can prove! And I know they all called him Ray."

Stephens then asked McFerren for an opinion as to who he believed was on the other end of the telephone that evening. After hesitating for several seconds, most likely unwilling to commit to a solid answer, McFerren eventually blurted out, "It was probably Ray, 'cause the scarred man said 'Ray' when he picked up the phone, but I can't say for sure."

Stephens pressed further. "But you don't think Ray killed King; is that correct?"

McFerren replied, "That's right. I think James Earl Ray was in a cahoots with Fat Frank and those people. But I don't think he done the actual killin'. I think Fat Frank and all them Mafias out there just set him up to be the fall guy."

McFerren's account of his arrival back to the southern outskirts of Somerville from the LL&L warehouse in Memphis on April 4 was the next topic Stephens asked his elder friend about. According to a number of news articles and books, it was McFerren's recollection that when he returned to his store around 6:00 p.m. or shortly thereafter, it was Viola who called him from the couple's nearby home to inform him of the heartbreaking shooting of Dr. King. Interested in hearing McFerren describe that part of the seldom-told story, Stephens inquired, "John, can you tell me what happened once you came back to the store on the day Dr. King was killed?"

McFerren took a brief second to think and then obliged his middle-aged interviewer with another answer. "Well, I left the warehouse sometime around five-fifteen that day and drove straight to the store so I could unload all my cold food and get it chilled down. See, I had it packed on dry ice in the truck, but I had to get it inside the store before it all spoiled. As I was unloadin' my meats and dairy supplies outta the truck about six-fifteen or so, the store phone rang, and I picked it up. It was Viola and she was callin' from our house. In a real scared kinda' voice, she told me that Dr. King had done got killed here in Memphis around three o'clock. But as soon as she told me, I told her it didn't happen at three 'cause I could already figure it out. It musta' happen after five fifteen or so, just after Fat Frank told someone on the phone to 'shoot the son-of-a-bitch on the balcony'. After a short while later that night, I found out from the newsman on the radio that the murder done happen around six o'clock. Right then I know Fat Frank had Dr. King killed, I knowed it."

Chapter 15

WEEKEND OF WORRY

ON FRIDAY MORNING, April 5, 1968, the day after Dr. Martin Luther King Jr. was murdered at the Lorraine Motel, John and Viola McFerren awoke to the latest broadcast concerning the heart-wrenching tragedy. By Saturday evening, April 6, the distraught couple had obtained the latest edition of *The Commercial Appeal*. On the front cover of its black-and-white pages, a hand-drawn composite of Dr. King's purported assassin had been published.

In addition to artist William "Bill" Herrington's drawing of the alleged killer, a written description was also included. Authored by *Commercial Appeal* journalist William "Bill" Sorrels, the description was embedded in a lengthy article detailing the suspected gunman's actions on the day of the shooting. By all accounts, Mr. Herrington, Mr. Sorrels, and an accompanying employee of the same newspaper named Robert H. Williams traveled early on Friday morning, April 5, to Bessie Brewer's 422½ S. Main Street rooming house. It was there that a former tenant named John Willard was alleged to have stalked and shot Dr. King from. After walking up the rickety staircase to the building's threadbare second-story level, the three newsmen met with Charles Quitman Stephens, a potential witness and current tenant inside room 6B. The newspaper employees also tried to speak with Mr. Stephens' fellow roommate and common-law wife, a woman named Grace Walden/Stephens.

By the conclusion of their interview with the severely hungover couple inside the South Main Street flophouse, the three *Commercial Appeal* journalists had written several pages of notes and completed a composite sketch of the John Willard whom Mr. Stephens claimed to have only seen the back of the evening before. Working feverishly throughout the rest of the day, the three reporters completed their article just in time for their deadline and the paper's Saturday morning edition, a copy of which ultimately made it into the hands of John and Viola McFerren.

Intent on hearing John's personal account of the April 6 newspaper topic, Randall Stephens asked his interviewee to go over the events of that day. After the request, McFerren, like he had most certainly done with Bill Pepper during the *King v. Jowers* trial, jumped around in the timeline by first describing the relationship the FCCWL shared with Dr. King's SCLC. Stephens, now only faintly annoyed, took a deep breath, smiled at his elderly friend, and listened patiently as Mr. McFerren proceeded.

"See, you gotta understand. We always stood side by side with Dr. King, all the way. Sometime about 1960, his ministry, the SCLC down in Atlanta, they gave the League, the Fayette County Welfare League, here in town a lotta money to help with our work. So me and Viola, all the black folks around here, this side of Tennessee, we all felt real close to Dr. King, and it was real hard on a lotta us here when he got killed. Now, when we got the paper that day, Viola read it to me a couple times, real slow, and I looked at the picture after. The picture was supposed to be the man that killed Dr. King. See, I knowed him from before at Fat Frank's business, and I already knowed that was him, the man I seen at the warehouse."

Stephens forgot all about his initial frustration with McFerren's circuitousness. Now fearful he might disrupt his new mentor's train of thought and flow of speech, he remained silent while McFerren continued.

"Now, me and Viola, we discussed it the rest of the day. I didn't want to get her and the children in any kinda' trouble. 'Cause once you become a snitcher around here, especially if you're a black man, the Klan, the White Citizens,...whoever, they'll all come after you and your whole family. Also, I was worried that if I told the polices about what I knowed, it could mess over my business. See, we'd already been cut off from buying our supplies here in town 'cause of the Somerville merchants and their blacklist, and I didn't want to have to stop goin' to another business, Fat Frank's business. If I told what I knowed, then I wouldn't be able to shop there no more. So Viola and me, we talked about it a long time. We was both worried about what we should do. Then, late that Saturday night, after we discussed it even further, we decided that we needed to talk to somebody else about it."

A Call to Bryant

The Rev. Sidney Baxton Bryant was a white Methodist minister, well-loved civil rights leader from the racially divisive South, and the eventual Director of the Tennessee Council on Human Relations. But unlike most of his contemporaries, Bryant was socially unreserved and thoroughly flamboyant in his social justice endeavors. Meant as a funny nod to the Methodist minister's outgoing personality and thinning coat of ginger-colored hair, Will Davis Campbell, who was a fellow pastor, civil rights leader, and longtime friend, once nicknamed

Baxton Bryant, "Booger Red," and the moniker stuck. But while he was inherently incapable of putting on faux Christian airs, the tremendous political and social influence the Rev. Bryant wielded in the United States was indisputable.

Just before noon on November 22, 1963, Bryant stood behind a wheelchair-bound woman on the tarmac of Love Field in Dallas, Texas, waiting patiently to shake the hands of his friends, President John Fitzgerald Kennedy and First Lady Jacqueline Bouvier Kennedy. After exiting Air Force One, the President greeted Bryant and then asked if they would see each other again at the Trade Mart later that day. After saying goodbye to Bryant and the rest of the crowd, JFK and Jackie departed the airport with the presidential motorcade. Then, while preparing to leave Love Field shortly after 12:30 p.m., Bryant heard a news bulletin being broadcast over his car radio, stating that President Kennedy had just been shot.

Less than five years later, on Thursday, March 28, 1968, Bryant stood on Beale Street in downtown Memphis next to another national leader and friend, Dr. Martin Luther King Jr. As Dr. King, the Rev. Ralph Abernathy, the Rev. James Lawson, and other local and national civil rights icons prepared to lead a peaceful march on behalf of the city's striking sanitation workers, Bryant joined King at the front of the rally. But like Booger Red's last meeting with President Kennedy in 1963, this day would also be marred in violence as a handful of young African-American men began rioting near the tail end of Dr. King's ultimately failed demonstration.

Then on Sunday, April 7, 1968, just three days after the repugnant murder of Dr. King, Bryant received a cryptic telephone call at his Nashville, Tennessee home. The person on the other end of the line was yet another civil rights leader and friend, a grocery and gas station owner from Fayette County named John McFerren. Sitting underneath the florescent lights inside the empty store, Stephens urged McFerren to again relay his version of the past events.

"I went ahead and called Baxton Bryant. Me and Viola knowed and trusted him. Anyhow, he was a white minister, but he was real honest and was a man we knowed we could talk to. So, I called him and asked him if he could drive over from Nashville to meet with us. I was tryin' to convince him to come without sayin' why, 'cause at the time, I thought maybe the phone was bugged, and I didn't want no one to eavesdrop on what I knowed happen to Dr. King. After he got here, probably around seven or so that evening, me and Viola talked with him for quite a while. He asked me a lot of questions and we spent a long time discussin' it further. I kept tellin' him why I didn't want to go to the police station in Memphis. But he kept pressin' and pressin' me to tell what I knowed. So, finally I said 'okay' and he promise me that he would talk to the polices for me in Memphis and protect me, like hide my name, if I talked to them."

As various other narratives have indicated, Bryant then departed the McFerrens' home and made the hour drive into Memphis. Immediately following his check-in at the Peabody Hotel, Bryant called MPD Director Frank C. Holloman at his Shelby County residence. As a Caucasian male and Christian minister from the South, Bryant was known for his well-honed ability to peacefully communicate with the typically all-white government and law enforcement authorities when advocating for the African-American community. And by this time, he and Holloman had become well acquainted due to the previous social unrest in Memphis in the days leading up to and following Dr. King's murder. After being awoken from his Sunday night slumber, the MPD director agreed to meet with Bryant at police headquarters.

Upon listening to the Methodist minister explain McFerren's incredible account, a now intensely curious, perhaps even nervous, Frank C. Holloman telephoned Chief Homicide Inspector N.E. Zachary and FBI Special Agent O.V. Johnson to request their added presence at his office. After Bryant's second rendition of McFerren's April 4 narrative, the three law enforcement officials decided to arrange a secret, low-profile meeting inside Bryant's 561 hotel room in which to interview the apprehensive McFerren. After calling Burch Porter & Johnson attorney David E. Caywood, asking him to represent McFerren at the future interview inside the Peabody, the Rev. Bryant departed Holloman's office around 12:30 a.m. on Monday morning to begin the hour drive back to Somerville to pick up McFerren.

Chapter 16

MONDAY MORNING MEETING

THE NEXT ISSUE Stephens felt compelled to clarify was the confusion surrounding McFerren's Monday morning, April 8 meeting with the Memphis police and FBI inside room 561 at the Peabody Hotel. Based on the various written accounts and McFerren's own present-day recollection, he entered the hotel room sometime around 2:30 a.m. Stephens then asked about the law enforcement officials who were inside room 561 at the time. While McFerren was foggy on the names of the government authorities he spoke with on the 8th, he again confirmed that Frank Holloman was one of the key individuals present that morning.

Now confident that Holloman (a potential player in the King assassination conspiracy and/or cover-up) was in attendance, Stephens began to form an opinion as to the reason the cagey Memphis police director's name was not officially listed as a participant in the MPD and FBI interviews. It was Stephens' belief that while Holloman was desperate to hear firsthand what McFerren really knew about the conspiracy involving Liberto and Ray, the MPD director instructed his chief homicide inspector, N.E. Zachary, and his former FBI coworker, O.V. Johnson, to keep his presence at the hotel out of their individual reports as a way of affording himself a thin layer of plausible deniability.

If asked in the future by members of the nosey news media about McFerren's allegations, the possible conspiracy involving the police-friendly Liberto, or Liberto's connection to the out-of-town fugitive, Holloman privately believed that he could keep his knowledge of the plot and early morning interest in McFerren's statements a secret by simply claiming that he wasn't present at the Peabody to hear the interview. In short, Holloman would simply feign ignorance and refer any pesky newsmen to Zachary and Johnson if asked about the Fayette County whistleblower.

Next, Stephens asked about the other men who were at the Peabody. As he had done countless times before, McFerren asserted that his friend, the Rev. Baxton Bryant was there as well as Lucius Burch's son-in-law, a young attorney in Burch's Memphis law firm named David E. Caywood. When Caywood's name came up, Stephens again used the statement as a segue into his next line of important questioning, asking McFerren about his 1968 use of the phrase "on the balcony."

According to true crime author Gerald Posner's 1998 book, *Killing the Dream*, Caywood was questioned approximately three decades after his participation in McFerren's April 8, 1968 interview at the Peabody. Based on Caywood's claim to Posner, it was his recollection that, when he and Baxton Bryant picked up McFerren just outside of Somerville and made the hour-long drive together back to the Peabody Hotel in Memphis, "McFerren left out the part of the story that claims Liberto said, 'Kill the son of a bitch on the balcony.'" Caywood went on to claim that it was only after the trio's arrival at the Peabody that the Fayette grocer mentioned the words "on the balcony" when speaking to the authorities. Posner continued to push the theory of McFerren's alleged embellishment and unreliability by writing in his book that when he (Posner) interviewed Caywood, the Memphis attorney stated:

> That would have jumped right out at me...It would have set off all kinds of bells because the day before King was shot, I was on that very balcony at the Lorraine with him. McFerren did say something about "shoot the son of a bitch," but there was nothing about the balcony in anything he told me.

Interestingly, the small group of men and women who made up Janet Reno's 1998-to-2000 DOJ team repeated Posner's allegations concerning the Caywood-McFerren issue in their supposedly independent investigative report. Disturbed, however, by the insinuation that McFerren may have exaggerated his story on the morning of the 8th, Marcus Holmes took it upon himself to personally question David Caywood in 2013. Upon his visit to Cayood's Clark Tower law office in Memphis, Holmes learned that the still-practicing attorney never spoke to McFerren again after that April 1968 morning. Caywood also admitted to Holmes that he was a very young, very inexperienced lawyer at the Burch Porter & Johnson law firm at the time. Additionally, he had lost sleep during the prior week while working on Dr. King's legal battle to lawfully protest in Memphis and was "in and out" of the 561 hotel room during the MPD and FBI's questioning of McFerren. Simply put, Caywood backpedaled when explaining to Holmes the thoroughness of his brief representation of McFerren in 1968 and the accuracy of his comments to Posner in the late '90s.

Even before his early 2016 interviews with McFerren, Stephens himself thought it odd that Caywood's recollection would hold any water in the first place. First, it was highly suspect that Caywood waited thirty years to refute McFerren's extremely consistent, much-publicized, decades-long claim. Second, what did it matter, Stephens wondered, if Caywood heard the phrase "on the balcony" or not? Maybe because of the early morning time frame, only a few hours after midnight, Caywood was simply too fatigued to pay complete attention to all of McFerren's predawn assertions. Or maybe McFerren simply made a conscious decision not to tell Caywood all of the details of his eyewitness account. Based on the statements of everyone involved, Caywood was a stranger to McFerren before that morning. Perhaps out of caution, McFerren simply gave the unfamiliar white attorney only small tidbits of information, fearful of revealing anything of major substance before speaking to the authorities. Whatever the case, Stephens was highly skeptical of Posner's original claim and Reno's regurgitated confirmation that McFerren supposedly added extra details to his story.

But when he finally raised the topic, Stephens was stunned by McFerren's reply. It was John's adamant claim that, despite the assertions of Caywood, Posner, or the government, Caywood didn't make the round-trip drive with Baxton Bryant from Memphis to Somerville on the early morning of the 8th to pick him up. According to McFerren, it was just himself and Bryant in the car during the predawn, 1:30 a.m. trek from central Fayette County to the Peabody in downtown Memphis. McFerren then claimed that he barely spoke with the unfamiliar Caywood when he first met him at the hotel before being quickly approached by Holloman and the other law enforcement officials.

And based on Caywood's own admission, the young lawyer had been up late for a number of days in a row prior to the 8th. Perhaps Caywood simply told Bryant that, because of his need for an extra two hours of sleep, he would forgo the long drive to Fayette County and back and simply interview McFerren upon his arrival at the Peabody in Memphis. If that was the case, Stephens thought, it was now completely clear why Caywood never heard McFerren's complete story. Furthermore, Stephens again scrutinized O.V. Johnson's April 8, 1968 interview and noted that the FBI 302 report itself indicated that McFerren only spoke to Viola and Baxton Bryant about the matter before discussing it with the authorities.

By all accounts, McFerren concluded his interview at the Peabody on the morning of the 8th, sometime around daybreak close to 5:30 a.m. During their drive back together from Memphis to Somerville along Highway 64, the Rev. Bryant spent the next hour naively reassuring his tired and uneasy passenger that he would stay in close contact with Special Agent O.V. Johnson and the ostensibly trustworthy Frank Holloman, and that he would update McFerren with any new information relayed by the two law enforcement officials in the days ahead.

Chapter 17

THURSDAY GUESTS

THE NEXT TOPIC Stephens broached with McFerren was the series of men, both official and unofficial, who visited the Fayette County gas and grocery business beginning on the morning of April 18, 1968. After ten days of nervous stirring, McFerren's first caller was an unexpected out-of-town gentleman who, among other things, was a former resident of the Somerville area, a reputed Tennessee gangster, and fellow gas station owner in New Orleans.

Robert Powers

The first person to make the Thursday trip to McFerren's Fayette County business was a white man named Robert Powers. As Stephens had earlier speculated, McFerren confirmed that the last name of the unwelcomed early morning visitor on April 18, 1968, was Powers and not Powell. He also told Stephens that Powers was previously incarcerated in a Tennessee state prison during the 1930s, was a known bootlegger in Fayette County, and later owned and operated a gas and grocery business just west of downtown Somerville on the corner of Highway 64 and Powers Store Road, or what is today Teague Store Road.

When Stephens asked about Powers' Louisiana connections, McFerren reiterated that the former Fayette Countian moved to New Orleans about twelve years before the death of Dr. King, opened a twenty-four-hour Gulf Oil truck stop on the corner of U.S. Routes 11 and 90, and used the Mafia-linked business as a front for illegal gambling, smuggling, and prostitution rackets. Finally, McFerren highlighted his earlier belief that someone, perhaps Frank Liberto, one of the conspirators in Somerville, or maybe even Frank's brother in New Orleans, called Powers to ask him to drive up to Fayette County in order to deliver the veiled threat. It was also not a coincidence to McFerren that Powers showed up on a Thursday, exactly two weeks to the day the grocer overheard Frank Frank screaming into a telephone. It was John's belief that the New Orleans resident made the unwelcomed visit on the same day he (McFerren) made his regular trips into Memphis as a way of underscoring the connection to the threat on behalf of Liberto. Not long after listening to McFerren's personal description of Powers, Stephens did some cursory checking.

It was already apparent to Stephens that at least one of Frank Holloman's MPD homicide officers, most likely Chief Homicide Inspector N.E. Zachary, interviewed Liberto sometime between April 8 and the 18th regarding Fat Frank's possible role in the MLK shooting and the issue of his injured finger. Given Zachary's prior interactions with McFerren on the 8th and then Liberto just days afterward, coupled with McFerren's failure to show up at the warehouse on Thursday, April 11, to buy his typical supplies, Stephens now believed that Liberto had been tipped off by Zachary and then called Powers in New Orleans, asking him to drive up to Fayette County to send a subtle message to the loud-mouthed grocer.

And according to multiple archived news articles, a since-demolished Gulf Oil truck stop did, in fact, once operate on the rural corner of U.S. Routes 11 and 90 east of Lake Pontchartrain just outside the metropolitan area of New Orleans. Lastly, Stephens discovered that the roadside corner where the truck stop used to be located was still affectionately referred to by area natives as "Powers Junction." Stephens' appetite for additional information on Robert Powers had been whetted by yet another confirmation, and he made a note to himself to dig up more buried morsels later on.

Fitzpatrick and Sloan

The next item Stephens questioned McFerren about was the alleged misidentification of Galt/Ray during the FBI's photo lineup on April 18, 1968. As indicated by FBI Special Agents Robert Fitzpatrick and Andrew Sloan in their own 302 report, McFerren failed to identify Eric Starvo Galt/James Earl Ray on multiple occasions, and only picked the suspect out of the photo lineup once he was told that Galt/Ray was the man being sought for the murder of Dr. King. But according to McFerren, just the opposite had occurred. Despite what Fitzpatrick and Sloan reported earlier, McFerren stood by his long-held claim that he picked Ray's photograph out the first time while viewing the lineup. When Stephens asked again, explaining to McFerren his signature on the 1978 HSCA affidavit, whereupon he acknowledged his own failure to identify Ray to the FBI in 1968, McFerren again defended himself by begrudgingly admitting that he had no way of knowing what he was signing in 1978 due to his illiteracy. In McFerren's words, "That Gene Johnson tricked me into signing them papers." Stephens then moved on to the final Thursday visitor, a man who was briefly hinted at near the end of Fitzpatrick and Sloan's 302 report. "John, can you tell me about the *TIME* reporter who was also here that day, Bill Sartor?"

William Dean "Bill" Sartor

Of all the names listed in Stephens' heaping pile of government reports and news articles, Bill Sartor was by far the least mentioned. Just as Holmes had attempted before, Stephens also tried to gain a firmer grasp of who Sartor was by asking McFerren to describe the time he spent with the reporter in the late '60s. According to McFerren, Sartor was a young, "mousey little fella" who looked like a beatnik. But he was also a fiercely brave reporter who was on the side of civil rights, eking out a living by working for *TIME* magazine and progressive Southern newspapers like Hodding Carter's *Delta Democrat-Times*. Immediately following the murder of Dr. King, Sartor drove from his Greenville, Mississippi home to Memphis to begin investigating the case on behalf of his editors at *TIME*.

In the late morning of April 18, 1968, the journalist received an urgent telephone call while reviewing his investigative notes inside room 400 at the Downtowner Motel in Memphis. At the recommendation of a concerned Baxton Bryant, McFerren called Sartor who then drove east to Fayette County around noon in order to interview McFerren about the murder, the possible conspiracy, and the earlier threat that morning at the hands of Robert Powers. But upon the later arrival of FBI Special Agents Fitzpatrick and Sloan at the same gas and grocery store, Sartor was forced to halt his barely-initiated interview. Making the most of his time, however, the reporter began taking snapshots of the two federal agents at work and lingered nearby until the G-Men completed their own inquiry with McFerren. Then, after Fitzpatrick and Sloan's completion of the photo lineup and their departure from the area, Sartor resumed his previous interview with the still-rattled black witness.

As illustrated in the eight-page report Sartor submitted to his editors at *TIME* on the morning of April 19, the Mississippi stringer outlined a number of crucial details concerning McFerren's eyewitness account as well as information pertaining to Frank Liberto's business associates. At the very top of Sartor's report, he wrote that "Eric Starve [sic] Galt…is sallow-skinned [and] has 'jungle rot.'" Sartor also stated that Galt worked "last fall" at a Memphis produce company, an enterprise that went on to become the "base from which the conspiracy plot was hatched or carried out or both."

The journalist also stated in the report, "There is strong indication that law officers (either local, state or county) or ex-law officers are involved." This potential connection between Fat Frank and the local authorities was emphasized by the typed statement, "the produce is a hangout for police, county officers and some state liquor officers." There it was again, the issue of Memphis's legal and/or illegal liquor industry. Given that Liberto's Scott Street warehouse was a notorious hub for smuggling, particularly when it came to the bootlegging of West Tennessee moonshine and other alcohol, it seemed incredible that a law enforcement official with the state liquor authorities would be a regular visitor there. Little did Stephens realize at the time, this singular clue in Sartor's report would later become essential in uncovering the connection between Memphis organized crime, West Tennessee law enforcement, and the New Orleans Mafia. Among the other countless details in the eight-page document, Sartor also stated that McFerren, after being shown the six photographs by the two FBI special agents just moments before, told the journalist immediately afterward, "I picked him [Galt] out as my first choice."

But as the April 26, 1968 *TIME* article eventually revealed, very little of McFerren's claims or Sartor's investigative report made it into print. In fact, Baxton Bryant later appeared in front of an NBC television news camera to not only defend his anonymous colleague's claims about Liberto and Ray, but to also protest as to why Ramsey Clark's DOJ, Hoover's FBI, and the editors at *TIME* didn't take McFerren's claims and Sartor's report more seriously. Undaunted by his editors' unwillingness to print the entire story, Sartor remained in Memphis after April and continued to personally investigate and record McFerren's unpopular MLK allegations. In fact, McFerren told Stephens that he personally drove Sartor around to various West Tennessee locales so that the reporter could hunt down new leads and interview additional witnesses.

McFerren explained that on one trip, in particular, he escorted Sartor to Bolivar, Tennessee, a small town just east of Somerville. It was McFerren's recollection that the two men stopped at a set of large red brick buildings located on the southside of Highway 64 in Bolivar and that when Sartor exited the vehicle, he went inside one of the imposing buildings, not returning until several minutes later. While McFerren didn't know the purpose for the trip at the time or what function the group of buildings served, Randall Stephens eventually discovered that John had unknowingly traveled to The Western Mental Health Institute in Bolivar.

It was Sartor's intention at the time to interview the recently committed psych patient and former MLK assassination witness, Grace Walden/Stephens. This, of course, was the same Mrs. Walden/Stephens who, along with her common-law husband, Charles Quitman Stephens, was a former second-floor tenant inside Bessie Brewer's 422½ S. Main Street flophouse at the time of King's death. Several years after McFerren and Sartor's trip to Bolivar, Mrs. Walden/Stephens was freed from the psych hospital by her eventual guardians and 1978 HSCA legal counsels, Memphis attorney Duncan Ragsdale and New York attorney Mark Lane.

Sadly, the relentlessly inquisitive Sartor was allegedly poisoned a few years later while still in the midst of his investigation. On the Thursday morning of December 9, 1971, while staying at his parents' home in Waco, Texas, Bill Sartor died. McFerren explained to Stephens his suspicion that, just before heading back to his parent's Texas residence, the thirty-five-year-old Sartor became sick immediately after eating at The Hut, a restaurant in downtown Somerville.

However, when Stephens looked into Bill Pepper's version of the Sartor story in *Orders to Kill*, it was the New York attorney's claim that the *TIME* stringer had been poisoned at a bar in Waco called The Hickory Stick. While McFerren's suspicion was plausible, and there was ample justification to doubt Pepper's willingness to convey accurate details regarding Somerville's connection to the King murder, Stephens still wanted to do his own research and compare McFerren's claim to Pepper's narrative concerning Sartor's mysterious death.

Stephens also noted that Pepper went on to write extensively about Sartor's independent investigation into the New Orleans Mafia connection and Don Carlos Marcello's possible role in the death of Dr. King. But as usual, Pepper's 1995 book somehow neglected to convey the since-deceased journalist's belief that Ray and Liberto were working jointly under Marcello. Without question, there was much more to the Sartor story, and Stephens promised John McFerren he would get to the bottom of it.

Chapter 18

POSTON AND THE POST

RANDALL STEPHENS NEXT reviewed the 1969 newspaper article written by Ted Poston, the same article that was subsequently attached to the DOJ's 1976 interview notes. Lovingly referred to by his collegues as the "Dean of Black Journalists," Theodore Roosevelt Augustus Major "Ted" Poston was one of the first African-American writers to work for a white-owned, nationally renowned newspaper. But more than that, he was a highly respected figure within the early civil rights community. "John," Stephens began, "can you talk to me a little bit about Ted Poston and the newspaper article he wrote about you and Frank Liberto in 1969?"

McFerren once more delved headfirst into a somewhat unnecessary prologue. But by this time, Stephens had grown fond of John's eccentric way of storytelling and somewhat hoped that the elderly wise man would include other details that, while not asked for, would be vital to the overall investigation. Stephens again sealed his lips, sat back in his steel and vinyl chair, and listened intently to McFerren's account of Poston's early work in Fayette County during the voter registration drive and Tent City era.

"Now let me explain all this to you so you'll understand. Back around 1959, 1960, we was up against the wall around here cause the white folks put out the blacklist. See, the list had all the black folks names on it that was registerin' to vote, and we couldn't do no shopping or business with any of the white merchants here in Somerville if our names was written down on that list. Soon after the list was made, we heard about it, and we had one of our undergrounds that worked for Dr. Morris get a hold of it...they sneaked it out from Dr. Morris's office here in town. Then we took the list and had it copied in Memphis by another black fella who was a banker." McFerren paused, leaned back in his chair, and stared up at the ceiling for a second, clearly trying to remember a crucial detail. Then, with a quick jerk back to his originally hunched position, he started again.

"Yeah, his name was Jesse Turner, and he was another leader in the movement who was workin' over at the Tri-State Bank in Memphis. So we took the list to Jesse Turner at the bank, and he made copies for us on his machine. Then, we drove back to Somerville and had our underground person that worked inside Dr. Morris's place put the blacklist back in his office, so it wouldn't look like we had messed with it or nothin'. Then, after that, we met with Ted Poston, and he worked for the *New York Post*. We gave him a copy of the blacklist to prove it was real, and he wrote about it in the newspaper in 1960."

Stephens was fascinated by the rich firsthand history lesson he was getting from McFerren regarding the local civil rights movement. But he was also focused on learning more about Poston's exposé on the King case. "John, can we fast forward a little bit? I'd like to talk about Ted Poston's 1969 article now, if we could."

Happy to oblige his interviewer, McFerren continued. "Okay, now about the same time Bill Sartor was visitin' here and drivin' around with me to different places, James Earl Ray confessed to killing Dr. King in March. As soon as that happen, everything around here got stirred up again, and Ted Poston asked if he could write about me and everything I had knowed about Dr. King and the killin'. After some thinkin' about it, I told him it was okay, and he set to writin' about Fat Frank in the newspaper."

Stephens pondered the timeline. Ray had, in fact, agreed to plead guilty to murdering Dr. King in order to avoid the death penalty and therefore testified in court on March 10, 1969, to doing so. Then on the 13th, the self-professed killer recanted his earlier confession, and by March 15, Poston's "King Murder: A Mystery Call" had been published in the *New York Post*. Stephens had studied the published editorial numerous times since first seeing it, and was, by this time, aware of several key details.

First, Liberto's name was never mentioned in Poston's article. Instead, the phrase "Memphis businessman" was used to describe the person who McFerren overheard screaming into the telephone. Second, Poston had obviously been granted permission by the once-anonymous McFerren to print his name in the newspaper, a fact that further confirmed McFerren's ongoing bravery to Stephens.

Next, the article reaffirmed McFerren's account of his return to Fayette County on the evening of April 4, 1968, and the subsequent telephone call that occurred between the store owner and his wife, Viola. As was described earlier to Stephens by McFerren, the article repeated the assertion that when Viola told John that Dr. King's shooting had occurred around 3:00 p.m., he instantly corrected her, already well aware that the horrific event had actually taken place sometime after 5:00 p.m.

Finally, a vast majority of the remaining article focused on the interview Poston conducted with the Rev. Sydney Baxton Bryant. Poston's report went on to describe the call that transpired between John at his Fayette County address and the Rev. Bryant in Nashville on April 7, 1968. Bryant was then quoted in Poston's article as saying that as soon as he arrived in Fayette County on Sunday, he spoke at length with the McFerren couple and then told John:

> ...that the authorities had to be told. After questioning him closely for several hours, I drove into Memphis and told the whole thing to Mr. Holloman.

Corroborating Stephens' earlier conclusions, Poston's article indicated that MPD Director Frank C. Holloman set up a meeting in room 561 at the Peabody Hotel in Memphis. The printed story also reaffirmed that the meeting lasted from 2:30 to 5:30 a.m. on Monday morning. And just as earlier asserted by McFerren to Stephens regarding Holloman's presence, Poston's article also confirmed that the meeting included "an FBI agent, Holloman, and the head of Memphis Homicide Division." Bryant then explained to Poston that the three law enforcement officials in the room that morning:

> ...took the names and addresses of both white men involved, and had McFerren draw a diagram of where he stood unseen while the telephone conversations were carried on. They promised him police protection and promised to take action immediately.

Stephens soon realized upon reading Poston's interview of Bryant that McFerren's initial drawing of the Scott Street warehouse (one that was never tracked down by Stephens) was created on April 8, 1968, and was the first in a series of three diagrams McFerren would continue to sketch for the DOJ in 1976 and HSCA in 1978. Stephens confirmed the minor detail by asking McFerren, "John, when you were at the Peabody that night, did you draw a diagram of Fat Frank's warehouse?"

McFerren replied instantly, "That's right. See, I wanted them polices to know I was really there and was tellin' the truth. So I proved to them that I knowed where everything was with my drawin'.'"

According to the article, Bryant also told the New York journalist, "he [Bryant] kept in touch with the FBI agent [O.V. Johnson]," who, although outwardly excited at first by McFerren's account, eventually "cooled down to where he said, 'We're not sure it's important.'" Poston's article then went on to detail the involvement of "a reporter for a national news magazine." Undoubtedly, the unnamed reporter being described by Bryant in Poston's article was *TIME* stringer Bill Sartor. Instantly, Stephens gave serious attention to the next section in Poston's piece. It stated that, as soon as Sartor submitted his report to the national publication's chief editors, a "conference" occurred between staff members at the "magazine's Washington bureau" and "officials of the Justice Dept." Bryant reinforced the suspiciousness of the situation by telling Poston:

> Naturally, I don't know what went on there...but–(the reporter) hinted that the Washington boys (Justice and the FBI) persuaded them not to print anything right then since it might hamper the hunt for the killer.

Before, Stephens had been confused as to why the April 26 issue of *TIME* contained almost nothing of Sartor's report on McFerren. But now it was clear. The strange Washington, D.C. bedfellows, the FBI, the DOJ, and the magazine's top editors, had decided as a collective to quash McFerren's claims. Again, Stephens could not help but wonder if the gutting of Sartor's submission was, in reality, the result of the federal government's possible fear of McFerren and his fly-in-the-ointment eyewitness account at the time.

Poston's editorial then detailed Bryant's third-person account of Sartor notifying Memphis Attorney Russell X. Thompson of McFerren's story. The newspaper article asserted that Thompson was "a Memphis lawyer who later was to become co-defense counsel for James Earl Ray, when he was finally apprehended as the trigger man in the killing." The article also stated that at the same time Poston was writing his piece, Thompson scheduled a meeting with Jack Greenberg, director of the NAACP's Legal Defense Fund in New York. Although not detailed in the article, Stephens learned later on that Thompson met with Greenberg to discuss Ray's alleged innocence in the shooting. The Rev. Bryant continued to speak on behalf of the apprehensive, now-always-on-alert McFerren in the article by telling Poston:

Someone has shot through the windows of his store [and] some Negroes smuggled whiskey, which is strictly forbidden, into his lunchroom. Some women he had never seen before started fights in his laundromat. He has expressed fears to me that someone may be hiring Negroes—members of his own race—to try to shut his mouth about what he heard.

In an effort to give government officials in both Memphis and Washington the opportunity to comment on McFerren's 1968 allegations, Poston wrote, "The Post learned the FBI had investigated McFerren's story and decided it was not true." The New York reporter's piece also stated:

In Memphis, Asst. Attorney General Robert Dwyer [former member of the Ray prosecution team led by D.A. Philip M. Canale Jr.] told The Post that Memphis police had checked the story out and found nothing to substantiate it. He said the man McFerren identified as receiving the call had been at home with his wife and a friend at the time McFerren said he was talking over the phone in his office.

Stephens contemplated the context of Poston's article and the impact it would have on McFerren's life in 1969. It seemed remarkable that, even before the March news story and the Anderson and McNeil attack in December, McFerren was already enduring veiled reprisals at the hands of paid, unfamiliar African-American agitators. It was also fascinating that Bryant's interview with Poston was printed just five months before the same white Methodist pastor traveled to Somerville to assist John and Viola in the local demonstrations. Given that an unnamed "Memphis businessman" had been implicated by a now publicly named John McFerren in the same news article, Stephens considered the August arrival of Bryant in Fayette County and the possible impression his presence had on an already nervous Mayor I.P. Yancey.

In the weeks and months following the Pulliams' August 12, 1969 attack on the Hobson women, Baxton Bryant's involvement in the future protests, and Dick Gregory's high-profile assistance in late September, the small town of Somerville would remain a powder keg of racial tension until the cold winter chill of December dulled everyone's fury. On September 28, 1969, an additional, thankfully nonlethal, shooting took place at McFerren's store, perpetrated once again by two white men. Nonviolent activists conducted sit-ins on the Fayette County Courthouse steps, only to be pelted with painful torrents of high pressurized water from local fire hoses. Somerville and Fayette County law enforcement officials, in an effort to keep the violent downtown clashes from being photographed and seen by the outside public, stole the cameras of visiting newsmen. And the area's angry white residents, resolute in their efforts to stoke the flames of racial hatred and inequality, showed up in droves to verbally and physically assault the peaceful activists.

When Stephens asked for a final comment concerning Poston and his March 15, 1969 article, McFerren dejectedly replied, "See, Ted Poston helped the League out with the voter registration drive and afterward with the Fat Frank story. So that's why when I made them tapes the year after, I figured he would want to write about them too."

Chapter 19

AUDIO REEL REVIEW

WHEN IT CAME time to discuss McFerren's secret recordings, there was little to clarify since no one had ever publicly acknowledged or refuted the contents of the audio reels. Leaving nothing to chance, however, Stephens questioned the former civil rights leader about his recordings and the underground network of African-American informants he maintained throughout the '60s and '70s. As he had already outlined to Holmes a few years earlier, McFerren again explained to Stephens that, due to the possible attempt on his life by the Anderson brothers and W.C. McNeil in the winter of 1969, he had taken it upon himself to record his informants. It was during these recording sessions that McFerren obtained damning information about Somerville Mayor I.P. Yancey, not only concerning the mayor's orchestration and financing of the '69 beating, but also regarding his involvement in maneuvering, protecting, and paying James Earl Ray both before and after the shooting of Dr. King.

Stephens wanted to be absolutely certain on a few points, the first of which was the exact date and time Ray's Ford Mustang was allegedly spotted at Yancey's Chevrolet garage. As before, McFerren again asserted that the date was April 2, 1968, and that it was extremely late in the evening when the Mustang was seen in Somerville. In McFerren's words, "Ray spent the night there." McFerren also confirmed to Stephens that according to Karl Mosby's mother, Mrs. Edna Coe, Yancey unexpectedly flew to London twice, once just before the shooting and then again immediately after. Just as Mosby asserted to Holmes, McFerren then told Stephens about aiding Mrs. Coe in her efforts to get out of town after being fired by Yancey. McFerren confided in Stephens that, "I gave her some money, but I got messed out of that deal too." When Stephens asked him to elaborate, McFerren half-jokingly commented that Mrs. Coe never paid him back the money he loaned her to flee the area.

Stephens then went on to ask about the Oakland, Tennessee pastor issue discussed on the recordings. According to both McFerren and Holmes, the recorded informant's name was Rev. Howard Massey. As heard on the tape, Massey claimed that two days before the assassination, late in the evening, an Oakland pastor named Harris had been visited at his home by an unnamed white man who claimed Dr. King was going to be killed during his next trip to Memphis. Holmes had speculated earlier that the anonymous white man was, in fact, James Earl Ray, and that Ray's comment to Harris was a late night, pre-assassination confession or warning of sorts. But Stephens wasn't so sure, and McFerren himself had almost no additional insight on the issue. Based on McFerren's inconclusive answers regarding the Oakland pastor issue, coupled with the topic's unclear importance within the investigation as a whole, Stephens ultimately decided to put it aside for the time being so that he could focus on other, more relevant leads in the case.

McFerren's audio-recorded statement about Russell X. Thompson was the next topic Stephens wanted to cover. McFerren verified that Thompson, a Memphis attorney who was later involved in Ray's initial defense with Attorneys Art Hanes Sr. and Jr., first traveled to Fayette County to interview both John and his wife Viola at their store a short time after Sartor's initial visit. McFerren stated in his recordings that during another meeting later that year, Thompson warned him to "keep it quiet...to yourself." When Stephens asked McFerren what Thompson meant when he told him to remain quiet, the grocer immediately replied, "He wanted me to keep my mouth shut about Fat Frank and James Earl Ray."

McFerren then went on to explain that Thompson eventually told him and Viola that, for safety's sake, they shouldn't be seen out in public together. Then, it was McFerren's claim that a number of years later while representing the Memphis Police Union, Thompson also legally assisted Viola in her request for a divorce. When Stephens asked McFerren why, in 1976, he told the DOJ that Thompson wanted to break up his marriage with Viola, McFerren again replied without hesitation, "Russell Thompson and John Wilder were buddies! He was helping the Memphis police and Wilder break up my family!" Based on McFerren's insights on Thompson, and Poston's description of the same Memphis attorney, Stephens realized there was much more to the subject and he scribbled a note to himself to look into Thompson at a later date.

Next, he broached the matter of McFerren's audio-taped statement about an African-American man he had referred to as John Thomas, a Fayette County resident and nearby business owner Stephens determined was actually named John Hardy Thompson. As McFerren claimed in the recordings, Thompson's brother was mixed up with the same "underworld gang" that put the contract out on Dr. King. When Stephens asked for clarification, McFerren again confirmed that the brother of his neighboring Fayette County friend and entrepreneur had been arrested for illegal liquor transportation and distribution. He also stated that the Memphis mobsters who the brother had been working for at the time were members of the same "syndicate" that Liberto and the other conspirators belonged to. With all of the previously established links between Liberto's illegal rackets in Memphis and the pool of African-American laborers in Fayette County, Stephens believed the bootlegging claim rang true.

Finally, the Big Fella concluded the secret audio reel portion of his interview by asking McFerren to list all of the people he had given, or tried to give, copies of the recordings to. McFerren confirmed that Hayward Brown, the DOJ, and Ted Poston all had duplicate copies in their possession by early 1970. But when Stephens asked McFerren if he could remember giving copies to any other journalists that same year, specifically Bill Sartor, McFerren said he couldn't remember. He did recall, however, trying to convince Robert Hamburger in 1971 and the DOJ in 1976 to look into the secret tape issue, but confirmed that both parties ultimately declined.

But McFerren's most memorable interaction regarding his secret tapes was his work with Kenneth Herman and Bill Pepper in 1977. As he had thoroughly explained to Holmes back in 2012, McFerren repeated his assertion that he took his last copy of the audio reels to Herman's Graham Street home in Memphis to have them duplicated at Pepper's request. When Stephens concluded his questioning by asking McFerren if he ever gave copies of the tapes to Gene and Ernestine Johnson or anyone else working for the House Select Committee in 1978, an instantly hostile McFerren replied in a loud and drawn out tone, "Nooo! Gene Johnson said I did in them papers, but I didn't! Them Johnson folks lied on me!"

Chapter 20

UNCLE SAM
AND THE SEVENTIES

BY THIS POINT in Randall Stephens' research, it was common knowledge that McFerren's contacts at the DOJ during the 1960s were well-known federal civil rights attorneys John Doar and Nick Flannery, and in the early '70s, perhaps the attorney general himself, John Mitchell. Also, a number of McFerren's 1976 statements to DOJ task force Attorneys Fred G. Folsom and James F. Walker regarding Ray's physical appearance, Mayor Yancey, Russell Thompson, Ted Poston, and the secret audiotapes had already been clarified. But when it came to the DOJ's typed interview notes, there remained a handful of issues Stephens still needed to ask McFerren about.

Folsom and Walker

The first item that needed to be clarified was McFerren's 1976 statement that his gas station's telephone had been bugged. It was

Mr. McFerren's long-held claim that, in an effort to convince a frightened Mrs. McFerren to divorce her doggedly outspoken husband, John Wilder began calling Viola on the couple's business telephone. As detailed by Holmes, McFerren became aware of the Fayette County lawyer's intrusive conversations with his impressionable wife. McFerren then informed the DOJ of the intrusion and requested that federal authorities wiretap his store's business line in order to capture Wilder's manipulative tactics.

In addition, McFerren was also of the staunch opinion that his store's payphone had been bugged as well. As outlined in Robert Hamburger's book, *Our Portion of Hell*, McFerren stated that the station's indoor coin-operated public telephone did not work most of the time and that he would place "two paper sacks and put one inside of the other one and put it over the receiver and hang it up." It was McFerren's contention that, after his attempts at muffling the receiver using the paper sacks, the payphone would eventually ring, and the operator on the other end of the line would ask him if he was having trouble with it functioning properly.

Stephens felt it important to differentiate the two telephone stories while also establishing a timeline. He first asked McFerren about the business line and Wilder's harassment. As he had done with Holmes, McFerren repeated his belief that Wilder was in violation of the 1962 federal landowners agreement by harassing Viola over the telephone. McFerren believed that, if these conversations were recorded by the DOJ, the Fayette County lawyer could be prosecuted for violating the McFerren couple's civil rights. McFerren also told Stephens that the payphone bugging and paper-sack solution was an altogether separate issue, that he never asked for the payphone to be installed at the business, and that he was suspicious when the telephone company placed it inside his store's main lobby. His suspicion that the government was using the payphone as a listening device grew in intensity when he tested his theory using the paper sacks, and the concerned operator suddenly called the same payphone to question McFerren about it.

Though it was a small, somewhat insignificant detail, Stephens was also curious about McFerren's claim to the DOJ that "he had someone from an electronics company inspect his telephone." Stephens, determined to leave no stone unturned, asked, "John, when you spoke to the Justice Department in 1976, you told them that you hired a man from an electronics company to inspect your phone for bugs. Can you tell me who you hired?"

McFerren answered, "It was Hayward Brown. See, he was a master electronics man around here, and he knew all about how to work on sound equipment like radios, tape recorders, telephones, and the like. So, I asked him to check out my phones one day 'cause I know they was bugged. I just didn't want to drag his feet through my mud, so I never told the Justice Department his name." While Stephens was skeptical whether Brown had actually determined if the phones inside the store were wiretapped or not, the reply McFerren gave was simple, made complete sense, and clearly answered the interviewer's question.

Although he was nearly convinced that McFerren, his regular cadre of underground civil rights visitors, and the gas station itself were, in fact, the targets of illegal FBI wiretaps or even bugs, Stephens decided to avoid discussing the legitimacy of McFerren's telephone bugging beliefs. Now satisfied as to why the Fayette businessman told the DOJ about the telephones in 1976, he tried to settle the issue with one last line of questioning. Curious if the paper-sack anecdote inside Hamburger's book could have been hijacked by Attorney General Janet Reno and used in her 2000 report, Stephens asked McFerren when he last remembered placing a paper sack over the payphone, and if he had ever done the same to his business line.

Adamant and immediate in his response, McFerren pointed to the naked, north indoor wall of the store's lobby and stated, "I only used the sacks on the payphone that was over there, and that was a long time ago. When they took it out, I never did use the sacks no more."

Stephens then inquired when the payphone was removed. McFerren replied, "I don't remember the exact date, but it was several years back." While the answer was extremely vague, Stephens still postulated that the individual who knew Hamburger, Reno, and McFerren used their knowledge of the book's paper-sack anecdote to help fill in the gaps within Reno's sketchy 2000 report. And when Stephens asked Holmes if he had ever witnessed McFerren place paper sacks over the receiver of the store's business line, Holmes' reply was an abrupt and simple, "Never! No way!"

However, the most pressing matter Stephens wanted to discuss concerned McFerren's 1976 statement that "Wallace was in on it" and "the same man that killed President Kennedy killed Dr. King." The next explanations were as enlightening as ever. As Stephens had earlier theorized, McFerren verified that he was indeed privy to the close relationship between the Wilders and the immediate family of Alabama Governor George C. Wallace. Based on his limited knowledge of Ray's temporary residence in Birmingham, Alabama, the alleged assassin's unofficial California campaign work for then-presidential candidate Wallace, and Wilder's relationship with the same Alabama governor, McFerren believed that the leadership within both the Tennessee and Alabama state governments helped direct the conspiracy to assassinate Dr. King. But there was more.

When Stephens asked him to clarify his allegations that Kennedy and King were killed by the same man, McFerren's array of scattered puzzle pieces began to fall into place. It was his claim that when he told the DOJ that the "same man" committed both assassinations, he didn't mean that both men were killed by the same triggerman. McFerren was merely trying to communicate his belief that both of the shootings had been orchestrated by the same mastermind. His curiosity now piqued, Stephens asked the next obvious question, "So, who was the man you believe planned both of the murders?"

McFerren paused for a moment to think and then spoke quietly and slowly. "I don't know the man's name, but what Bill Sartor told me years ago was, it was the head Mafia man down there in New Orleans who done most of the plannin'." Stephens was familiar with who was being referenced due to his prior research into Bill Sartor and the HSCA, and the name Carlos Marcello instantly popped into his mind.

The final item Stephens wanted to question McFerren about concerned the gunshot wound he suffered on September 10, 1976, the same gunshot wound that DOJ attorney James Walker brushed aside. McFerren went on to describe the events that unfolded that night to Stephens. McFerren explained that he had been warned of the impending attack by one of his informants inside Liberto's warehouse. Prepared with a holstered sidearm of his own, McFerren returned fire through the building's plate glass window just after being shot in the abdomen. After confirming his multi-day stay at St. Joseph's Hospital in downtown Memphis, McFerren reiterated his earlier belief that the shooting was directly related to his knowledge of Ray's work with Liberto and that the Scott Street businessman no doubt hired someone to kill him in September of that year.

Stephens went on to share with McFerren that on September 17, just one week after the shooting in front of the Fayette County business, a very crucial and long-contested bill finally passed the House of Representatives in Washington, D.C., authorizing the formation of the House Select Committee on Assassinations. This was again the very same HSCA that would go on to question McFerren about Liberto for the next two years.

Johnson and Johnson

The issue of McFerren's extremely contentious dealings with the House Select Committee's lead MLK investigators had already been thoroughly covered and documented by both Holmes and Stephens. But as a matter of due diligence, Stephens went over the conflict one last time while he still had McFerren in the hot seat. As before, the former civil rights activist again confirmed that HSCA investigators Gene and Ernestine Johnson visited him at his place of business on a number of occasions in 1977 and 1978.

McFerren also told Stephens that during his multiple interviews, he tried to explain James Earl Ray's connection to "Fat Frank," Somerville Mayor Yancey's involvement with Ray, and Yancey's friendship with Memphis Mayor Henry Loeb. As he had repeatedly stated before, McFerren then explained to Stephens that he never made the admission to the Johnson team that he failed the 1968 Galt/Ray photo lineup, nor did he ever hand over his last copies of the secret audio reels to the pair of HSCA interviewers. The frustrated Fayette Countian once more reasserted to Stephens that, because of his inability to accurately read what had been erroneously typed in the 1978 affidavit, he naively followed Johnson's instructions by signing the document and handwritten sheet of yellow legal paper. Still under the assumption that he would be given the opportunity to testify at the public hearings in Washington, McFerren was overcome by harrowing confusion when an overtly unfriendly Gene Johnson told him that he would not be allowed to speak and that he needn't bother making the trip to D.C. to do so.

Chapter 21

SLICK WILLY

BOTH MARCUS HOLMES and Randall Stephens had already devoted a tremendous amount of personal time and energy to the topic of Bill Pepper's long, selfishly one-sided relationship with John McFerren. But as was now customary, Stephens reviewed the matter once more while McFerren was still his captive subject. For the sake of continuity, Stephens again asked McFerren when he first met Pepper, and as before, he stated that it was sometime in 1977 during the HSCA's investigation, prior to the 1979 date Pepper claimed in his book, *Orders to Kill*. Then, just as he had told Holmes, McFerren reiterated that it was during this same period that he drove to Kenneth Herman's Memphis home to have his audio reels duplicated.

McFerren told Stephens he just assumed that, after Herman copied the tapes, the Memphis music producer and part-time private investigator mailed the duplicates to Pepper, and that the New York attorney kept them for himself. McFerren learned only after Holmes' own investigation that Herman, under Pepper's direction, mailed at least one of the duplicate reels to someone at the DOJ. But before Stephens could ask his next question, McFerren volunteered his opinion on the issue. "I can't be sure, but I'm thinkin' now, since me and Marcus talked to Kenneth Herman, that them Johnsons got copies of my tapes from Pepper."

Stephens moved on to the next question on his list. "Did you know that you were being filmed for Pepper's documentary movie back when he came to visit your store in 1989?"

Once again appearing robust in his sincerity, McFerren retorted with a quick and simple, "Nooo!"

Stephens continued, "So Pepper never told you that he wanted you to speak on camera or that there was a film crew outside that day?"

Again, the grocer forcefully replied, "No, nuh-uh! Pepper never said nothing to me about it, and I didn't know I was in that movie until Marcus showed it to me a couple years back."

McFerren then confirmed to Stephens, just as he had to Holmes, that in 1993 during the filming of the HBO mock trial, he drove to Memphis to testify in court, but that only after a brief moment or two of speaking on the witness stand, Pepper told him that he was no longer needed and that he could leave the courtroom.

Next, Stephens asked, "Did Pepper ever send you a copy of one of his books?" Trying not to look embarrassed, McFerren confessed that the *Orders to Kill* author was aware of his inability to read. Unsatisfied with the answer, Stephens restated the question, "So, he never mailed you a copy of one of his books so that someone could possibly read it to you?"

Again McFerren quickly replied, "No, uh-uh."

Stephens followed up by asking, "Has anyone ever read Pepper's books to you, maybe a family member or a friend?"

McFerren explained, "No, nuh-uh. The only people who has ever read those Dr. King books to me is you and Marcus." While he instinctively understood the real purpose behind Pepper's failure to provide McFerren with copies of his two MLK books before 2015, Stephens thought it odd that of all of McFerren's adult children who lived in the Memphis area, none had taken the time to purchase Pepper's authored works and recite to their father what had been written about him. Was there a reason McFerren's nearby daughters wanted him to remain in the dark?

The next topic Stephens discussed was the short list of African-American witnesses named in *Orders to Kill* who knew Frank C. Liberto, the men Pepper allegedly met through McFerren. Looking up at his interviewee each time for some type of acknowledgment, Stephens recited the names out loud, one by one from Pepper's own authored list. "Old Pal? Robert Tyus? O.D. Hester? Someone named 'Slim?' Columbus Jones? How about Tango?" After each name, McFerren simply shook his head and then spoke after Stephens was finished.

"Look here, I already been through all this with Marcus. The only folks I told Pepper about was Freddie Granberry, Ezell Smith, T.R. Wright, and my divorce lawyer who was Hughie Ragan. All them other names, I don't know. But also, Marcus found out later that Granberry used to get money from Pepper to show him around town, you know, so that he could meet more people. So maybe Pepper met them other people that way."

Stephens took a moment to think about McFerren's corroboration of Holmes' earlier findings. In his first book, Pepper had, in fact, written a fair amount about Ezell Smith, Tommy Wright, and Jackson, Tennessee Attorney Hughie Ragan while making only a one-time, extremely insignificant mention of Freddie Granberry. But as Holmes first discovered and then later explained to Stephens, Granberry was a Fayette County neighbor of McFerren's, had been kicked out of his home during the Tent City era, and was in need of quick cash in the '80s and '90s. Granberry eventually worked quietly behind McFerren's back to rectify his financial woes while satisfying Pepper's

hearty appetite for new West Tennessee leads. According to Robert
Lee Bell, who had been a Tent City resident along with Granberry,
it was through this financial arrangement between Granberry and
Pepper that the New York attorney came into contact with Frank C.
Liberto's previous black employees and other underworld associates.
Eventually, Granberry introduced Pepper to Bell at the hospital
while the now wheelchair-bound man was recuperating from his leg
amputation.

As if now fearful the quiet, introspective Stephens was equating
him to Granberry's past work as one of Pepper's greedy secret
informants, McFerren interrupted Stephens' completely unrelated
thought process by loudly declaring, "Look here, I never took one red
copper from Pepper!"

After informing McFerren that he already knew Pepper never
paid him for information, Stephens smiled, reassured his new friend
that he didn't view him in that kind of light, and moved on to the
topic of Pepper's first encounter with Robert Bell.

Stephens asked, "John, did you know Pepper spoke to Robert
Bell?"

McFerren didn't have to think about the question before
answering. "Yes, but see, I didn't tell Pepper about him 'cause, like I
said before, he was workin' for Fat Frank up there at the warehouse,
and I didn't want him to get hemmed up with them Mafias out
there over somethin' I said to Pepper or anybody else. One day, the
one-legged man just came in here and told me that Pepper showed up
to talk to him, and that was it."

Based on his familiarity with Pepper's habit of changing people's
identities to obscure the truth, Stephens now wondered if one of those
unfamiliar names printed in *Orders to Kill* was, in fact, a pseudonym
the author assigned to Robert Bell. As Bell told Holmes, Granberry at
one time brought Pepper to visit Bell while he was in the hospital. And
of all of the so-called connections Pepper said he had met through

McFerren, and who had been researched by Stephens, "Tango" was the only person who fit Bell's profile the best, and who could not be verified through public records.

Also, it was absolutely understandable to Stephens why Pepper might obscure Bell's name. If the attorney wanted to hide Bell's 1967-drive with Willie Green and Ray from Only, Tennessee, to the Scott Street warehouse, or the work Bell did on the red-to-white Mustang on behalf of Liberto, then changing Bell's name to "Tango" made complete sense. And finally, Stephens was able to track down the federal court records related to Bell's interstate transportation of the stolen Kellogg's cereal boxes for Liberto in 1984. According to the large stack of court documents, the FBI-DOJ case against Bell was successfully tried and prosecuted by local U.S. Attorney Lawrence Joseph "Larry" Laurenzi, a man who, as of Stephens' 2016 interviews with McFerren, still lived in nearby Germantown, Tennessee. Stephens made yet another note to look deeper into Bell, the federal case against him, and the other players who were involved.

He then addressed the issue of Ezell Smith and the Browning rifle Smith likely outfitted for Liberto just before the shooting. "John, can you tell me about your friendship with Ezell Smith?"

As if only yesterday, McFerren again wasted little time in explaining to Stephens who Ezell was and the role he played in the past. "Alright now, early on, my brother Robert owned this business before me. The first building, the smaller one that Robert was runnin', was just south 'a here, next door. But when the blacklist started, and Rube Rhea dug up his gas tanks, Robert got beat down and quit the business. So, I took it over from my brother and got into the gas and grocery business back around 1959 and '60. Then, I bought new gas tanks and gas pumps to replace the ones that was taken up by Rube Rhea. But when this fella come out to dig the holes for the new tanks, he got the heat put on him by his higher ups, the white men who had a money grip on him. So, after only diggin' for half a day, he got scared and quit 'cause he was helpin' us Negroes with our independent oil business. Now, the company I bought the tanks and pumps from had a top engineerin' man, a black fella, who helped me bury the tanks anyhow, and his name was Ezell, Ezell Smith. So Ezell showed us how to dig the holes on our own with tractors and scoops, and later on after a lotta diggin', we got the tanks in the ground."

Stephens was again impressed by McFerren's ability to recall the early endeavor. But as was typical by now, he was more interested in Ezell's involvement with Liberto in 1968. Once more, Stephens tried to gently nudge the dialogue forward. "John, what about Ezell's work with Liberto and the rifle? Can we talk about that?"

McFerren proceeded. "Okay, so after the killin' was done, Dr. King's killin', Ezell came by the store and he was real nervous. And I could tell he wanted to talk to me about somethin' important. Now, this was before I started tape recordin' my underground folks, so I never got this recorded. But, Ezell and me, we walked outside 'cause I didn't want any of the bugs in the store to catch what he might say. So, we went outside, and he told me he worked on a rifle, a Browning, for Fat Frank just before the killin of Dr. King took place. Later, when Pepper started comin' around, I told him about Ezell and the Browning rifle, and Pepper wenta lookin' for him so they could talk about it. But that was all I knowed until Marcus started lookin' into things, and that's when we found out that Kenneth Herman talked to Ezell."

At first, it was Holmes' educated suspicion that Granberry had provided the introduction between Ezell Smith and Pepper's private investigators, despite the New York author's claim that they failed to locate Smith before his death. Ezell Smith, who was a longtime mutual friend of both McFerren and Granberry, had long claimed that he had attached a sling and a scope to a Browning 30.06 rifle for Liberto just before the death of Dr. King. He also asserted that Liberto's Browning, purchased from the Stratton-Warren Hardware

Company once located on the corner of Front Street and East Carolina Avenue in downtown Memphis, was the actual murder weapon used in the assassination.

Smith's statement to McFerren concerning the make of the alleged murder weapon was later verified when Holmes spoke to Kenneth Herman about the matter over the telephone. Herman, on the outs with Pepper and living in Florida in 2012, was happy to confirm to Holmes his earlier interview of Ezell Smith. The Florida resident also confirmed that Smith claimed that the rifle he assembled for Liberto was a Browning and that the weapon was purchased from the now-defunct Stratton and Warren hardware business.

Holmes eventually concluded, as did Stephens, that Pepper lied about his inability to find Smith because Ezell's testimony concerning the Browning could be associated with the Browning cardboard box Ray allegedly left near the murder scene. This piece of information might link Ray to Liberto and was, therefore, omitted in Pepper's book. Stephens wondered, was the Browning rifle indeed separated from its box by Liberto? And was that box then given to Ray and used to transport his Remington? Stephens would obviously need to look into the issue much further.

The final and perhaps most delicate Bill Pepper subject that needed to be addressed revolved around the notion that Ray worked for Liberto and McFerren's failure to say so at the 1999 Loyd Jowers civil trial. Choosing his words very carefully, Stephens asked, "John, can you tell me why you didn't talk about Ray's work for Liberto when you were on the witness stand at the 1999 civil trial?" What followed was an immediate uneasy silence, one that made Stephens somewhat nervous. Fearful he had just offended McFerren or indirectly accused him of being easily swayed by the New York attorney, the interviewer watched nervously as the blue-eyed proprietor stared for a moment through the gas station's dingy plate glass windows toward the three-way intersection outside.

Coming out of his reverie, McFerren finally started to speak. "Let me put it to you like this. I knowed Pepper for more...now let me see, yeah. I knowed him for more than thirty years by the time I started tellin' Marcus about this mess, and when I say 'I'm with you,' I keep my word and stick with you. You can take it to the bank! And at that time, I was stickin' only with Pepper, all the way. Also, I didn't think Ray had done the actual killing, and neither did Pepper. So, when he asked me to keep quiet about Ray knowing Fat Frank, I just done what he asked me." Confirming his earlier suspicion that Pepper coerced McFerren into silence, the straightforward answer satisfied Stephens' curiosity, and he immediately dropped the subject.

Stephens' next question concerned the date of Liberto's death as recorded in the 1999 Jowers trial transcript. Looking directly into McFerren's piercing blue eyes, as if to underscore the importance of the question, Stephens asked, "In the trial, you said Frank Liberto died in 1996. Did you find out what year Liberto died on your own, or did Pepper tell you the date before you came to court?"

This time there was no drawn-out, uncomfortable silence to contend with. McFerren answered his interviewer swiftly and matter-of-factly, "Pepper told me. See, I never went to that Scott Street warehouse again after Dr. King got killed. So as far as I knowed, Frank died... the way I got a hold of it was through Pepper."

Already aware that it was a shot in the dark, Stephens followed up the question anyway by asking, "Do you know for certain when Fat Frank actually died?"

Again, McFerren did not hesitate, "All I knowed is what Pepper told me."

Stephens, adamant in his need to clarify every minuscule detail in the case, asked another obvious question. "So, Robert Bell never told you when Liberto died?"

McFerren's answer was immediate, "The one-legged-man and me, we never did discuss it after he got outta prison." Confident in

McFerren's candid answers, Stephens was more certain than ever that Ray's former New York attorney had manipulated the Fayette grocer over a period of several decades. With nearly all of his Bill Pepper questions answered, the Big Fella now moved on to the topic of yet another backhanded lawyer from McFerren's past.

Chapter 22

NEARBY NEMESIS

WHILE THE COUNTLESS personal conflicts between John Wilder and John McFerren fascinated the history-hungry investigator, Randall Stephens dedicated little effort to the matter at first during his multiple interviews with John. As he had done numerous times before, McFerren simply repeated his former assertion that, in cooperation with the wealthy white power structure of Somerville and the county, John Wilder spent the better part of the '60s and '70s trying to break up his family, shut down his business, and ruin his life.

Stephens then moved on to the meat and potatoes of his inquiry by asking McFerren to again confirm his knowledge of Wilder's relationship with Frank C. Liberto. John once more explained that, according to an informant named T.R. Wright, Frank Liberto frequently drove to Somerville on Saturdays to meet with Wilder at his law office located on the east side of the downtown square. Stephens wanted to be certain as to the time periods. "John, can you tell me if you remember when Liberto visited Wilder? Was it before 1968? After 1968? Around 1976, or maybe during the House Select Committee hearings?"

McFerren glared at Stephens, most likely irritated by the suggestion that his mind was failing him, and then barked sharply, "Hey, I know! Look here, it was before and after '68, and a long while after that! You don't think I remember? Look, when I tell you something, you can take it to the bank!"

Stephens smiled softly and tried to ingratiate himself. "I'm sorry, John. I didn't mean to question your memory. I just need to make sure I get your story straight."

As a follow-up question, Stephens broached the matter of John's former divorce attorney in Jackson, Tennessee, and the lawyer's possible knowledge of Wilder's underworld ties. "John, Pepper wrote in his book that your divorce lawyer knew all about Wilder's relationship with local mobsters and other criminals. Is that right? Did your lawyer know about Wilder and Liberto?"

McFerren's answer was immediate, "That's right. See, I told Pepper about my divorce from Viola. My lawyer's last name was Ragan, and he was out in Jackson. Now, when I was going through my divorce, Ragan helped me, and I told him all about Wilder, Russell Thompson, the polices, and Fat Frank, and the Mafias, and how they was all in a cahoots to break up my marriage. But Ragan told me he already knowed about Wilder and all his work with the Mafias out in Memphis."

The next question he posed to McFerren related to Wilder's familiarity with Robert Bell. Stephens asked, "How about the one-legged man? Did Wilder know him too?"

McFerren again frowned at his much younger counterpart. "Of course he knew him! Wilder helped black folks around here find work all the time, and he's the one who helped Robert get a job out there with Fat Frank at the warehouse. When Robert got in trouble back awhile for selling that cereal for him [Liberto], supposedly now, I only heard this from Marcus, Wilder was the one who talked to Robert and Fat Frank about it. But that's all I know."

Stephens then rattled off a list of prominent Southern figures that had come up earlier in the investigation. "Besides Liberto, I want to read you some names, and then when I'm done, I want you to tell me if these people knew Wilder and if you think they were involved in the assassination of Dr. King." McFerren nodded quietly as his new friend proceeded. "Okay, Judge Paul Summers, Mayor I.P. Yancey, Mayor Henry Loeb, Frank Holloman, and Governor George Wallace?"

McFerren grinned slyly, raised his head and looked at Stephens. "You think I just gettin' started in this thing, don't ya?" A long silence filled the space as Stephens hesitated to respond, now unsure how to appease the elderly man's half-facetious accusation. Then, McFerren continued. "Look, I been doing this awhile, okay? So I know! All them people you named, they was all in a cahoots! All them people was working together with Wilder and Liberto in some kinda way to help in the killing of Dr. King, or to help take the killing and go under the barnyard with it! I know it!"

Stephens had heard McFerren's barnyard terminology before and knew immediately that the grocer was referring to the post-assassination cover-up. The last John Wilder topic Stephens felt compelled to cover was the Somerville lawyer's possible link to fellow attorneys Lewis K. Garrison and Bill Pepper. "Okay John, this is really important. Do you know if Wilder and Lewis Garrison ever met, or if they knew each other?"

McFerren took a second to think, "I don't know if they knew each other or not, but they probably did. 'Cause hey, how can they not know each other if they was both living here in Fayette County?"

Stephens concluded with one final question regarding Garrison's partner in crime, "What about Pepper? Did Wilder know him?"

John did not wait to answer, "I can't be sure, 'cause I never did see them together. But I talked to Pepper about James Earl Ray, Fat Frank, Wilder...all of them, I talked about all them fellas all the time, and he knew where to find Wilder up there on the east side of the courthouse. Also, one time, when Pepper was here, John Wilder's boy came in here with a couple of other fellas for no reason, and just stared me down, and then he left. I told Pepper who he was, but I don't know for sure if he checked into it or not."

Now satisfied with John's personal insights into the former lieutenant governor of Tennessee, Stephens moved on to the DOJ interview that allegedly took place in March of 1999, and the absolutely astonishing link both McFerren and Wilder had to one of the key people involved in the federal investigation.

Chapter 23

DIFFICULT DISCUSSION

ON THE SURFACE, most would have assumed that there was little to discuss regarding the March 1999 interview the DOJ purportedly conducted with the former Liberto whistleblower, particularly since Holmes had already explained to Stephens that McFerren had no recollection of speaking with members of Attorney General Janet Reno's MLK investigative team. But in his now sickened gut, Stephens realized on a profoundly emotional level that this would be, by far, one of the most difficult topics to cover with his new friend.

Still, he began with the obvious, "John, back in 1999, do you remember speaking with the Justice Department about the Dr. King case?"

Confidently, McFerren answered without waiting, "They tried to get me to talk, but like I said before, I was stickin' with Pepper at the time, and I knew he wanted me to wait until I had a chance to tell about it in the trial."

Already aware of what the answer would be, and deeply preoccupied with the difficult questions that lie ahead, Stephens heard little of McFerren's reply. Taking a deep breath, and remembering his recent promise to Holmes to broach the touchy subject with McFerren, Stephens proceeded. "Okay, the next question I need to ask you concerns John Wilder's relationship with your family. After Viola divorced you, how involved was Wilder in the lives of your ex-wife and children?"

McFerren sat quietly for a moment and then replied, "I know he helped them all the time. He done a lot of stuff for Viola. Why you asking me that?"

Stephens' stomach ache grew more intense. "Well, when I was doing my research, I discovered that your youngest daughter graduated from Yale University and then again from Harvard Law School. Is that right?"

Proudly, McFerren sat straight up in his chair and confirmed Stephens' claim. "That's right, my baby girl graduated from both them schools and became a lawyer up there in Washington."

Trying to subliminally walk McFerren down the uncomfortable path by merely looking into his eyes, Stephens reluctantly continued. "So, do you know, did Wilder help her get into those universities? In other words, do you know if he wrote letters of recommendation for your daughter?"

Again, McFerren, still oblivious to where Stephens was leading him, answered without hesitation. "Yeah, I know he helped her get in them schools, 'cause that's what her mama told me. He did."

His suspicion now confirmed, Stephens swallowed hard and prepared to tackle his most difficult question yet. "Okay, John, can I ask you, did you ever find it strange that after she graduated and became a lawyer, your own daughter got a job at the Department of Justice?"

The proverbial silence was deafening. What was probably less than a few seconds of muted tension seemed to stretch out for an eternity. As he continued to watch McFerren, now terrified he would be verbally thrown out of the store and therefore unable to ask his remaining questions, Stephens continued. "In my research, I discovered that she worked for the DOJ at the same time they were conducting their Dr. King investigation. Also, after she left the DOJ, your daughter immediately attained a top-level position at the University of Memphis as the Director of the Benjamin Hooks Institute. I'm not sure if you're aware of this or not, but the tallest building on the campus is dedicated to John Wilder, and his son David gave a lot of money to the university."

The elderly black man, while admittedly illiterate, was an extremely competent and keenly perceptive individual and now realized what Stephens was driving at. Unwilling to admit the obvious, however, McFerren simply replied, "All I know is she got some help from Wilder, but she done real good with herself all on her own."

Just as any lovingly dedicated parent would, John McFerren was quick to defend his youngest daughter and her ability to climb the professional ladder within Washington and Memphis on her own, despite what Stephens had tried to gently hint at. Sensing that John's immediate endorsement of his daughter's work ethic and professional aptitude was, in truth, a subtle warning not to pursue the delicate family matter any further, Stephens kept the details of Ms. McFerren's employment under U.S. Attorney General Janet Reno quiet, considered himself lucky to still be inside the gas station, and quickly moved on to his final line of questioning.

Chapter 24

VERY VERY DANGEROUS

RANDALL STEPHENS WAS struck by the irony that, despite being perhaps the most important topic of his entire King investigation, there was very little for him to inquire about regarding the man nicknamed Very Very Dangerous, especially since John McFerren knew almost nothing about Dr. King's other alleged assassin. Nevertheless, the now-fatigued middle-aged white man proceeded with his brief inquiry.

As he had with Holmes, McFerren explained to Stephens that for several years prior to 2012, he believed a young African-American man from Fayette County who worked for Frank C. Liberto alongside Robert Bell was, in fact, the gunman who ended Dr. King's life. When Stephens asked McFerren who the man was, the grocer happily uttered the same name he divulged earlier to Holmes. Despite his serious reservations concerning the now highly distinguished man's past involvement, Stephens scribbled a note in the margins of his questionnaire and promised his new friend that he would look into the unlikely shooter at a later date.

Finally, it was time to cover the issue of the elderly African-American man identified only as J.P. and the much-talked-about red dot he made inside McFerren's threadbare telephone book. In an attempt to confirm the identity of the informant Holmes had named just before heading off to prison, Stephens asked, "John, I want to talk to you next about the red dot inside your phonebook. Can you tell me the name of the man who made it?"

McFerren did not wait to reply. "Yes, his name is James Prayer [sic], and he lives out there on Fortune Road near Moscow. I knowed him a long time, and he helped with Tent City. See, like I told Marcus a few years ago, I always heard someone on Fortune Road had something to do with the killing of Dr. King. But I only got a hold of it, I only found out who the man was when Prayer [sic] came in here and made that dot. He told me the name of his neighbor who he knowed done the killing and then marked it for me so I could keep it for my records."

Realizing there was little else to question McFerren on, Stephens began to wrap up his inquiry by asking the grocer to confirm his strange 2013 encounter with the adult son of Very Very Dangerous. Just as he had told Holmes two years prior, McFerren repeated his assertion to Stephens that the unfamiliar man was white, yet dark-complected, tall, bald-headed, and wearing a law enforcement uniform. McFerren proceeded to explain that the uniformed man entered his store, asked a few questions about Dr. King's death, and then stated that a relative of his had been involved in the event somehow. McFerren concluded his claim by telling Stephens that the man left his business card and that, upon showing the card to Holmes, McFerren learned that the burly-looking visitor was the alleged assassin's son.

Wrap Up and Warning

With all of his present questions adequately answered, Stephens began to bid his new friend farewell for the day. But just as he stood up to leave, McFerren asked him to sit back down for a moment. Curious to hear what other revelations might emerge from the once-secretive business owner, Stephens happily complied. Yet, what followed was a lengthy heartfelt warning from McFerren.

"Look here, when Marcus was lookin' into all of this, before he got hemmed up with Bobby Riles and all of them folks, I tried tellin' him to watch himself. See, I know these people out here, and they will do anything to keep this under the barnyard. I also talked to Marcus's daddy about all of this, so if he got messed over, he would understand before it happen. Now, Marcus wouldn't let me talk to his wife, 'cause now I know she ain't too happy that he's been workin' on this, but I told him to make sure she knew what was comin' down the path, too. See, I ain't just getting started in this. I've been doin' this a long time. So I know, just like they tried to break me down and make my wife leave me, they also tried to do that to Marcus. Now, I'm tellin' you this 'cause I want you to understand what you're in for. If these people out here did it to me, and did it to Marcus, they will try to do it to you, too, if you go too far."

The overly confident Stephens, being somewhat naive about his personal safety and future involvement, dismissively replied, "I understand, Mr. McFerren. I don't plan on letting this interfere with my life on a long-term basis. I told Marcus, just before he went back to prison, that I would look into the story while he was gone. So, when he comes back, I'll most likely give him all of my new evidence and notes and let him take it from there."

Thanking McFerren for his trust, time, and words of caution, Stephens said goodbye and exited the excessively warm building. While it wouldn't be the last time he sat down to interview McFerren concerning the murder of Dr. Martin Luther King Jr., Stephens was pleased with what he had garnered from his time with his elderly friend. But as he entered his vehicle, turned the ignition key, and started for home, a strong urge suddenly overtook him, compelling Stephens to visit some of the more notable locations of Fayette County.

Part Three

CONCLUSIONS AND QUESTIONS

Chapter 25

FAYETTE COUNTY TOURIST

RANDALL STEPHENS EDGED slowly out of John McFerren's gas station parking lot, looked for oncoming traffic at the precarious three-way junction, turned left onto Tennessee Highway 195, merged onto Highway 76, and headed north toward the Somerville downtown square. Almost immediately, and just as he was prone to doing while sitting behind the wheel, Stephens' mind began to wander. After passing the entrance to the Bill Kelley Justice Complex where Sheriff Bobby Riles and his deputized minions did most of their lying and scheming, Stephens looked to his right at the decaying building of the former Somerville Elementary School.

Completing the short three-minute drive, he reached the Somerville town square, stopped at the red light draped across the intersection of Highways 76 and 64, and looked in the direction of a drab stone building just off to his immediate right. The uninviting, gothic-like structure housed the infamous Somerville Bank and Trust Company, the same bank that secretly barred a blacklisted group of Fayette County African Americans from conducting financial business in the early 1960s, and the same bank that was led for a time by Mayor I.P. Yancey, James "Preacher" Shelton, and Preacher's first cousin, John Shelton Wilder.

Stephens next laid his eyes upon the previous law office of Wilder himself. Watching stoically over the town square a little less than thirty-six yards north of the bank's gray facade, the two-story red brick building was trimmed in green and bore the signage of Wilder's last law partner, Attorney Lee Saunders. Turning his head slightly to the left, Stephens then shifted his gaze as well as his thoughts to the Fayette County Courthouse. Pondering the building's long history as a quiet witness to the area's racial evolution, Stephens was reminded of the bronze bust of John Wilder that continued to sit proudly in the courthouse's rotunda.

Interrupting his angry contemplation, the stoplight turned green, and Stephens pulled forward. After creeping between Wilder's old legal firm and the adjacent courthouse the nearby senator undoubtedly helped corrupt, Stephens rounded the courthouse circle and continued his short twenty-second drive north until reaching I.P. Yancey Park. Aside from its tiny west-facing sign, corner landscaping, white-pillared gazebo, and plaque honoring Tennessee's longest-serving mayor, the park looked to Stephens to be little more than a well-manicured yard. But to John McFerren, the property was a haunting reminder of Somerville's dark past. As the former location of the Burnette Chevrolet car dealership where James Earl Ray allegedly parked his Mustang on the evening of April 2, 1968, the unassuming greenspace dedicated to the dealership's longtime owner and president, Isaac Perkins Yancey, once served a more nefarious purpose in the local conspiracy to assassinate Dr. Martin Luther King Jr.

Stephens continued driving north on Highway 76 for less than a half-mile and looked to his left toward the northern tip of West

Street and the African-American ghetto known as Winfrey Bottom. Not much had changed. While most of the dilapidated cabins on the segregated strip had been torn down or slightly updated since the *Ebony* photograph was taken in 1960, a set of equally oppressive apartment buildings called Westview Manor now reigned where several of the former shanties once stood. He continued his drive for several more miles, reached the two-way split, and then headed northwest on Highway 59. After passing the John S. Wilder juvenile detention center on his left and the recently shuttered Jefferson Elementary School on his right, Stephens drove for five more miles and arrived at two more significant Fayette County landmarks.

Slowing to a thirty-mile-an-hour crawl and looking to his left toward the rural home of the uniformed man who tried to interrogate McFerren in 2013, Stephens' mind shifted to the man's father who Marcus Holmes had nicknamed Very Very Dangerous. Quickly looking to his right, just across the two-lane highway from the son's residence, Stephens also observed the meager home of the uniformed man's mother, the same woman who, according to Holmes, was the previous wife of Very Very Dangerous and present friend of New Orleans residents Anna Mae and Tony Angelo.

After an additional four-and-a-half-mile trek along Highway 59, Stephens finally reached the pinnacle of his Fayette County and King conspiracy tour. Off to his left was the former Longtown home, immense land holdings, and cotton processing plant of the now-deceased Lt. Gov. Wilder. Stephens pulled off to the side of the desolate two-lane road, placed his vehicle in park, and looked down at his iPhone. He was amazed by the intimate proximity of the locations. According to his phone's recently installed GPS app, all of the key waypoints on Stephens' Fayette County tour, McFerren's business, Wilder's law office, Yancey's garage, the homes of the VVD family, Wilder's Longtown Gin, all of the locales fell inside a circle with a geographical radius of only six and a half miles.

Stephens looked up from his cellphone, slipped it into his jacket pocket, stepped outside, and surveyed with intense bitterness the plantation-era origins of Wilder's previous financial and political power. But unlike his numerous other drives to the locale, Stephens was suddenly struck by the bleak emptiness that surrounded him. It was January, and the harvest season had been over for several months. On full view for the entire world to see, the Wilder family's once-welcoming fields of fluffy white cotton had now been replaced by the browning melancholy of barren cotton burrs and gangly decaying stems. To Stephens, this was perhaps a small sign from the Almighty that the whitewashed veil of secrecy long coating Fayette County was lifting as well, finally revealing the area's authentic, albeit ugly, conspiratorial roots.

Chapter 26

UNSUNG HERO

BASED ON JOHN McFerren's familiarity with Frank C. Liberto coupled with the multiple eyewitness accounts linking James Earl Ray to West Tennessee, Randall Stephens now had to conclude that Ray was likely a reluctant, albeit paid, underling of Liberto in the plot that killed Dr. King. As he had repeatedly stated, McFerren was a weekly, eight-year customer at the 814 Scott Street produce warehouse in Memphis and witnessed Ray working there on at least three separate occasions before the shooting. McFerren also accurately identified Fat Frank in the two photographs Stephens showed him. Next, Stephens verified that Frank C. Liberto was a longtime Memphis Italian American, wholesale tomato salesman, reputed organized crime figure, and smuggler with deep family and mob ties in New Orleans.

Also, it was common knowledge that members of both the Memphis Police and Shelby County Sheriff's Departments were on the take and hung around the produce market in order to conduct illicit business with Liberto and the sometimes visiting "Memphis

Godfather." In addition to the Liberto and Ray issue, more than one of McFerren's underground informants had been tape-recorded stating that they spotted Ray's 1966 Springtime Yellow (cream-colored) Ford Mustang parked at Yancey's Burnette Chevrolet car dealership on the late evening of April 2, 1968, just two days prior to Dr. King's death. This, of course, was just the first half of the Yancey and Ray theory, the second of which consisted of Mrs. Edna Coe's claim that Yancey flew to London, England, immediately before and after Ray's trip to the same country.

And while there was still much to research when it came to John Wilder's involvement in the conspiracy and cover-up, Stephens had to strongly consider McFerren's physical proximity and ability to observe the Somerville statesman, as well as Wilder's extremely close associations with both Liberto and Yancey. As for the totality of McFerren's longstanding claims and official testimony, nothing seemed outlandish. While there were still a number of highly crucial details to sort out and investigate, including McFerren's staunch belief that Ray was a patsy, Stephens was now comfortable with the overall plausibility of McFerren's still consistent Liberto, Ray, Yancey, and Wilder statements. However, Stephens and Marcus Holmes were by no means the first men to stand behind McFerren and his claims.

Public Supporters

Only weeks after McFerren gave his statement to the MPD and FBI on April 8, 1968, Baxton Bryant, a prominent civil rights leader and friend of both President JFK and Dr. King, stood in front of an NBC television news camera to publicly support his anonymous friend's Liberto and Ray assertions. Also, magazine and newspaper stringer, Bill Sartor, worked diligently from April 18, 1968, until his mysterious death in December of 1971 to get McFerren's story told in print. And journalist Ted Poston also ostensibly placed his support behind McFerren when he wrote his "King Murder: A Mystery Call" newspaper article, which was published in the March 15, 1969 edition of the *New York Post*. While the list was admittedly short, it was obvious to Stephens that McFerren had been supported by men of great moral integrity and credibility before being degraded by less than trustworthy law enforcement officials, biased members of the media, and various corrupt attorneys.

Public Detractors

Even before Stephens began his investigation in 2015, Marcus Holmes spent an inordinate amount of time and energy trying to explain the multiple efforts made by those who had tried to hide or distort McFerren's various statements. But it wasn't until Stephens started his own extensive digging that he realized just how accurate Holmes had been. The first group of these outspoken detractors, and unquestionably the most vicious in their public attacks on McFerren, were officials within local, state, and federal government. Stephens once again mulled over MPD Director Frank C. Holloman and Inspector Nevelyn E. Zachary's inexcusable "dismissal" of McFerren's April 8, 1968 eyewitness account. But Holloman and Zachary were just the first two badge-wearing puppets on Stephens' list. Several special agents from Holloman's former Memphis FBI field office, including Orville Vernon Johnson, Robert Fitzpatrick, Andrew Sloan, Joseph C. Hester, and Robert Jensen, were also involved in dismissing and/or discrediting McFerren's April 1968 account.

Next, there were the two separate federal investigations conducted in the late 1970s to consider. Not only did DOJ Attorneys Fred G. Folsom and James F. Walker exclude McFerren's 1976 interview from their final report, but DOJ and HSCA Attorney Gene R. Johnson and his D.C. Metro Police partner Ernestine G. Johnson manipulated McFerren in 1978 into signing documents he couldn't read, and then hostilely barred him from publicly testifying in Washington. Finally, Stephens again pondered the 1998-through-2000 McFerren character assassination orchestrated by President Bill Clinton's handmaiden, Attorney General Janet Reno, and her DOJ minions led by Attorney Barry Kowalski. Despite their combined efforts to paint the former Fayette County civil rights leader as unreliable, Stephens now viewed all of the government's criticisms as attempts at covering up John McFerren's true knowledge of the conspiracy.

The second list of detractors Stephens compiled consisted of book authors and members of the typically biased print-and-television news media. While there was still a mountain of research to be conducted, Stephens had yet to find a single mention of McFerren's Liberto and Ray account in the local 1968 newspapers, specifically inside the black-and-white pages of Memphis's daily rag, *The Commercial Appeal*. But this late 1960s media blackout was not limited to West Tennessee at the time. It was also a matter of public record that, in spite of Bill Sartor's best efforts, his editors at *TIME* fell under the fearful spell of the FBI and DOJ's warnings, and therefore gutted his McFerren report in their April 26, 1968 issue of the national magazine.

Further, while Ted Poston was willing to at least publish the phone call portion of McFerren's Liberto account in March of 1969, the *New York Post* reporter brushed aside McFerren's 1970 secret audiotapes, which outlined Mayor Yancey's possible link to Ray. And without so much as a cursory vetting of the recordings, *Our Portion of Hell* author, Robert Hamburger, also ignored McFerren's humble 1971 request to investigate the Yancey and Ray connection. But this tradition of turning a blind eye or reporting only small, incomplete pieces of McFerren's story in the national news cycle continued over the next several decades.

As detailed earlier, Bill Pepper's 1989 work with U.K. tabloid film and news producers John Sergeant and John Edginton falsely portrayed McFerren as a terrified witness. Although McFerren's phone call account was briefly summarized in the *Inside Story: Who Killed Martin Luther King?* documentary, absolutely nothing about Ray's probable work with Liberto was mentioned by Pepper or the Sergeant and Edginton production team. Then, in 1993, Pepper and his U.K. partner and producer, Jack Saltman, kept McFerren quiet by editing out his brief testimony in the HBO mock trial. Also, Sam Donaldson of ABC's *Primetime Live* television news program, in collaboration with Bill Pepper, only broadcast a small portion of McFerren's Liberto account during the April 2, 1997 episode. And adding to this reemergence of journalistic suppression in the late 1990s, author Gerald Posner's MLK assassination book, *Killing the Dream*, went on sale in 1998 and sought to finish off McFerren's already smeared statements and character. Yet, Posner was not alone in his 1998 efforts to stifle the Fayette Countian's enduring voice.

During a public MLK gathering at Rev. James Lawson's former Centenary United Methodist Church in Memphis on the evening of April 3, 1998, investigative journalist Marc Perrusquia, a Posner acolyte and self-appointed King assassination authority, made an appearance to cover the event for his employers at *The Commercial Appeal*, the same Memphis newspaper that failed to publish a word of McFerren's Ray and Liberto story thirty years earlier. In the midst of Marcus Holmes' own research, he discovered that Perrusquia mysteriously departed the church's MLK gathering earlier that evening, apparently sometime before John McFerren approached the pulpit to address the crowd. By the following day, the less-than-hard-hitting reporter's cynical critique of the church event and its numerous speakers, minus any mention of McFerren or his public comments, was being read by hundreds of local *Commercial Appeal* subscribers.

Incidentally, it was also Marc Perrusquia who later broke the Ernest C. Withers story in 2010. Withers was the same nationally renowned civil rights photographer, Memphian, and confidential informant who spied on John McFerren for the FBI during the

1960s. Yet, in spite of Perrusquia's own discovery of a collusive effort by Withers and FBI Special Agent William H. Lawrence to spy on McFerren, and the reporter's knowledge of McFerren's connection to the King case, Perrusquia remained a staunch opponent of anything related to an alleged MLK murder conspiracy, never reporting on McFerren's claims.

Stephens was dismayed by the journalist's dismissive unwillingness to investigate or write about the case. Given Perrusquia's personally acquired government intelligence on McFerren's ties to both Withers and the black underground in Fayette County, and the same newspaper reporter's expertise in the King case, Stephens found it strange that Marc chose not to write about McFerren's personal account of Liberto's alleged handling of Ray. But the third and final assemblage of detractors on Stephens' list included two of the most corrupt men he had yet to investigate.

It was no secret by now that, among the small group of private attorneys who sought to quash McFerren's voice, John Shelton Wilder had been the most ruthless. Emboldened by his own deep-rooted Southern wealth and status as a high-level Tennessee state politician and legal expert, Wilder used his unhinged power to repeatedly attack McFerren over the course of several decades. In addition, Stephens verified several close connections between the former Somerville lawyer and possible members of both the pre-shooting conspiracy and post-assassination cover-up. But beyond Wilder's multi-decade hatred of McFerren, it was the conniving, two-faced work of Attorney Bill Pepper that outraged Stephens the most. For close to forty years, the slick New York lawyer used his deceitful influence over McFerren and their so-called friendship to obscure the humble black man's knowledge of Ray's partial involvement in the conspiracy to kill Dr. King.

At the conclusion of Stephens' analysis, it was clear that proponents of both the official and conspiratorial sides of the James

Earl Ray debate had feared McFerren and his inconvenient assertions, and therefore did everything in their power to twist his story and assassinate his good name. Due to the United States' centuries-old bigotry toward McFerren's routinely subjugated race, John's rural background, and his lack of formal education, the brave entrepreneur and social advocate was viewed by the local and national elite as a malleable target, easily silenced and smeared. But what the corrupt purveyors of deceit underestimated was McFerren's militant ability to live a long, healthy, and economically independent life, retain his sharp memory, and continually repeat his unwavering eyewitness account.

John McFerren's Word

Randall Stephens was now determined to set the record straight concerning John McFerren's character and claims, and he began to do so by first transcribing his personal observations. The first item Stephens jotted down was that under no circumstances had John McFerren been too scared to speak. While the reclusive Fayette County grocer was indeed cautious as to what he said and whom he said it to, McFerren came across as an extremely courageous individual. Not only was he a survivor and combat veteran of the European campaign during World War II, but the outspoken African American was also a Tennessee civil rights pioneer who, as a leader on the front lines, was one of the first men to publicly defy the white authority's violent stranglehold on the racist South.

Throughout his gutsy work assisting other black Fayette County residents in their own endeavors to vote, live peaceably in the area, receive an adequate education, and ultimately thrive as free human beings, McFerren also managed to build a profitable family business while simultaneously facing down illegal local monopolies, threats of physical violence, severe beatings, and numerous heart-stopping gun attacks. In spite of all that he had financially, legally, physically, and emotionally endured, McFerren still traveled the country in order to detail his civil rights story and speak out against social injustice. And when it came to the inevitable threats posed by the sleazy likes of Frank C. Liberto and his bought-and-paid-for cadre of Memphis police officers and Shelby County deputies, McFerren stared danger in the face, putting himself and his family's lives at risk by exposing what he saw and heard between 1967 and 1968.

Furthermore, McFerren continued to speak out about the 1968 event for nearly fifty years to throngs of law enforcement officials, lawyers, authors, journalists, and crowds of MLK researchers and conspiracy enthusiasts. To be clear, Stephens was appalled by Bill Pepper's characterization of McFerren as someone who was too terrified to explain himself. To have done so was an intentional slap in the face of a fearless hero who, for all intents and purposes, deserved to have his name and lengthy achievements engraved in solid gold.

Next, Stephens evaluated McFerren's overall credibility. It seemed extremely odd that the stark divide between McFerren's apparent ability to provide accurate information and his subsequent lack of complete reliability was only established by the local and federal government after April 8, 1968. In other words, if the Fayette County witness was not a credible source of local intelligence, why did the FBI field office in Memphis and Special Agent William H. Lawrence dedicate thousands of federal tax dollars and countless man-hours to surveilling McFerren through Fayette County Sheriff C.E. Pattat, paid confidential informants Ernest C. Withers and Allen Yancey Jr., and illegal wiretaps?

It was not until he exposed the conspiratorial link between the government's prime suspect and Frank C. Liberto that McFerren's credibility suddenly came into question. Stephens now believed that the federal government already knew McFerren to be a reliable source of underground civil rights intelligence, and therefore had to discredit him after his April 8 statement in order to protect Liberto, local law enforcement, and the more prominent members of the West Tennessee conspiracy to kill Dr. King.

In his twilight years, McFerren was also verbally attacked by numerous individuals and groups who exploited his age and lack of formal education for the benefit of their dishonest hidden agendas. While Stephens had to concede that McFerren had become verbally wandering in his chronology and sometimes unable to clearly articulate himself, that slightly diminished ability to communicate did not make John's original eyewitness account wrong. Moreover, Stephens also conceded that McFerren had slipped a smidgen when it came to his memory.

Indeed, the aging grocery and gas station owner was not infallible, and had made some documented mistakes in 1999 with regard to simple details such as the exact day agents Fitzpatrick and Sloan interviewed him. But overall, Stephens was repeatedly amazed throughout his investigation by McFerren's elevated level of intelligence, memory, consistency, and accuracy. Although the elderly former civil rights leader was eccentric by all accounts, his primary claims had remained the same for close to fifty years. As part of his final estimation, Stephens placed a great deal of faith in McFerren's moral compass, honesty, and credibility.

In the end, the brave unsung hero from Fayette County had simply endured by telling the same truthful story, over and over again, until someone like Marcus Holmes finally listened. Just as the conspirators failed to predict McFerren's interference beginning in the late 1960s, the West Tennessee power structure, along with Bill Pepper, also failed to predict the nosey involvement of Holmes five decades later. Stephens took a second to marvel at the fluke occurrence he had been blessed to investigate.

For the first time in almost half a century, John McFerren, the rural African-American shut-in, was finally getting the objective in-depth investigation he had long hoped and prayed for, simply because of the insatiable curiosity of Marcus Holmes, a middle-aged construction contractor from Somerville, Tennessee. Stephens could not ignore the awesome reality he was now emersed in. Crucial evidence related to one of the most painful events in U.S. history had been somehow passed down from one generation to the next through the simple act of genuine kindness and mutual respect between two friends. Yet, aside from Stephens' solidified confidence in McFerren and the plausibility of his steadfast account, there still remained a number of unanswered questions that needed to be addressed.

Chapter 27

MORE RABBITS TO CHASE

ALTHOUGH HE WAS now confident in John McFerren's personal character and the general plausibility of his account, Randall Stephens was well aware of the additional rabbit holes that still needed to be thoroughly explored and linked together. It was his ultimate wish to further vet and perhaps even corroborate many of the minuscule, seemingly improbable details McFerren had asserted in his overall narrative.

A Forest of Frank Libertos

The first enigma Stephens viewed as crucial to decipher was the widespread confusion over who Memphis crime figure Frank C. Liberto was and the other Memphis businessmen who shared his first and last name. During his so-called comprehensive investigation, Bill Pepper inflicted severe damage on the already murky Liberto topic when he deliberately entangled Frank C.'s death with the passing of both Frank J. Liberto in 1977 and Frank H. Liberto in 1996. However, while he knowingly exploited the confusion over the Liberto family commonalities in order to distance Frank C. from James Earl Ray, Pepper was not the first nor the last alleged expert to make the grossly inaccurate misidentifications.

When Frank J. Liberto passed away in 1977, rumors spread quickly throughout the country that it was the famous Memphis Hull-Dobbs Ford car salesman Frank H. who had recently died. The national mix-up was so rife that several newspaper articles were subsequently written between 1977 and 1978 in order to straighten out the perplexing issue. But the late '70s were additionally plagued by yet another Frank Liberto misunderstanding when the HSCA clumsily requested all known FBI and DOJ documents on Frank J. in addition to Frank C. Next, former Memphian and well-respected conspiratorial researcher, Mary Ferrell, also erroneously stated in a 1993 letter to fellow MLK researcher, Harold Weisberg, that the 814 Scott Street produce business owner was the same Frank Liberto who owned The Green Beetle tavern and restaurant on South Main Street. In truth, however, the former owner of the still-operational Green Beetle in downtown Memphis was not Frank C. but Frank J.

And as recently as October of 2017, the Mid-South historian and columnist, Vance Lauderdale, wrote and published a full two-page color article in *Memphis Magazine* describing the long history of The Green Beetle bar and grill. The only problem with the article was that Lauderdale inserted a large black-and-white portrait of car salesman Frank H. Liberto into his allegedly well-researched piece on Frank J.'s famous establishment. Adding insult to injury, Lauderdale wrote a tongue-in-cheek correction in a subsequent edition of the same magazine after being contacted numerous times by Frank J.'s family and friends. In part, Lauderdale wrote:

In the column, I ran a photo of the establishment's founder and owner, a nice fellow named Frank Liberto. I had located a photo of Frank shutting the doors to the cafe when it closed for a while in the 1970s. But since I didn't think you could see him very well in that particular photo, I also ran a larger image of the man. And that's when various members of his family began to call the Lauderdale Mansion, disturbing my slumbers with an unusual complaint. WHO, they wanted to know, was the fellow I had so clearly identified as Frank Liberto? I ignored these pesky calls for as long as could. After all, the Lauderdales are rarely wrong about anything. Finally, though, I took the time to look over the column, and I had to admit that the man shown in one photo (closing the doors to the restaurant) didn't look a whole lot like the fellow I had also said was Liberto. So that's when I realized my foolish mistake. It was indeed the wrong person!

It is important to note that, while the numerous official and private Frank C. Liberto conspiracy investigations were being conducted in Memphis, Frank J., his wife Mary Holloway Parrent Liberto, and their daughter Linda endured unfair harassment due to the widespread confusion. So, while Mr. Lauderdale was willing to make sarcastic light of his mistake in the 2017 *Memphis Magazine* correction, the same egregious lack of accuracy and emotional distress had been earlier inflicted on the family of the misidentified Green Beetle owner, Frank J. Liberto.

In addition to his deep desire to sort out and accurately document, once and for all, the various Frank Libertos who used to live in Memphis, Stephens also wished to examine all of the past interviews of Frank C. and his associates by local and federal law enforcement. He also hoped to verify the identities and activities of Frank C.'s West Tennessee family, friends, and business connections, most specifically the local liquor distributor and organized crime boss who McFerren referred to as the "Memphis Godfather." Finally, there was the additional murkiness surrounding Frank's purportedly mob-connected brother in

New Orleans. Undoubtedly, a thorough investigation into the various connections between the Memphis gang of organized crime figures and the Mafia-controlled sister city in Louisiana was in order.

Sister City of the South

Early in his research, Stephens was uncertain as to who Frank C. was referring to during his April 4, 1968 telephone call when he screamed, "Go down to New Orleans and get your $5,000 from my brother." The only item Stephens could find at the time that pointed to a specific person was the description in the HSCA's 1978 report in which they stated, "an indirect link between Liberto's brother, Salvatore [sic], and an associate of New Orleans organized crime figure Carlos Marcello was established." But by early 2016, Stephens was still running into brick walls of intentionally misleading descriptions, deceptive identities, and false spellings of the name "Salvatore." Inside the pages of the HSCA's inaccurate report and Pepper's extremely untrustworthy books, Stephens found a number of highly erroneous references to the elusive "Sal Liberto." Obviously, a tremendous volume of questions still needed to be answered concerning Frank's brother and who he knew inside Marcello's Crescent City Mafia.

Additionally, Stephens would need to further examine former Fayette County resident Robert Powers, his Powers Junction Gulf Oil truck stop located on the east side of Lake Pontchartrain, and the possible Mafia links between Powers and the alleged Memphis and New Orleans cabal. Next, Stephens was faced with the issue of researching Bill Sartor's unfinished investigation into Carlos Marcello's possible leadership role in the assassinations of both President John F. Kennedy in 1963 and Dr. Martin Luther King Jr. in 1968. And finally, Sartor's theory that Liberto and Ray conspired with Marcello and other powerful men living in The Big Easy and elsewhere in the South needed to be looked at by Stephens as well.

James Earl Ray and Associates

During his cursory look into the official documentation pertaining to James Earl Ray's alleged role in the MLK assassination conspiracy, Stephens was able to construct a rudimentary timeline illustrating Ray's travels beginning with his prison escape on April 23, 1967, and ending with the shooting of Dr. King on April 4, 1968. Between those two dates, Ray traveled to and resided in a number of locales throughout North America. After his escape from the Missouri State Penitentiary in Jefferson City, Missouri; Ray journeyed to Chicago, Illinois; Quincy, Illinois; St. Louis, Missouri; Southeast Canada; Birmingham, Alabama; three cities in Mexico; Los Angeles, California; New Orleans, Louisiana; Atlanta, Georgia; and Memphis, Tennessee. Then on May 6 of 1968, Ray fled North America on a flight from Toronto, Canada, to London, England. But Stephens also found large gaps in this timeline, gaps that neither the authorities nor Ray himself were able to credibly explain.

Stephens began to hypothesize that perhaps these gaps in the official timeline coincided with the sightings of Ray at Liberto's warehouse and the eyewitness accounts of the Springtime Yellow (cream-colored) Ford Mustang parked at Yancey's business. Also, the issue of Ray's darkened skin tone and flaking neck, as seen by McFerren in the winter of late '67 and early '68, was a matter that still needed to be properly vetted and maybe even corroborated.

Sparking his future research into the topic of Ray's possibly altered flesh, Stephens' initial breakthroughs would come, ironically, by way of Gerald Posner's 1998 *Killing the Dream* and the 2010 book *Hellhound on His Trail* written by Memphis native, noted historian, and bestselling author Hampton Sides. Tucked between the inconspicuous pages of both Ray-was-the-lone-assassin books, extremely brief descriptions were included regarding the alleged killer's pre-1968 attempts at secretly staining and darkening small sections of his skin using a "walnut dye." It was alleged by his fellow inmates that, while serving time inside the Jefferson City state prison, Ray boasted about his test use of the dye, his future plans to escape to the warmth of Mexico, and his intentions to blend in with the local population by appearing Hispanic.

Additionally, there was the topic of Ray's other suspected associates that still needed to be investigated, particularly the alleged assassin's temporary links to West Tennessee residents Robert Lee Bell and Willie Green. And lastly, Stephens wanted to take a deeper look into Ray's indirect associations as alleged by McFerren, including the convict's potential secondary tie to John Wilder's family friend, Governor George C. Wallace.

But of course, none of these issues were as important as the ultimate James Earl Ray question: Could he and did he actually pull off the murder of Dr. King as described by the official record? By now, it was a foregone conclusion that Stephens would have to also conduct an extremely thorough examination of the physical evidence and location where Dr. King lost his life on the evening of April 4, 1968.

Memphis Crime Scene

Before even stepping foot into the Memphis crime scene arena, Stephens made a short list of the general categories he needed to carefully research. The first category on his list was the crime scene geography. Stephens thought it necessary to construct an extremely detailed computer-generated model of the buildings, their floor plans, and the surrounding outdoor landscape as it all existed on April 4, 1968. But the task would be more difficult than he originally believed. Because of the major modifications that the NCRM had since made to the former Lorraine Motel on Mulberry Street, the adjacent cluster of South Main Street buildings where James Earl Ray allegedly shot

Dr. King from, and the crime scene's encompassing grounds, Stephens would be relegated to digitally reconstructing the area using seldom-published black-and-white photographs, original building schematics, and old crime scene drawings. Also, Stephens himself would have to make countless visits to the Mulberry and Main Street locale to photograph, video record, sketch, and personally compare the multiple building interiors and exteriors where Dr. King was killed.

The second category to be dealt with on Stephens' list was the crime-scene witnesses. This, too, was going to be a daunting task to overcome. Stephens needed to compile vast witness subcategories that differentiated motel staff from the out-of-town guests, Memphis residents, and local law enforcement officials who were at the scene that day. He also needed to track down the physical documents and digital archives of the nearly fifty-year-old eyewitness accounts that were scattered throughout Memphis and across the internet. A painfully methodical and time-consuming search of typed government interviews, additional MLK books, newspaper articles, audio recordings, photographs, old television news footage, documentary film clips, and other historical archives would be necessary to formulate a complete eyewitness narrative.

Third, it was crucial, no matter how technically overwhelming, for Stephens to study the official crime scene evidence and forensics, most specifically the government's reports on the Remington 30.06 rifle, the ballistics, and Dr. King's autopsy. While he was by no means an expert on the subject, Stephens had learned enough through his own military training and experience as a decorated combat veteran to understand the specifics of covertly shooting a grown man from various distances away. With this core knowledge from his time traveling the crater-filled roads of war-torn Iraq, along with a further study of crime-scene forensics, Stephens believed he could adequately compare the handful of assassin scenarios and bullet trajectories as purported by the government and the opposing independent ballistics and firearms experts.

Finally, he needed to generate several unique shooting timelines and conclusions by integrating all of the information from the three categories. In the end, Stephens understood how necessary it was to positively ascertain whether Ray had indeed shot Dr. King as the multiple government investigations indicated, or if the man who assassinated the acclaimed civil rights leader was someone else, perhaps the Fayette County resident who Marcus Holmes had recently nicknamed Very Very Dangerous.

Fayette's Prime Suspect

In spite of his steadfast assertion that James Earl Ray had been involved in the initial planning of the conspiracy to kill Dr. King, John McFerren was equally as adamant that Ray was not the actual triggerman, but a mere patsy who was most likely set up by Liberto and company. And although he had long believed that an African-American employee of Liberto's had been the shooter, McFerren's opinion started to change in the sweltering summer of 2012. After a Moscow, Tennessee friend and former Tent City comrade named James Puryear Sr. made an unexpected visit to his store, McFerren's suspecting finger began pointing in the direction of an address located on Fortune Road in Fayette County.

Admittedly, the alleged connection between Very Very Dangerous and the West Tennessee conspiracy was purely circumstantial at this point, and Stephens would need to do a lot more digging if he was going to be convinced of the recently identified suspect's guilt. The first step in Stephens' plan included a short drive to Puryear's Fortune Road home to interview the longtime friend of McFerren. Next, Stephens needed to use his information about the Memphis crime scene to pinpoint VVD's precise whereabouts and movements on the day of the shooting. As Stephens had already discovered, it was a well-documented and extremely significant fact that at 6:01

p.m. on April 4, 1968, VVD was located across the street from the same 306 motel room doorway where Dr. King's life was tragically taken.

Next, Stephens would need to conduct an exhaustive and sometimes-risky investigation into VVD's relationships. This would include research into the suspect's parents and upbringing as well as potential interviews with his spouse and son, the same overly curious son who made his own unannounced and suspicious visit to McFerren's store in 2013. Also on Stephens' list of possible interviewees were the multiple West Tennessee associates of VVD. This obviously included his past friends, neighbors, and former coworkers. But most intriguing to Stephens were the two New Orleans pals of the suspect's spouse. According to her own Facebook page, the wife of VVD was a longtime family friend of an unidentified woman and man named Anna Mae and Tony Angelo, both of whom resided in the Crescent City. By now, Stephens understood the extreme importance of investigating the mysterious Louisiana couple, their possible connections to other alleged MLK conspirators in both Memphis and New Orleans, and their conspicuous friendship with Very Very Dangerous and his raven-haired bride.

Cotton Coated Cover-Up

The final component of Stephens' future investigation would require digging deeper into the multiple cover-ups that ensued the moment Dr. King was struck down by the assassin's fatal bullet. Already outlined, a nearly fifty-year effort to hide the truth had been orchestrated by various levels of government. But there were specific members within those governing bodies that Stephens still wanted to thoroughly investigate. Among them, Shelby and Fayette County politicians and law enforcement officials topped the list. Second, Stephens felt it vitally necessary to climb the potential chain of obstruction by looking into specific members of Tennessee state government. Aside from State Senator and Lt. Gov. John Shelton Wilder, Stephens had isolated as potential suspects several additional General Assembly members, state district attorneys, and past Tennessee governors.

Third, Stephens knew he needed to focus on individual members of the FBI. Yet, there was a specific member of the Bureau who topped his list: a special agent named Franklin Lewis Johnson. Johnson's name and employment with the FBI surfaced early on during Stephens' original research into Fayette County and Tent City. As a member of the two-man team that included then Special Agent in Charge Frank Holloman, Johnson was removed by the DOJ from the 1959 Fayette County black voter registration inquiry due to his suspected collusion with the county's racist sheriff's department. As Stephens had since discovered, Fayette County civil rights attorney James F. Estes was correct in his assertion that Johnson harbored dual loyalties to the FBI and the county's white power structure.

As it turned out, Johnson was born and raised in Fayette County in the small town of Moscow. Most shocking to Stephens, however, was that the same FBI special agent and Moscow native was also assigned to personally investigate the April 4 actions of Very Very Dangerous in the days immediately following Dr. King's murder. The fact that both Agent Johnson and VVD once lived in the vicinity of the sparsely populated Fayette County town of Moscow raised serious flags in Stephens' mind. It goes without saying that both Special Agent Franklin L. Johnson and his superior, Special Agent Joseph C. Hester, cleared VVD of any wrongdoing in the FBI's 1968 investigation.

Nearing the end of his list, Stephens felt it crucial to dive headfirst into the backgrounds of the various DOJ and HSCA officials who were also unquestionably involved in the multi-decade cover-up. And lastly, Stephens felt compelled to investigate the numerous private attorneys who represented James Earl Ray and the mountain of West Tennessee witnesses. But among these legal experts, it was wealthy cotton baron and private attorney John Wilder who fascinated Stephens the most. The crafty Fayette County legal professional and powerful politician seemed to lurk behind every dark MLK corner, not just in connection with the pre-assassination conspiracy, but also with regard to the post-assassination cover-up.

But the question remained: Was all of this even remotely possible? Was Wilder capable of keeping a lid on the multi-tentacled conspiracy and cover-up for more than forty years? Naturally, the only way for Stephens to solve this all-important riddle was to dig even deeper into the Somerville attorney's past by way of one-on-one interviews and additional archival searches. However, the most crucially unanswered question of all still lingered in Stephens' mind...did he actually want to keep digging?

Fork in the Road

Randall Stephens had an extremely crucial decision to make. If he continued to dredge up the evil roots of Fayette County's cotton-coated past, what were the possible consequences for his own life? How much was he willing to risk? How much did Stephens value the safety of his family and that of himself? If he persisted down this path, his future efforts would not be limited to simple armchair investigating. While internet and archival research would remain important throughout his overall examination, Stephens would need to do the additional, treacherous work of physically knocking on doors and calling on sometimes frightened or even hostile witnesses. Without question, it was vital for him to consider the potential dangers he was facing if he proceeded any further, and Stephens need only look at the lives of two men to understand the likely West Tennessee pitfalls that lie ahead.

In 1959, John McFerren became one of the first African-American men to bravely confront, dig up, and publicly expose Fayette County's historically racist cornerstones. Yet, as time would tell, the former civil rights leader was often digging his own potential "barnyard" grave, the very grave in which the county's white power structure tried to repeatedly bury him and the truth under. Stephens thought back to McFerren's recent statement in which he cautioned, "If these people out here did it to me, and did it to Marcus, they will try to do it to you, too, if you go too far." Now taking serious heed of McFerren's sage-like words of warning, Stephens also pondered the fast and furious downfall of Marcus Holmes.

Chapter 28

DAPHENE
AND THE D.O.J.

IN 2012, MARCUS Holmes and John McFerren met privately with Ms. Daphene Rose McFerren, Mr. McFerren's youngest daughter, inside the concrete block walls of the McFerren Grocery and Oil Company. In addition to discussing their recent investigation into John Wilder, the secret audiotapes, and her father's additional King assassination knowledge, Holmes and McFerren also tried to explain to Daphene their recent efforts to contact her alleged half-sister, Angela K. Frazier, who lived in Waukesha, Wisconsin. The two men went on to describe their desire to ask Ms. Frazier to submit to a DNA-based paternity test, thereby providing incontrovertible proof that she was not Mr. McFerren's biological daughter.

However, only minutes into their discussion, Ms. McFerren became extremely hostile toward Holmes. In front of both men, Daphene became "spitting angry" while listening to Holmes review the mountain of evidence. Scolding both her father and his younger counterpart, she then proceeded to furiously bark aloud her belief that Marcus was going to get her father killed. Additionally, when Daphene begrudgingly admitted to her father during the same heated exchange that the King case had been officially closed for some time, the elder McFerren, obviously left in the dark for the last several years, exclaimed in shock, "You never told me they closed the King case!"

As described to Stephens, an unsuspecting Holmes was also stunned and confused by Ms. McFerren's sudden outburst and unwillingness to gratefully embrace the evidence he had voluntarily hunted down on behalf of her embattled father. Per Holmes' personal account of the verbal confrontation that day, Daphene became so inexplicably enraged that she was eventually unable to speak and stormed out of her father's business. According to a subsequent comment made by an equally-bewildered John McFerren, he had never seen his daughter that angry before. Then, in 2013, Holmes again observed Ms. McFerren become visibly aggressive, this time toward a young African-American journalist from the *West Tennessee Examiner* named Tyron Tony Reed Jr. While Mr. Reed was in the process of interviewing her father for a series of upcoming 2014 newspaper articles, Daphene "got up in the guy's face" and tried to abrasively discourage him from speaking to her father in the future.

After a somewhat thorough investigation into Ms. McFerren, Holmes and Stephens eventually came across some rather incredible details. According to her own LinkedIn profile, Ms. McFerren graduated from Yale in 1984 and Harvard Law School in 1989. After a position at the Securities and Exchange Commission in Washington, D.C., John McFerren's youngest daughter became an Assistant United States Attorney at the Washington office of the Department of Justice in 1995. But it was her next assignment at the DOJ that raised the eyebrows of both Stephens and Holmes.

As indicated on her own résumé, Ms. McFerren became the legal counsel to the Attorney General of the United States, Ms. Janet

Reno, in December of 1999 and remained by Reno's side until January of 2001. Incredibly, Ms. McFerren began working one-on-one with Reno at the same time the attorney general was overseeing the King investigation, and only nine months after Reno's team members allegedly interviewed Daphene's own father in March. But the flabbergasting revelations didn't end there.

Ms. McFerren also later indicated in a self-authored online article dated November 7, 2016, that while she worked alongside the attorney general, both women discussed Robert Hamburger's 1973 book, *Our Portion of Hell*. In the article dedicated to the cherished memory of her since-deceased DOJ boss, Ms. McFerren wrote:

> However, I did not voluntarily tell Ms. Reno of my parents' civil rights activism, or that a book, *Our Portion of Hell* (Hamburger 1973), had been written about my parents' activism and the struggle for civil rights in Fayette County, Tennessee. I did share this book with a fellow colleague and he, unbeknownst to me, gave the book to Ms. Reno to read. When I walked into her office one morning, Ms. Reno stood up and announced that she was going to have all of her department heads at the DOJ read *Our Portion of Hell*. While I should have been flattered, I was horrified that DOJ attorneys would sit around the table in the Attorney General's conference room and read about my life, and then have a book club discussion about it.

Then, sometime in 2002, Ms. McFerren's current associate and friend, Ms. Barbara Andrews, developed a new exhibit at the National Civil Rights Museum in Memphis. At the time, Ms. Andrews was the Director of Education and Interpretation at the NCRM. In preparation for the January 2003 grand opening of the museum's annexed buildings on South Main Street, which included Loyd Jowers' old bar and grill building and the 422½ address where James Earl Ray allegedly shot

Dr. King from, Ms. Andrews crafted a permanent exhibit dedicated to Daphene's father. As it so happens, this exhibit mentioned nothing of Tent City or Fayette County's civil rights struggle, but was instead focused solely on John McFerren's previous allegations regarding Frank C. Liberto and the Dr. King conspiracy case.

By June of 2006, Ms. McFerren had also become a visiting scholar at the Benjamin L. Hooks Institute located on the campus of the University of Memphis. After approximately a year of working in that capacity, Daphene attained a full-time position at the same U of M institute in January of 2008, becoming its executive director. Today, she is also one of the curators of a large collection of documents and archival items located in the Special Collections room at the U of M library. Not surprisingly, this massive collection details her parents' lengthy civil rights struggles in Fayette County.

There were a number of undeniable observations Stephens drew from the layers of evidence pertaining to Ms. McFerren's career and various relationships. First, as part of the entrance process into Yale University, it was once an unofficial rule that applicants submit at least one letter of recommendation from an extremely influential figure. Stephens believed it likely, just as Daphene's father had confirmed, that it was her mother's post-divorce benefactor, Lt. Gov. John Shelton Wilder, who wrote and submitted one of these much-needed letters of recommendation on Daphene's behalf.

Indeed, this powerful support would have forged a deep bond between Daphene and Wilder, therefore solidifying the DOJ attorney's profound sense of lifetime gratitude toward the aging state senator. Also, Stephens again considered the timeline, noting that the divorce between John and Viola McFerren was finalized in 1980, the same year Daphene began her studies at Yale. Was some type of quid pro quo established between the elder Mrs. McFerren and the neighboring John Wilder that assisted Daphene that year?

Next, Stephens found it remarkable that after the DOJ's alleged March 1999 interview of John McFerren, and John's documented unwillingness to discuss the case at the time, Ms. Daphene McFerren was brought on board by Reno herself in December of 1999, a full six months before the MLK investigative team published its June 2000 report, which included a scathing character assassination of Daphene's own father.

Then, there was the matter of the curious paper-sack anecdote that had been outlined in the pages of Robert Hamburger's *Our Portion of Hell*, a book that was being read and discussed by both Ms. Reno and Ms. McFerren at the time. Stephens shook his head in amazement when he realized that the same paper-sack story depicted in Hamburger's 1973 book made it into Reno's report as an event that occurred during the DOJ's interview of John in March of 1999. Upon further research, Stephens also discovered that Robert Hamburger was a close friend of Daphene, so close, in fact, that the author forfeited his copyright and royalty claims to the book, donating them to Ms. McFerren instead. As of today, John McFerren's daughter has yet to republish *Our Portion of Hell*, and limited copies of the out-of-print title sell online for upwards of hundreds of dollars, making it extremely rare and therefore difficult to obtain and study.

Stephens also wanted to thoroughly vet Daphene's connection to Ms. Barbara Andrews and the John McFerren exhibit inside the National Civil Rights Museum annex on South Main Street. Interestingly, Stephens was completely taken aback upon visiting the large exhibit at the NCRM. The first example of grossly inaccurate information he noted within the McFerren display read as follows:

John McFerren, a Somerville, Tennessee, businessman, testified that on April 3, while in Frank Liberto's produce store, he overheard Liberto talking on the telephone with his brother in New Orleans.

Stephens was astonished. How in the world, he wondered, had a simple, albeit crucial, mistake like that made it into the museum's final exhibit? At no time, not even according to some of the slightly suspicious government reports, had McFerren stated that he overheard Liberto's telephone conversations on Wednesday, April 3. And it was not Liberto's brother who was on the other end of the telephone line that day! Yes, the Liberto brother was mentioned, but Fat Frank was undoubtedly speaking to a would-be assassin who had been ordered to pick up the contract money from the Liberto brother in New Orleans. Now outraged, the next so-called mistake Stephens found was even more jaw-dropping. In another section related to the McFerren narrative inside the museum, the permanent signage claimed:

> After first reporting to authorities that Liberto had said, "Kill the S.O.B on the balcony," McFerren changed his story, shifting from the previous day to the previous hour, and including a role for James Earl Ray that was not described initially. Reno's investigators concluded that these changes made his account suspect.

Stephens' blood was now boiling. Again, John McFerren had stated from the very beginning that his Liberto telephone observations occurred around 5:15 p.m. on April 4, 1968. Not once did John change his story or shift the timeline "from the previous day to the previous hour." Also, during his very first interview with the MPD and FBI investigators on April 8, it was McFerren's firm belief that Liberto had harbored the alleged gunman sometime in late 1967. John's initial claims about Liberto and Ray were never added at a later time. With his brow furrowed, Stephens read aloud the same disturbing section more than a dozen times. While it was undeniably erroneous, the confusing paragraph smacked of something similar he had remembered reading elsewhere. And then it hit him. Stephens recalled seeing the following in the footnotes of Gerald Posner's 1998 *Killing the Dream*:

> McFerren, meanwhile, was a civil rights activist and president of Somerville's Civic and Welfare League, and might have actually thought after King's murder that the remark he heard the previous week did indicate some level of foreknowledge on the part of Liberto. In order to boost the impact of his statement, he may have moved it up to an hour before the assassination and added in some details he knew about how King was killed.

Obviously, Ms. Andrews, when creating the museum's McFerren and Liberto exhibit in 2002, couldn't even get the details right when plagiarizing the erroneous from-the-week-before-to-the-hour-before assumptions made by Mr. Posner four years earlier. Stephens was again appalled by the sloppy attempt at twisting John's long-consistent narrative. Yet it was the third example of rewritten history that angered Stephens the most. According to still another section of the museum's McFerren display, Liberto had his finger treated not on April 3 as claimed in Reno's report, but this time on the 4th. The museum's printed description under the heading "Liberto's Alibi" stated:

> The Justice Department was able to substantiate Liberto's alibi that he was at home at the time of McFerren's allegations. Liberto, now deceased, had told the Memphis Police Department and the FBI that he left work early on the afternoon of April 4 and went home because of an injured finger. His partner and his wife corroborated his alibi, as did medical records which showed that Liberto had his finger "lanced" on April 4.

Although Stephens was highly skeptical of the produce man's originally tenuous alibi, Reno did, in fact, state in her June 2000 report that Liberto claimed to have left work early on the 4th. But the attorney general and Barry Kowalski's report also stated that the lancing of Liberto's infected finger, according to medical records, occurred not on the 4th, but on the 3rd, which was the day before Dr. King's death. To be precise, Reno and Kowalski clearly stated in the summer of 2000:

> Liberto told detectives that on the afternoon of April 4, 1968, he left work early and was at home because of an injured finger. His partner corroborated his alibi, as did his wife. Medical records further established that Liberto had his finger lanced the day before Dr. King was killed.

Stephens' head pulsated with piercing hues of maddening red and mystifying grey. Did Ms. McFerren's and Ms. Andrews' friendship date back as far as 2002, the year the McFerren and Liberto display was being assembled? Did Daphene, in an effort to perpetuate the narrative published by her DOJ boss in 2000, assist Ms. Andrews in contorting Mr. McFerren's allegations? Had Mr. McFerren's daughter simply mirrored John Shelton Wilder's unashamed willingness to rewrite family history to suit a social or political agenda? And if not, why didn't she demand that Ms. Andrews and/or the NCRM correct the exhibit at a later date? It is public knowledge that Ms. McFerren has been a welcome guest at the NCRM for a number of years, and is a well-connected colleague of those who work inside the museum's leadership.

Whatever the case, Ms. McFerren's present friend, Ms. Barbara Andrews, had at best, negligently publicized outrageous errors regarding John McFerren's 1968 claims, and at worst, intentionally propagated blatant fabrications as historical truth in order to fool the museum's thousands of unassuming annual visitors. Stephens' mind harkened back to an often-cited quote most typically attributed to Winston Churchill, although the accidental investigator discovered through his now OCD-like research that the quote was originally spoken, coincidently, in the same German tongue used by the Wilder family's ancestors.

Sometime just before his suicide on October 15, 1946, former Nazi leader Hermann Göring stated during the Nuremberg trials, "Der Sieger wird immer der Richter und der Besiegte stets der Angeklagte sein." Loosely translated into English, Göring defiantly declared, "The victor will always be the judge, and the vanquished the accused." Stephens was struck by the inescapable parallels. Just like Göring's German quote, the vanquished John McFerren had been deviously accused, and his testimony inaccurately rewritten upon the inner walls of the National Civil Rights Museum. And bolted to the adjacent building at the same historical landmark, mere feet from where the vanquished Dr. Martin Luther King Jr. took his final blood-spattered breath, an outdoor metal plaque honoring the victor, Lt. Gov. John Shelton Wilder, continued to look judgingly across Mulberry Street in the direction of Mr. McFerren's distorted and accused claims.

Adding to the layers of intrigue, Ms. McFerren became the Executive Director of the Benjamin L. Hooks Institute at U of M in January of 2008. Was it a coincidence that she obtained this position less than three months before an extremely-powerful Senator Wilder announced his self-imposed departure from the Tennessee General Assembly? With all of the influence the Wilders had over the university, specifically the financial assistance the former lieutenant governor's wealthy son showered upon U of M, Stephens found it unsurprising that Ms. McFerren secured a top-level position within the same institution immediately before John Wilder's political influence over West Tennessee weakened in March of 2008.

Unsatisfied, however, with the purely circumstantial evidence pointing toward Ms. McFerren's deep loyalty to Wilder and perhaps biased participation in the DOJ's MLK investigation, Stephens tracked down a number of electronic communications between Janet Reno and Daphene during her time as the attorney general's legal counsel. According to the information provided to Stephens by the National Archives, Ms. McFerren and Ms. Reno exchanged a number of emails between 1999 and 2001 that included the proper names of MLK investigative team members Yvonne Bonner, Brad Farnsworth, Lisa J. Stark, Seth Rosenthal, and Barry Kowalski. But that was not all.

Sixty-four additional emails between the two DOJ attorneys also contained the word "Fayette" and two more contained the name "Liberto." In total, the Freedom of Information Act redaction staff at the National Archives indicated that no less than one-hundred-and-three emails between Daphene and the attorney general included keywords that were directly related to the King investigation. Now supported by semi-concrete evidence that Ms. McFerren, despite a glaring conflict of interest, worked quietly behind the scenes at the DOJ as an uncredited member of their King conspiracy investigative team, Stephens was able to form some fairly clear conclusions.

It was now his firm belief that, after the attorney general and her DOJ team's failure in March of 1999 to convince a stubbornly reticent John McFerren to discuss his audiotapes and knowledge of Dr. King's murder, Reno specifically sought out Daphene at the DOJ and hired her internally as her legal counsel in December of that same year. Now, cleverly hidden under the protective legal blanket of Ms. McFerren and Ms. Reno's attorney-client privilege, the U.S. attorney general and her lead MLK investigator, Barry Kowalski, were free to secretly piece together their imaginary March 1999 interview of Mr. McFerren by using chunks of his old government statements, Gerald Posner's *Killing the Dream*, Robert Hamburger's *Our Portion of Hell*, and Ms. McFerren's personal family insights. The DOJ team also used this information in their June 2000 report to illustrate John McFerren's "quirky behavior" and erroneous beliefs regarding Somerville Mayor I.P. Yancey's handling of Ray.

Intensely hungry to gain favor with her politically powerful, high-profile employer, Ms. McFerren refused to openly support her rurally isolated father's already criticized beliefs concerning Wilder, Yancey, Liberto, Ray, the 1968 conspiracy, the 1970 confidential recordings, and the cover-up at the hands of the very DOJ she was working for at the time. The youngest and most ambitious of McFerren's children willingly surrendered her loyalty to her father in exchange for job security and future advancement. By now, it was clear, the interview of John McFerren in March of 1999 never took place, the DOJ lied yet again, and Ms. McFerren was anonymously complicit in the federal government's fourth MLK cover-up and character assassination of her father.

Based on the statements made by a number of unnamed sources currently inside Memphis's African-American civil rights community, Ms. McFerren, while more than willing to publicly exploit her father's past Tent City leadership for the benefit of her own professional gain, is paradoxically militant in her ongoing denial to those who wish to speak to John McFerren about his involvement in the King case. Viewed by many of her colleagues as the self-appointed gatekeeper to her father and his crucial, albeit suppressed, MLK knowledge, Daphene McFerren has earned a notorious reputation in West Tennessee for being suspiciously evasive, combative, and sometimes verbally abusive in her efforts to prevent John McFerren from speaking to other, more inquisitive parties.

To Stephens, the answer to the multi-decade equation was simple. Based on Ms. McFerren's lifetime loyalty to her mother and John Wilder, her willing participation in the federal government's campaign to further discredit her own father, her possible propagandist work with Barbara Andrews at the National Civil Rights Museum, and her currently lucrative top tier position at the University of Memphis, Stephens could only conclude that Ms. McFerren's motivations boiled down to little more than a matter of dollars and cents. As one anonymous source privately commented to Stephens about Ms. McFerren's refusal to publicly broach her father's MLK involvement, "Talking about her daddy's connection to the King case around here is just bad for business."

Stephens was now certain that it was Ms. McFerren who supplied the '99 DOJ investigative team with the negative critique of her father's audio-taped information regarding I.P. Yancey and James Earl Ray. Stephens was also sure that Daphene purposely hid important information from the elder McFerren, specifically Ernest C. Withers' and Allen Yancey Jr.'s past reconnaissance work. Stephens went on to discover that Ms. McFerren was herself a close personal friend of both Allen Yancey Jr. and Rosalind Withers, the daughter of the famed Memphis civil rights photographer.

By 2010, Daphene would have been keenly aware of the FBI's past collusion with the two confidential informants from her study of *The Commercial Appeal* article detailing Marc Perrusquia's findings, through her relationships with Allen Yancey Jr. and the Withers family, or by way of her position at the DOJ. Yet incredibly, it was not Ms. McFerren who, out of respect, enlightened her oblivious father, but Marcus Holmes. After obtaining Perrusquia's since-declassified and publicly-accessible FBI files, the brash African American again made the drive to John's gas station to explain to McFerren that his past civil rights comrades, Withers and Yancey, had regularly spied on him in the 1960s on behalf of the FBI field office in Memphis.

It was also clear that Daphene had forged some type of unspoken, mutual understanding with Bill Pepper in the mid-to-late '90s, specifically throughout the *King v. Jowers* trial. During her heated exchange with her father and Marcus in 2012, Ms. McFerren, in another moment of unguarded anger, blurted out to her father, "Daddy, Pepper didn't do you no favors!" The sharp remark was telling in the eyes of both Holmes and Stephens. Knowing full well that the slithery New York attorney and her "Uncle Wilder" had a longstanding agreement to hide the truth from the American public, Ms. McFerren, even with her sharp legal skills and high-level DOJ connections, sat idly by for a number of years, thereby permitting Pepper to sidle up to her father and trample on his already vilified reputation.

Conversely, Stephens also believed that, upon learning of Mr. McFerren's and Holmes' combined efforts to investigate Wilder and the secret tapes in 2012, a terrified Ms. McFerren spent the remainder of that year and 2013 trying to undermine Holmes' work and relationship with her father. This would have included her use of the DOJ web server to scrutinize Marcus's FayetteFiles.com website as well as her behind-the-scenes collusion with Wilder's old West Tennessee political disciples in their endeavors to demolish Holmes' already teetering legal standing.

Cotton Coated Consequences

He had already forced his family and business to take a back seat to his investigation. Without question, the time and energy Stephens had devoted to the McFerren and Dr. King question was taking its toll. But was he to become the third person to be buried underneath the heavy layers of the West Tennessee cover-up? It was now January of 2016, and Stephens raised his weary head to look at the calendar, noting that Holmes, the individual who had convinced him to dive headfirst into this mess, wouldn't be released from prison for at least the next year. But what was Stephens' next move?

Obviously, he could end his research now, hand over his evidence to Holmes when he returned, and then walk away. That would clearly be the safe move. On the other hand, he could continue the exciting, obviously dangerous path that lie ahead. It was an understatement to say that the accidental investigator was torn; did Stephens give in to his own insatiable curiosity, growing need for adrenaline, and quest for justice, or did he protect himself and his family from future harm?

Epilogue

DIVIDED BY DAPHENE

FOLLOWING THE COMPLETED rough draft of this book in early 2019, Ms. Daphene Rose McFerren, with the assistance of her attorney, Lynn Wilhelm Thompson of the Apperson Crump law firm in Memphis, officially filed for and successfully attained co-conservatorship over her father, John McFerren. As a part of the probate court's decision, Ms. McFerren was granted shared authority over Mr. McFerren's entire estate, which included his Fayette County business and personal collection of MLK-related archives. Through the same ruling by Judge Kathleen Nalani Gomes of the Probate Court in Shelby County, Tennessee, Daphene was also triumphant in her attempts at physically and permanently removing John McFerren from his cherished Fayette County gas station, closing the business's doors, and legally barring several of Mr. McFerren's friends from communicating with her father in the foreseeable future.

As part of her extreme efforts at ensuring Mr. McFerren never spoke to anyone about the MLK case again, Daphene confiscated her father's flip phone, shackled him with a GPS ankle monitor, and hired Ms.

LaTina Moore (a woman with several documented legal and financial issues) to privately watch over Mr. McFerren during visitation hours at the nursing home where he spent the remainder of his days. Thankfully, Ms. McFerren and Attorney Lynn Wilhelm Thompson, after filing an injunction against Clear Lens Publishing, LLC in Shelby County Probate Court, failed in their illegal efforts to prohibit the author and editors of this book from using John McFerren's name, likeness, and photograph.

Sadly, however, John McFerren and his fellow MLK investigators never had the pleasure of seeing each other or speaking again after the court's decision in 2019. After Judge Gomes' ruling, Mr. McFerren spent the remainder of his time on earth confined to a nursing home bed and took his final breath on April 4, 2020, the fifty-second anniversary of Dr. Martin Luther King Jr.'s murder. Rubbing salt in the already stinging wound, a public funeral was not held at the time for Mr. McFerren due to the COVID-19 outbreak of that year. A number of his friends were relegated to simply driving by his shuttered grocery and gas station, now adorned with a black wreath, and saying their private goodbyes to John at the Morris Chapel Cemetery located on Highway 195 just southwest of McFerren's former Fayette County business. Today, Mr. McFerren lays at eternal rest next to his cherished son, John McFerren Jr., who passed away in September of 2012 as a result of an automobile accident. As of the copyright date of this publication, Ms. Daphene Rose McFerren could not be reached for comment through Attorney Lynn Wilhelm Thompson.

Appendices

McFERREN
PHOTOS & EVIDENCE

The following items and others are also available online at:

cottoncoated.com

Fayette County Courthouse in Somerville

John S. Wilder bust

John S. Wilder law office in Somerville

*Former Somerville Bank and Trust
(now Trustmark National Bank)*

I.P. Yancey Park in Somerville

(top)
*John McFerren and
original McFerren
Grocery and Oil Co.*

(center)
*Second McFerren
Grocery and Oil Co.*

(bottom)
*Tent City marker and
second McFerren
Grocery and Oil Co.*

Second McFerren Grocery and Oil Co.

Second McFerren Grocery and Oil Co.

UNITED STATES DEPARTMENT OF JUSTICE

FEDERAL BUREAU OF INVESTIGATION

MAY 4 1961

Detroit, Michigan
April 7, 1961

RACIAL SITUATION
FAYETTE COUNTY, TENNESSEE
RACIAL MATTERS

On the night of January 29, 1961, Sheriff
C. E. Pattat, Jr., Fayette County, Somerville, Tennessee,
telephonically advised a representative of the Memphis
Federal Bureau of Investigation Office of the following
information:

Sheriff Pattat stated that on January 29, 1961,
two cars of white people, consisting of four white boys and
one white girl, had been seen in the vicinity of Tent City.
Sheriff Pattat stated that Tent City is a settlement
consisting of numerous tents occupied by Negro families
who were allegedly evicted from their Fayette County tenant
farms in recent months and these Negroes are claiming to
have been evicted by reason of their registering to vote
and attempting to register to vote in Fayette County,
Tennessee. Sheriff Pattat stated that one of the automobiles
was a 1951 Dodge, bearing 1960 Michigan license BG 9651.

On February 2, 1961, Sheriff Pattat advised he
had determined the correct identities of the four white
boys and one white girl who were in the vicinity of
Somerville, Tennessee, on January 29, as Sandra Cason,
Charles Erickson and Don Tillerson from the University of
Texas and Dave Giltrow and Tom Hayden from the University
of Michigan.

The records of the Michigan Secretary of State's
Office, Lansing, Michigan, indicate as of March 22, 1961,
that 1960 Michigan license BG 9651 has been issued to John
F. Hayden, 605 Edison Avenue, Detroit, Michigan.

Sheriff C.E. Pattat's Tent City report to FBI
(page 1)

Racial Situation
Fayette County, Tennessee

The records of the Registrar's Office of the
University of Michigan, Ann Arbor, Michigan, as furnished
by Mrs. Mayme Swisher, indicate that Thomas Emmett Hayden
was currently attending the University of Michigan and is
the 1960-1961 editor of the "Michigan Daily", University
of Michigan student publication. The above records indicate
that Hayden is the son of Mr. and Mrs. John F. Hayden who
resided at 3333 Parker, Royal Oak, Michigan, at the time
of Hayden's registration.

The 1958 Detroit City Directory as well as the
current Detroit telephone directory indicates that John F.
Hayden resides at 605 Edison, Detroit, Michigan.

Detroit T-1, who has furnished reliable information
in the past, advised on August 6, 1960, that Thomas E. Hayden,
undergraduate student at the University of Michigan, was a
Michigan campus leader and incoming editor of the "Michigan
Daily" during the fall semester of 1960. Detroit T-1 stated
that Hayden was a member of the Student Government Council
of the University of Michigan and University of Michigan
delegate to the National Student Congress. During the
summer of 1960, Hayden visited campuses throughout the
United States regarding National Student Association affairs.
Detroit T-1 described Hayden as a responsible, aggressive
student leader whom he regards as a completely loyal citizen
of the United States. Detroit T-1 stated that in Hayden's
three years at the University of Michigan, he has never known
him to participate in subversive activities nor to express
pro-Communist sympathies. Detroit T-1 stated that Hayden's
responsible work was crusading and he possessed inexhaustive
energy which takes him in every interest to leadership capacity.
Detroit T-1 stated that Hayden possessed a passion for
unpopular causes and will counsel with all factions on any
particular issue.

Detroit T-1 stated that as a member of the Student
Government Council, student governing body, University of
Michigan, Hayden supported the Student Government Council's
endorsement of "sit in" demonstrations in the South and has
worked diligently on integration matters. Detroit T-1 stated

- 2 -

Sheriff C.E. Pattat's Tent City report to FBI
(page 2)

that Hayden's activities on controversial issues were
based on sincere personal conviction. Detroit T-1 stated
that Hayden has not been a member or sponsor of any student
organization in the University of Michigan known to the
Informant to have contained Communists or Communist sympathizers
and that he has not associated with individuals known to
Detroit T-1 as Communist or Communist sympathizers.

Detroit T-2, who has furnished reliable information
in the past, advised in August, 1960, that Thomas Hayden,
editor of the "Michigan Daily", was national coordinator
of a non-violence movement in connection with Hiroshima and
Nagosaki Day activities on August 6 and 9, at San Francisco,
California. Detroit T-2 stated that demonstrations consisting
of marching and picketing were scheduled at San Francisco
on August 6 and 9 and that Thomas Emmett Hayden, editor of
the "Michigan Daily", University of Michigan student
publication, had indicated that there was no official
organization connected with this demonstration but it was
a racial theme "No More Hiroshima - Youth Wants Peace".
Detroit T-2 stated that Hayden had also indicated that he
was not connected officially with the Communist Party, but
does have many similar sympathies with them and that he
would welcome a visitor from the Communist Party when he
returns to the University of Michigan.

The Communist Party, USA, has been designated by
the Attorney General of the United States pursuant to
Executive Order 10450.

This document contains neither recommendations nor
conclusions of the FBI. It is the property of the FBI and
is loaned to your agency; it and its contents are not to be
distributed outside your agency.

- 3 -

Sheriff C.E. Pattat's Tent City report to FBI
(page 3)

SAC (170-70 Sub)   5/12/64

SA WILLIAM H. LAWRENCE   FOIA(b)(7) - (D)

ERNEST C. WITHERS
CS(R)

On 4/28/64 ERNEST C. WITHERS, Confidential
Source (Racial), orally advised SA WILLIAM H. LAWRENCE
that JOHN MC FERRIN, Negro leader in Fayette County,
Tennessee, who has received national publicity in
connection with his efforts concerning Negro voter
registration in Fayette County and who is a highly
controversial Negro, recently visited WITHERS and
stated that he was on his way to New Orleans, La., to
see Dr. JAMES DOMBROWSKI and some of his associates at
the National Office of the Southern Conference Education
Fund, Inc. (SCEF) at 822½ Perdido Street, New Orleans.
MC FERRIN did not say why he was going to New Orleans.
MC FERRIN did brag that about two years ago when he
was in Chicago, Ill., on a speaking engagement that
ELIJAH MUHAMMAD, national leader of the NOI, had contacted
MC FERRIN and had tried to convert him to Islam. MC FERRIN
stated that he did not show any interest in Islam or the
NOI despite the fact that MUHAMMAD wanted MC FERRIN to
go back to Fayette County and organize a group of his
followers into the NOI.

With regard to the forthcoming 1964 Democratic
Primary local election in Fayette County, Tennessee,
MC FERRIN told WITHERS that it had been generally reported
that he and his followers would support the white male
namely L. T. REDFERN, who has claimed that he will run
for Sheriff in the Democratic Primary. MC FERRIN told
WITHERS that he is distrustful of REDFERN and that he
does not feel that many Negroes will support him inasmuch
as they feel that REDFERN is an opportunist and is merely
trying to use the Negroes as a stepping stone to the Sheriff's
Office. He did not elaborate. He did state that ODELL

1 - 170-70 Sub (WITHERS)

1 - 100-4003 (Southern Committee to Abolish the HUAAC)
1 - 100-92 (SCEF)   100-92-589
1 - 105-160 (NOI)
WHL:gmh   SEARCHED _____ INDEXED _____
(5)   SERIALIZED _____ FILED _____
                                MAY 12 1964
                              FBI -- MEMPHIS

*One of Ernest C. Withers and William H.
Lawrence's FBI reports on John McFerren*

FD-36 (Rev. 12-13-56)

FBI

Date: 8/6/65

Transmit the following in _____
                                    (Type in plain text or code)

Via ___ AIRTEL _____
                                    (Priority or Method of Mailing)

- -

TO: DIRECTOR, FBI

FROM: SAC, MEMPHIS (173-New) (P)

PROPOSED FREEDOM MARCH,
BROWNSVILLE, TENNESSEE,
AUGUST 7, 1965
PA; CRA 1964

          Re Memphis tel to Bureau 8/5/65.

          Enclosed herewith for the Bureau are 8 copies of
a letterhead memorandum dated and captioned as above. The
extra copy is being disseminated inasmuch as this is
tantamount to a racial matter in which normally 8 copies
of LHM are submitted. The first source of the LHM is
ERNEST C. WITHERS, Confidential Source, Memphis, Tenn.,
who furnished information to SA WILLIAM H. LAWRENCE.
The second source is [   ] Somerville,
Tennessee, Source of Information-R, who furnished information
to SAs CYRIL F. BUSCH and WILLIAM H. LAWRENCE.

3 - Bureau (Enc-8)
14 - Memphis (2 - 173-New)
        1 - 157-646 (WEST TENNESSEE VOTERS PROJECT)

        1 - 157-109 (SNCC)
        1 - 170-70 Sub (ERNEST C. WITHERS)
        1 - 100-4114 (DANIEL S. BEAGLE)
        1 - 100-4124 (ROBERT GABRINER)
        1 - 100-4123 (VICKI GABRINER)
        1 - 100-   DEBORAH RIB
        1 - 173-109 (BOYCOTT OF NEGRO SCHOOLS, FAYETTE CO., TENN.)
        1 - 173-104 (BOYCOTT OF NEGRO SCHOOLS, TIPTON CO., TENN.)
        1 - 100-3572 (CORE)

NW: 849 DocId: 59171028 Page 81

                                        100-3572-222

Approved: _____ Sent _____ M Per _____
            Special Agent in Charge

William H. Lawrence's FBI report indicating
a "second source" in Somerville

FD-36 (Rev. 3-31-77)

● FBI ●

TRANSMIT VIA: PRECEDENCE: CLASSIFICATION:
☒ Teletype   ☒ Immediate   ☐ TOP SECRET
☐ Facsimile   ☐ Priority   ☐ SECRET
☐ _____   ☐ Routine   ☐ CONFIDENTIAL
                                                       ☒ E F T O
                                                       ☐ CLEAR
                                              Date _____7/17/78_____

FM MEMPHIS (66-2197) (P)

TO DIRECTOR (62-117290) IMMEDIATE

BT

UNCLAS E F T O

ATTENTION CONGRESSIONAL INQUIRY UNIT, RECORDS MANAGEMENT DIVISION.

HOUSE SELECT COMMITTEE ON ASSASSINATIONS (HSCA).

RE BUREAU TELETYPE DATED JULY 14, 1978.

ON JULY 15, 1978, THE SOURCES LISTED BELOW WERE CONTACTED

AND ADVISED OF THE NATURE OF THE INQUIRY AS OUTLINED IN REFERENCED

TELETYPE. EACH OF THEM STATED HE DOES NOT WANT HIS IDENTITY

DISCLOSED TO HSCA. EACH EMPHATICALLY STATED HE WANTS HIS FORMER

RELATIONSHIP WITH THE FBI TO REMAIN STRICTLY CONFIDENTIAL.

SOURCES CONTACTED ARE AS FOLLOWS:

FORMER ME 352-R, CATO JOHNSON, JR.

FORMER ME 339-R, ALLEN YANCEY, JR.

FORMER ME 338-R, ERNEST C. WITHERS.

AN FD-302 REGARDING THE INTERVIEW OF THESE INDIVIDUALS

66-2197-67

ALL INFORMATION CONTAINED
HEREIN IS UNCLASSIFIED
DATE 7-18-02 BY 60229ac/bcp/kl   SEARCHED
                  #42711/42713   SERIALIZED
BFJ:sad   INDEXED
(1)   FILED
AAB

Approved: _____   Transmitted _____   Per _____
                                          (Number)   (Time)   FBI/DOJ
NW 55244 DocId:32989819 Page 71

Fayette County resident Allen Yancey Jr. named as
FBI confidential informant

Frank C. Liberto

Frank C. Liberto

814 Scott Street warehouse
(now a lumberyard)

North side of 814 Scott Street warehouse
with northeast dock entrance and office window

For Assassin's Plan

A Southern Drawl, A Few Steps, A $20 Bill And The Scene Was Laid For Murder

By WILLIAM SORRELS

Dr. Martin Luther King Jr.'s assassin said his name was John Willard.

He spoke with a Southern drawl.

He paid for his $8.50 a week room with a crisp $20 bill, fishing it out of his right front pocket and holding it in both hands before handing it to the landlady at 422½ South Main.

He wore a dark suit and appeared to have little in common with men forced to stay in a flophouse.

He took no more than 13 steps when he walked from Room 5, where a 50-watt light bulb snapped off when he pulled a ceiling chain, to a dingy bathroom where he lay in wait to shoot Dr. King.

His mission was accomplished at 6:01 p.m.

With unerring aim, he cut down Dr. King, standing alone on the balcony of the Lor-

Reward In Dr. King's Death Leaps To $100,000—Body Taken To Atlanta

By JOHN MEANS

The reward fund for the arrest and conviction of Dr. Martin Luther King Jr.'s murderer grew to $100,000 yesterday while the search for the assassin spread throughout the nation.

The City Council guaranteed yesterday to underwrite $50,000 to be added to the $25,000 offered Thursday by The Commercial Appeal and an additional $25,000 put up by Scripps-Howard Newspapers for the reward fund.

The body of the 39-year-old civil rights leader left Memphis yesterday morning in a bronze casket and a chartered airliner. The departure came shortly after the arrival of the nation's top law enforcement officer, United States Atty. Gen. Ramsey Clark, who conveyed President Johnson's personal sympathy to Dr. King's widow.

April 6, 1968 Commercial Appeal article

Commercial Appeal sketch of shooting suspect

James Earl Ray FBI wanted poster April 19, 1968

DEPARTMENTAL   COMMUNICATION

TO: ████████████   RE: REV. MARTIN LUTHER KING MURDER

FROM: INSP. N. E. ZACHARY

DATE: APRIL 12, 1968

RESTRICTED INFORMATION DELETED
PER FOIA ██████████ (7)c
BY__EKL__ ████, DATE __9|17|96____.

Sunday night, April 7, 1968, at approximately 10:30 p.m., the undersigned was contacted by
Fire and Police Director Frank Holloman by telephone at home requesting that I meet with
Mr. Braxton Bryant and Attorney David Kaywood, and a person they had who wanted to give
information concerning this murder. After two or three telephone conversations, at 2:30 a.m.,
Monday morning, April 8, 1968, I was contacted by Mr. Bryant, stating that he had the subject
and was at the city limits and requested that I meet him in a room at the Hilton Peabody.

After contacting Mr. ████████████of the FBI, we then went to the Hilton Peabody where we
met Mr. Bryant, Kaywood, and a subject I will call J. M., whom they had picked up and brought
to Memphis for the purpose of passing information he had to us.

According to J. M., he was in Memphis on Thursday, April 4, 1968, where he picked up some
chickens on Front St., and at about 3:45 p.m. he arrived at the Fineburg Packing Co., at
2875 Starling, where he picked up some meat, and left around 4:20 to 4:30 p.m., and went to
the market on Scott St. to pick up some produce; that he went to the L. L. and L. Produce Co.
at 814 Scott. As he went into this company, he heard a man on the telephone say to someone,
"Kill the son of a bitch on the balcony. Get the job done! You'll get your five thousand."
That he went on, got his vegetables, and he wanted some apples that this man had, but he
referred him to a Jew on the end of the building to get the apples, and some red onions.
He stated that as he came from the produce area with his vegetables, a smaller man with a
scar on his neck answers the telephone and tells a man who he had heard on the phone previously that someone was on the phone, and the man then made the statement over the phone,
"Don't come out here. Go to New Orleans. You know my brother. Get the money from him."
After hearing this, he went to the Jew's, got his apples and onions, arrived at his home
about 6:05 p.m., got a call from Wm. C. Anderson at 6:15 p.m. that King was shot. Some time
later he learned that he had died.

J. M. stated that about a week prior to this, he was in the same place, heard the same man
talking to some other men, he believed to be on Monday after the snow, and heard the same man
make the statement, "We ought to kill King, the son of a bitch." After he got his vegetables,
the man asked him what he thought about King and his men, and he told him that he tried to ter
to his own business, and made no further comment. He described the man doing the talk as
being a big man of mixed breed, weighing at least three hundred pounds, and that last fall
he had another mixed breed working for him that appeared to be a mixture of Cuban and Mexican
or Indian, that had only worked four or five weeks, and that he had jungle rot on his neck.
He described this subject as being mixed breed, about 25, 5'9", 140, slender keen built, that
he looked exactly like the sketch in the paper.

He stated that he and his wife talked about this after King's death, and he told Mr. Brya
about it at 7:00 p.m., April 7, 1968. He was very fearful of retaliation, should his id ititj
be revealed, and stated we might learn something from this from a big male colored with back trouble whi
worked on the east end of the building where this conversation took place. He was assured
we would try to conduct this investigation without revealing his identity, if at all possible

#145   This memo cleand by memo # 186
C.P.A To 3.5.2.   3333
4-12-67

N.E. Zachary's MPD report on John McFerren

FL ..AL BUREAU OF INVESTIGATION

Date 4/11/68

1

██████████████ Somerville, Tennessee, was
interviewed at the Peabody Hotel, Memphis, Tennessee, in
the presence of Inspector ███████████ Mr. ████
of the Tennessee Council on Human Relations, and Attorney
█████████████ stated that he had some
information he wished to furnish concerning the shooting of
Dr. MARTIN LUTHER KING, JR.

████████████ advised that on the afternoon of
April 4, 1968, he traveled from Somerville, Tennessee, to
Memphis, Tennessee, to pick up his supplies for his grocery
store. He advised that he departed from the ███████████
Company, █████████ Memphis, at approximately 4:20
P.M. He said he traveled directly to the Farmers Market
located on Scott Street and after arriving purchased a sack
of potatoes from a Negro man, name unknown, at the market.
He then went to the place where he normally buys his produce
and stated he does not know the name of this particular firm
but said it was possibly the ████████████████████
He said this business is operated by a large, heavy set white
man, who weighs approximately 300 pounds and is of possible
Puerto Rican extraction and who can be identified because his
teeth are set apart from each other. ████████ stated after
arriving at this company he walked up to the door to the
office and noticed that the heavy set man was sitting at his
desk with his back to the door and talking on the telephone.

████████████ stated that the heavy set man did not see
him at that time. He stated he heard the heavy set man say,
"Kill the S.O.B. on the balcony and get the job done. You
will get your $5,000." According to ████████ a white
man who is thin in build and who has a scar on his right cheek,
saw him about that time and asked him what he wanted. ████
replied that he was there to pick up some produce and this
man told him to go on to the back and help himself.

████████████ said he went back to the rear portion of
this office and shortly thereafter heard the telephone ring.
The phone was answered by the man with the scar, and ████████

On 4/8/68 at Memphis, Tennessee ___ File # Memphis 44-1987:

by SA ████████████████ ___ Date dictated 4/9/68

This document contains neither recommendations nor conclusions of the FBI. It is the property of the FBI and is loaned to
your agency; it and its contents are not to be distributed outside your agency.

2

O.V. Johnson's FBI 302 report on John McFerren
(page 1)

ME 44-1987
2

said he could not hear what this man said. The man then
handed the phone to the heavy set man, and ████████ said he
heard this man say, "Don't come out here. Go to New Orleans
and get your money. You know my brother." ████████ continued by advising that he bought his produce and wanted
to purchase two bushels of apples. He said he saw apples at
████████ but they referred him to another
store and told him that he could get his apples there.
████████ believes that he was only at ████████
Company for approximately ten minutes and this was sometime
between 4:45 P.M. and 5:15 P.M.

████████ continued by advising that approximately a week prior to April 4, 1968, he was at ████████
████████ at which time the heavy set man, the man with
the scar, and approximately three other white men were in
a group talking. He said he heard the heavy set man say at
this time, "They ought to shoot the S.O.B." ████████ advised
that immediately after this the heavy set man walked over
to him and said, "What do you think about King and his mess?"
████████ told the heavy set man that he tended to his own
business.

████████ advised that he arrived at his store in
Somerville at approximately 6:15 P.M. He said immediately
thereafter ████████ telephonically advised him that
KING had been shot. He said on the following day his wife
told him about the description of the person who possibly
shot KING, and he said according to this description the
individual was approximately 5'6" tall. He said he saw the
sketch which appeared in the Commercial Appeal and which
was supposed to be a likeness of the unknown individual who
shot KING and when he compared the descriptions furnished by
his wife from the paper and the sketch which appeared in the
paper he thought of a person who was employed at ████████
████████ sometime last summer. He thinks this man
might be identical to the person who actually shot KING and
stated that this individual is a cross between an Indian, a
Cuban, or a Mexican. According to ████████ this person
has a very yellow complexion, has "jungle rot" on his neck,
and definitely gives the impression of being a Puerto Rican
or a Cuban and definitely not an American. ████████ also
said, "This person is not 5 feet 6 like they said in the
paper, but he is real tall. He is at least 5 feet 9."

3

O.V. Johnson's FBI 302 report on John McFerren
(page 2)

ME 44-19█
3

█████ also advised that the person who he thinks might be
identical to the person who shot KING weighs 140 pounds,
has a slender build, and is approximately 25 years old. He
could furnish no further description regarding this person or
any further information of value to identify him.

█████ stated that he discussed what he had
heard on the afternoon of April 4, 1968, with his wife and
also discussed with his wife the possibility that he knows the
identity of the person who shot KING. He said he was afraid
to tell any person other than his wife and did not mention
it to anyone except █████ whom he advised at
approximately 7:00 P.M. on April 7, 1968.

O.V. Johnson's FBI 302 report on John McFerren
(page 3)

FEDERAL BUREAU OF INVESTIGATION

Date ____4/22/68____

JOHN MC FERREN, Route 4, Box 133 A, Somerville,
Tennessee, was interviewed at his place of business, Somerville,
at which time he furnished the following information concerning
the shooting of Dr. MARTIN LUTHER KING, JR:

On the morning of April 4, 1968, at 8:00 a.m., he
traveled to Memphis, Tennessee, from Somerville to pick up his
supplies for his grocery store in Somerville. Before obtaining
these supplies he went to his brother's house regarding income
tax returns to be filled out by his brother, ROBERT MC FERREN.
_ _ _ his wife at home at approximately 2:30 p.m. and some-
_ _ _ thereafter, at approximately 3:00 p.m., he departed his
brother's place of business to go to a "chicken place" near the
Greyhound Station on Front Street to purchase some meat. He
arrived at the "chicken place" a little before 3:15 p.m. and
thereafter departed to go to Fineberg Meat Company, 2875 Starling
Road, Memphis, Tennessee, arriving there at approximately 3:45
p.m. He bought $72 worth of meat at this place and a white
female waited on him. He left Fineberg Meat Company at approximately 4:15 p.m. enroute to the Farmers Market located on Scott
Street and arrived there at approximately 4:25 to 4:30 p.m.
Upon arriving at the Farmers Market, he went to the east shed
to purchase a sack of potatoes from a Negro male, name unknown.
He put these potatoes in the bed of his truck and then proceeded
to LL & L Produce Company, 814 Scott Street, Memphis. He
described this produce market as a large warehouse type building
with a garage type door.

He stated that as he passed this door he heard a white
male yell, "Kill the son-of-a-bitch on the balcony" and, "I don't
care how you get the job done, just get it done." At the time
he heard this remark he did not know just what it meant.

He stated the LL & L Produce Company is operated by a
large heavy-set white male who weighs approximately 250-300
pounds, has straight hair, is approximately 6' tall, has gapped
teeth, was wearing a red sport shirt and sitting in an office in

On __4/18/68__ at __Somerville, Tennessee__ File # __Memphis 44-1987__

SA ROBERT FITZPATRICK &
by __ANDREW SLOAN:RF: cjz:hb__ Date dictated __4/22/68__

This document contains neither recommendations nor conclusions of the FBI. It is the property of the FBI and is loaned to
your agency; it and its contents are not to be distributed outside your agency.

*Robert Fitzpatrick and Andrew Sloan's FBI 302 report
on John McFerren
(faded and unredacted - page 1)*

FEDERAL BUREAU OF INVESTIGATION

1   Date ___ 4/22/68 ___

████████████████████████████████████ Somerville,
Tennessee, was interviewed at his place of business, Somerville,
at which time he furnished the following information concerning
the shooting of Dr. MARTIN LUTHER KING, JR:

On the morning of April 4, 1968, at 8:00 a.m., he
traveled to Memphis, Tennessee, from Somerville to pick up his
supplies for his grocery store in Somerville. Before obtaining
these supplies he went to his brother's house regarding income
tax returns to be filled out by his brother, ████████████████
He called his wife at home at approximately 2:30 p.m. and sometime thereafter, at approximately 3:00 p.m., he departed his
brother's place of business to go to a "chicken place" near the
Greyhound Station on Front Street to purchase some meat. He
arrived at the "chicken place" a little before 3:15 p.m. and
thereafter departed to go to Fineberg Meat Company, 2875 Starling
Road, Memphis, Tennessee, arriving there at approximately 3:45
p.m. He bought $72 worth of meat at this place and a white
female waited on him. He left Fineberg Meat Company at approximately 4:15 p.m. enroute to the Farmers Market located on Scott
Street and arrived there at approximately 4:25 to 4:30 p.m.
Upon arriving at the Farmers Market, he went to the east shed
to purchase a sack of potatoes from a Negro male, name unknown.
He put these potatoes in the bed of his truck and then proceeded
to ██ Memphis.

He stated that as he passed this door he heard a white
male yell, "Kill the son-of-a-bitch on the balcony" and, "I don't
care how you get the job done, just get it done." At the time
he heard this remark he did not know just what it meant.

He stated ████████████████████████████ is operated by a
large heavy-set white male who weighs approximately 250-300
pounds, has straight hair, is approximately 6' tall, has gapped
teeth, was wearing a red sport shirt and sitting in an office. In

On 4/18/68 at Somerville, Tennessee   File # Memphis 44-1987

SA ROBERT FITZPATRICK &
by ████████████████████   Date dictated 4/22/68

*Robert Fitzpatrick and Andrew Sloan's FBI 302 report
on John McFerren
(clear and redacted - page 1)*

2

an office in this warehouse-type building at a desk with a telephone and was facing into the produce department area. He stated the individual had dark skin and was possibly of Puerto Rican or some "foreign" extraction. MC FERREN stated he walked up to the door of this office and noticed the heavy set man was sitting at the desk with his back to the door talking on the telephone. This man did not notice him, MC FERREN, at the time.

At this time another individual, whom he described as a white male, clear skin, over 6' tall, 200 pounds, with a hat on, wearing casual clothes, and a scar on the right side of his throat, known by MC FERREN to be another boss at the LL & L Produce Company, approached him and asked him what he wanted. According to MC FERREN, this man said, "Go ahead and wait on yourself." MC FERREN advised that he then went back to the rear portion of the warehouse and purchased $16 worth of produce.

When he was coming out of this warehouse-type building, he heard the telephone ring which was answered by the man with the scar on his throat and he heard this individual mumble something to the heavy set man but he could not hear what this man had said. The man with the scar then handed the telephone to the heavy set man and he heard the heavy set man say, "Go to New Orleans and get your $5,000 and don't bring your ass near my place and don't call me any more—you know my brother in New Orleans." MC FERREN advised that he had already purchased $16 worth of produce but decided he wanted to purchase approximately two bushels of apples. He had seen the apples at the LL & L Produce Company but stated the heavy set man and the man with the scar on his face acted very nervous and told MC FERREN "to go next door and get your apples." MC FERREN stated that he was in the warehouse for approximately 30 minutes and to the best of his knowledge the telephone call took place about 5:15 p.m. MC FERREN advised that he bought two cases of apples from a Jewish fellow on the west side of the Farmers Market and then left to return to his home in Somerville, Tennessee.

MC FERREN advised he arrived back at his store in Somerville at 6:15 p.m. and learned from WILLIAM C. ANDERSON, a friend of his, who telephonically advised him that Dr. KING had been shot. He stated that late that night, after talking with his wife and discussing the description of the person who

Robert Fitzpatrick and Andrew Sloan's FBI 302 report
on John McFerren
(faded and unredacted - page 2)

ME 44-1987
2

an office at this warehouse-type building at a desk with a
telephone and was facing into the produce department area.
He stated this individual had dark skin and was possibly
of Puerto Rican or some "foreign" extraction. ██████████
stated he walked up to the door of this office and noticed
the heavy set man was sitting at the desk with his back to
the door talking on the telephone. This man did not notice
him, ██████████ at the time.

At this time another individual, whom he described
as a white male, clear skin, over 6' tall, 200 pounds, with
a hat on, wearing casual clothes, and a scar on the right
side of his throat, known by ██████████ to be another boss
at ██████████ approached him and asked him
what he wanted. According to ██████████ this man said, "Go
ahead and wait on yourself." ██████████ advised that he then
went back to the rear portion of the warehouse and purchased
$16 worth of produce.

When he was coming out of this warehouse-type
building, he heard the telephone ring which was answered
by the man with the scar on his throat and he heard this
individual mumble something to the heavy set man but he
could not hear what this man had said. The man with the
scar then handed the telephone to the heavy set man and he
heard the heavy set man say, "Go to New Orleans and get your
$5,000 and don't bring your ass near my place and don't call
me any more-you know my brother in New Orleans." ██████████
advised that he had already purchased $16 worth of produce but
decided he wanted to purchase approximately two bushels
of apples. He had seen the apples at ██████████
██████████ but stated the heavy set man and the man with the scar
on his face acted very nervous and told ██████████ "to go
next door and get your apples." ██████████ stated that he was
in the warehouse for approximately 30 minutes and to the best
of his knowledge the telephone call took place about 5:15 p.m.
██████████ advised that he bought two cases of apples from a
Jewish fellow on the west side of ██████████ and then
left to return to his home in Somerville, Tennessee.

██████████ advised he arrived back at his store in
Somerville at 6:15 p.m. and learned from ██████████
a friend of his, who telephonically advised him that Dr. KING
had been shot. He stated that late that night, after talking
with his wife and discussing the description of the person who

*Robert Fitzpatrick and Andrew Sloan's FBI 302 report
on John McFerren
(clear and redacted - page 2)*

ME 44-1987

2

... ., he figured the conversation he had heard
... ... had to nothing to do with the murder of Dr. KING.

        MC FERREN stated that on the following day he saw
a sketch appearing in The Commercial Appeal which was supposed
to be a likeness of the unknown individual who shot KING and
he compared the description furnished by his wife from the
... ... which appeared in the newspaper and
thought this to be a person who was employed at the LL & L
Produce Company sometime in the late fall or early winter
of 1967. He stated this man, described as a light tanned
or Puerto Rican type individual with long straight, coarse
black hair, "jungle rot" on his neck, slender build, drop
... ..., white male, 5'10" - 5'11", 160 pounds, not a day
over 25, as being identical with the individual who shot
KING. He stated this individual was a cross between an Indian,
Cuban, and Mexican and he could possibly identify this individual
again. MC FERREN stated he saw this individual for approximately
one to two days at the LL & L Produce Company in the late fall
or early winter and has not seen him since that time at the
produce company.

        MC FERREN advised another reason for his suspicions
is that on a Thursday, a week before April 4, 1968, he was
at the LL & L Produce Company at which time the heavy set man,
the one with the bear, said to him, "What do you think about
your buddy?" MC FERREN said he replied, "Who are you talking
about?" The heavy set man then said, MARTIN LUTHER KING", to
which MC FERREN replied, "I tend to my own business." MC FERREN
stated the heavy set man then said, "Somebody ought to shoot the
son -of-a-bitch." MC FERREN stated he again replied, getting into
his truck, "I tend to my own business" and drove off. MC FERREN
stated this was the first time the heavy set man had ever spoken
to him regarding a racial matter.

        MC FERREN advised that he had discussed what he had
heard on the afternoon of April 4, 1968, with his wife and had
also discussed with his wife the possibility he knew the identity
of the individual who shot KING.

        MC FERREN stated that on the morning of April 18, 1968,
between 8:30 and 9:00 a.m., a beige, late model 1966 or 1967
Cadillac with a golden emblem on the front license plate, license
plate not noticed, drove into his driveway at Route 4, Box 133 A,

7   151

*Robert Fitzpatrick and Andrew Sloan's FBI 302 report
on John McFerren
(faded and unredacted - page 3)*

ME 44-1987
3

possibly shot KING, he figured the conversation he had heard
may have had something to do with the murder of Dr. KING.

████████████ stated that on the following day he saw
a sketch appearing in The Commercial Appeal which was supposed
to be a likeness of the unknown individual who shot KING and
he compared the description furnished by his wife from the
paper and the sketch which appeared in the newspaper and
thought this to be a person who was employed at ██████████
██████████ sometime in the late fall or early winter
of 1967. He stated this man, described as a light tanned
or Puerto Rican type individual with long straight, coarse
black hair, "jungle rot" on his neck, slender build, drop
shoulders, white male, 5'10" - 5'11", 160 pounds, not a day
over 25, as being identical with the individual who shot
KING. He stated this individual was a cross between an Indian,
Cuban, and Mexican and he could possibly identify this individual
again. ████████ stated he saw this individual for approximately
one to two days at ████████████████████ in the late fall
or early winter and has not seen him since that time at the
produce company.

████████████ advised another reason for his suspicions
is that on a Thursday, a week before April 4, 1968, he was
at ██████████████████████ at which time the heavy set man,
the man with the scar, said to him, "What do you think about
your buddy?" ████████ said he replied, "Who are you talking
about?" The heavy set man then said, MARTIN LUTHER KING", to
which ████████ replied, "I tend to my own business."
stated the heavy set man then said, "Somebody ought to shoot the
son-of-a-bitch." ████████ stated he again replied, getting into
his truck, "I tend to my own business" and drove off. ████████
stated this was the first time the heavy set man had ever spoken
to him regarding a racial matter.

████████████ advised that he had discussed what he had
heard on the afternoon of April 4, 1968, with his wife and had
also discussed with his wife the possibility he knew the identity
of the individual who shot KING.

████████████ stated that on the morning of April 18, 1968,
between 8:30 and 9:00 a.m., a beige, late model 1966 or 1967
Cadillac with a golden emblem on the front license plate, license
plate not noticed, drove into his driveway at ████████████████

*Robert Fitzpatrick and Andrew Sloan's FBI 302 report
on John McFerren
(clear and redacted - page 3)*

LD 44-1987

... .n Avon, Somerville, Tenn. ..., An individual,
identified a _JOHN POWERS_ and his wife, approximately
... years old, run the Powers House in Somerville, Tennessee,
and thereafter left to live in New Orleans, Louisiana, or that
vicinity ... advised this individual operated an all-night
truck stop in Louisiana at the intersection of Route 11 and Route
... McFerren stated this individual has house trailers on
the property.

He stated POWERS and his wife got out of the car to
shake hands with MC FERREN and stated they were "glad to see
him." MC FERREN stated they asked him questions concerning
his itinerary for that day and he told them he was going to
Memphis at approximately 4:00 p.m.

MC FERREN stated that POWERS asked, "Are you putting
out a lot of weight?" and then asked if the road behind the
Powers Store Road still came out into Old Macon Road. MC FERREN
advised he "acted dumb" and after a while POWERS left. POWERS
told MC FERREN he was leaving tonight or tomorrow night.
(April 18-19, 1968). MC FERREN advised that POWERS did not
threaten him in any way and he was very suspicious and connected
this incident with the telephone call at LL & L Produce Company
because the "white man shook my hand." According to MC FERREN,
it is very uncommon for white men to shake black men's hands in
his part of the country.

MC FERREN stated he can tell when individuals are
wearing guns and stated many times in the past he has seen
people who appeared very suspicious to him and who, he thought,
were a threat to him inasmuch as they stared at him and acted "funny."
He advised he always looks at individuals to see whether or not
they are wearing shoulder holsters or sidearms or "45's" in their
back pockets. MC FERREN pointed out that he always acted dumb
so that people will not give him a hard time when in reality he
is actually very smart.

MC FERREN was shown six photographs, five of which were
random photographs of individuals who have been arrested in
various parts of the country in the past. These photographs are
of NORMAN JAMES BURKETT, FOLSE JOSEPH BERTAUT, JR., JOSEPH FRANK
ANGONE, RONALD FRANCIS SCOTT, DEAN VINCENT PATREN, and JAMES EARL
RAY, also known as ERIC STARVO GALT. MC FERREN immediately
eliminated the photographs of RAY PATREN, and SCOTT and looked
closely at the three remaining photographs. He stated that the

8   1517

Robert Fitzpatrick and Andrew Sloan's FBI 302 report
on John McFerren
(faded and unredacted - page 4)

ME 44-1987
4

▪▪▪▪▪ Somerville, Tennessee. An individual,
identified as ▪▪▪▪▪ and his wife, who approximately
twelve years ago ran ▪▪▪▪▪ in Somerville, Tennessee,
and thereafter left to live in New Orleans, Louisiana, or that
vicinity. He stated this individual operates an all-night
truck stop in Louisiana at the junction of ▪▪▪▪▪
▪▪ He further stated this individual has house trailers on
the property.

He stated ▪▪▪▪▪ and his wife got out of the car to
shake hands with ▪▪▪▪▪ and stated they were "glad to see
him." ▪▪▪▪▪ stated they asked him questioned concerning
his itinerary for that day and he told them he was going to
Memphis at approximately 4:00 p.m.

▪▪▪▪▪ stated that ▪▪▪▪▪ asked, "Are you putting
on a lot of weight?" and then asked if the road behind the
▪▪▪▪▪ still came out into Old Macon Road.
▪▪▪▪▪ he "acted dumb" and after a while ▪▪▪▪▪ left.
told ▪▪▪▪▪ he was leaving tonight or tomorrow night.
(April 18-19, 1968). ▪▪▪▪▪ advised that ▪▪▪▪▪ did not
threaten him in any way and he was very suspicious and connected
this incident with the telephone call at ▪▪▪▪▪
because the "white man shook my hand." According to ▪▪▪▪▪
it is very uncommon for white men to shake black men's hands in
his part of the country.

▪▪▪▪▪ stated he can tell when individuals are
wearing guns and stated many times in the past he has seen
people who appeared very suspicious to him and who, he thought,
were a threat to him inasmuch as they stared at him and acted "funny."
He advised he always looks at individuals to see whether or not
they are wearing shoulder holsters or sidearms or "45's" in their
back pockets. ▪▪▪▪▪ pointed out that he always acted dumb
so that people will not give him a hard time when in reality he
is actually very smart.

▪▪▪▪▪ was shown six photographs, five of which were
random photographs of individuals who have been arrested in
various parts of the country in the past. These photographs are
of ▪▪▪▪▪
▪▪▪▪▪ and JAMES EARL
RAY, also known as ERIC STARVO GALT. ▪▪▪▪▪ immediately
eliminated the photographs of ▪▪▪▪▪ and ▪▪▪▪▪ and looked
closely at the three remaining photographs. He stated that the

*Robert Fitzpatrick and Andrew Sloan's FBI 302 report
on John McFerren
(clear and redacted - page 4)*

photograph of SUBJECT looks like the unknown individual he
saw in the Farmers Market in the late fall or early
winter but states he may be "too short."

MC FERREN did not desire to furnish a signed
statement regarding this individual stating he "did not want
to get in trouble" if this should be the wrong person.
He could not be certain this was the man in this photograph,
he saw but stated he/she was the man, he and the same "jungle
growth" on his neck, and the person was similar to that of the
person by the individual shown in the newspaper. The
individual picked out by MC FERREN was born September 28, 1943,
is 5'5"tall, weighs 152 pounds, medium build, brown hair,
brown eyes, and was last known to be residing in New Orleans,
Louisiana.

MC FERREN was shown a photograph of JAMES EARL RAY,
also known as ERIC STARVO GALT, who was identified to MC FERREN
as being the individual wanted by the FBI for the murder of Dr.
KING. At this point, MC FERREN took the photograph of RAY
and intimated this individual, too, resembled the man he saw
at the Farmers Market in late fall or early winter, 1967. He
stated, "I would be honest, the hair is combed the same way
and there was some similarity in the individual he was attempting
to describe. MC FERREN was reminded that he had positively
eliminated RAY on three occasions and he thereafter stated he jus
"was not sure."

During the interview with MC FERREN, an individual who
was known to be a Times Magazine reporter was taking photographs
of Agents interviewing MC FERREN and during the interview it was
felt that the distraction caused by this Times Magazine reporter
necessitated moving MC FERREN to a more secluded spot so that an
effective and penetrating interview with him could be accomplished.

The following description of JOHN MC FERREN was obtained
through observation and interview:

Race:	Negro
Sex:	Male
DOB:	October 28, 1924
POB:	Somerville, Tennessee

9

*Robert Fitzpatrick and Andrew Sloan's FBI 302 report
on John McFerren
(faded and unredacted - page 5)*

ME 44-1987
5

photograph of ███████████ looked like the unknown individual he
had seen in ███████████ in the late fall or early
winter but stated he may be "too short."

███████████ did not desire to furnish a signed
statement regarding this individual stating he "did not want
to get him in trouble" if this should be the wrong person.
███████████ noted certain similarities in this photograph,
namely, the hair style was the same, he had the same "jungle
rot" on his neck, and the profile was similar to that of the
sketch by the Commercial Appeal artist in the newspaper. The
individual picked out by ███████████ was born ███████████ 1943,
is 5'5"tall, weighs 152 pounds, medium build, brown hair,
brown eyes, and was last known to be residing in New Orleans,
Louisiana.

███████████ was shown a photograph of JAMES EARL RAY,
also known as ERIC STARVO GALT, who was identified to ███████████
as being the individual wanted by the FBI for the murder of Dr.
KING. At this point, ███████████ took the photograph of RAY
and intimated this individual, too, resembled the man he saw
at ███████████ in late fall or early winter, 1967. He
stated, "Now let's be honest, the hair is combed the same way
and there was some similarity in the individual he was attempting
to describe. ███████████ was reminded that he had positively
eliminated RAY on three occasions and he thereafter stated he just
"was not sure."

During the interview with ███████████, an individual who
was known to be a Times Magazine reporter was taking photographs
of Agents interviewing ███████████ and during the interview it was
felt that the distraction caused by this Times Magazine reporter
necessitated moving ███████████ to a more secluded spot so that an
effective and penetrating interview with him could be accomplished.

The following description of ███████████ was obtained
through observation and interview:

Race:
Sex: Negro
DOB: Male
POB:

ME 44-1987
6

Height:	5'9"
Weight:	178
Hair:	Black
Eyes:	Gray
Complexion:	Light brown
Social Security #:	
Occupation:	

Robert Fitzpatrick and Andrew Sloan's FBI 302 report
on John McFerren
(clear and redacted – pages 5 and 6)

January 10, 1970

Mr. Elmo Spencer
Route 4 Somerville, Tennessee - Old Macon Road
Resides west of Brown's Grocery, located on Old Macon Road west of W.P.
Ware High School. Mr. Spencer has worked for Mayor I.P. Yancey's
Chevrolet Co. since 1946. Mr. Spencer is approximately 50 years old.

Mr. Spencer saw Kyle Wilbourne, of Highway 64 west of Somerville,
pass money to the Anderson men and W.C.McNeil after beating me. Kyle
Wilbourne is also a collector for the Chevrolet Garage.

Dean Gammel lives on Tapp Drive the first street on the left after
entering city limit on Highway 76 from the south. Gammel was also in
the passing of the money, there were five or six other white men that
gave money, but Spencer did not know their names. Spencer saw those
men give the Anderson brothers and W.C. McNeil money after the incident.

William Finnie (Mathes Finnie) a Negro worker for the Chevrolet Garage
also saw the passing of the money. Finnie lives on Route 3 west of
Shaws Grocery, located on the Old Jonican Road.

Miss Bettie Mae Jones lives on Northwest Street, Somerville, Tennessee
(a Negro), sent word by John McFerren's cousin, James Jones, that the
City Police had given Ernestine McNeil Fields, a Negro woman about 28
years old, (Ernestine is a party of the black group that beat John up)
a gun to shoot John McFerren with. Bettie heard some whites discussing
this at a party at W.S. Shinault Sr's house on South Marginal, Somerville, Tennessee.

James (Sonny) Porter, a Negro man who resides on East Street accross
from Johnson Mays Cafe, and the next building from Shinault's Laundromat, says he was in Johnson May's Cafe when Otho Lee Anderson made the
statement that Mayor Yancey was going to give them a car for them to
do away with John McFerren. At that time they had not received the car
tho Lee was getting upset about it and made the statement he was going
to give Mayor Yancey two more days, if he didn't present the car somebody would know something. Later Porter saw, Otha Lee Anderson driving
1961 green & white Pontiac car. Otha Lee said, see there I told you
he was going to gove it to me. When the first statement was made about
the car the four Anderson brothers, Otha Lee Anderson, Alex Anderson,
lfonso Anderson, Robert Lee Anderson and W.C. McNeil along with his
sister, Ernestine McNeil Fields, were sitting around a table in Johnson
May's Cafe. James (Sonny) Porter also states the Merchants have
something like a donation boy going from store to store raising money
or this black group.

John Hardy Thompson, a Cafe owner next door to McFerren's Grocery, Hwy
64 at Old Macon Road, has heard the above statement by others. Thompson claims that the Anderson group was also given $300.00 in cash.
Thompson's address is Route 1 Box 151, Oakland, Tennessee. Phone 465-
932.

Johnny Hussey, a brother-in-law to Ernestine McNeil Fields and W.C.
McNeil, stated that he believes that Paul Burrow, City Chief of Police,
gave W.C. (Shorty) McNeil a sawed-off pump and a double barrell shot
gun and shells. Johnnie Hussey lives on the Old Jonican Road, .
metines called the Mt. Olive Road, Somerville, Tennessee, about 2 ½
Miles southeast of Somerville.

John McFerren's letter to the
DOJ's Civil Rights Division
(page 1)

+l Mosby lives on Highway 59, north of Somerville, Phone 465-2062,
l works at H. & C. Table Co., at Somerville, Tennessee. He states
it Alfonzo Anderson, Otha Lee Anderson, Loeb McNeil, of Memphis, and
;. McNeil came up to John Thompson's Cafe. Two entered through the
:k door and two entered through the front door looking for a Negro
1 called Yate (Saint John the Killer). Otha Lee Anderson pulled his
v 38 Special with a shoulder holster and showed it to Carl Mosby.
te (Saint John the Killer) was not at the Cafe at that time. Carl
iimes 'cause men shoot guns around town like mad and the Police don't
:n question this action.

vie McDaniel, or Davie Coe lives on the Old Jackson Road at the
;y limits near the railroad, and works at Boswell Feed Store (Purina
:d Store), 215 North Main Street. He has worked there since 1959.
vie McDaniel claims that Tom Day and Alden Feathers, City Police,
ie to Boswell's Feed Store and Boswell took them into his office and
ve them ten or fifteen dollars from his cash register. Paul Burrow
llected money on the side of town of the Somerville Bank & Trust Co.
1 Day and Feathers also went into Parson's Grocery collecting money.
nk Boswell was laughing and talking to the policemen, Day and
ithers, about my getting beat up. Parson, the grocerman, said they
ild shoot marbles on my coat tail when I was running trying to get
iy from the gang that beat me up.

: Anderson brothers live at the City limits by the old railroads, on
: Old Jackson Road. W.C. McNeil lives in Winfrey Bottom just off N.
st Street, northwest of Somerville, Tennessee.

is is information as it has been given to me concerning the December
th attack on me.

Signed:

John McFerren, President of the
Original Fayette County
Civic & Welfare League, Inc.
Route 4 - Box 133A
Somerville, Tennessee
Phone 901 - 465-3659 - Residence
       901 - 465-9936 - Grocery

*John McFerren's letter to the
DOJ's Civil Rights Division
(page 2)*

*John McFerren's
3 3/4 speed audio reel*

Memorandum of Interview of John McFerren, Somerville,
Tennessee, July 9, 1976

John McFerren was interviewed by team members Folsom and
Walker at his gasoline service station and general grocery store
located on Highway 76 and Old Macon Road, Somerville, Tennessee.

McFerren escorted Folsom and Walker to a rear room of the
grocery store which he had set up as a conference room. After
Folsom and Walker displayed their credentials and McFerren was
assured of their identities, the purpose of the task force was
explained. McFerren immediately said that "Wallace was in on it"
and that the same man that killed President Kennedy killed Dr. King.
McFerren said he knew this because he had been doing some checking
on his own and he had the evidence on tapes, one of which he had
mailed to the Justice Department. He said the first time he mailed
the tape to the Justice Department it came back but he remailed
the tape by certified mail and it did not come back.

It was explained to McFerren that we were particularly interested
in the conversation that he told the FBI he overheard at the LL& L
Produce Company, Memphis, Tenn., on the afternoon of April 4, 1968.
McFerren stated that he had been trading with the LL & L Produce
Company for about 8 years and he went there sometime after 4:00 p.m.
on April 4, 1968, to buy produce for his grocery store. He said he
knew where everything was in the warehouse and drew a diagram which
is attached to this memorandum. McFerren said the office is located
to the left of the entrance to the warehouse. The door to the office
was standing ajar when he entered and he saw the man whom he identified
for the FBI only as "the fat man," using the telephone. McFerren

Fred G. Folsom and James F. Walker's DOJ notes
on John McFerren
(page 1)

stated that he knew the man was Frank Liberto, but he did not want
to give his name to the FBI because of the danger involved. Continuing,
McFerren said he stood near the door to the office and overheard Liberto
say: "Shoot the S.O.B. on the balcony or anywhere, I don't care how
you get the job done." By that time the handy man, whom McFerren
described as a thin white man with a scar on his neck running from
ear to ear, walked up to him and asked him what he wanted. McFerren
told him that he wanted to purchase some produce and the handy man
told him to go get it.

McFerren said he proceeded to the produce bins and selected
his produce. When he returned to the area of the office, McFerren said
the phone rang again. The handy man answered the phone and told Liberto:
"Ray wants to speak to you." McFerren said that Liberto took the phone
and he overheard him say; "Don't bring your ass near this place. You
know my brother in New Orleans. Go there to get your money."

It was pointed out to McFerren that he did not tell the FBI that
Liberto had mentioned Ray's name. McFerren said that he did not mention
any names to the FBI, but gave them only descriptions. He said that,
in fact, Ray had put groceries in his car. He stated that Ray had worked
for the LL & L Produce Company either before Christmas or after Christmas.
McFerren described Ray as a thin man with coarse black hair and fungus
on his neck which he said he called "jungle rot." McFerren said at the
time he thought this man was a Mexican or an Indian rather than a white
man.

Continuing, McFerren said he left the produce company about 5:15 p.m.
and drove back to Somerville arriving there about 6:00 p.m. He said
he did not think too much about the conversations he had overheard until

*Fred G. Folsom and James F. Walker's DOJ notes
on John McFerren
(page 2)*

he heard that Dr. King had been shot. After he discussed the matter
with his wife, he decided he would report the information to the police.

McFerren stated that Robert Powell, a small time gangster
of New Orleans who formerly lived in the Memphis area, came to see
him on Tuesday after the assassination. Powell asked McFerren how he
was and questioned him about the roads leading to and from McFerren's
house. McFerren said he was suspicious of this visit and played dumb.

Two weeks later McFerren said three black men came to his store
and attempted to shoot him. McFerren's brother was behind the counter
and McFerren was sitting at a table when the men came into the store.
The men mistook McFerren's brother for him. McFerren said that when one
of the men pulled his gun, he grabbed him and they chased them away.

McFerren stated that he was attacked by five blacks on the
Somerville courthouse steps about six months to a year after the
assassination. He said he ran to the front yard of Mrs. Fair, a white
lady, who came out with her shotgun and broke up the attack. The city
police came and took him away, but made no arrests. McFerren said his
jaw was broken and some of his teeth were knocked out during the attack.
He believes the men were paid to beat him up. McFerren gave Folsom
and Walker a copy of a memorandum, dated January 10, 1970, which he said
contained the evidence that the men were paid to beat him. The memorandum
is signed by John McFerren, President of the Original Fayette County
Civic & Welfare League, Inc. and is attached to this memorandum.

McFerren said he was also suspicious of Russell Thompson, an attorney
who formerly handled cases for the NAACP Legal Defense Fund but now
represents the Memphis Police Union. McFerren said Thompson represents
his wife in a divorce action filed against him. He reasoned that the

Fred G. Folsom and James F. Walker's DOJ notes
on John McFerren
(page 3)

MPD could have been in on the assassination; that Thompson is protecting them through the police union and is now trying to destroy him by breaking up his marriage.

McFerren gave Folsom and Walker a copy of an article from the March 15, 1969 issue of the New York Post. The article (attached to this memorandum) was written by Ted Poston and is titled: "King Murder: A Mystery Call." The article is McFerren's story about the overheard conversations at the LL & L Produce Company. McFerren said he and Ted Poston, who is now deceased, were very close. He sent a tape of evidence to Poston and he believes his widow will give us access to the tape.

McFerren said a lot of money had been collected in Somerville for Ray. When asked what his source of information was, he said the cooks for various people such as the Mayor gives him the information. He tapes their conversations and telephone calls on a small pocket size tape recorder and transfers these conversations to a master tape. McFerren said he had sent four of these master tapes to various places in the country, including the Justice Department.

McFerren stated that his telephone was "bugged." He said he knew this because he had someone from an electronics company inspect his telephone. Therefore, he does not discuss certain matters on the telephone and he recognizes people by their voices rather than by their names. Once he hears a voice, he said he never forgets it.

Fred G. Folsom and James F. Walker's DOJ notes
on John McFerren
(page 4)

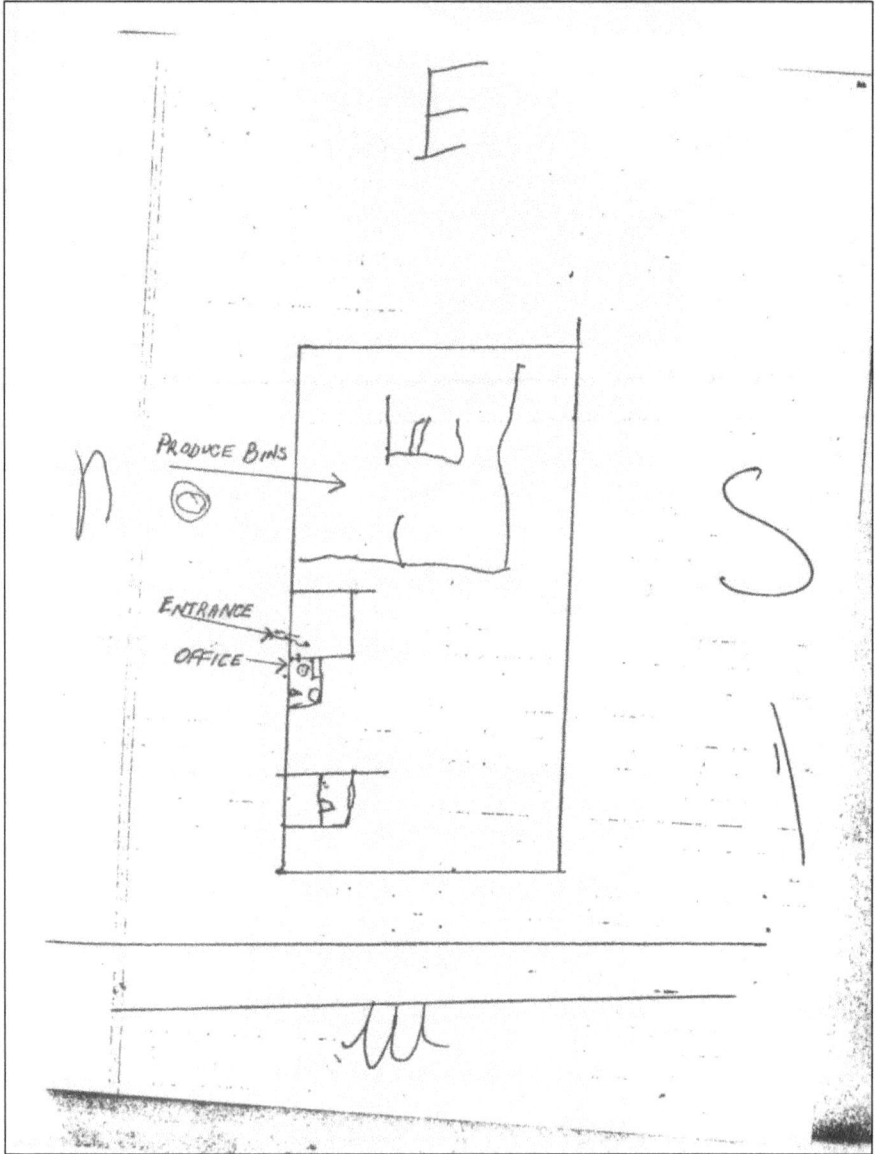

John McFerren's sketch of 814 Scott Street Market given to Fred G. Folsom and James F. Walker

Memorandum of Telephone Call   From
John McFerrin
_____

On November 16, 1976, John McFerrin of Somerville, Tenn.
telephoned me before I arrived at the office. Upon
returning McFerrin's call, he stated that he got shot right after we
were down there and that he spent 8 days in the hospital. McFerrin
also stated that his wife had left him and was suing him for a
divorce. He believes Russell Thomas, his wife's attorney, is instigating the whole thing.

McFerrin inquired whether the Department of Justice knew
he had been shot as the NAACP said they would notify the Department.
I advised McFerrin that the Task Force reviewing Martin Luther King, Jr.'s
assassination had not been informed. In response to questions,
McFerrin said that he was shot in the lower part of his stomach on
September 10, 1976, at about 12:30 a.m. when he was closing up his
laundry mat. He stated that a car drove up with one white male, two
black males and a woman and one of the black males shot him through
the glass door. McFerrin said he got his gun and shot one of the black
males after which they all got in the car and left.

McFerrin stated that no one was arrested and inquired
whether the Department of Justice was going to investigate the matter.
He insisted that "they" were out to get him. When asked who "they"
were he said the police were in on it and he could not talk about it
now because his phone was tapped.

I informed McFerrin that I was, indeed, sorry to hear that he
had been shot, but the situation appeared to be a purely local matter
involving his local activities. He was advised that the Department of
Justice in general and the Task Force in particular did not have
jurisdiction to investigate the shooting. Therefore, I suggested that
he should pursue the matter through the local sheriff's office.

McFerrin said that he understood and that he guess he would
not be hearing from us anymore. I informed McFerrin that the Task
Force would complete its work in about two months and would then be
dissolved.

JAMES F. WALKER, Attorney
Department of Justice

*James F. Walker's DOJ notes on
John McFerren's follow up call*

<pre>
                     A F F I D A V I T

        JOHN MCFERREN, being duly sworn, makes oath as
follows:

        That on April 4, 1968, I travelled from Somerville,
Tennessee, where I live, to Memphis, Tennessee, for the purpose
of picking up supplies for my grocery store located in Somerville.

        That during the course of this trip I went to the
LL & L Produce Company located at 814 Scott Street, Memphis,
Tennessee at approximately 4:30 p.m. for the purpose of pur-
chasing supplies.

        That while at LL & L Produce Company I initially
overheard a loudly uttered statement which I recall as con-
sisting of the following words: "Kill the son-of-a-bitch on
the balcony: I don't care how you get the job done; just get
it done" - or words to that effect.

        That this statement was made by an individual known
to me as Frank Liberto, a large, heavy-set, white male also
known to me as one of the operators of LL & L Produce Company,
as that person spoke over the telephone in an office of the
building which housed LL & L Produce Company.

        That immediately after overhearing this statement I
was approached by another large - but not so large as the
first - white male with a scar on the right side of his neck,
also known to me as one of the operators of LL & L Produce who
asked me what I wanted and who then advised me to help myself.
</pre>

John McFerren's HSCA affidavit taken by
Gene R. Johnson and Ernestine G. Johnson
(page 1)

That several minutes later as I was exiting the
building after making a purchase in the rear I heard the
telephone in the office ring. I observed the white male
with the scar on his neck who had previously spoken to me
hand the receiver to the heavy-set white male known to me
as Frank Liberto whom I had overheard earlier. I, then,
overheard the following words spoken into the telephone
receiver by Frank Liberto: "Go to New Orleans and get your
$5,000; you know my brother; don't come here." - or words to
that effect.

That the approximate time of the latter phone call
was 5:15 p.m.

That after overhearing this second conversation I
left LL & L Produce Company and returned home to Somerville
where I learned at approximately 6:15 p.m. that Dr. King had
been shot.

That approximately four days later I described to
Inspector N.E. Zachary of the Memphis Police Department the
aforementioned incident.

That approximately ten days thereafter I was interviewed
by agents of the Federal Bureau of Investigation with respect
to this incident at which time I was shown several photographs
one of which I immediately chose as closely resembling an individual whom I had seen working at LL & L Produce Company
for a short period of time during the preceding fall or early
winter. This individual was a lightly tanned or Puerto Rican-
type individual with black hair, slender build, and a height of
approximately five feet, nine-to-ten inches, readily recognizable

John McFerren's HSCA affidavit taken by
Gene R. Johnson and Ernestine G. Johnson
(page 2)

due to skin abrasions on his neck which I would most accurately describe as "jungle rot." The photograph which I chose was identified to me by the FBI agents as being that of someone other than James Earl Ray.

That this individual closely resembled a sketch of Dr. King's assassin which appeared in the Commercial Appeal on April 5, 1968.

That about a week prior to Dr. King's assassination while at LL & L Produce Company I was told by the large white male with a scar on his neck with reference to Dr. King: "Somebody ought to shoot the son-of-a-bitch."

That in and about 1968, I maintained an underground intelligence network composed of cooks, butlers, and bellboys from which I learned that former-Mayor Yancy of Somerville, Tennessee, a friend of former-Mayor Loeb of Memphis, collected money from local businessmen to pay for the assassination of Dr. King; made two trips to London, England, to assist James Earl Ray; and harbored James Earl Ray for the two days immediately prior to Dr. King's assassination.

That I have been threatened, beaten, and shot since the aforementioned incident and believe these threats, beatings, and shootings to be related to my observations at said LL & L Produce Company on April 4, 1968, and my relation of these observations to law enforcement authorities.

That I have been interviewed by staff members of the House of Representatives, Select Committee on Assassinations on several occasions including March 12, 1977, May 13, 1977, and February 9, 1978 during which times I have communicated

John McFerren's HSCA affidavit taken by
Gene R. Johnson and Ernestine G. Johnson
(page 3)

-4-

to them the extent of my knowledge concerning circumstances
which I believe to be connected to the assassination of Dr.
Martin Luther King, Jr.

   Further affiant saith not.

                                        John McFerren (signature)
                                        JOHN MCFERREN

   Sworn and subscribed to before me on this _22nd_
day of June, 1978.

                                        Ora Fowler (signature)
                                        NOTARY PUBLIC

My Commission Expires:

May 20, 1991 (signature)

John McFerren's HSCA affidavit taken by
Gene R. Johnson and Ernestine G. Johnson
(page 4)

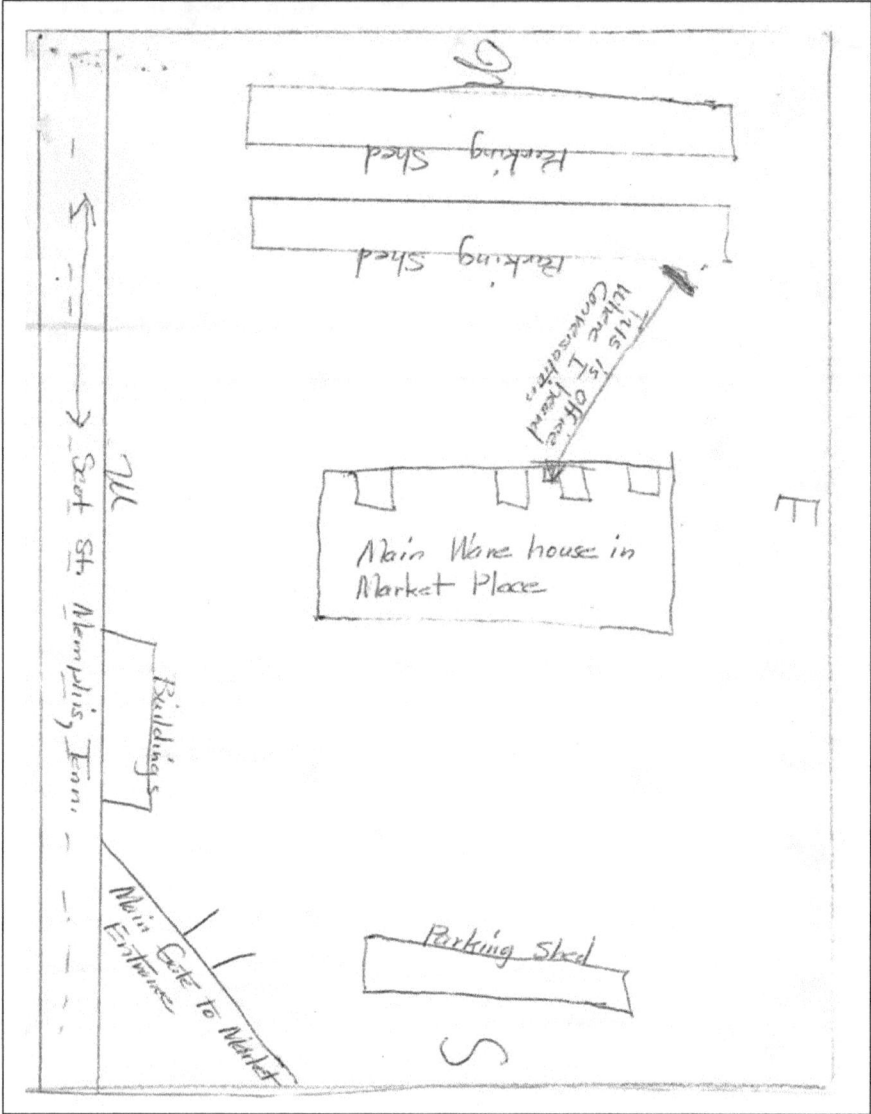

John McFerren's sketch of 814 Scott Street Market given to
Gene R. Johnson and Ernestine G. Johnson

April 3. 1978
3:26 PM

RECEIVED from JOHN McFERREN

ONE Tape SPEED 3 3/4
(reel to reel)

Those Present: Gene R. Joh

John mcferren

Ernestine G. Johnson

Informal 3 ³/⁴ speed audio reel receipt given by
Gene R. Johnson and Ernestine G. Johnson
to John McFerren

(b) John McFerren

The committee's review of Memphis FBI files revealed that John McFerren approached agents on April 8, 1968, with information concerning the assassination. (129) McFerren said that on the afternoon of April 4, 1968, while he was shopping at the Liberto, Liberto, and

Page 386

Latch Produce Store in Memphis, he overheard a "heavy, set white male," later identified as Frank Liberto,7 the company's president, talking on the telephone. (130) McFerren asserted that Liberto indicated that his brother in New Orleans, La. was going to pay $5,000 to someone to kill a person on a balcony.(131) After hearing of Dr. King's death, later that day and observing a sketch of the assassin in the newspaper the following day, he felt an individual that had been employed at Liberto, Liberto and Latch Produce during the last year might be the fugitive assassin.(132) Based on McFerren's story, a writer, William Sartor, hypothesized that organized crime was responsible for the King assassination. In his investigation, Sartor attempted to connect Frank Liberto with organized crime figures in Memphis and New Orleans. (133)[8]

In its 1968 investigation of McFerren's allegation, the FBI and Memphis Police Department interviewed Liberto and members of his family in New Orleans, and James W. Latch, vice president of Liberto, Liberto, and Latch Produce. All those interviewed denied any involvement in, or knowledge of, Dr. King's assassination. Both Frank Liberto and his business partner, Latch, however, admitted making disparaging remarks about Dr. King in the presence of their customers. (134)

Because Liberto lived in the Memphis area and because of reports that he had displayed pronounced racial bias, the committee determined that McFerren's story warranted additional investigation. It conducted extensive interviews of Liberto, (135) members of his family, (136) neighbors (137) and business associates, (138) in addition to checking the backgrounds of Liberto and his brother through the FBI and municipal police departments. Liberto and members of his family provided the committee essentially the same information they had given the FBI in 1968. Liberto stated under oath that, while on occasion he had made disparaging remarks concerning Dr. King, he did not recall making the April 4, 1968. statements attributed to him by McFerren. (139) Although an indirect, link between Liberto's brother, Salvatore, and an associate of New Orleans organized crime figure Carlos Marcello was established. (140) no evidence was found to substantiate the claim that Frank Liberto or Carlos Marcello were involved in the assassination.

HSCA's 1979 findings on John McFerren
(page 1)

In its attempt to evaluate McFerren's credibility, the committee interviewed local police and FBI agents who had received information from him. McFerren had a reputation for furnishing the officials with information that could not be substantiated. (141) The committee noted, however, that this evaluation by law enforcement officers may have been tainted by McFerren's work as a Black civil rights activist who frequently lodged complaints of police brutality.

Extensive interviews of McFerren by the FBI in 1968 (142) and the committee (143) revealed inconsistencies in his basic allegation that could not be reconciled. For instance, McFerren had told the original investigators, as well as the committee, that James Earl Ray had worked at the Liberto produce company before the assassination,

7 The committee received additional allegations with respect to Frank Liberto from Morris Davis (see sec. IIc(5) (a) infra.)

8 See text, infra, at subsection IIc(3) (a) for a discussion of Sartor's information.

Page 387

either in the fall or early winter of 1967.(144) McFerren also told members of the committee staff that at this time, Ray had "jungle rot" on his cheek and neck. (145) The committee, however, had no evidence of Ray's presence in Memphis during the period alleged by McFerren, and persons who had seen Ray during that period did not recall a similar skin disease.

McFerren also claimed he had positively identified James Earl Ray to the FBI as the individual who worked at the produce company before the assassination. (146) An FBI memorandum concerning this incident revealed that McFerren eliminated all photographs (including one of Ray) of Bureau suspects that he reviewed. McFerren only claimed that Ray closely resembled the person who worked at the market after a picture of Ray was pointed out to him. (147)

On the basis of witness denials, lack of corroborating evidence and McFerren's questionable credibility, the committee concluded that his allegation was without foundation and that there was no connection between his story and the assassination of Dr. King.

HSCA's 1979 findings on John McFerren
(page 2)

JOHN McFERREN

Having been first duly sworn, was examined and testified as follows:

DIRECT EXAMINATION BY MR. PEPPER:

THE COURT: Sit back and relax.

THE WITNESS: Yes, sir.

THE COURT: Thank you.

Q. (BY MR. PEPPER) Good afternoon Mr. McFerren.

A. Glad to be here.

Q. Thank you for coming. Would you state your full name and address for the record, please.

A. My full name is John McFerren, spelled J O H N, capital M C F ER R E N, McFerren.

Q. And your address, Mr. McFerren?

A. 7615 Highway 195, Somerville, spelled S O M E R V I L L E, zip code is 38068.

Q. Thank you. John, would you just tell the Court, please, and the jury a bit of your background, how you come to be where you are today.

A. First of all, I'd like to say my granddaddy was brought here five years before the Civil War in chains. He was a slave. And lesser than a mile and a half from the store, the record will show in 1867 he gave seven dollars and a half for four hundred acres of land. We have some of that in the family yet.

Q. John, did there come a time in 1959 or 1960 that you became involved in civil rights activity, voter registration activity, in Fayette County and the area of Somerville?

A. Well, I'd like to please the Court to go back a little bit further than that how I got deeply involved. I met Gerald Estes in Camp Ellis, Illinois, and later I met him again in 1957. In 1957 he was a young practicing attorney. He came to Somerville to defend Burton Dotson.

Q. John, what opposition did you meet when you started, though, moving -- I'm moving forward -- when you started the voter registration project in Fayette County?

A. According to the way I got the records together, before 1960 there was no negroes registered to vote in that county. In 1957 me and Mr. Estes and the others got together. He was the legal counsel. We formed a league called the Fayette County Civic & Welfare League to set out to get negroes registered to vote. At that time the negroes didn't have no chance, and the law, they would pick them up, sentence them, and put them out on the road, and a negro didn't have no chance. The only way we could figure out to change that landscape was through the ballot box.

Q. What did you do?

John McFerren's transcribed testimony during
King v. Jowers - November 16, 1999
(page 1)

A. We formed this group. It was the first -- around about April or May in 1959 to get the negroes registered to vote. We got a small majority of negroes registered, and we had a local sheriff election. The local man that we was supporting was named L. T. Redbanks. He run for sheriff against the local sheriff. The Democrat party refused to let us vote. That's how it got started. That's how it got started. When they refused to let us vote, on August the 12th, 1959, Gerald Estes filed a suit against the Democratic party asking for us to have the right to cast our ballot.

Q. What happened as a result of that action?

A. Well, that was in 1959. In 1960, the early part of 1960, we was still pushing to get negroes registered to vote, and the local editor of the Fayette Falcon was named Coaster. The wavy understand it, the Commercial Appeal man name here was named Coaster. They was kinfolks. When we got it going, he put an ad in the Fayette Falcon and the Commercial Appeal that they was going to make a thousand negroes move off the land in 1960, that winter. During that time in 1960, if you registered, you had to move. The leaders of the movement, the citizen council and the Klu Klux Klan, they had a list that later that we got ahold to it through by borrowing it from the Klu Klux Klan's secretary. Ebony magazine published the list. We got ahold of it, forwarded it -- we got a photostatic copy of it, and the made carried it back and put it in the safe and they never knew how we got the list. The list in this Ebony magazine had all -- had A's behind it, that you couldn't buy nothing nowhere. I was the leader of the group, and they run me out of every wholesale house in Memphis.

Q. Now, this was an embargo list, this was a list of people who no wholesale house should sell any products of any sort. Is that what you are saying?

A. Wouldn't sell them for money at no price.

Q. Moving on now, John, what kind of business were you in, what kind of business did you take over?

A. Well, my brother, he had the store. And he had an education and always followed saw mills and such. He said, I'm going to move, I'm just going to leave. He thought he was the one that was behind the movement all the time, and I was the one who was spearheading the movement with the people. He moved to Memphis and left them out there. When he moved to Memphis, then Gulf Oil Company, they jumped in the squeeze. In 1960 no oil company would sell no black farmers no gasoline, no oil and no seed in 1960. It was a liberal at Eades named Ben Roafer. He told all the farmers to come down there to him and he'd sell them what they want. He had more business than he could look at. During that time I made friends with the underworld. What I mean by the underworld, they run me out of every wholesale house in Memphis but Malone & Hyde. The bread companies wouldn't sell nothing to me. There was a young bread man who said, tell you what you do, you meet me out there on Summer Avenue and I'll sell you off the bread off the truck. I would come to Memphis and meet him on Summer Avenue in Memphis in a 1955 Ford car. That's what I had. I would come to Memphis and meet him on Summer Avenue and get bread. They Klan would get after me every night or two. I had -- which I'm a top mechanic myself on the old models. To make a car run fast and turn curves faster, if you noticed, a 1955 Ford has got a solid frame in the front. We took the torch and cut two inches out of the frame in the front. That brought the front wheels in and let the back wheels be wider, and we had chains on -- see, a 1955 Ford has got straight springs behind it. That let the car wheels up when it would go around

John McFerren's transcribed testimony during
King v. Jowers - November 16, 1999
(page 2)

a sharp curve, it would slide around. At that time, which I could see a nail in the highway now, at that time my vision was better and I could drive just like I was standing still, and when they'd get after me, I'd cut over in them back roads, and them new cars couldn't turn good like me. At that time wasn't no two-way radios in cars. During that time we had Tent City going.

Q. John, let me stop you there. Would you just tell the Court and the jury what Tent City was?

A. Tent City, we went to Washington, and me and my attorney, Carrie Porter Boyd and one other guy. At that time this was under the Eisenhower Administration, and they filed an injunction against the landowners from stop making the tenant farmers move. And this was under the Eisenhower Administration. That was in 1961. President Kennedy got elected in 1961 in November, and he took office in 1962.

Q. Well, John, let's back up a minute. It is a historical fact that John Kennedy was elected in 1960, took office January 20th of 1961. So it is a year back.

A. A year back. I'm just --

Q. That's okay. Continue.

A. And during that time that I was leading my folks and all this was -- we'd have meetings to discuss it, and I decided the only way to be successful in political ranks would be independent from the citizen's council and the Klu Klux Klan. What I mean by being independent, stay out of the Klan's pocketbook. When you borrow money from the Klan, he squeeze up on you in a minute.

Q. John, what kind of business do you run today?

A. I run a grocery store and oil company.

Q. How long have you run that business?

A. I've been running that business since 1960.

Q. That's when you took it over from your brother?

A. That's when I took it over from my brother. But now let me run back back just a second. Shaw, a fellow named Shaw, bought it from my brother first. He stayed in it about a month and a half. Because of me going into the business after then -- there was an eighty-three year old man named John Lewis. He said, John, he says, they will starve us to death, we need somebody in that business who knows how to do and feed us. At that time a test was going. If you get Jet magazine, you can see some of the people were so poor, they were starving. Of course, you take most of the people at that time, they had never been nowhere or no-how to maneuver out of oppression. The Jet magazine published some pictures how poor the folks were at that time.

Q. In Fayette County?

A. In Fayette County.

Q. Let's move on. You have run this business all these years?

John McFerren's transcribed testimony during
King v. Jowers – November 16, 1999
(page 3)

A. That's correct.

Q. How many days a week is your business open?

A. The onliest time -- at that time the business was -- we were running seven days a week. I had a family. But after I lost -- the Klan tore my family up. I only shuts it up when I go to pick up merchandise.

Q. Now, where do you buy your merchandise?

A. All over Memphis.

Q. Where have you always bought your merchandise?

A. Well, I bought all over Memphis. I'd buy from Frank Liberto's Produce, I'd buy from the meat houses, Morrell Meat Company, Fineberg Meat Company. I know every one in Memphis.

Q. You sell produce and meats as well?

A. That's correct.

Q. And you sell fuel oil and gasoline?

A. That's correct.

Q. In 1968 where did you buy your produce?

A. From on market street.

Q. Was there a market there?

A. There was a market there when I first started coming there.

Q. What did you buy at this market?

A. I'd buy -- on that street, the street runs north and south, and on that street, the banana house, the tomato house, and Frank Liberto sold most of the produce and sometimes bananas.

Q. So you bought produce from a warehouse run by --

A. Frank Liberto.

Q. -- a man framed Frank Liberto. In 1996?

A. That's correct. I did before then. See, I knew him way before then. Around about 1960, 1960 or 1961, I got to know him real well.

Q. How many years had you been buying produce from Mr. Liberto?

A. Since 1906 or 1961.

Q. Since 1960 or 1961 he ran that warehouse?

A. He was there then, but I didn't know his name. When I first started going there, I didn't know his name like I did later.

John McFerren's transcribed testimony during
King v. Jowers - November 16, 1999
(page 4)

Q. What day of the week -- do you recall what day of the week did you go to pick up your produce in the year 1968?

A. It was on a Thursday, around five-fifteen.

Q. So you would -- why would you go there around five-fifteen every Thursday?

A. Well, you've got to understand how I made the runs. I first started with Malone & Hyde on south -- Malone & Hyde was on South Parkway.

Q. Right.

A. I'd make that run, the dry grocery run. Then I would come on up and I'd have it to put my meat on ice and produce on ice. I'd make them's two places my last pick-ups.

Q. So Liberto's warehouse was your last pickup?

A. Was the last pickup.

Q. You would get there around five-fifteen?

A. I got there that day at five-fifteen exactly.

Q. We're coming to that day. April 4th was a Thursday, the day Martin Luther King was assassinated was a Thursday.

A. That's correct.

Q. Did you go to Frank Liberto's place that day?

A. I went there that day.

Q. You arrived there at what time?

A. Around five-fifteen. Now --

Q. Would you describe what the layout of the place was and what you did when you arrived at that warehouse?

A. That warehouse faced east and west, but you enter in the gate on the south side, and when I drove around to the north side and come up about fifteen feet of the door, I stopped my truck. At that time I had a three-quarter ton pickup truck with a canvass on it, a cloth canvass over it.

Q. Okay.

A. When I drove up to the -- when I stopped the pickup truck out in front of the door, this door is on the north side, and there is a big door that could you rollback and back a truck up in. Coming in from the north side on the right side there is a little small office, and when I got within ten to fifteen feet of this office, why, Latch was standing up.

Q. Who was Mr. Latch?

A. Mr. Latch had a scar around his neck like this.

John McFerren's transcribed testimony during
King v. Jowers - November 16, 1999
(page 5)

Q. What was his relationship to Mr. Liberto?

A. He was a handyman. I never did know, because I was always scared of Mr. Latch. You see, if you looked at him, he had a scar from right here to right there, and he would always be mean, but Mr. Liberto was always friendly. I wouldn't fool with Mr. Latch. I would stay away from him if I could.

Q. So you walked in that afternoon, into the entrance and the office. You said you were how far from the office?

A. Ten to fifteen feet.

Q. Ten to fifteen feet from the office?

A. That's correct.

Q. Then what happened next?

A. The phone rang. When the phone rang, Latch picked it up. When Latch picked it up, Latch said, that's him again. He give it to Mr. Liberto. Mr. Liberto said, shoot the --

Q. You can just say what he said.

A. Shoot the son-of-a-bitch on the balcony. Well, at that time they didn't have noticed me. I was just standing up a little closer to them just looking. I was a cash-paying customer. He would always tell me, you go get what you want and come by the office and pay for it. If the warehouse hadn't been changed, the doors, you have a line formed going in there.

Q. Let's go back over what you saw. You heard Mr. Liberto talking on the telephone?

A. Telephone.

Q. Around what time of the day was this?

A. I'd say that was around five – ten minutes after, five-fifteen, around five twenty-five, not quite five-thirty.

Q. Five twenty-five to five-thirty you heard him talking on the telephone?

A. Telephone.

Q. He received a phone call. What did you hear him say once again?

A. Shoot the son-of-a-bitch on the balcony.

Q. Shoot the son-of-a-bitch on the balcony. Then what happened after that?

A. Then he looked around and seen me. Then they said, go on and get your merchandise. The locker is made with two doors, you open one door, then you walks in and open another door. I went on in and got my merchandise, come on back out. Then when I was coming back out, the phone rang again. Latch picked it up and give it to Mr. Liberto. And Mr. Liberto told him to go to his brother in New Orleans and get his $5,000. Mr. Liberto wrote me a ticket. I never would buy nothing from nowhere without a bill. He give me a bill. I took the bill, put my merchandise in the truck, then I went on the back side of the

John McFerren's transcribed testimony during
King v. Jowers – November 16, 1999
(page 6)

company out on that street and I come around to hit Summer Avenue and hit old 64 home. When I got home, my wife called and says, do you know Dr. King done got killed? I says, I know it. It all come back to me in my mind what I had heard. That's what I told her, I know it.

Q. John, did you tell this story at that time to anyone?

A. I didn't tell it to no one until it got to worrying me, I wondered what they know I heard. You know, when you gets kind of itchy -- that was on a Thursday. So on a Friday or Saturday, no later than Saturday morning, Mr. Baxton Bryant, who was a Baptist white minister that I know in Nashville, I called him and told him what I had heard. So that Sunday evening he said, John, I'm in church now. Says, I'll be there about four o'clock tomorrow evening. When he came down about four o'clock that Sunday evening, we talked it over, and in meantime he had contacted Mr. Lucius Burch's son-in-law to meet me and him with the FBI down here in Memphis.

Q. And did you have a meeting with the FBI and any local law enforcement people in Memphis on that Sunday?

A. Well, that night, that Sunday night, we met with the FBI. Now, I didn't know whether or not that they was local police or somebody else. But the only somebody I know was the FBI -- one was a tall and one was a lower.

Q. Did you tell them this story, these details?

A. I gave them the same details. They questioned me two or three hours over the same thing, the same thing. They questioned me two or three hours over the same thing.

Q. Did you give these details to them on any other occasion?

A. That Monday, two little young FBI come out to the store and stayed there half a day questioning me the same thing. So that Tuesday Robert Powell from New Orleans come there, which he used to run a store out there on 64 highway, and I wasn't at the store when he came, he -- the lady where I hide was named Ms. Ida Mae. The record will show that in my deposition with the FBI. She told them that I was at the house. So Robert – I stayed about an hour and a quarter from the store. Robert Powell drove on out there to the house, and when he come out this to the house -- I knowed him -- I never did have no dealings with him, but I knowed him, and he come out there to see me, and he talked with me, and at that time he had a big Gulf station in New Orleans tied up with the Mafias, I know it. I wouldn't say much to him, but the onliest questions he asked me was how to get to my house from the back roads. It jumped curious in my mind that all this done happened and he wanted to know how to come to my house through the back roads.

Q. John, you told this story. What happened as a result of your giving this information to the officials?

A. Well, in the meantime, Hal Flannery, which I've got his phone in my pocket right now, he was in the Justice Department. Of course, he had been working with us on the landowners' case. I called him that Tuesday and told him about Robert Powell had been there and I was scared of him. See, when you buy from groups, you begin to know who is who.

John McFerren's transcribed testimony during
King v. Jowers - November 16, 1999
(page 7)

Q. Who has happened as a result of the information that you gave the officials? Has anything happened in succeeding years?

A. First of all, Dean Milk Company run my mama down, caught her on the road, run over the truck. After then they hired Marion Yancy and Rue Grady hired the Andersons to beat me up, beat me to death. And they give a 1961 Pontiac and three hundred fifty dollars to beat me to death. They got out at the courthouse and run me in Ms. Fair Theater's yard. That's the person who owns the theaters in Somerville now. They still own it. When we was fighting in the yard, she come out there with her gun, said, if you all don't quit beating him, I'm going to kill you.

Q. John, were you put in the hospital as a result of that?

A. Well, I come to my family doctor -- and I'd rather not discuss his name, because something else I'm going to bring out, I don't want any reprisals against him – I come to my family doctor, and by my grandparents on my daddy's side come up in slavery, I learned a lot about nerve doctors. When you take mullet and boil it down, which mullet has got a little stickers on, it looks like a catfish, you can boil it down and take Vaseline and make a salve and take iodine salt and lay in it and draw a sweat out. That's what I did. I come to the doctor. They examined me and said I didn't have no -- I didn't break no bones.

Q. John, I want to move along because of the time constraints we have.

A. I understand.

Q. Were you ever asked to go to Washington and testify before the House Select Committee on Assassinations and tell what you have told us here today?

A. Let me bring one other point up.

Q. John, no, stay, please, with me and answer this question.

A. All right. Gene Johnson came down investigating for the Select Committee. Me and him went over all the records. I discussed what I know, what I knew with him. And when the time come for me to if to Washington to testify before the Select Committee, he come out there with the papers for me to sign, and when he come out there with the papers for me to sign, I noticed that he had gotten a little hostile towards me. Somebody had got, in my opinion, to him and changed his attitude. That's my thinking. I signed the papers and got everything ready. I says, John -- he says, John, he says, I'll call you before you come up and testify before the Select Committee. And the Select Committee was going on. Two to three days before I was supposed to go, he called me up and said, John, we don't need you.

Q. So the answer to the question is that at the end of the day, you were not called to testify before the Congressional committee?

A. I was not called.

Q. That's what you heard.

MR. PEPPER: No further questions.

John McFerren's transcribed testimony during
King v. Jowers - November 16, 1999
(page 8)

THE COURT: Let's take about fifteen minutes.

(Jury out.)

(Short recess.)

(Jury in.)

THE COURT: All right. Mr. Garrison.

CROSS-EXAMINATION BY MR. GARRISON:

Q. Mr. McFerren, you and I have talked before about all of the things that you know. You knew Mr. Liberto quite a long time, did you, Frank Liberto, over a period of years?

A. I know him from 1960 up until 1996, I was in his business once or twice a week.

Q. Okay. After the assassination of Dr. King, did you ever see him anymore after that?

A. I never did see him personally after that.

Q. Okay. And during the time that you were around Mr. Liberto, Mr. McFerren, did you ever hear him mention the name of Loyd Jowers, ever hear him ever mention that name to you?

A. Not to me.

Q. All right. Let me ask you this, sir: After you saw Mr. Liberto when you would go for your produce to buy it -- am I correct, sir?

A. That's correct. Ninety percent of the time he would be there, but sometimes Latch would be there.

Q. All right, sir. You've lived in Somerville many, many years, in the town of Somerville, am I correct, sir?

A. I've been there all my life. The only time I've been away is when I was in the Army.

Q. Do you know Mr. Liberto visited Somerville -- are you aware that he visited Somerville on occasion?

A. He would -- I wouldn't say every Saturday morning, but he would visit John Wilder's office, which is on the east side of the courthouse. Now, let me explain this to you so you'll understand. When the assassination committee of Dr. King was going on in Washington, getting ready to go on, he went to visiting John Wilder's office regular. Now, the way I got ahold of it, I had some of our underground watching. Two to three weeks before James Earl Ray broke pen out of Brushy Mountain, I called Washington and told the Select Committee that they was going to kill James Earl Ray or something was going to happen to him. I talked to Mr. Gene Johnson, which I've got his phone numbers, I've got Mr. Flanders' phone numbers in my pocket now, I've got Mr. Dole's phone numbers in my pocket now. I was in correspondence with all of them. The Justice Department, what I said before, the Justice Department covered it up. When I said they covered up the barnyard, I mean they covered it up. Now, if you look at the records, the assistant to the United States Attorney General at that time was -- it was

John McFerren's transcribed testimony during
King v. Jowers – November 16, 1999
(page 9)

under the Nixon administration. He had a heavy voice. I talked to him one time. I says, I know Dr. King's killings, who is in it, they trying to set me up to get me killed. Mitchell, that was his name. If you ever talked to him on the phone, he has got a gross voice like a bullfrog.

Q. All right. Let me ask you this, Mr. McFerren: Since all this started and you started the civil rights movement, have you ever been shot?

A. I've been shot, I've been beat up twice. The citizen council and the Klu Klux Klan hired a man named Benefield, gave him eighteen hundred dollars to kill me. He got chicken and didn't kill me. He sent word to me by Reverend Frank Jones. He came to my brother's house. He didn't even know which one of the houses I stayed in. Myself, Reverend Frank Jones and Mr. Benefield come down here on Vance. Our lawyer's office was at 860 Vance Avenue. That's Gerald Estes office on Vance. He filed -- he made an affidavit with the law and sent it to the Justice Department that he was hired to kill me. It hit on a dead ear. Nothing come about it.

MR. GARRISON: I appreciate it. Thank you, sir.

REDIRECT EXAMINATION BY MR. PEPPER:

Q. Is it true that almost thirty-one years ago you told the same story that you have told to this jury and this Court this afternoon?

A. That's correct.

Q. And is that story true to the best of your recollection and knowledge today as it was then?

A. That's correct.

Q. And have you ever had an opportunity to tell this story before in a court of law?

A. This is the first time.

MR. PEPPER: John, thank you very much. No further questions.

THE COURT: All right. You may stand down, sir. You can remain in the court room or you are free to leave.

THE WITNESS: Thank you.

(Witness excused.)

John McFerren's transcribed testimony during
King v. Jowers – November 16, 1999
(page 10)

Section 2a: Liberto's alleged threat

On April 8, 1968, John McFerren, the owner of a small gas-station store in Somerville, Tennessee, informed the FBI that less than an hour before the assassination, he was in Liberto's Memphis market, where he often went to buy produce. According to McFerren, while shopping he overheard Liberto say over the telephone, "Kill the S.O.B. on the balcony and get the job done. You will get your $5,000." In a second telephone conversation a short while later, McFerren claimed to have heard Liberto say, "Don't come out here. Go to New Orleans and get your money. You know my brother."

McFerren later told the FBI that the man depicted in a police sketch of the purported assassin, which appeared in a newspaper the day following the shooting, had worked in Liberto's market in 1967. The sketch depicted James Earl Ray, who at that time had been identified only by his alias, "Eric Galt." According to McFerren, the man he knew was of Cuban, Mexican, or Indian descent with coarse black hair and "jungle rot" on his neck. Based on McFerren's claims, the FBI showed him an array of six photographs, which included Ray's picture. McFerren excluded Ray and instead tentatively identified three others, who did not resemble Ray, as the man who had worked for Liberto. One of the men was in prison and the other two were never known to have been in Memphis.

Despite McFerren's misidentifications, both the Memphis Police Department and the FBI investigated his report of the telephone conversation. First, they interviewed Liberto and his business partner, both now deceased. Liberto told detectives that on the afternoon of April 4, 1968, he left work early and was at home because of an injured finger. His partner corroborated his alibi, as did his wife. Medical records further established that Liberto had his finger lanced the day before Dr. King was killed.

Both Liberto and his partner also denied being involved in an assassination plot or participating in any telephone conversations discussing shooting Dr. King. While they frankly admitted making derogatory remarks about Dr. King's activities in Memphis and Liberto even conceded the possibility of saying in jest that someone ought to kill him, each explained that his comments would not have been made over the telephone or on the afternoon of the assassination. In any event, such comments have no significance since they were, at the time, unfortunately unremarkable among many whites, who continued to revile Dr. King.(32)

Liberto also informed investigators that any comments about money and New Orleans would have been inconsequential as he often transacted business involving large sums of money by telephone and made frequent business trips to New Orleans to purchase produce and visit family. Following up on that information, as well as McFerren's

Janet Reno and DOJ's findings
on John McFerren - June 2000
(page 1)

reference to overhearing Liberto mention "[his] brother" and "New Orleans," FBI agents interviewed Liberto's mother and three brothers in New Orleans. They confirmed that Liberto did business in New Orleans and visited regularly. They provided no information suggesting Liberto's involvement in the assassination.

In the end, neither the FBI nor the Memphis police corroborated any part of McFerren's report suggesting Liberto had involvement in the assassination. Accordingly, McFerren's allegation fell into the same category as literally hundreds of other alleged threats on Dr. King's life, which, after investigation, proved either unsubstantiated or idle.

A decade after the Memphis police and FBI investigation, the HSCA conducted its own detailed inquiry into McFerren's allegation. Liberto, then still alive, gave a sworn affidavit denying involvement in the assassination and repeating that he was at home with an injured finger when McFerren claimed to have seen him in his market. The HSCA also interviewed Liberto's relatives, friends, neighbors, and business associates. It found nothing to support McFerren's accusation that Liberto plotted to kill Dr. King or had a suspicious telephone conversation on the day of the assassination.

For several reasons, we, too, have concluded that McFerren's account is not reliable. Most importantly, we, like the HSCA, found no independent evidence to establish either that McFerren witnessed what he claimed or, more generally, that Liberto played a role in the assassination.

In addition, in statements to the 1976 Department of Justice Task Force, the HSCA, and our investigation, McFerren significantly expanded his account to incorporate James Earl Ray, who had not yet been identified at the time of McFerren's initial April 1968 statement to the FBI. In 1976, McFerren added for the first time that when Liberto's partner answered the telephone, he referred to the caller by name telling Liberto, "Ray wants to speak to you"(emphasis added). Later, McFerren falsely claimed that he had identified Ray's photograph when interviewed by the FBI in April 1968, and, notwithstanding Ray's known whereabouts around Christmas 1967, insisted that Ray had worked at Liberto's market at that time. Additionally, contrary to well-documented evidence of Ray's travels, McFerren later reported that Ray stayed at the Mayor's house in his hometown, Somerville, for two days prior to the assassination.(33)

During King v. Jowers, McFerren again related Liberto's alleged telephone conversation. He did not, however, repeat his contention that Liberto's partner named Ray as the caller. In fact, McFerren did not mention Ray in his testimony at all. Since McFerren focused on Ray for years, including during our interview of him in March 1999, this recent omission further undermines his credibility. Indeed, it seems McFerren may have tailored his

Janet Reno and DOJ's findings
on John McFerren – June 2000
(page 2)

testimony to fit the theory advanced by Dr. Pepper at trial -- that Ray was not involved in the assassination.

There is also some possibility that McFerren exaggerated at the very beginning. On April 8, 1968, immediately prior to giving his original statement to the FBI, he told his story to David Caywood, a lawyer and then president of the local chapter of the ACLU, who accompanied him to the FBI interview. Caywood told our investigation that while he recalled McFerren's recounting that Liberto had said something like "get the SOB," he did not remember whether McFerren claimed that Liberto included the words "on the balcony." Caywood explained that had McFerren used those words, he likely would have remembered it since Caywood had been on that same balcony with Dr. King the day before. The apparent omission is obviously significant, because it is only the words "on the balcony" that connect Liberto's alleged statement to the assassination.

McFerren's account also appears unreliable because of his quirky behavior and beliefs. When members of our investigative team spoke to McFerren, he locked his door and asked that we speak quietly because his phone was "bugged." He then placed a paper bag over the telephone receiver to prevent the conversation from being overheard. During the interview, he asserted that according to his "intelligence network," the Ku Klux Klan and the Mafia had met concerning him the day before and had been after him for 30 years. In addition, he maintained that Klan control of the Small Business Administration had interfered with his obtaining a business loan. He further added that he was in great danger because of his knowledge of the connection between the King and Kennedy assassinations but insisted on withholding the information until he could testify for Dr. Pepper in court. Finally, he repeated his erroneous assertion that Ray had stayed at the mayor's home in Somerville (McFerren's hometown) before the assassination.

McFerren related similarly strange information to the 1976 DOJ Task Force and the HSCA. For instance, he advised investigators that the same person killed both President Kennedy and Dr. King and that unidentified persons had tapped his phone, were "out to get him," and had made several attempts on his life.

McFerren's inconsistent accounts, peculiar behavior, and bizarre, uncorroborated claims, some of which contradict known facts, render his story about Liberto unreliable. Thus, McFerren does not offer any credible evidence to corroborate Jowers' contention that Liberto participated in the assassination.

Janet Reno and DOJ's findings
on John McFerren - June 2000
(page 3)

Section 3: Liberto's alleged connection to the Mafia

Others besides Jowers have accused Liberto of having Mafia connections. Whitlock, for instance, claims that Liberto disclosed that he was acquainted with Mafia boss, Carlos Marcello, when the two were children in New Orleans. McFerren also alleges that the backroom in Liberto's produce market was used as a Mafia meeting place.

The HSCA investigated the possibility of Liberto's involvement with organized crime. According to HSCA documents, neither the FBI nor the New Orleans Police Department had any record of such involvement. However, HSCA records include information from the New Orleans police that Liberto's brother, Salvatore, associated with a bail bondsman who was believed to be affiliated with Carlos Marcello. The HSCA found nothing more than this potential "indirect link" between Salvatore and the Mafia.

Because of the allegations made by Jowers, McFerren, and Whitlock, and the speculative report regarding Liberto's brother Salvatore, we initiated a review of Department of Justice and FBI organized crime investigative records. We found no information in these records showing that either Frank or Salvatore Liberto had any affiliation with the Mafia. Our review of the remaining historical record also revealed nothing to support the claims concerning Liberto's Mafia involvement.

Ultimately, the allegations of Liberto's Mafia ties come from unreliable sources and lack any corroboration. Moreover, even if Liberto had some connection with the Mafia, we found no credible evidence to suggest that organized crime was involved in the assassination.

Janet Reno and DOJ's findings
on Frank C. Liberto's alleged ties to Carlos Marcello
and the New Orleans Mafia - June 2000

John McFerren, Sam Donaldson, and Bill Pepper
at 814 Scott Street Market - April 1997

Re: F.O.I.A. Response Letter ███████

cer <cer@nara.gov>
███████████████

To: cer <cer@nara.gov>
Cc: ████████████████████████████

📎 1 attachments (31 KB)
File List.xlsx;

███████████████

We are responding to your message of ██████████ in which you narrowed your search of documents and emails within the Electronic Records of Daphene McFerren (National Archives Identifier 83832638) and the Email Records Daphene McFerren (National Archives Identifier 86663816). This message is in response to FOIA Request Reference Number ██████████

After conducting a search of the email records using the twelve (12) proper names that you provided, we located a total of 104 email messages, noted below by search term. For your information, there are more than 6400 email messages in the email records of Ms. McFerren.

- Bonner – 7 messages
- Farnsworth – 1 message
- Fayette – 64 messages
- Kowalski – 6 messages
- Liberto – 2 messages
- Rosenthal – 12 messages
- Stark – 12 messages

National Archives email linking Daphene R. McFerren
to Janet Reno's DOJ-MLK investigation

A Memphis–New Orleans Connection?

1 JOHN MCFERREN, a Somerville, Tennessee, businessman, testified that on April 3, while in Frank Liberto's produce store, he overheard Liberto talking on the telephone with his brother in New Orleans. They were talking of a plan in which Liberto's brother would pay someone $5,000 to kill another person on a balcony.

1 JOHN MCFERREN. After first reporting to authorities that Liberto had said, "Kill the S.O.B. on the balcony," McFerren changed his story, shifting from the previous day to the previous hour, and including a role for James Earl Ray that was not described initially. Reno's investigators concluded that these changes made his account suspect.

LIBERTO'S ALIBI
The Justice Department was able to substantiate Liberto's alibi that he was at home at the time of McFerren's allegations. Liberto, now deceased, had told the Memphis Police Department and the FBI that he left work early on the afternoon of April 4 and went home because of an injured finger. His partner and his wife corroborated his alibi, as did medical records which showed that Liberto had his finger "lanced" on April 4.

Erroneous displays at National Civil Rights Museum regarding John McFerren and Frank C. Liberto

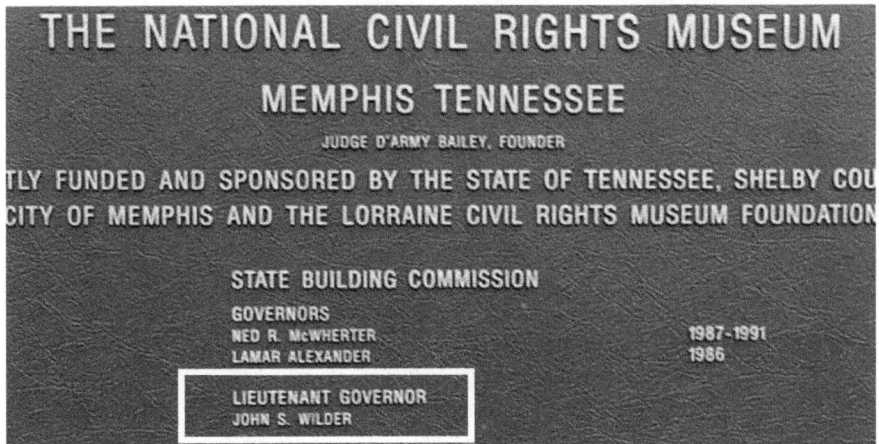

THE NATIONAL CIVIL RIGHTS MUSEUM
MEMPHIS TENNESSEE
JUDGE D'ARMY BAILEY, FOUNDER

TLY FUNDED AND SPONSORED BY THE STATE OF TENNESSEE, SHELBY COU
CITY OF MEMPHIS AND THE LORRAINE CIVIL RIGHTS MUSEUM FOUNDATION

STATE BUILDING COMMISSION
GOVERNORS
NED R. McWHERTER   1987–1991
LAMAR ALEXANDER   1986

LIEUTENANT GOVERNOR
JOHN S. WILDER

National Civil Rights Museum plaque honoring John S. Wilder

*Investigative Team Member and John McFerren
listening to McFerren's secret audio reels*

*Front and back cover of John McFerren's
2005 BellSouth telephone book*

Robert Lee Bell and Investigative Team Member

*1984 interstate theft and transportation case against
former Frank C. Liberto employee, Robert Lee Bell*

(opposite page)
John McFerren and
Investigative Team
Members

(top of this page)
Mourning wreath
on the door of McFerren
Grocery and Oil Co.
April 2020

(bottom of this page)
John McFerren
gravesite at Morris
Chapel Cemetery in
Fayette County

Acknowledgments

This book has been in the making since the birth of John McFerren on October 28, 1924. However, the majority of the investigation, writing, editing, and publishing process began in 2012 and ended in the latter months of 2020. For those eight years, a number of incredibly intelligent and dedicated individuals contributed to the completion of this manuscript. Author John Roberts and Clear Lens Publishing, LLC would like to thank the following:

First and foremost, we would like to bestow our deepest and most heartfelt thanks to Mr. John McFerren for his lifelong pursuit of truth and justice. Were it not for his selflessly enduring work within West Tennessee's civil rights movement, none of this would be possible. He is a shining example to all people, regardless of race or religion, of what a true hero should be.

Next, the various independent investigators who assisted the author and our publishing company need to also be recognized. While all of them have asked to remain anonymous, we would like to thank the men and women who fact checked and thoroughly vetted this manuscript, especially the West Tennessee resident who interviewed Mr. McFerren in early 2016.

The past work of now-deceased historians, researchers, and authors should also be highlighted. Brilliant men and women on both sides of the MLK conspiracy debate, and who investigted other related side issues, dedicated large portions of their lives to the discovery and communication of truth. While a number of these experts were at odds with one another and would probably disagree with our conclusions, we would like to thank their eternal spirits, nonetheless. These past individuals include the late Hank Hillin, Harold Weisberg, Mary Ferrell, Philip Melanson, John Davis, Wayne Chastain, Renfro Hayes, William Bradford Huie, Gerold Frank, Dick Gregory, Mark Lane, James Earl Ray, Baxton Bryant, William Sartor, Ted Poston, George McMillan, Jack Lait, and Lee Mortimer. In a category all her own, Fayette County historian and author Dorothy Morton laid the groundwork for the opening pages of this book and deserves our posthumous appreciation.

Among the living who have contributed to the amazing body of work on this and periphery subjects, we also extend our profound thanks to David Garrow, Michael Honey, Earl Caldwell, Selwyn Raab, Winfield Dunn, Keel Hunt, Robert Gordon, Jerry Mitchell, Frank J. Palisi III, Joseph Maselli, Dominic Candeloro, Robert Caro, Maureen Hughes, Lyndon Barsten, Mike Vinson, Martha Bragg, Tamara Carter, Judge Joe Brown, Ryan Jones, Lamar Waldron, Thom Hartmann, Donald Wilson, Kenneth Herman, John Billings, Marc Perrusquia, Gerald Posner, John Emison, Hampton Sides, Stuart Wexler, Larry Hancock, Preston Lauterbach, Robert Hamburger, Rodney E. Stanley, P. Edward French, Brian Dominski, and yes... Bill Pepper. Were it not for Mr. Pepper's enduring shenanigans, several of this book's more intriguing sections would be otherwise unremarkable.

The local and online archival institutions who aided in this endeavor should also be recognized. This list includes the staff at the Memphis Library's Memphis & Shelby County Room, specifically Mr. G. Wayne Dowdy. The staff at the Special Collections room at the University of Memphis Library also deserves our sincere gratitude. The men and woman who work at the Register of Deeds offices in both Fayette and Shelby Counties were invaluable to our research. The folks at maryferrell.org, The Harold Weisberg Archive, newspapers.com, the Fayette County Tennessee Historical Society, Ames Plantation, and orig.jacksonsun.com/civilrights are also extremely deserving of our appreciation. Additionally, we owe a huge debt of gratitude to the genealogical experts who work at the Tennessee Genealogical Society.

Ms. Daphene McFerren and her Benjamin Hooks Institute staff continue to provide a wealth of Tent City information at memphis.edu/tentcity and deserve to be thanked as well. The staff at Rhodes College who acquired and maintain the *Memphis World* collection deserve much praise. The staff at the Howard Gotlieb Archival Center at Boston University was instrumental in helping us tie-up loose ends. Of course, we need to thank the men and women at the National Archives who are forever dedicated to helping people find needles in haystacks. Naomi Van Tol and her exemplary Fayette County slave research also merits a tip of the hat. A huge "thank you!" goes out to Mr. Carter Jackson for his crucial cemetery research. We would also like to thank the rough and tumble crowd at the Crescent City Mafia Facebook group for their lively discussions and profound knowledge on Louisiana's criminal underbelly.

Another final mention of Mr. Lyndon Barsten must be included here as well. In a spur of the moment decision, Mr. Barsten graciously donated his entire collection of MLK and James Earl Ray documents to our investigative team. It should be noted that this massive collection will eventually be digitized for online viewing and then donated to one of Memphis's archival institutions. Your selfless contribution, Mr. Barsten, will never be forgotten.

A number of previous witnesses and experts, named, unnamed, living, and passed, deserve to be thanked as well. The following were willing to discuss their personal knowledge and/or involvement in the case, the alleged conspiracy, local history, or other periphery issues. These people include Karl Mosby, Robert Lee Bell, Richard Shorter, both James Puryear Sr. and Jr., Jim Emison, Robert French, Nathan Whitlock, Jules Ron "Ricco" Kimble, Barbara Rabbito, Gene R. Johnson, Robert Fitzpatrick, Shelley Murphy, Jon Land, Joseph Rosenbloom, G. Robert Blakey, Jim Douglass, Bill Morris, Barbara DuFour, Ronald Maley, Amelio Guasco, Lewis K. Garrison Sr., David E. Caywood, Dr. Raymond Winbush, members of the Brewer family, Calvin Taylor, Duncan Ragsdale, Lucian Pera, Eades Hogue, and Anthony Radosti. We are also appreciative of the families of the late Earl Clark and Jim Green for their willingness to speak to our investigators as well as the momentary discussions our team had with Leta McCollough, Frank Strausser, and Gene Barksdale.

The firemen at Fire Station 2 in Memphis have been incredibly gracious when impromptu tours have been requested. We would be remiss if we did not acknowledge the past advice and ongoing vigilance of Ms. Jacqueline Smith who continues her steadfast watch outside the Lorraine Motel. In addition, we would like to thank the members of the various Liberto families for their willingness to be interviewed. The past co-workers, neighbors, friends, and relatives of John Wilder, I.P. Yancey, and the VVD family also deserve our extreme gratitude for their willingness to bravely divulge crucial information pertinent to this book series. Of course, none of this would be possible were it not for the other discussions that took place between our team of investigators and the countless anonymous witnesses who still call Shelby and Fayette Counties home.

The editorial and art production staff at Clear Lens Publishing, LLC are more than deserving of recognition for their tireless dedication to this project. We would also like to extend a special thanks to our four independent editors who span the country. We are sincerely appreciative of P.L. on the east coast, S.W. in northern Illinois, M.V. in central Tennessee, and W.A. in Memphis for your combined editorial insights and work. The guys at the Malliard Report podcast, specifically Jim Malliard, are worthy of a shout out for their moral support and willingness to give us airtime. We also want to thank Josh Huckaby and his crew at The Green Beetle for their hospitality and serving up great suds and comfort food whenever we visit the Bluff City. The friendship and past encouragement bestowed upon me by fellow McFerren and MLK history buffs Jeff, Pete, and Phillip will always be cherished. You know who you are.

Finally, as the author, I would like to personally thank my incredible family. Without your patience, love, and undeserved loyalty, none of this would have taken place. I love you with all my heart. Thank you for putting up with me.

May 18, 2021

Dear Reader,

Clear Lens Publishing, LLC would like to take this opportunity to extend our sincerest apologies to you, the reader of *Cotton Coated Conspiracy, Book One: John McFerren's Word*. As of this day, May 18, 2021, it came to our attention that a former member of our investigative team had illegally taken possession of a pirated, unpublished copy of this manuscript with the intention of publishing it on his own. Despite our best efforts to explain to this irrational, underhanded individual that he was in violation of copyright law, we felt compelled to rush to publish it before he had the chance to do so.

While the main portion of this manuscript has been complete for some time, our editors were in the process of compiling an extensive Notes and Index section to aid in any potential research endeavors. We, unfortunately, due to the vile actions of the above-referenced individual, were unable to complete those two sections on time and have, therefore, rushed to publish the manuscript as is.

As compensation, Clear Lens Publishing, LLC will soon be offering a free PDF version of both sections on our website, www.cottoncoated.com. Until the second edition of this book is published with curently missing sections, we ask that you download the PDF Notes and Index sections as they become available online.

We are sincerely appreciative of your interest in this book and again apologize for the inconvenience.

Sincerely,

Editorial Staff at Clear Lens Publishing, LLC.

Check back periodically for the PDF downloads of our Notes and Index Sections

cottoncoated.com

www.ingramcontent.com/pod-product-compliance
Lightning Source LLC
Chambersburg PA
CBHW021500090426
42739CB00007B/392